Discourse of Opportunity

How Talk in Learning Situations Creates and Constrains Interactional Ethnographic Studies in Teaching and Learning

D1715252

Discourse and Social Processes
Lesley A. Rex, series editor

Discourse of Opportunity: How Talk in Learning Situations
   Creates and Constrains Interactional Ethnographic Studies
   in Teaching and Learning
       Lesley A. Rex

forthcoming

Narrative Analysis for Literacy Teacher Education: Sociolinguistic
   Tools for Understanding Teacher and Learning Interactions/
   Dialogues/Classroom Talk
       Lesley A. Rex and *Mary Juzwik* (eds.)
Doing Classroom Discourse: A Guide for Teachers
       Betsy Rymes
Action, Reflection and Social Justice: Integrating the Study of Moral
   Reasoning into Professional Education
       Edward P. St. John

Discourse of Opportunity

How Talk in Learning Situations Creates and Constrains Interactional Ethnographic Studies in Teaching and Learning

edited by

Lesley A. Rex
University of Michigan

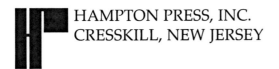

HAMPTON PRESS, INC.
CRESSKILL, NEW JERSEY

Copyright © 2006 by Hampton Press, Inc.

All rights reserved. No part of this publication may be reproduced, stored in a retrieval system, or transmitted in any form or by any means, electronic, mechanical, photocopying, microfilming, recording, or otherwise, without permission of the publisher.

Printed in the United States of America

Library of Congress Cataloging-in-Publication-Data

Discourse of opportunity:how talk in learning situations creates and constrains
   interactional ethnographic studies in teaching and learning/edited by Lesley A. Rex.
    p. cm.
  Includes bibliographical references and index.
  ISBN 1-57273-644-5 (cl) —ISBN 1-57273-645-3 (pb)
   1. Communication in education—Research. 2. Discourse analysis—Research. 3. Educational anthropology—Research. I. Rex, Lesley A.

  LB1033.5.D57 2006
  306.4307'2—dc22   2005055136

Hampton Press, Inc.
23 Broadway
Cresskill, NJ 07626

Contents

Foreword   *vii*
   Annemarie Palincsar

1   Introduction   *1*
     Lesley A. Rex

2   Considering Discourse Analysis as a Method   *37*
     for Researching Professional Development
     Katherine A. Morris

**PART I   Assessing the Opportunities for Learning Made
             Available for Students**

3   Establishing a Positive Classroom Climate: An Experienced   *73*
     Teacher in a New School Setting
     Alexandra Miletta

4   Mentoring Non-Latino Tutors in a Biliteracy Latino   *127*
     After-School Program
     Mary M. Yonker

5   Using Sociocultural and Developmental/Cognitive   *155*
     Lenses to Inform Classroom-Based Assessments
     of Children's Reading
     Carol McDonald Connor and *Lesley A. Rex*

**PART II   Applying Intertextuality to Examine an Instructional
              Approach**

6   Constructing Anatomy Literacy: Use of Computer-   *193*
     Based Media in a Dissecting Laboratory
     Silvia Wen-Yu Lee

7   Facilitating Exploration of Theory and Practice   *229*
     in a Teacher Education Study Group
     Jacob Foster

PART III   Exploring and Building Conceptual Knowledge

8   What Does It Mean to Build Conceptual Knowledge?   263
     Ruth Piker
9   Connecting the Microscopic View of Chemistry   297
     to Real Life Experiences
     Hsin-Kai Wu

**PART IV   Studying the Social Positioning of Students'
            Roles and Identities**

10   Extending Opportunities, Expanding Boundaries: 331
     Addressing Gendered Discourse Through Multiple
     Subjectivities in a High School English Classroom
     Sharilyn C. Steadman

Author Index   361
Subject Index   367

Foreword

At first blush, it may be difficult to apprehend what unites the study of children at play in a Headstart class, first-year medical students dissecting a cadaver, a struggling reader across the school day, a tutor and child in an after-school biliteracy program, an experienced teacher enculturating a new class of students into ways of behaving that are morally acceptable, a group of college students exploring their development as teachers, the interactions between high school students and their teachers in chemistry classes, a teacher's efforts to disrupt the traditional, gendered, ways in which young males participate in an English class, and meetings among educators working to improve their teaching of mathematics. What unites these topics, in addition to their constituting the foci of this important volume, is that they are all investigations of arguably the most complex of human activities—education—as it occurs in an array of complex social contexts.

In this preface, I wish to speak to several remarkable features of this volume, beginning with its contribution to methodology in educational research. Self-conscious regard for methodology serves to stimulate a field, to bring about new conceptions of what can be known and how it can be known. The recent publication of *Scientific Research in Education* (National Research Council, 2002) and the debate it sparked in journals (e.g., Educational Researcher, 2002) and public forums (e.g. at the annual meeting of the *American Educational Research Association*), testify to the fact that the development of methodology for the human sciences, perhaps particularly in education, is still very much a work in progress.

Polkinghorne (1983) has argued that methodological questions are best answered in the practice of research. This book exemplifies that process. The nine research projects reported in this volume were guided by the tenets of Interactional Ethnography. Collectively, these studies constitute a rare—but highly desirable—test of a method. Each reveals the assumptions, as well as the complement of tools (e.g., discourse analysis) and constructs (e.g., intertextuality and intercontextuality) that are characteristic of this method.

Furthermore, given the array of purposes and contexts in which this method was employed, the studies speak to the capacious nature of Interactional Ethnography and its close relatives. In this volume we encounter a range of questions, multiple sources and forms of data, and a number of theories, including: critical literacy theory, cognitive theory, and sociocultural theory. The congeniality of Interactional Ethnography is a welcomed feature in the complex field of educational inquiry.

A third remarkable characteristic of this volume is that it features initial forays, by novice researchers, into the practices of adopting and adapting Interactional Ethnography. In contrast to experts, for whom a number of practices are second-nature, these novices are explicit about the problems they confronted and the choices they made. For example, we are privy to their decisions regarding: the problem space, the grain size for analyses, coding, the issue of what should constitute the foreground, and the conduct of ethical inquiry.

Finally, this volume is remarkable because of the project it represents. As a doctoral student, the editor, Professor Lesley Rex, was a participant in a community of practice known as the Santa Barbara Classroom Discourse Group. In turn, she has propagated yet another community of practice with her own graduate students. In doing so, she has provided an extraordinary opportunity for these students to both learn about and advance educational inquiry. This volume is testimony to the value of this innovative model of graduate education.

Annemarie Sullivan Palincsar
June 12, 2004

REFERENCES

Educational Researcher (2002), *31*(8).

National Research Council (2002). *Scientific research in education.* Committee on Scientific Principles for Education Research (R. J.Shavelson & L. Towne, eds.). Center for Education. Division of Behavioral and Social Sciences and Education. Washington, DC: National Academy Press.

Polkinghorne, D. (1983). *Methodology for the human sciences.* Albany: State University of New York Press.

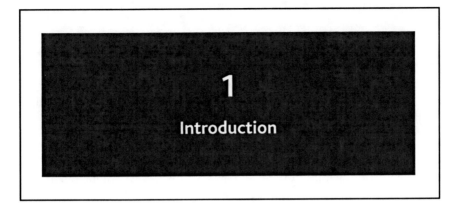

1

Introduction

Lesley A. Rex

THE OPPORTUNITY AND THE CHALLENGE

The community of authors in this volume share the good fortune of having found an intellectual and methodological home for pursuit of their research interests. That home is interactional ethnography. The ensuing chapters present beginning researchers' initial explorations in using this approach for researching issues of deep concern to them and to society, often what drew them to graduate school. These chapters reflect work in the process of evolving into professional scholarship, work its authors hope will eventually make a difference. Although they drew sustenance from the publications of senior researchers and scholars, especially interactional ethnographers, the authors did not imitate that work. Rather, they strove to emulate it in order to find their own ways of conceptualizing and designing studies that inform important issues in their fields.

This collection of studies reflects different commitments, frameworks, and designs for research, and yet all of them began with interactional ethnography. All the chapters share the same question: How do the practices and processes of teaching and learning create and constrain opportunities for teaching and for learning? All the researchers want to study and represent these processes in action, that is, the practices of groups as they teach and learn together. This goal presents a difficult research challenge. The studies aim to accurately render in inert media, such as text and graphs, a dynamic phenomenon, whose dynamics are complex and interactive. Each researcher assumed it was necessary to tackle this challenge by viewing teaching and learning as inseparable and by studying them as interactional events. Their studies analyze and represent teaching and learning events as unique, as situated in particular contexts, and as meaningfully related across time. They demonstrate how these events are performed through discourse in social situations, and are uniquely meaningful and purposeful to the social groups involved.

The chapter authors have discovered that working with the same approach, different research questions, and a common purpose has been a powerful opportunity for our own learning. We have developed new ways of understanding how processes and practices in various sites create or constrain opportunities for teaching and learning. To do that, we have had to create ways of representing the motions of teachers' and learners' actions, discourse, and texts. Although each study represents only a small slice of the complexity it seeks to describe, we are hopeful that as we expand our repertoire of representational strategies we are moving closer to understanding and representing what is so difficult to capture—sustenance, instantiation, and change.

ORIGINS OF THE VOLUME

The Santa Barbara Classroom Discourse Group

The intensity that erupts when a need meets a means feels magical, and that feeling inspires the work represented in this book. I felt that way when Judith Green arrived at the Graduate School of Education at the University of California, Santa Barbara in 1990. My long search for a way of studying classroom teaching and learning of literacy through classroom talk was over, I thought. Actually, it was just beginning. Judith joined with colleague Carol Dixon (Dixon, de la Cruz, Green, Lin, & Brandts, 1992; Dixon, Frank, & Brandts, 1997; Dixon, Green, & Frank, 1999), who brought to the partnership scholarship in reading and expertise in the writing project model through her 11-year co-direction of the South Coast Writing Project (in 1990). Together they immersed classroom teachers and graduate students in the Santa Barbara Classroom Discourse Group (SBCDG) and I in learning and elaborating what has come to be called interactional ethnography.

That explosive moment in the elaboration of interactional ethnography occurred during SBCDG's foundational years, from 1990 to 1997, when individual teachers, faculty, graduate student researchers, and visiting researchers met officially once, and sometimes twice, a week. Actually, our time together spilled over beyond those meetings to evolve and disseminate, through professional development, instruction, and publication, a significantly rich body of work. For example, third-grade teacher, Sabrina Tuyay's study of her own classroom, with Carol Dixon and Louise Jennings, elaborated the concept of interactional "opportunities for learning" (Tuyay, Jennings, & Dixon, 1995; see also, Tuyay, 1999, 2000; Tuyay, Floriani, Yeager, Dixon, & Green, 1995). Beth Yeager's study of her sixth-grade classroom (Yeager, 2003; Green & Yeager, 1995; Yeager, Floriani, & Green, 1998), and other SBDG members such as Maria Rech from Brazil (Rech, 1998), Ana Ines Heras from Argentina (Craviotto, Heras, & Espindola, 1999; Heras, 1993, 1995), and Maria Franquiz, now at the University of Texas, San Antonio (Franquiz, 1995, 1999; Franquiz, Green, & Craviotta, 1993), expanded our view of powerful bilingual learning of subject matter (SBCDG, 1995). Both Sabrina (Tuyay, 2000) and Beth (E. Yeager, 2003) have since written dissertations and assumed university positions in education related to social justice initiatives (B. Yeager, Pattenaude, Franquiz, & Jennings, 1999) More recently, they, along with Carol Dixon, Judith Green, and Ana Floriani represent the SBCDG as editorial consultants for the Research Tools Sidebar columns for the National Council of Teachers of English (NCTE) journal, *Language Arts*.

Many of us who are now tenured faculty at research institutions, took the lead to expand this early work in various directions through our dissertations and publications while still doctoral students: Ana Floriani, at University of Southern Illinois, theorized intercontextuality (Floriani, 1993, 1997); Louise Jennings, University of South Carolina, worked with Sabrina Tuyay on "opportunities for learning (Jennings, 1996; Tuyay, 1999; Tuyay, Jennings, & Dixon, 1995); LeAnn Putney, University of Nevada, Las Vegas, built the concept of consequentiality (Putney, 1997; Putney, Green, Dixon, Duran, & Yeager, 2000); Carolyn Frank, California State University of Los Angeles demonstrated how "ethnographic eyes" can serve preservice teachers (Frank, 1997, 1999; Jennings, 1998); Lichu Lin, now at National Chung Cheng University, evolved the concept of language "of" and language "in" the classroom (Lin, 1993, 1994, 1994); and I have theorized how students orient to classroom expectations for literacy performance (Rex, 1997, 2000, 2001, 2002, 2003; Rex & McEachen, 1999; Rex, Murnen, Hobbs, & McEachen, 2002; Rex & Nelson, 2004).

I took these rich experiences of what it meant to work as a doctoral student with me when I joined the faculty in the School of Education at the University of Michigan. There I found doctoral students, often former classroom teachers, who shared my interest in making usefully transparent the social complexity of teaching and learning, some of whose work appears in this volume. Together we have found it not only possible, but also productive to use the interactional ethnographic approach, which is characterized by the following theoretical constructs for where and how to focus our research:

- Examine how members of a classroom construct the patterns of everyday life through face-to-face interactions (Green & Dixon, 1993).
- Examine what is constructed in and through the moment-to-moment interactions among members; how they negotiate events through these interactions; and the ways in which knowledge and texts generated in one event become linked to, and thus a resource for, members' actions in subsequent events (Castanheira, Crawford, Green, & Dixon, 2001).
- Focus on understanding what members of a classroom need to know, do, predict and interpret in order to participate in the construction of ongoing events through which cultural and subject matter knowledge of that classroom is developed (Dixon, Green, & Frank, 1999; Green & Dixon, 1993).
- Take a holistic and comparative perspective; that is, seek to understand the customary actions, beliefs, knowledge, and attitudes of a classroom or social group within it from an insider's perspective, and then compare patterns identified in other settings, events, or groups. (Green, Dixon, & Zaharlick, 2003); Zaharlick & Green, 1991.
- Transcribe discourse as a theoretically driven process that seeks to represent what classroom members accomplish through conversation (Green, Franquiz, & Dixon, 1997).
- Analyze discourse to understand who can say or do what to and with whom, when and where, under what conditions, in relation to what actions or artifacts, for what purposes, and with what outcomes? (Castanheira et al., 2001, Santa Barbara Classroom Discourse Group, 1992b).
- Look for variability and change, which always exists in a community, in the roles and relationships that are situationally constructed in the actions and interactions among members over time (Green & Dixon, 1993).

By the time Judith Green came to Santa Barbara, she had already accumulated an influential body of foundational work for interactional ethnography. Green (1977), with a series of colleagues—Cynthia Wallat (Green & Wallat, 1979, 1981a; Wallat & Green, 1979, 1981), Judith Harker

(Green & Harker, 1982, 1989; Harker & Green, 1985), and Ginger Weade (Weade & Green, 1989; Green & Weade, 1987, 1986; Green, Weade, & Graham, 1988)—had pioneered an analysis of classroom conversational shifts across time and explained a method for mapping instructional conversations, for what at the time she referred to as sociolinguistic analysis within an ethnographic approach (Green & Wallat, 1981b); and, with Amy Zaharlick (Zaharlick & Green, 1991), had articulated an ethnographic approach suited to studying classrooms. Green reviewed research on teaching as a linguistic process in *Review of Research in Education* (Green, 1983) and had edited with Judith Harker (Green & Harker, 1988), accounts of classroom data from different analytical perspectives (see Green, Harker, & Golden, 1987).

The evolution of interactional ethnography has never been documented and requires a dedicated historical reconstruction that I do not attempt here; however, I offer my account as a resident 4-year participant in the transitional phase from 1993 to 1997. Interactional ethnography came into being as a lived as well as a conceptual and methodological approach. It was co-constructed in the weekly meetings, late-night writing sessions, and protracted sortings out by members of the "Blob," as the SBCDG came to call itself. Carol Dixon recognized an analog between the behavior of the eponymously titled movie's leading character and our group. Like the viscous creature in the movie, *The Blob*, as people left the group to assume academic positions elsewhere, we seemed to split off and disperse both proximally and intellectually without losing our core organic identity. Every time a new person entered the base group or satellite groups, we "blobbed," or grew in even more powerful conceptual and methodological configurations.

Roots of the Interactional Ethnographic Approach

The early core versions of interactional ethnography were based in the ground breaking interactional sociolinguistic work of Judith's mentor, John Gumperz (1982; Gumperz & Herasimchuk, 1972; Gumperz & Hymes, 1972). Early versions also drew from anthropological ethnography, especially the ethnography of communication with Dell Hymes (1972, 1974). In addition, they were inspired by followers of sociologist Harold Garfinkel's ethnomethodology (Baker, 1991; Garfinkel, 1967; Heap, 1991, 1992). Interactional ethnography developed out of a pragmatic need by members of the SBCDG to have a way of seeing, understanding, and investigating classroom teaching and learning that was particular to their research interests and questions. It was an epistemological and ontological framework and a related repertoire of inquiry methods and methodologies that allowed them to examine the classroom co-construction of literacy demands in various subject matters in relation to the discursive and social moves and expectations of the participants.

This framework arose out of and in reaction to the limits of traditional sociolinguistics, one of the longest established social approaches to language, which itself had developed in response to the limits of traditional linguistics by pushing against the concept of language as an abstract, self-contained symbolic system (Gumperz & Hymes, 1964, 1972). Retaining an interest in the structure of language, sociolinguists are concerned mostly with spoken language and with differences in pronunciation, grammar, and style. This focus leads them to study the differences of spoken language among social groups and between individual speakers as they change the way they speak to other individuals who may or may not belong to their social group, share their purpose, or have a similar understanding of the purpose for the conversation. These shifting structural qualities of speech led to understandings about the relationship between language and society, and the role of language in determining variable positions people can assume within society's social structures.

The SBCDG was interested in these concerns, and wanted further to understand how kinds of knowledge were signaled as important in student and teacher interactions. John Gumperz's (1986; Cook-Gumperz & Gumperz, 1991) interactional sociolinguistics added this dimension. This approach pinpoints how social order and understanding are created or constrained as interactants read and act on contextualization cues in their partner's speech. To mark important knowledge, interactional sociolinguists focus on variations in aspects of interaction such as turn-taking, conventions for indicating acknowledgment and agreement, and the prosodics, or sound landscapes, of utterances (Gumperz, 1992; Gumperz & Herasimchuk, 1972). These analytical features served the Blob group's interest in describing how ordinary discursive and social practices in classrooms came to be in moment-to-moment interchanges.

A central principle of ethnomethodology, another approach to studying talk-as-interaction to observe how social order is produced and reproduced in the ordinary conversations of daily life, also became important to the elaboration of interactional ethnography. Ethnomethodologists (who gave rise to a way of analyzing talk referred to as conversation analysis) assume that social actors are not governed by externally imposed social rules (Garfinkel, 1967; Heritage, 1984). Rather, they posit that speakers are agentive and actively engage in creating social order as they conduct everyday conversations. Scholarship about the analytical tools of context (Erickson & Schultz, 1981) and frame (Goffman, 1974; Tannen, 1979, 1993) were central in our descriptions of the discursive creation of this social order. The agentive and orderliness qualities of ordinary classroom talk provide for interactional ethnographers a way of observing how teachers and students act in and through their talk to build and sustain what they think the classroom is meant to be doing and for which particular reasons.

Interactional Ethnography Emerges as a Means of Inquiry

As interactional ethnography took on its own conceptual identity, the central question for any interactional ethnographic study of a classroom came to be who can say or do what to and with whom, when and where, under what conditions, in relation to what actions or artifacts, for what purposes, and with what outcomes? (Castanheira et al., 2001; Green & Dixon, 1993) This orienting question implicates a number of related questions that direct data collection and analysis (Table 1.1):

To pursue the questions put forth in Table 1.1 in a way that addresses the unique opportune and constraining qualities of particular class-

Table 1.1. Questions Guiding Data Collection and Preliminary Analysis

Who:	Which members provide opportunities for learning academic literacies?
	Which members are provided with opportunities?
	Which members take up opportunities?
What:	Which academic literacies are available to learn?
With whom:	Who are the interactional partners with whom the members will be learning?
When:	On what occasions, with what frequency, and in what timely fashion do teaching and learning opportunities occur?
Where:	In which interactional spaces?
	In what physical spaces
How:	How are learning opportunities provided?
	How are they taken up?
	How are the literacies constructed?
Under what conditions?	In which social and power relationships are literacy practices constructed?
	With what material resources?
	With what social resources?
	With what cultural resources?
For what purposes?	What are the goals and expectations for performance of classroom members, dominant members, divergent members, individual members?
With what outcomes?	What performances count?
	How are they assessed and valued?
	How is capability determined?

rooms and of situated educational processes in which individuals engage, the conceptual and analytical lenses needed expansion. In addition to individual interactions, the "groupness" quality of classroom discourse needed to be included. The Santa Barbara group sought to further understand how speakers demonstrate and construct communicative competence as members of a classroom community.

Whereas interactional sociolinguists can demonstrate the accomplishment of communication among interactants, it is ethnographers of communication (Gumperz & Hymes, 1972; Saville-Troike, 1982) who can make visible the use of language in relation to a larger culture in which it occurs. This is an important distinction for interactional ethnographers, because each classroom evolves its own unique set of cultural practices as the school term goes on (Collins & Green, 1990). Like ethnographers of communication, interactional ethnographers are interested in studying patterns of communication as an aspect of cultural knowledge and group membership behavior. They assume there are diverse communicative practices among members of a classroom that are negotiated into commonly agreed upon rules of "how things work and what matters here" (Green & Dixon 1993; Rex, 2000). Finding out what counts for the members of a particular speech community like a classroom, provides insight into the social norms and expectations themselves. Such insights inform how those norms serve particular purposes as routinized practices and rules for perceiving, believing, acting, and evaluating (Goodenough, 1981) beyond individuals' creation of those practices. For example, the Blob was inspired by Derek Edwards and Neil Mercer's (1987) work in the United Kingdom. Edwards and Mercer were exploring how knowledge was socially constructed in classrooms, which suited the Blob's interest in understanding the construction of subject matter knowledge. As the group studied "opportunities" for learning important academic and subject matter knowledge, the general orienting question expanded to include questions about the construction of subject matter knowledge. (Table 1.2).

Inquiry into the dynamic relationship between the discursive practices of individuals and the cultural norms and practices of the group is the general methodology pursued through interactional ethnography. The Santa Barbara group evolved this approach to understand the nature of the relationship between opportunities for learning and social and discursive practices within and across events of life in classrooms and their consequences for students. In the introduction to their 1993 special issue of *Linguistics in Education*, Judith Green and Carol Dixon relate that the volume's studies show that life in a particular classroom has particular consequences for students in that they are able to construct situated models of learning in content areas (Green & Dixon, 1993). "In each classroom,

Table 1.2. Questions Guiding Analysis of Subject Matter Teaching and Learning Practices

---

What counts as subject matter knowledge?

Where, when, and how was subject matter knowledge constructed?

What patterns of activity were opportunistic for subject matter knowledge construction in this classroom?

When and how did the teacher provide opportunities for particular subject matter knowledge to be taken up?

How, through his or her discourse actions with the class as a group, did the teacher provide opportunities for students new to the subject matter knowledge to become recognized as capable members?

What particular kinds of learning opportunities did particular kinds of students recognize and take up, and in what ways?

students were constructing situationally defined repertoires associated with particular models for being students, [which] existed even when content, task, goals, materials, and group were the same" (p. 237). The articles in this seminal volume are footprints of the early interactional ethnographic framework for studying the complexity of social and discursive actions among classroom members in constructing subject matter knowledge.

In her study, Lichu Lin (1993) conceptually separated language "in" and language "of" the classroom to distinguish between language students and teachers use for social interaction—language as means, and language as subject matter—that counts as the literate language of academic texts and academic practices. In making this distinction, Lin's study analytically teases apart the two language uses with two sets of heuristic questions. Questions whose focus is language "in" the classroom look at the social life to explore communicative processes, and patterns of use within a social group. This focus can provide information about access and opportunity observed within and across discourse events and repertoires of events and practices. Questions concerned with language "of" the classroom presuppose that the researcher has already identified the range of verbal practices of the classroom. Questions applied at this point explore the conditions and uses of these practices as a pattern of language use. When related to information gathered from the first set of questions (i.e., "in"), the second set (i.e., "of") can link occasion, type and frequency of social access opportunities to particular kinds of literacy knowledge and practices.

By making visible the intertextual ties between discourse practices and knowledge construction, Lin's study described how what counted as "language and all of its uses" as a subject matter was built over the first 9 days of an English class. In particular, the analysis foregrounds the English teacher's actions in consciously and systematically helping students construct what counted as "language" by making intertextual relationships among discourse events that supported particular ways of engaging with texts, of communicating with others, and of constructing texts (SBCDG, 1992b).

In examining what counts as knowledge and how that knowledge is constructed in and through interactions by members, Blob member Ana Ines Heras (Heras, 1993) explored how institutional positions and interactive positionings were constructed in various interactional spaces in a classroom (e.g., whole class, table group, pairs, and individuals). An interactional space is distinguished by certain features: organizational pattern, time, physical space, and purpose, as well as participants. Positions and positionings are two features of the range of features shaping opportunities students have to construct knowledge. The others are temporality, interactional spaces, intertextuality, and knowledge as constructed through interactions. Heras' study made visible the relationship between different kinds of knowledge and the various interactional spaces in which they are constructed on different occasions over time. The study makes a link between time, space, knowledge and the discursive practices of interactants.

Heidi Brilliant-Mills' (1993) study of the situated construction of what counts as mathematics in a sixth grade classroom described the intertextual discourse construction of what counts as the academic discipline of mathematics. Brilliant-Mills elaborated on the concept of a "field" of intertextual relationships among prior and present events that frame assumptions about what counts as the subject matter of a discipline of study. Classroom members drew on these intertextual assumptions to guide their discursive practices in present and future events. Brilliant-Mills' study provided a view of academic content knowledge as socially and discursively constructed over time in and through the interactions of members of a social group, rather than presenting it as an abstract body of knowledge and practices.

These studies contributed to theoretical understandings and raised further questions about the complexity and influence of context in conceptualizing literacy teaching and learning. Green and Wallat's (1979) earlier question, "What's an instructional context?, which arose when mapping instructional conversation shifts over time, became a central theoretical issue for Blob during this period. Ethnographic analysis of discourse, by providing information about social and cultural conditions and forces, enriched the possibility of what could be viewed as contextual factors (Green & Bloome, 1995; Moerman, 1988). The ethnographically conducted discourse studies expanded notions of what counts as context under the assumption that the relationship between language and context is a mutually constitutive one. In addressing the role of context in ethnographic research in educational settings, Fred Erickson and Jeffrey Shultz (1981), asked the question "When is a context?" They theorized assumptions about contexts that are fundamental to understandings of social competence linked to textual construction and intertextual relationship. The interactional ethnographers of this period tested these assumptions and found them useful:

- Contexts are constituted by what people are doing and where and when they are doing it.
- People in interaction become environments for each other.
- Contexts consist of mutually shared and ratified definitions of situation and of the social actions people take on the basis of these definitions.
- Contexts are embedded in time, can change from moment to moment, and are meaningfully socially related across time.
- With each context change, the roles and relationships among participants are redistributed to produce differing configurations of concerted action.
- Mutual rights and obligations of interactants are continually amenable to subtle readjustment and redistribution into different configurations of concerted action called participation structures.
- Multiple participation structures occur within a single occasion.
- Participants read and provide contextualization cues for each other in their discourse.

In interactional ethnography, context refers, then, to the common orientation and pattern of activity among interactants that leads to the construction of a common text—oral or written. Contexts, like texts, and text-producing events, are shaped by and shape the interactions as they occur over time.

The studies also raised the question of what is a text and how are discourse and texts related? When texts were understood to be written or spoken discourse, students and teachers were seen to bring prior texts to the building of new texts. They drew from an expansive range of textual and material references that were imported from outside and inside the classroom. These imported texts were made relevant through social interaction, when they are socially identified, acknowledged, and validated in classroom conversations (Bloome, 1991). In addition, David Bloome, currently at the Ohio State University and an early protégé of Judith Green's, and Ann Egan-Robertson, once his doctoral student (Bloome & Egan-Robertson, 1993), note that recent scholarship and research locates intertextuality in new ways:

> Reflecting the current diversity of linguistic, literary, and educational views of language, intertextuality is variously located in the reader (and his or her previous readings), in the interaction between a reader and a text (or perhaps more accurately in the transactions among readers and texts), in social interaction, in the social semiotics of language, in classrooms (viewed as diverse linguistic environments), in the discourse structures of various institutions in which we live as well as in how we contest the confines of these discourses, among other locations. (p. 255)

Intertextuality is used by interactional ethnographers to suggest that all social and intellectual relationships can be construed as texts that are themselves intertextual, wherein texts are always under construction and in shifting relational juxtaposition. Intertextuality, as a central concept of interactional ethnography, is a means of describing the links in classrooms between texts, of describing current and previous text linkages to someone's experience, and of describing the processes through which knowledge is co-constructed by teachers and students (who are in social relationships) through textual connections.

Ana Floriani (1993), in a study linking intertextuality to the interactional frames of reference within which students construct knowledge, coined the term "intercontextuality" for the relationship between text and the person(s) who produce(s) it. Floriani's analysis of students working together in collaborative pairs over time to write a common text attempts to define context by identifying a written text and considering how participants are constructing the text within each unfolding event that is shaping its form and substance. Central to this analysis is the view that texts are never single-person constructions, but are always interactive, and that a relationship always exists between the persons engaged in producing them.

Evolving Programs of Research Develop the Interactional Ethnographic Approach

These studies and subsequent generations of work have extended the conceptual framework, approach, methods of analysis, focal interests, and purposes of interactional ethnographic research. They have helped to build constructs central to interactional ethnography:

- Classrooms are unique cultures within institutional cultures of schooling whose practices and values as they accrue become ordinary and invisible to members (SBCDG, 1992a).
- In and through language and actions observed in moment to moment discourse interactions that become patterned over time, teachers and students construct and constitute their classroom norms and expectations for what counts as meaningful academic knowledge (Edwards & Mercer, 1987; Green et. al., 1988).
- What counts as academic knowledge is built and maintained in and through social processes that can be identified by examining who can say or do what, to and with whom, under what conditions, in what ways, when, where, for what purpose(s), and with what outcome(s) (Zaharlick & Green, 1991).
- Classroom discourse interactions are constituted by and, in turn, construct interactional spaces and contexts of understanding which are characterized by interactants roles and relationships and the knowledge and values brought forward into the interaction (Heras, 1993; Tuyay, Jennings, & Dixon, 1995).
- A dynamic, mutually constitutive relationship exists between the kinds of knowledge brought forward and taken up, the activity to which it is applied, and the interactional contexts in which members give it meaning (Green & Wallat, 1981b).
- The nature of this relationship is visible in intertextual and intercontextual links across time among classroom events that students and teachers construct during discourse interactions. (Bloome & Bailey, 1992; Bloome & Egan-Robertson, 1993; Floriani, 1993)
- Over time, particular kinds of commonly held understandings of what counts as literate thinking, literate actions, literate products and being literate are visible as patterned intertextual and intercontextual relationships (SBCDG, 1992a, 1992b).
- The dynamic, historical network of intertextual and intercontextual relationships in classroom cultures inscribe fields of meaning visible to, available to, and kept in motion by members in the social interplay of classroom discourse. These fields of meaning have consequences for which students can participate and how, and for the subject matter and school knowledge students can learn (Brilliant-Mills, 1993; Lin, 1993; Rex & McEachen, 1999; Rex, 2000, 2001).

As may be evident in these principles, interactional ethnography is undergirded by the extensive anthropological tradition of ethnographic research in education. The foundational scholarship of George and

Louise Spindler (Spindler, 1982; Spindler & Spindler, 1992) laid out the dimensions of ethnography as applied to the study of education. For the Spindlers, the ultimate purpose of ethnography is to provide source material for analysis, wherein "analysis is inference governed by systematic models, paradigms, and theory" (p. 22). No single or constant model, paradigm, or theory governs interactional ethnography. Nevertheless, theoretical positions about the construction of knowledge and the tools to study it are consistently evoked in interactional ethnographic studies. In rejecting the central tenet of positivism, that there can be a neutral, impersonal scientific language to describe and interpret human activities, interactional ethnography follows in the footsteps of Charles Taylor's (1987) seminal thinking in "Interpretation and the Sciences of Man." There exists no structure of meaning for a phenomenon independent of the interpreter's interpretation of it. In addition, those engaging in interactional ethnography assume that knowledge does not exist independent of those who create and use it.

This postmodern interpretivist and constructivist view of knowledge "as actively constructed—as culturally and historically grounded, as laden with moral and political values, and as serving certain interests and purposes" has been summarized by philosopher of science, Kenneth Howe (2001, p. 202). Howe's explanation of the dilemma this interpretivist position creates for social science researchers argues for two camps of interpretivist research: the postmodern and the transformationist. Given Howe's distinction between the two, interactional ethnography would fall into the transformationist camp. Those who use the interactional ethnographic approach "see their task as working out defensible conceptions of knowledge and rationality that have contingent human experience as their basis. . . . continuous with the emancipatory project of modernity" (p. 202).

Returning then to ethnography as the approach taken by interactional ethnography, ethnography is a means to intimately study the lived experience of knowledge and rationality of a group culture. In addition, the process of that study has an ethical responsibility to not only represent that lived experience as consistent with the range of interpretations of cultural insiders, but also to provide a study with transformative power. That is to say, those who engage in interactional ethnography negotiate not only their interpretations with those they study, they also evolve research questions and study designs that will elicit knowledge of that site that can contribute to positive change in education. Such a contribution should be made to both the local participants and to the larger community of educators and educational researchers and scholars.

Multiple later generations of researchers in the interactional ethnographic tradition have applied and extended these principles and concerns. Each elaborated the interactional ethnographic conceptual and methodological framework. I developed a cluster of linked studies to theorize how students "orient" to classroom expectations for successful subject matter as they engage in the co-construction of those expectations (Rex, 2001, 2002; Rex & McEachen, 1999; Rex et. al., 2002). LeAnn Putney (Putney, Green, Dixon, Duran, & Yeager, 2000) conceptualized "consequential progressions" as a means of observing the consequential nature of classroom events. One elaboration that strongly influenced the studies in this volume is Tuyay, Jennings, and Dixon's (1995) elaboration of the concept of "opportunities for learning" as a socially signaled and recognized phenomenon that is context- content-, time-, and participant-dependent. Their logic that the researchers in this volume found so compelling was that if, as previous studies have established, subject matter learning is socially constituted and constructed through intertextual and intercontextual classroom interactions around texts that build intellectual knowledge, then student access to such interactions is central to effective learning. Identifying the range and repertoire of interactions that could provide access, and defining the kind of access that is granted, is one of the purposes of interactional ethnography.

In 1982, Green and Harker had preliminarily explored this issue in a study of students' attempts to gain access to the teacher or to group discussion at times other than their designated turn or when the floor was open. Their study showed that students were sensitive to implicit shifts in expectation and could extract information necessary for a socially appropriate performance. In later studies, Alton-Lee and Nuthall (1992) analytically isolated critical elements of student opportunity to learn by surveying available opportunities for interaction with content. Assuming students needed a "critical mass" of numbers of opportunities, and that this mass is built up over time, the study developed a retrospective predicative model for student performance outcomes. The researchers acknowledged that time and critical mass as significant factors in determining opportunity to learn are necessary but not sufficient. They recognized that the teacher's skill is pivotal in providing opportunities considered appropriate within the social, cultural and instructional contexts of the classroom.

Using the lens of interactional ethnography, Tuyay, Jennings, and Dixon (1995) appropriated and expanded these concepts of opportunities to learn by applying an ethnographic "insiders" perspective. They studied different student groups' interaction patterns as they each collaboratively drafted a writing task. They demonstrated how different interactions by different groups of students in different interactional spaces built different knowledge and constructed different opportunities to learn, even when the task was the same. This study confirmed that a range of opportunities to learn are available as a configuration of the student roles and relationships within a particular group and their attendant interactional patterns. The study also made visible how a common task was negotiated and renegotiated on different occasions over time by the teacher and students as the teacher made contingent responses (see Wells & Chang-Wells, 1992). Key to the work in this volume, by describing patterns of interaction within classroom instructional events, this study demonstrated how, through the weaving together of ethnographically obtained data of patterned events across time, a web of opportunities for learning could be made visible.

A Recent Illustration of The Interactional Ethnographic Approach

A more explicit and instructive explanation of interactional ethnography as an approach linked to a logic of inquiry which implies types of transcripts and analyses, appears in a later *Linguistics and Education* (Castanheira, Crawford, Green, & Dixon, 2001) article. This study of Judith Green's and Carol Dixon's, with members from a later Blob generation, Maria Lucia Castanheira and Teresa Crawford, illustrates the approach through a broad range of analyses that comparatively describe what counts as text, as literate practices, and as participation in each of five subject area classes taken by Aaron, an Australian high school student. The authors tell us the following:

> The interactional ethnographer . . . must look at what is constructed in and through the moment-by-moment interactions among members of a social group; how members negotiate events through these interactions, and the ways in which knowledge and texts generated in one event become linked to, and thus a resource for, members' actions in subsequent events. (p. 357)

In this representation of the central interactional ethnographic constructs, the generation of and linkage between events has taken a dominant role. Although intertextuality appeared as an important construct in early interactional ethnographic work, it has come to assume an even more theoretically integrated and methodologically explicit role. In order to examine the opportunities for learning and the knowledge available to Aaron within his vocational education program, the researchers studied each of his five classrooms. They inquired into a broad spectrum of intertextual relationships to describe how subject specific literate practices worked together to shape daily classroom events and students' knowledge construction.

As is typical in an ethnographic approach, the researchers began with an overarching or orienting question, which guided their analyses of their data: "How can we understand the ways in which literate practices are shaped, and in turn shape, the everyday events of classroom life, and thus, the opportunities that Aaron, and his peers, had for learning?" To construct an answer to this question they began a series of representations of the data, each of which generated and was guided by a question that emerged from the prior analysis. These representations took the form of transcripts, data tables, and domain analyses (Spradley, 1980). In a first set of analyses, the researchers analyzed what was happening—the events—in each class by tracing who Aaron interacted with, about what, in what ways, for what purposes, when and where, and with what outcomes. They wanted to understand what events constituted the activity and semantic world of each classroom. This first phase analysis of video tapes produced three transcripts or structuration maps (see Giddens, 1979; Green & Meyer, 1991): a time-stamped running record of classroom activity, an event map representing the episodic nature of members' activity, and comparative timelines of the events and phases of activity. These became core texts for the rest of the analytical process. By tracing Aaron's interactions across time and events, they provided representations of subject matter knowledge teaching and learning practices, including opportunities and demands for its display.

In the second set of analyses, the researchers compared and contrasted the demands for being literate in each subject-area class in order to understand "How was literacy talked and acted into being within and across classrooms?"; and, "What is the role of the individual in the sociocognitive activities identified?" To perform this analysis, they focused on the role of a frequently used text, the workbook, in framing opportunities for learning. To do so, they contrasted event maps across classrooms, they applied contrasting methods (i.e., event mapping, transcript/discourse analysis, and domain analysis); and they compared stated and observed curriculums. For example, they contrasted activity timelines to compare how time was spent in each subject area. In addition, they compared events that occurred in multiple classrooms, like test-taking, to observe the range of interactional spaces, the norms and expectations for performance, and the roles and relationships observable in actions, talk, and texts. The analyses surfaced the ways of being and acting as a student afforded Aaron in each classroom as well as the unique and comparable opportunities for learning available to him as he engaged with workbooks in each setting.

A third set of analyses identified who shaped the opportunities previously identified. By comparing and contrasting the curriculums as observed with statements about curriculum in official documents, comparisons were made between what was said to be happening and what was happening in terms of vocational education for Aaron. To perform this analysis, the researchers conducted domain analyses of the literate demands and actions in all five classrooms. From these domain analyses, they constructed a taxonomy of kinds of written text and a taxonomy of kinds of literacy-related interaction. They next constructed a summary table of statements related to the official curriculum drawn from educational documents. They performed a type of critical discourse analysis to understand the institutional positions and identity relationships that are inscribed in and through the various discourses.

One outcome of the study was a detailed description of how Aaron acted "appropriately" as a student in all his classes and how he was afforded radically different kinds of opportunities in his English and mathematics classes. In mathematics he could expand his conceptual understanding of math terms and computational practices through direct interaction with the teacher; whereas in English, where his interactions were limited to workbook activities *about* English literacy knowledge, he had less opportunity to engage *in* literate practices. Because both the official texts and the workbook expected engagement in literacy practices, the study provides empirical descriptive evidence of the lack of support on the part of the English course and the presence of learning opportunities in the mathematics class for Aaron's literate capacity-building.

There is a danger in using a single study to illustrate the methods of interactional ethnography. A single portrayal privileges and essentializes a single, unique application. Interactional ethnography is a constantly evolving approach to studying teaching and learning in classrooms, and as such should not be confused with a step-by-step research plan or system. Although it is guided by conceptual and procedural principles and utilizes self-referential methods of transcription and analysis, no single set of guidelines exists for conducting an interactional ethnographic study. With the elaboration of theoretical tools for observing educational settings and teaching and learning, and with the expansion of teaching and learning into new educational sites beyond the traditional classroom, interactional ethnography continues to evolve. The questions interactional ethnographers ask and the analyses they perform expand into these new conceptual and physical territories as will be noticeable in the studies that follow. Nevertheless, certain key principles remain constant: (a) the subject of study is a complex social phenomenon; (b) that a group of people intentionally engaged in teaching and learning form a culture; (c) the conceptual and procedural constructs of ethnography and discourse analysis are key ways of studying the actions of such a group; and (d) complexity is productively studied through analysis of relationships between parts and wholes within single instances and across situations and time.

OVERVIEW OF THE CHAPTERS: THE APPLICATION AND ADAPTATION OF INTERACTIONAL ETHNOGRAPHY

In the nine chapters that follow, beginning researchers try on interactional ethnography as a means of building empirically evidenced understandings about how teaching and learning interactions create and constrain opportunities for learning. Before becoming chapters for this volume, each study began as a paper with a more extensive conceptual framework and methods section. We decided to shorten these sections to eliminate unnecessary redundancy, and to instead describe the theories and approaches as we have in the beginning of this introduction. We kept the results sections intact so that readers could observe the methods, means, logics, and outcomes of the disparate analyses.

How and Why I Chose Interactional Ethnography

Chapter 2 by Kathy Morris is not a research study. Rather it is an explanation of why the author applied discourse analysis methods and frameworks for studying classrooms to the study of professional development. The chapter evolved from Kathy's need to find a way of studying teacher learning in professional development workshops, because such research is in its infancy. She began with the assumption that methods that have been successful in studying K–12 classroom teaching and learning should be fruitful in studying adult groups, and narrowed those methods to ones that analyze the discourse of teaching and learning interactions. After reviewing the K–12 classroom discourse literature and the wide variety of discourse-analytic approaches and methods, she selected conversational analysis (CA) and interactional ethnography (IE), having determined that both have proven track records in educational research.

We thought it fitting to begin the volume with Kathy's chapter because it provides a window into the stage in her research process, which is usually absent from the methods sections of research articles— when she had to decide which methods would be best suited to explore the phenomenon she has chosen. Although it is not written as a narrative, embedded in her chapter is Kathy's recursive, dialectical thinking process as she pondered the reflexive relationship between what she wanted to study and what methods she would use. In her explanation to us of why she selected CA and IE to investigate teacher learning in professional workshops, we see the series of intellectual choices she had to make.

These choices about what comprises the object of study and how to study or know it, referred to by scholars as the ontology and epistemology of research, are intimately and influentially related. For example, Paul

Ricoeur (1981), writing about scientific study of the social world, addressed this relationship as one between how we know what we know, how we know we know it, and the actions we take based on these conceptual interrelationships. He illuminates how meanings and subsequent related actions emerge from our (the researcher's and the consumer's of research) relationship to language. Ricoeur posits that the question to be asked is no longer "How do we know?" but rather, "What is the mode of being of that being who exists only in understanding?" (p. 54). Understanding, which emerges from the interpretation of language used to construct meaning, creates phenomena, the creation of which leads to our decisions about ways of dealing with them. To determine her object and her methods of study, Kathy engaged in a circular, constant comparison building of understanding of what she would end up with as her subject if she studied it in a particular way.

Kathy's challenge in Ricoeurian terms is the challenge to locate language that reflects understanding being built—the particular professional development phenomenon to study, and to represent that teaching and learning language using research language that reflects an understanding of it—a valid way of knowing the phenomenon. Kathy first addresses this challenge as an issue of transcription. She makes the important point that a transcript is a particular type of representation that foregrounds certain features and backgrounds or eliminates others—quite often the contextual and "groupness" features. Transcribing is a political act that empowers some ideas, situations, outcomes, and people while marginalizing others.

She introduces us to the CA elements—among them, turn-taking, adjacency pairing, and back channeling—that she finds helpful in studying the structural qualities of coherence and cohesiveness (understandings under construction) of professional development interactions. Kathy illustrates what these CA analytical tools can make visible through before and after transcriptions of the same interaction. She notes that professional developers talk like teachers who habitually control teaching–learning interactions in a particular sequence of teacher initiation, student response, and teacher evaluation or feedback. Kathy demonstrates that to some extent studying discourse structures can afford a view of their semantic content or of the meanings that are constructed in the moment through engagement in those structures.

Returning to a consideration of the phenomenon that these structural tools provide, Kathy confronts the differences between adult to adult professional development (PD) and adult-to-child classroom relationships. She selects additional discourse analysis features of frame, footing, and alignment to study ever-changing relationships between PD interactants that complicate their "learning." A reconsideration of the PD phenomenon and what CA can understand of it leads Kathy to note the method's limitations. CA can inform us about how PD groups participate in and maintain conversation, but studying discrete moments of conversation could not help her view how teacher learning is constructed over time in ways that are meaningful to the participants to improve PD. So she turns to IE as a potential method for looking at that sort of phenomenon. To understand "whether" and "how" learners (or in this case teachers as learners) have come to new understandings about particular subject matter (i.e., learning) requires studying the reconstruction of old understanding and knowledge.

Assessing The Opportunities for Learning Made Available for Students

The studiers in chapters 2–4 use discourse analysis to locate and demonstrate student take up of opportunities for learning. Alexandra Miletta's (Chapter 3) study describes the opportunities provided by the teacher's interactions with students to build their own respectful manner and their classroom's respectful environment as they engage in inquiry. In Chapter 4, Mary Yonker is concerned with how tutors and immigrant children in an after-school bilingual literacy tutoring program build trust and reading instruction knowledge. Next, in Chapter 5, Carol Connor and I focus on the opportunities for struggling and able readers to obtain effective reading instruction.

Alexandra's study explores the possibility of making visible the moral aspects of teaching. In this initial foray into the subject, which she eventually elaborated for her dissertation (Miletta, 2003), Alexandra utilizes IE to see how a teacher and her students incorporate what they believe is fair, right, and just into the daily life of their elementary school classroom. Alexandra is breaking new ground in this area by bringing IE to the classroom to investigate how a teacher, Darlene, and her students construct what counts as morally acceptable behavior through verbal, nonverbal, and written communication in order to establish what they view as a "good" classroom climate. Alexandra selects five interactions, which she has ethnographically determined as episodes in which Darlene took advantage of a regular instructional moment in order to co-construct with her students an understanding of morally acceptable behavior. Each of these interactions is selected to serve as a telling, rather than a typical, case. A telling case, as originally conceptualized by ethnographer J. Mitchell (1984), is selected not because it is representative of the culture, although it may be, but rather because it offers an occasion for surfacing previously obscure theoretical relationships. Comparative analysis of the five particular cases of in-action teaching of moral action engendered speculative theories about how morally acceptable behavior was built in the classroom.

Alexandra's study is also noteworthy for another aspect common to IE—the intimate involvement of the teacher (or main participants) in the research process. From the beginning of the study, Darlene and Alexandra worked together to collect and analyze the data. Their continual dialogue about what Alexandra was collecting and interpreting influenced every aspect of the study. Darlene's reflections on her own intentions as she reviewed and interpreted video-tapes of her teaching became additional data, and her assessments of Alexandra's interpretations of what was accomplished in the moments of her teaching served as a constant member check. Alexandra also applied student data to complement Darlene's point of view and arrive at claims for her study that benefited Darlene and her students by promoting positive classroom climate. By using cases like Darlene's to illustrate "how" to engage students in behaving in more respectful and responsible ways, managing student behavior is represented as a more complicated issue than classroom management.

Similar to Alexandra, Mary Yonker was concerned that an important educational phenomenon had been insufficiently explored. For Mary, that phenomenon was after-school tutoring programs. A bilingual beginning researcher, she was concerned with the potential risks for failure of immigrant children who were suddenly immersed into English-only classrooms. As a teacher, she helped support a voluntary after-school program designed to sustain immigrant children's biliteracy while improving their English reading. In Chapter 4, Mary presents her study of the after-school reading instruction activities in that program. She is interested in understanding how the program director loosely trained the college student tutors, how the tutors taught reading, and how the children responded.

From her ethnographically collected data corpus, she selected "rich points" (Agar, 1980, 1994) for discourse analysis to understand whether biliteracy practices were established, and if so, how. These data points seemed to her to be rich with promise for offering insight into her questions and were all interactions that occurred during circle time, a routine group meeting that involved reading. Mary chose IE because it focused on language, which for her was central to the biliteracy dilemma faced by the teachers, tutors, and children in the program. In addition, in emphasizing culture, the approach allowed Mary to foreground the communal aspect of the program so important to the Mexican immigrant teachers, parents, and children. In addition to teaching bilingual reading, the program was expected to operate as a community based on *confianza*, or mutual trust, between the families and the members of the program and among the program participants. Capturing the quality of trust as it relat-

ed to reading instruction was as important to Mary as assessing the quality of the instruction and learning. Mary's analysis indicated that the children's experience of community and trust was positive and supportive of
their acculturation. However, the quality of reading instruction they were
experiencing was not as positive. Although not meant as a program
assessment tool, her study served to open a dialogue with the program
director about the issues raised by the study.

In Chapter 5, Carol Connor and I combine a cognitive lens for evaluating struggling readers against standard developmental benchmarks
and a sociocultural lens to assess their performance as readers within the
literate activities of their classrooms. By combining the two lenses in the
study, the contrasts between each are readily apparent and highlight the
epistemological differences between cognitive and sociocultural
approaches for assessing educational phenomena like reading. However,
we have worked hard to complementarily combine the two.

Carol is a former speech-language pathologist and keenly aware of
the recent expansion of the role of speech-language pathologists in working with reading specialists and classroom teachers on interventions to
improve students' literacy. Although standardized tests remain important evaluation instruments, classroom-based assessments have become
critical for guiding interventions. At the time of the study, combining the
two approaches was an untested challenge in need of theoretical and
practical guidance. Carol and I took up this challenge using an IE
approach for studying two African-American fourth-grade boys' classroom reading performances.

For the study, we combined the results of the boys' reading and language tests and their classroom reading performances to assess the two
readers' capabilities, to inform an intervention, and to work collaboratively with the teacher. The tests indicated that one of the students was an
able reader and the other struggled. By analyzing the boys' reading
actions within the classroom norms for reading and in relation to the
teacher's pedagogical practices, the classroom study provided a rich,
contextualized description of their capabilities and weaknesses. It was a
description to which the teacher contributed and from which Carol could
find footholds for approaching the teacher about assessing her teaching.
Structuration maps and transcriptions of telling sequences of interaction
made visible and concrete what was happening during reading instruction and classroom activity that required reading. In addition to observation, interviews with the teacher provided information about her beliefs
and knowledge about the boys as readers and about her knowledge of
reading instruction. From the study, Carol was able to ascertain that the
teacher provided different kinds of reading opportunities for the boys,
some of which the boys interacted with effectively and some of which

they could not. By depicting how reading instruction and classroom demands for reading influenced the kind of readers the boys could be in the classroom, the study could make suggestions for general changes in the classroom curriculum and in teaching strategies that could benefit the struggling reader while keeping in place the practices that already served the able reader.

Applying Intertextuality to Examine an Instructional Approach

In chapters 5 and 6, intertextuality becomes a dominant conceptual and methodological lens for analyzing learning territory that requires creative means for data collection and analysis. Wen-Yu Lee (Chapter 6) incorporates computer process video texts with discourse transcripts to understand how a cadaver-dissecting team learns together as it proceeds. In Jake Foster's (Chapter 7) study of a voluntary study group for student teachers, intertextual analysis is taken to the scale of discursive message units. Jake observes micro moves in discussions about theory and practice to see how together he and the students navigate their way through conceptual and practical topics toward greater understanding.

A medical school dissection lab is the setting for Wen-Yu's chapter study of anatomical literacy learning. Not conventionally considered a classroom, Wen-Yu found the lab a rich site for studying medical students' computer uses as they learn anatomy knowledge. She applied an interactional ethnographic approach to analyze the discourse of a six-member dissecting team over the course's 14 lab sessions. Her purposes were to find out when and why students used computer technology during the dissection lab and to understand how social interaction functioned as an educative milieu during the lab. She wanted to know what knowledge sources students drew on and what knowledge they built together as they worked on their cadaver during the 3-hour lab. She wanted to understand how anatomical literacy-building occurred during occasions of computer use.

Intertextual analysis was central to her study. Referring to videotapes of the students' dissection conversations and of their computer screen (using ATLASplus), Wen-Yu looked for significant intertextual relationships between students' speech and physical actions and the medical texts. She was able to demonstrate how different media for anatomy literacy were incorporated simultaneously into the learning practices of the dissection group. Wen-Yu's three levels of data analysis began when she represented the group's learning events with the computer in a complexly integrated structuration map and time line. In her second analytical step, she categorized five patterns among these events, or learning themes, for uses of the computer. Finally, she located occasions when the group conversed to construct intertextual knowledge utilizing the computer. In her chapter, she presents three illustrative cases of intertextually observed anatomical literacy learning. Through her study, Wen-Yu observes the important role intertextuality played in students' collaborative achievement and in individual anatomy literacy building.

Intertextuality was also central to Jake Foster's study of a teacher education study group. As a science teacher educator, he was interested in understanding how, during discussions of their student teaching, members of a study group explored relationships between the theoretical concepts from their university courses and the immediate experiences of teaching science. He also wanted to assess the effectiveness of his facilitation, grounded in sociocultural constructivist learning theory, during conversations among the four group members over their six sessions. To conduct his IE study, he applied the concept of intertextuality to understand relationships between multiple influences, perspectives, and/or events considered by the group in the social discourse.

On a participant–observer continuum, Jake was a key participant in the phenomenon he was studying. In choosing his analytical approach, he was keenly mindful of the importance of having a method of analysis that would provide an analytical distance from the phenomenon under study, to strengthen the validity of his interpretations. First, from the videotapes, he mapped and examined the events of all the group discussion sessions to describe the topics and issues the student teachers found most important and relevant. Next, Jake identified topical interactions that embedded theory–practice connections by viewing each interaction in relation to the discussion in which it was embedded to identify participant moves, content, and function of the statements.

At this point, he performed an intertextual analysis to examine the nature of the theory–practice relationships discussed and provide a profile of his facilitation moves in the discussion. By following David Bloome and Ann Egan-Robertson's (1993) conceptual construct for social intertextuality, he was able to make visible how intertextual juxtapositions were accomplished and what they produced in terms of significance for group members. Jake's close attention to ascertaining the social significance of certain discursive moves and intertextual links made it possible for him to describe how theory–practice relationships were promoted and facilitated in the study group.

Exploring And Building Conceptual Knowledge

In the studies in Chapters 8 and 9, Ruth Piker and Hsin-Kai Wu focus on studying the building of conceptual knowledge. Ruth's goal is to understand how the unorthodox instructional approach of a preschool teacher provides opportunities for her students to understand concepts they otherwise might not. Hsin-Kai explores innovative attempts to improve student learning of traditionally challenging chemistry knowledge.

A former preschool teacher, Ruth Piker's interest is in improving preschool education. She was concerned that documents advocating improvement call for the "building of conceptual knowledge" but do not define what is meant by that phrase nor do they provide instructional guidelines for its achievement. Observing a Head Start preschool classroom in which, she surmised, students were building conceptual knowledge, she used IE to understand how the classroom's routines and ways of interacting assisted the children in socially constructing conceptual knowledge. Her aim is to understand what conceptual development and change might look like in a preschool classroom. As part of her analysis, she observes how common ways of interacting offered opportunities for students to challenge and be challenged for conceptual change. Living in the classroom for 28 days over 8 months as a participant- observer, Ruth collected ethnographic data. Within the view of the classroom, the teacher, and the children afforded by her data corpus, Ruth focused on the language used in the classroom as well as on the activity-participation structures.

After providing descriptive examples of what she has speculated are instances of conceptual knowledge building, Ruth turned to psychologist's theories of conceptual knowledge. She carefully compares what she has observed to what theorists suggest constitutes conceptual learning and concludes that within their particular learning environment the children did build understandings of being on a plane, of people with special needs, of a papoose, of eating rabbits, and of insects' characteristics. Ruth's study highlights the application of educational theories to analyze classroom performances as related to opportunities for learning.

In Hsin-Kai Wu's study, she describes how high school chemistry class members interactionally constructed meanings for chemical representations by connecting them to their life experiences. She observes this dynamic in relation to the way in which the experienced teacher and the student teacher used content knowledge to shape the students' connections. A common problem in chemistry education is the difficulty students have in understanding the representations of chemical molecules and processes. A recommended approach for resolving that difficulty is to guide students in linking chemical properties and reactions to common facets of their daily lives. Hsin-Kai bases her study on the assumption that cognitive processes or mental representations are made accessible through social and discursive interactions among teachers and students and are rhetorically and contextually dependent. She collected ethnographic data daily at a high school for 7 weeks in order to focus on an 11th-grade science class' unit on toxins centered around the inquiry question "Is my drinking water safe?" Working from her videotapes and observational fieldnotes of instruction, Hsin-Kai first transcribed the class activities to identify the events, their duration, and the chemical concepts that were covered. She then mapped each event and subevent to understand how they were interrelated within the whole cycle of activity of the unit. Using these event maps, she selected discourse segments of subevents to transcribe. She was guided in her choices by her research questions, and so chose those segments in which microscopic representations were talked about, connected to life experiences, or elaborated by the teachers. She triangulated her transcriptions and interpretations of the video data with the curriculum materials and observational fieldnotes she had collected.

In reporting what she learned from the study, Hsin-Kai uses similar strategies performed by other studies in the volume. She includes her structuration maps in the appendix and presents a few interactional excerpts to illustrate patterns that emerged from her part–whole analyses within and across all her ethnographic data and discourse analyses. This compression selection strategy allows the reader to see in condensed form descriptive evidence of the phenomena the researcher claims is occurring. Hsin-Kai's three segments show how connections were initiated and completed by the class members, by teachers while interacting with student responses, and as solely constructed by the teachers. In choosing these segments, Hsin-Kai is making an effort to provide a view of the classroom that fairly represents its culture and practices. Although the segments themselves are not necessarily typical, they reflect what is typical about the classrooms' discourse and knowledge-building practices.

Studying the Social Positioning of Students' Roles and Identities

Although most of the applications of the IE approach have been directed at understanding teaching and learning interactions or the construction of subject matter knowledge, Sharilyn Steadman's (Chapter 10) two-stage study points in a different direction—at identity. First, she studied the discursive culture of the classroom and how it shaped the opportunities for student learning, and then attempted to improve those opportunities by applying what she had learned. Her first study noted the presence of gender-differentiated discourses in the classroom and their role for the boys in establishing and maintaining their social identity. Her second study was an experiment to see if a targeted change in teaching approach could expand the boy's identity positions and consequently their social learning opportunities beyond being "players."

Sharilyn had noted that for the boys "playing" and being perceived as "players" was their highest priority, whereas in relation to the boys, girls took on the role of "teacher." The consistent patterns of the students' and teacher's discourse throughout the term defined social and classroom participation that consistently limited the scope of the intended learning. For the next term's class, Sharilyn and the teacher reconstructed the curriculum and her teaching approach to expand the way students related to each other and to the curriculum. They required both boys and girls to act as teachers for the rest of the class. In the study's second phase, Sharilyn investigated the boy's discursive patterns prior to the change and noted they consistently took on the role of player, as had the first group. She observed how their roles contributed to the material social relations in the classroom. She then analyzed the discourse generated in the class during the changed curriculum to observe whether the boys acted as teachers as well as players. She also investigated whether the change had an enduring effect on the social and material reality of the classroom as a learning environment. In documenting the success of the intervention, Sharilyn's study became a bold attempt to qualitatively measure the affect of an intentional change in the way students participate in their learning.

About the Process

At the beginning of each section that follows, the authors of the chapters in that section reflect on the major issues, decisions, and problems they encountered in their quest to realize their studies. They make reference to the advanced methods course for doctoral students I taught for 4 years in the School of Education at the University of Michigan: Introduction to Interactional Ethnography. All of the studies presented in the chapters that follow began as projects for that course. Some of the data were collected prior to the course, whereas others were acquired after they began. Students read about the anthropological, sociolinguistic and discourse-analytic approaches from which interactional ethnography draws, while reading literature that illustrated versions of the approach and research that applied it. Working in collaborative groups of three to four members, the students "tried out" the concepts and methods on their data. They evolved research questions, designed a logic of inquiry, conceived rationales for selection of data to transcribe and analyze, evolved transcription methods, and developed their interpretations and claims. They also analyzed the rhetorical structures of IE research articles and served as critical readers of each others' drafts as they wrote up their studies. Because

I was present for each of the four courses, I can attest to commonalities students reported in their dispositions, knowledge, and activity during their intense 13 weeks of saturated study. They developed reflexivity throughout the research process, heightened awareness of the responsibility visited on those of us who engage in interpretive research, and care in exercising it through increased respect for the powerful relationships among what we say, what we think, and what we do.

REFERENCES

Agar, M. (1994). *Language shock; understanding the culture of conversation.* New York: William Morrow.

Agar, M.H. (1980). *The professional stranger: An informal introduction to ethnography.* New York: Academic Press.

Alton-Lee, A., & Nuthall, G. (1992). Children's learning in classrooms: Challenges to developing a methodology to explain "opportunity to learn." *Journal of Classroom Interaction, 27*(2), 1-7.

Baker, C.D. (1991). Literacy practices and social relations in classroom reading events. In C. Baker & A. Luke (Eds.). *Toward a critical sociology of reading pedagogy* (pp. 161-190). Philadelphia, PA: John Benjamins.

Bloome, D. (1991). *Interaction & intertextuality in the study of classroom reading and writing events: Microanalysis as a theoretical enterprise.* In the Proceedings of the II International Conference on Classroom Ethnography, Mexico City, June 26-28.

Bloome, D., & Bailey, F. (1992). Studying language through events, particularity, intertextuality. In R. Beach, J. Green, M. Kamil, & T. Shanahan (Eds.), *Multidisciplinary perspectives on literacy research* (pp. 181-210). Bloomington, IL: National Conference for Research in English/National Council of Teachers of English.

Bloome, D., & Egan-Robertson, A. (1993). The social construction of intertextuality in classroom reading and writing lessons. *Reading Research Quarterly, 28*(4), 305-333.

Brilliant-Mills, H. (1993). Becoming a mathematician: Building a situated definition of mathematics. *Linguistics and Education, 5*(3 & 4), 301-334.

Castanheira, M., Crawford, T., Green, J., & Dixon, C. (2001). Interactional ethnography: An approach to studying the social construction of literate practices. *Linguistics and Education, 11*(4), 353-400.

Collins, E., & Green, J. (1990) Metaphors: The construction of a perspective. *Theory Into Practice, 29*(2), 71-77.

Cook-Gumperz, J., & Gumperz, J. (1991). Changing views of language in education: The implications for literacy research. In R. Beach, J. Green, M. Kamil, & T. Shanahan (Eds.), *Multidisciplinary perspectives on literacy research* (pp. 151-179). Urbana, IL: National Council of Teachers of English.

Craviotto, E., Heras, A.I., & Espindola, J. (1999). Cultures of the fourth-grade classroom. *Primary Voices, 7*(3), 25-36.

Dixon, C., de la Cruz, E., Green, J., Lin, L., & Brandts, L. (1992). Do you see what we see? The referential and intertextual nature of classroom life. *Journal of Classroom Interaction, 27*(2), 29-36.

Dixon, C., Frank, C., & Brandts, L. (1997). Teacher in writer's workshop: Understanding the complexity. *CliPs: Journal of the California Literature Project, 3*(1), 31-36.

Dixon, C., Green, J., & Frank, C. (1999). Classrooms as cultures: Understanding the constructed nature of life in classrooms. *Primary Voices. K-6, 7*(3), 4-8.

Edwards, D., & Mercer, N. (1987). *Common knowledge: The development of understanding in the classroom.* New York: Falmer Press.

Erickson, F., & Schultz, J. (1981). When is context? Some issues and methods in the analysis of social competence. In J. L. Green & C. Wallat (Eds.), *Ethnography and language in educational settings* (pp. 147-160). Norwood, NJ: Ablex.

Floriani, A. (1993). Negotiating what counts: Roles and relationships, content and meaning, texts and context. *Linguistics and Education, 5*(3 & 4), 241-274.

Floriani, A. (1997). *Creating a community of learners: Constructing opportunities for learning and negotiating meaning in a bilingual classroom.* Unpublished dissertation, University of California, Santa Barbara.

Frank, C. (1999). *Ethnographic eyes.* Portsmouth, NH: Heinemann.

Frank, C. R. (1997). *The children who owned all the words in the world: An ethnography of writing workshop in second grade.* Unpublished dissertation, University of California, Santa Barbara.

Franquiz, M. (1999). Learning in transformational space: Struggling with powerful ideas. *Journal of Classroom Interaction, 34*(2), 30-44.

Franquiz, M. E. (1995). *Transformations in bilingual classrooms: Understanding opportunity to learn within the change process.* Unpublished dissertation, University of California at Santa Barbara. (Winner of the Outstanding Dissertation Award for 1996, National Association for Bilingual Education.)

Franquiz, M., Green, J., & Craviotta, E. (1993). What is meant by quality of teaching?: Toward a social constructivist perspective on teacher education. *Educational Research and Perspective, 20*(1), 13-24.

Garfinkel, H. (1967). *Studies in ethnomethodology.* Englewood Cliffs, NJ: Prentice-Hall.

Giddens, A. (1979). *Central problems in social theory: Action, structure, and contradiction in social analysis.* Berkeley: University of California Press.

Goffman, E. (1974). *Frame analysis.* New York: Harper and Row.

Goodenough, W. H. (1981). *Culture, language, and society.* Menlo Park, CA: Cummings.

Green, J. (1977). *Pedagogical style differences as related to comprehension performance: Grades one through three.* Unpublished dissertation, University of California, Berkeley.

Green, J. L. (1983). Research on teaching as a linguistic process: A state of the art. In E. Gordon (Ed.), *Review of research in education* (Vol. 10, pp. 152-252). Washington, DC: American Educational Research Association.

Green, J.L., & Bloome, D. (1997). Ethnography and ethnographers of and in education: A situated perspective. In S. B. Heath, J. Flood, & D. Lapp (Eds.),

Handbook for research in communicative and visual arts (pp. 181-202). New York: MacMillan.

Green, J. L., & Dixon, C. D. (1993). Introduction to talking knowledge into being: Discursive and social practices in classrooms. *Linguistics and Education, 5,* 231-240.

Green, J., Dixon, C., & Zaharlick, A. (2003). Ethnography as a logic of inquiry. In J. Flood, D. Lapp, J. Squire, & J. Jensen (Eds.), *Handbook of research in teaching English language arts* (pp. 201-224). Mahwah, NJ: Erlbaum.

Green, J., Franquiz, M., & Dixon, C. (1997). The myth of the objective transcript. *TESOL Quarterly, 31,* 172-176.

Green, J. L., & Harker, J. O. (1982). Reading to children: A communicative perspective. In J. Langer & M. T. Smith-Burke (Eds.), *Reading meets author: Bridging the gap.* Newark, DE: International Reading Association.

Green, J. L., & Harker, J. O. (Eds.). (1988). *Multiple perspective analyses of classroom discourse.* Norwood, NJ: Ablex.

Green, J. L., & Harker, J. O. (1989). Gaining access to learning: Controversial, social, and cognitive demands of instructional conversation. In L. C. Wilkinson (Ed.), *Communicating in the classroom* (pp. 183-222). New York: Academic Press.

Green, J. L., Harker, J. O., & Golden, J. M. (1987). Lesson construction: Differing views. In G. Noblit & W. Pink (Eds.), *Schooling in social context: Qualitative studies* (pp. 46-77). Norwood, NJ: Ablex.

Green, J. L., & Meyer, L. A. (1991). The embeddedness of reading in classroom life: Reading as a situated process. In C. Baker & A. Luke (Eds.), *Toward a critical sociology of reading pedagogy* (pp. 141-160). Philadelphia: John Benjamins.

Green, J. L., & Wallat, C. (1979). What is an instructional context? An exploratory analysis of conversational shifts across time. In O. Garnica & M. King (Eds.), *Language, children, and society* (pp. 159-174). New York: Pergamon.

Green, J. L., & Wallat, C. (Eds.). (1981a). *Ethnography and language in educational settings.* Norwood, NJ: Ablex.

Green, J. L., & Wallat, C. (1981b). Mapping instructional conversations—a sociolinguistic ethnography. In J. L. Green & C. Wallat (Eds.), *Ethnography and language in educational settings* (pp. 161-205). Norwood, NJ: Ablex.

Green, J. L., & Weade, R. (1986). Reading between the words: Social cues to lesson participation. *Theory Into Practice, 24*(1), 14-22.

Green, J. L., & Weade, R. (1987). In search of meaning: The sociolinguistic perspective on lesson construction and reading. In D. Bloome (Ed.), *Literacy and schooling* (pp. 4-30). Norwood, NJ: Ablex.

Green, J. L., Weade, R., & Graham, K. (1988). Lesson construction and student participation. In J. L. Green & J. Harker (Eds.), *Multiple perspective analyses of classroom* (pp. 11-48). Norwood, NJ: Ablex.

Green, J., & Yeager, B. (1995). Constructing literate communities: Language and inquiry in bilingual classrooms. In J. Murray (Ed.), *Celebrating difference, confronting literacies* (pp. 97-111). Sydney: Australian Reading Association.

Gumperz, J. (1982). *Discourse strategies.* New York: Cambridge University Press.

Gumperz, J. (1986). Interactional linguistics in the study of schooling. In J. Cook-Gumperz (Ed.), *The social construction of literacy.* New York: Cambridge University Press.

Gumperz, J. (1992). Contextualization and understanding. In A. Duranti & C. Goodwin (Eds.), *Rethinking context* (pp. 229-252). New York: Cambridge University Press.

Gumperz, J., & Herasimchuk, E. (1972). Conversational analysis of social meaning: A study of classroom interaction. In R. Shuy (Ed.), *Sociolinguistics: Current trends and prospects*. Washington, DC: Georgetown University Press.

Gumperz, J., & Hymes, D. (1964). The ethnography of communication (special issue). *American Anthropologist, 66*(6), part 2.

Gumperz, J. J., & Hymes, D. (Eds.). (1972). *Directions in sociolinguistics: The ethnography of communication*. New York: Basil Blackwell.

Harker, J. O., & Green, J. L. (1985). When you get the right answer to the wrong question: Observing and understanding in the classroom. In A. Jagger & M. T. Smith-Burke (Eds.), *Observing the language learner* (pp. 221-231). Newark, DE: International Reading Association, National Council of Teachers of English.

Heap, J. L. (1991). A situated perspective on what counts as reading. In C. Baker & A. Luke (Eds.), *Toward a critical sociology of reading pedagogy* (pp.103-140). Philadelphia, PA: John Benjamins.

Heap, J. L. (1992). Seeing snubs: An introduction to sequential analysis of classroom interaction. *The Journal of Classroom Interaction, 27*(2), 23-28.

Heras, A. (1993). The construction of understanding in a sixth-grade bilingual classroom. *Linguistics and Education, 5*(3&4), 275-300.

Heras, A. I. (1995). *Living bilingual, interacting in two languages: An ethnographic and sociolinguistic study of a fourth-grade bilingual classroom*. Unpublished doctoral dissertation, University of California, Santa Barbara.

Heritage, J. (1984). *Garfinkel and ethnomethodology*. Cambridge, MA: Polity Press.

Howe, K. (2001). Qualitative educational research: The philosophical issues. In V. Richardson (Ed.), *Handbook of research on teaching* (pp. 201-208). Washington, DC: AERA.

Hymes, D. (1972). Introduction. In C. Cazden, V. John, & D. Hymes (Eds.), *Functions of language in the classroom*. Prospect Heights, IL: Waveland Press.

Hymes, D. (1974). *Foundations in sociolinguistics: An ethnographic approach*. Philadelphia: University of Pennsylvania Press.

Jennings, L. B. (1996). *Multiple contexts for learning social justice: An ethnographic and sociolinguistic study of a fifth grade bilingual class*. Unpublished doctoral dissertation, University of California, Santa Barbara.

Jennings, L. B. (1998). Reading the world of the classroom through ethnographic eyes. *The California Reader, 4*(31), 11-15.

Lin, L. (1993). Language of and in the classroom: Constructing the patterns of social life. *Linguistics and Education 5*, 367-410.

Lin, L. (1994a). *Literate practices and the construction of intertextuality in a secondary English classroom: An ethnographic study of writing and reading as instructional resources*. Unpublished doctoral dissertation, University of California, Santa Barbara.

Miletta, A. (2003). *Managing dilemmas: Uncovering moral and intellectual dimensions of classroom life*. Unpublished doctoral dissertation, University of Michigan.

Mitchell, J. C. (1984). Typicality and the case study. In R.F. Ellen (Ed.), *Ethnographic research: A guide to general conduct* (pp. 238-241). New York: Academic Press.

Moerman, M. (1988). *Talking culture: Ethnography and conversation analysis.* Philadelphia: University of Pennsylvania Press.

Putney, L. (1997). *Collective-individual development in a fifth grade bilingual classroom: An interactional ethnographic analysis of historicity and consequentiality.* Unpublished dissertation, University of California at Santa Barbara.

Putney, L., Green, J., Dixon, C., Duran, R., & Yeager, B. (2000). Consequential progressions: Exploring collective-individual development in a bilingual classroom. In C. Lee & P. Smagorinsky (Eds.), *Constructing meaning through collaborative inquiry: Vygotskian perspectives on literacy research* (pp. 86-126). New York: Cambridge University.

Rech, M. (1998). *Redefining history in a Brazilian classroom: An ethnographic study of history in the making.* Unpublished dissertation, University of California at Santa Barbara.

Rex, L. A. (1997). *Making-a-case: A study of the classroom construction of academic literacy.* Unpublished dissertation, University of California at Santa Barbara.

Rex, L. A., (2000). Judy constructs a genuine question: A case for interactional inclusion. *Journal of Teaching and Teacher Education, 16*(2), 315-333.

Rex, L. A. (2001). The remaking of a high school reader. *Reading Research Quarterly, 36*(3), 288-314.

Rex, L. A. (2002). Exploring orientation in remaking high school readers' literacies and identities. *Linguistics and Education, 13*(3), 271-302.

Rex, L. A. (2003). Loss of the creature: The obscuring of inclusivity. *Communication Education, 52*(1), 30-46.

Rex, L. A., & McEachen, D. (1999). "If anything is odd, inappropriate, confusing, or boring, it's probably important": The emergence of inclusive academic literacy through English classroom discussion practices. *Research in the Teaching of English, 34*(1), 65-129.

Rex, L. A., Murnen, T., Hobbs, J., & McEachen, D. (2002). Teachers' pedagogical stories and the shaping of classroom participation: "The Dancer" and "Graveyard Shift at the 7-11." *American Educational Research Journal, 39*(3), 765-796.

Rex, L. A., & Nelson, M. (2004). How teachers' professional identities position high stakes test preparation in their classrooms. *Teachers College Record, 106*(6), 1288-1331.

Ricoeur, P. (1981). *Hermaneutics and the human sciences: Essays on language, action, and interpretation* (J. Thompson, Ed. & Trans.). Cambridge: Cambridge University Press.

Santa Barbara Classroom Discourse Group. (1992a). Constructing literacy in classrooms: Literate action as social accomplishment. In H. Marshall (Ed.), *Redefining student learning: Roots of educational change* (pp. 119-150). Norwood, NJ: Ablex.

Santa Barbara Classroom Discourse Group. (1992b). Do you see what we see? The referential and intertextual nature of classroom life. *Journal of Classroom Interaction, 27*(2), 29-36.

Santa Barbara Classroom Discourse Group. (1995). Two languages, one commu-
    nity: An examination of educational opportunities. In R. Macias & R. Garcia
    (Eds.), *Changing schools for changing students: An anthology of research on lan-
    guage minorities, schools & society* (pp. 63-106). Santa Barbara: U.C. Linguistic
    Minority Research Institute.
Saville-Troike, M. (1982). *The ethnography of communication: An introduction.*
    Oxford: Blackwell.
Spindler, G. D. (1982). *Doing the ethnography of schooling: Educational anthropology
    in action.* New York: Holt, Rinehart & Winston.
Spindler, G., & Spindler, L. (1992). Cultural process and ethnography: An anthropo-
    logical perspective. In M. LeCompte, W. Millroy, & J. Preissle (Eds.), *The hand-
    book of qualitative research in education* (pp. 53-92). New York: Academic Press.
Spradley, J. P. (1980) *Participant observation.* New York: Holt Rinehart & Winston.
Tannen, D. (1979). What's in a frame? Surface evidence for underlying expecta-
    tions. In R. Freedle (Ed.), *Advances in discourse processing* (Vol. 2, pp. 137-181).
    Norwood, NJ: Ablex.
Tannen, D. (1993). *Framing in discourse.* New York: Oxford University Press.
Taylor, C. (1987). Interpretation and the sciences of man. In P. Rabinow & W.
    Sullivan (Eds.), *Interpretive social science: A second look* (pp. 33-81). Los
    Angeles: University of California Press.
Tuyay, S. (1999). Exploring the relationship between literate practices and oppor-
    tunities for learning, *Primary Voices K-6, 7*(3), 17–24.
Tuyay, S. (2000). *Becoming academically literate: An interactional ethnographic study of
    opportunities for learning in a bilingual elementary classroom.* Unpublished doc-
    toral dissertation, University of California, Santa Barbara.
Tuyay, S., Floriani, A., Yeager, B., Dixon, C., & Green, J. (1995). Constructing an
    integrated, inquiry-oriented approach in classrooms: A cross-case analysis of
    social, literate and academic practice. *Journal of Classroom Interaction, 30*(2), 1-
    15.
Tuyay, S., Jennings, L., & Dixon, C. (1995). Classroom discourse and opportunities
    to learn: An ethnographic study of knowledge construction in a bilingual
    third grade classroom. *Discourse Processes, 19*(1), 75-110.
Wallat, C., & Green, J. L. (1979). Social rules and communicative contexts in
    kindergarten. *Theory Into Practice, 18*(4), 275-284.
Wallat, C., & Green, J. L. (1981). The construction of social norms. In K. Borman
    (Ed.), *The social life of children in a changing society* (pp. 97-122). Hillsdale, NJ:
    Erlbaum.
Weade, R., & Green, J. (1989). Reading in the instructional context: An internation-
    al sociolinguistics perspective. In C. Emihovich (Ed.), *Locating learning across
    the curriculum: Ethnographic perspectives on classroom research* (pp. 17-56).
    Norwood, NJ: Ablex.
Wells, G., & Chang-Wells, G. L. (1992). *Constructing knowledge together.*
    Portsmouth, NH: Heinemann.
Yeager, B., Floriani, A., & Green, J. (1998). Learning to see learning in the class-
    room: Developing an ethnographic perspective. In A. Egan-Robertson & D.
    Bloome (Eds.), *Students as researchers of culture and language in their own com-
    munities* (pp. 115-139). Cresskill, NJ: Hampton Press.

Yeager, B., Pattenaude, I., Franquiz, M., & Jennings, L. (1999). Rights, respect, and responsibility: Toward a theory of action in two bilingual classrooms. In J. Robinson (Ed.), *Elementary voices: Teaching about genocide and intolerance* (pp. 196-218). Champaign-Urbana, IL: National Council of Teachers of English.

Yeager, E. (2003). *"I am a historian": Examining the discursive construction of locally situated academic identities in linguistically diverse settings.* Unpublished doctoral dissertation, University of California, Santa Barbara.

Zaharlick, A., & Green, J. (1991). Ethnographic research. In J. Flood (Ed.), *Handbook of research on teaching the English language arts* (pp. 205-225). Champaign-Urbana, IL: National Council of Teachers of English.

2

Considering Discourse Analysis as a Method for Researching Professional Development

Katherine A. Morris

Table 2.1. Transcript A

1	Lampert:	I think that if you look at these numbers—What happens?
2		The numbers over here. Anthony?
3	Anthony:	Times three all the time?
4	Lampert:	It's always three times bigger than the one over there, is that what
5		you were thinking Donna Ruth?
6	Donna Ruth:	Yeah, and um, and it's like even and odd.
7	Lampert:	That's true too.
8		Okay, I think we really need to stop now. Let's have the pens
9		collected and have you put your notebooks in your desks please.

Note. Words and punctuation are preserved, although line breaks have changed from Lampert's (2001, pp. 463-464) original transcript.

Even in the most adventurous teaching, one knows instantly that
Anthony and Donna Ruth are students and Lampert is their math teacher
because of the immediately recognizable the teacher–student–teacher
pattern in instructional interactions. In many ways, the transcripts presented in Tables 2.2 and 2.3 look similar.

Table 2.2. Transcript B

10	Nanette:	Okay, so you said, the two came from the two new perimeters
11		from the adjacent sides, is that what you said?
12	Nicky:	Well, units of perimeters, uh, I guess. Two new units.
13	Nanette:	Two new units?
14	Nicky:	I don't know, it's probably not very good English...
15	Gregg:	Can I share our work?
16	Nanette:	Uh-huh.
17	Gregg:	It's... you're adding three, and you're taking away two...
18	Nanette:	Okay, so, adding three to what?
19	Gregg:	To the... to whatever shape it was...whatever you started with.
20	Nanette:	Okay.

Note. Data used with permission, VCMPD (NSF: ESI-9731339, 1998–2003).

Table 2.3. Transcript C

21	Nanette:	So any other thoughts around this, the Lindsey...
22	Nicky:	I think she was correct.
23	Nanette:	Lindsey was correct?
24	Nicky:	Yes. She just never had a opportunity to explain what she thought
25		the T equaled which in this case would be the middle pieces or T
26		minus two. Total pieces minus two. She never elaborated what her,
27		on what the T for her meant.
28	Nanette:	Uh hum. So you think Lindsey is correct in the way in which she
29		was doing it but didn't have a chance to come to it or formal...
30	Nicky:	Uh hum, explain it was just, what did that T really, because they
31		were coming up with T, what did T really, symbolize.
32	Nanette:	Why do you think she didn't have the chance to explain?

Note. Data used with permission, VCMPD (NSF: ESI-9731339, 1998–2003).

Here, too, the roles of the interactants and alternating teacher–student–teacher pattern are recognizable, but there are also intriguing differences between these two interactions and those represented in Table 2.1. For example, although no one in Lampert's class was interrupted, interruptions seem frequent in Nanette's class: Notice that when Gregg interrupts another student, his teacher permits him to continue, although she later interrupts him herself (lines 14-18); and the teacher, Nanette, is repeatedly interrupted by her student Nicky (lines 21-22 & 29-30).

Looking closely at the variations in the interactional patterns of instructional discourse represented in these two classes is of particular interest because Lampert and Nanette teach in two very different instructional settings. In fact, Lampert's students are children, whereas Nanette's students are teachers attending an in-service professional development. For nearly three decades, discourse analysis has been used to study interactions between teachers and their students in classrooms. This chapter explores that literature and grapples with the question of what these methods and frameworks can bring to the study of professional development.

PROFESSIONAL DEVELOPMENT

In an age of educational reform, teachers are expected to continuously improve their teaching practice (e.g., Darling-Hammond & Sykes, 1999; McLaughlin & Oberman, 1996). In their review of the professional development (PD) literature, Wilson and Berne (1999) point to some of the complexities inherent in the field as well as the limitations of current research. Both the contents and contexts of PD are complex. PD supports teachers in their study of a seemingly endless number of topics relevant for teaching, including K–12 subject matter content (e.g., math, art, history, or physical education), instructional resources (e.g., textbooks, tools, or technologies), and teaching practices and strategies (e.g., for working with diverse learners, assessment, or classroom management). Not only do teachers study a myriad of topics in the PD, they do so in a vast array of contexts. They study in groups, with partners or mentors, and independently; schools and school districts provide PD workshops and courses as do universities, regional professional organizations, and teacher study groups; PD may entail a few hours after school, many days during the school year, or weeks during the summer; teachers may pay or be paid to participate.

This chapter focuses on a kind of PD that shares many surface features with K–12 classroom instruction: a series of monthly meetings for mathematics teacher leaders that is both content-based and district-sponsored. Both have a fairly stable community of learners, instructional objectives, instructional materials, and an instructor within a defined spatial and temporal context. Mirroring the K–12 classroom, teachers tend to stay seated at tables like students while the professional developer tends to stand near the front of the room with easy access to a chalkboard, chart paper, and overhead projector but is free to move around at will. In addition to occupying a unique physical space, the professional developer is in charge of the flow and content of instruction as well as the flow of talk among the teachers. That is, like the classroom teacher, the professional developer grants (or does not grant) permission for participants to interact with one another and he or she determines what tasks the group will work on, how they will work, how long they will work, and what they will do when they are done. From a research perspective, then, similarities between these two instructional contexts suggest that methods that have been successful in the study of K–12 instruction should be fruitful in the study of PD.

WHY DISCOURSE?

In the introduction to her seminal book, *Classroom Discourse: The Language of Teaching and Learning*, Cazden (1988)[1] points to three key features of instructional institutions that might lead educational researchers to study discourse: (a) language is the medium of both teaching and expressing learning; (b) unlike other crowded spaces such as bus stops and restaurants where "simultaneous autonomous conversations are normal," in classrooms one person controls the talk, "not just negatively, as a traffic policeman, but also positively, to enhance the purposes of education"; and (c) people express their identities in and through language (pp. 2-3). She names these three: the propositional language of curriculum, the social language of control, and the expressive language of personal identity respectively.[2]

The languages of curriculum, control, and personal identity are pertinent in the PD as they were in the classrooms Cazden studied. In both contexts, language is the medium of teaching and the medium through

---

[1]Although Cazden (2001) has recently updated and re-released *Classroom Discourse*, this chapter refers to the original edition.

[2]Jackson's (1968) list of key characteristics from *Life in Classrooms* provides an interesting comparison to Cazden's list. He nominates *crowds, praise,* and *power* as the most salient characteristics of classrooms. Cazden's *control* seems to overlap Jackson's *crowds* and *power* and her notion of *personal identity* seems to relate to his *praise* and *power*. But it is noteworthy that although Cazden lists curriculum first, Jackson's list includes neither content nor learning.

which learners demonstrate what they learn. That is not to say that the discourses of PD and K–12 education are the same. One major difference is the context in which what is learned is to be demonstrated and used. For K–12 students, the classroom context is central because the classroom is where students study, demonstrate their learning, and use their learning through discussions, assignments, and assessments. In contrast, for teachers involved in PD there are *two* central contexts. Teachers first study and demonstrate their learning through the language they use within the PD context; they then must demonstrate and use what they have learned in the classroom context through the language they use to ply their "new and improved" teaching practices with their students.

Clearly, focusing on the language teachers use in the PD context as a means of studying what teachers learn is theoretically warranted, but that is not enough; for one must choose from a myriad of discourse-analytic methods. Titscher, Meyer, Wodak, and Vetter (2000) identify nearly 40 theories and methods of discourse and text analysis that inform the 12 methods they explore throughout their book (pp. 50-51). Schiffrin (1994) limits her introductory text to six methodological approaches, explaining her goal of looking "in a more systematic and theoretically coherent way" at the explosion of discourse analysis (p. 6). In his book, Gee (1999) investigates just one approach, all the while cautioning the reader that no approach is uniquely suited. He explains that "different approaches often fit different issues and questions better or worse than others" and that he aims "to 'lend' readers certain tools of inquiry, fully anticipating that these tools will be transformed, or even abandoned, as readers invent their own versions of them or meld them with other tools embedded in somewhat different perspectives" (pp. 4-5).

Following these scholars' lead, I narrow this chapter's focus a second time. In addition to focusing specifically on school district-sponsored, content-based PD, this chapter focuses on only two methods of discourse analysis, conversation analysis (CA) and interactional ethnography (IE), both of which have proven track records in educational research.

TRANSCRIPTION

Before exploring distinctions between CA and IE approaches to studying discourse, it is important to consider an element common to both: transcripts of interactions as data. Transcripts are representations and as such should not be confused with the actual "in-the-moment talk" they represent. Transcribing naturally occurring speech is both complex and theoretically driven (Baker, 1997; Ochs, 1979). How much talk comprises a unit of analysis? Which verbal and nonverbal features of discursive events are to be captured in the transcript? Does it matter if the speaker said "uhm" or "uh," that someone interrupted the speaker, or that there was a long pause within or between speakers' turns? The researcher must base decisions about whether and how to transcribe discursive features such as these on her research questions and theoretical framework. The researcher must also decide how to present the transcript.

Transcription decisions inherently reflect the researcher's biases, assumptions, and perspectives; as such, far from being objective representations of talk, transcripts are necessarily political (Green, Franquiz, & Dixon, 1997; Psathas & Anderson, 1990).

> Transcribing, therefore, is a *political act* that reflects a discipline's conventions as well as a researcher's conceptualization of a phenomena [sic], purposes for the research, theories guiding the data collection and analysis, and programmatic goals. . . . Following this logic, what is **re**-presented is data **constructed** by a researcher for a particular purpose, *not* just talk written down. (Green et al., 1997, p. 1)[3]

The political implications of choosing standard or nonstandard orthography in a transcript (e.g., said or *sez*, asks or *aksez*) may be fairly obvious because it is clear that through such representation the researcher constructs a certain kind of identity for a speaker (West, 1996), but the politics can be far more subtle. Ochs (1979) explains that even presentational format can show symmetrical or asymmetrical power relationships among speakers. "Leftness is linked with priority and also with inception of a statement or entire discourse . . . the overwhelming tendency is for researchers to place the adult's speaker column to the left of the child's speaker column" (p. 49). She asserts that positioning on a transcript may reflect the researcher's interpretation of dominance and control in a discursive situation.

Transcripts of classroom interactions tend to obscure a quintessential aspect of the context—*crowds* (see Jackson, 1968). Although there may be a room full of 30 official or *ratified* participants (Goffman, 1981) in a classroom, the transcript may only represent the names of a few speakers. Although all are expected to be active participants in whole-group conversations whether speaking or not, nonspeakers can become invisible when not named in the transcript. Decisions to name or not are political, as are decisions about how to name. These decisions include whether to use surnames, first names, honorific/professional titles, or all three; whether or not to use names that are marked for the ethnicity or gender

---

[3]Note that throughout this chapter, bold and italics within cited text is as it appeared in the original text.

of the speaker, such as *Juan Antonio, Ting Lee,* or *Courtney Fisher;* and even whether to identify speakers by names at all or simply identify *Speaker A* and *Speaker B.*

Although perhaps subtle, issues of transcription are not trivial. In fact, nearly all of the aforementioned issues can be seen in the deliberate choices made in selecting and representing the three transcripts that began this chapter. Transcript A in Table 2.1 represents just a few seconds from a vast multimedia data set that captures a year of fifth-grade mathematics teaching and was selected from Lampert's (2001) book *Teaching Problems and the Problem of Teaching,* in which she uses transcripts to illustrate particular aspects of her teaching practice. Transcripts B and C (Tables 2.2 and 2.3) come from videorecordings of the PD I studied as part of my work on the Professional Development through Video Project (Principal Investigator: Magdalene Lampert, funded by a grant from the MacArthur Foundation). In all three transcripts, I decided to represent the naturally occurring talk such that the instructor had the first and last word, highlighting the teacher's power in these conversations. My labeling decisions are also noteworthy: In Transcript A, by referring to the teacher by her last name (Lampert) and the students by their first (Anthony and Donna Ruth), I highlight the teacher's status; in the PD transcripts, all speakers are labeled with their first names (Nanette, Nicky, and Gregg) suggesting that their status is more comparable. With their permission, both instructors are represented with their real name, whereas pseudonyms label their students to protect their anonymity. I have chosen to use standard orthography, although I maintained the speaker's grammatical errors such as when Nicky says "a opportunity" (line 24). Judging it to be more accessible to my target audience, I formatted these transcripts in a familiar "drama-like" style rather than introducing the more esoteric Jeffersonian notation (Atkinson & Heritage, 1999) that is introduced along with other forms of transcription in order to illustrate concepts in CA and IE later in this chapter.

CONVERSATION ANALYSIS IN GENERAL

Jefferson's system was developed as part of her work with conversation analysts Sacks and Schegloff (Atkinson & Heritage, 1999). These scholars worked to explicate the implicit rules that enable native speakers to engage successfully in conversations (e.g., how to open, maintain, and close conversations). They rely on fine-grain transcriptions that carefully attend to the cohesion between and among pairs of adjacent turns (Schegloff & Sacks, 1973). Schiffrin (1994) explains the centrality of the *adjacency pair* as follows:

> From a speaker's point of view, next-position thus offers a location in
> which to find the recipient's analysis of the utterance—to see whether
> an anticipated response is confirmed. From a recipient's point of
> view, next-position offers an opportunity to reveal aspects of the
> understanding of prior talk to which own talk will be addressed. . . .
> Thus, next position is a crucial location for the building of intersub-
> jectivity: each next turn provides an environment in which recipients
> can display many understandings. (p. 237)

Deciding to focus on turn-taking mechanisms is obviously theoretically driven, but so is deciding what counts as a turn. For conversation
analysts, turns contain one or more "transition-relevant places" (Sacks,
Schegloff, & Jefferson, 1974), that is, places where a new speaker could
begin talking. A turn "is neither a 'natural message' nor an activity but a
slot in adjacency pairs" (Edelsky, 1993, p. 202); consequently, utterances
are not necessarily considered turns. For instance, when a speaker utters
an encourager such as "uhm huh" while another is talking, this may or
may not be interpreted by participants or researchers as a turn. (If it is not
considered a turn, this kind of talk is called *back channeling*.)

A number of conversation features have been analyzed within this
research tradition including pauses and hesitations (Schegloff, Jefferson,
& Sacks, 1977), repetitions and repairs et al. overlapping speech in which
two speakers are talking simultaneously (Sacks et al., 1974), latching
speech in which a new speaker immediately follows the previous speaker without a pause between turns (Sacks et al., 1974), and kinds of turns
(Edelsky, 1993). To illustrate these conversation analytic concepts, lines
28-32 from Transcript C are retranscribed in Table 2.4 and then analyzed
using many Jeffersonian transcription devices.

Within this notation system, two square brackets, one directly below
the other in an adjacency pair (lines *b* and *c*) are used to indicate the point
at which overlapping speech begins in the conversation. To avoid ambiguity when there are two consecutive pairs of overlapping speech, the
second incident is conventionally marked by double square brackets
(lines *d* and *e*). Underlining indicates emphasis (lines *f* and *h*) and the
equal sign is used to indicate adjacent turns in which the second speaker
latches on to the first (lines *g* and *h*). Periods within parentheses are used
to indicate 1-second pauses (lines *a*, *d*, *e*, and *f*). In the original version of
Transcript C the three-dot ellipsis is used to indicate a point where the
speaker's tone indicated she might continue (lines 21 and 29). In this
notation, three dots would indicate a 3-second pause in order to avoid
ambiguity, the ellipsis is replaced with an em dash (line *d*).

Perhaps the most obvious change in this new version is the redistribution of turns, but the Jeffersonian version reveals far more, enabling a
level of analysis and interpretation of the instructional conversation that

Table 2.4 Jeffersonian Version of Transcript C, lines 28-32

a	Nanette:	Uh hum. So you think Lindsey (.) is correct
b		[in the way in which she was doing it,
c	Nicky:	[uh hum
d	Nanette:	but didn't have a chance to (.) [[come to it or formal—
e	Nicky:	[[Explain it was just (.) what did that T
f		really (.) Because they were coming up with T (.) What did T <u>really</u>
g		symbolize? =
h	Nanette:	= <u>Why</u> did you think she didn't have a chance to explain?

was simply not available through the original script-like transcript. The new transcript shows that Nanette pauses between "Lindsey" and "is correct." She may be hesitating, but her pauses might also be interpreted as pedagogical moves intended to provide enough *wait time* for the teachers to recall what Lindsey did.

This new transcript reveals that on two occasions Nicky's speech overlapped Nanette's. The first time might be interpreted as Nicky back channeling her agreement as it comes at a point where Nanette has not signaled a transition-relevant place. Despite Nicky's simultaneous talk, Nanette continues her turn (lines *a* and *d*). The second time, however, Nicky begins her overlap after Nanette has paused—a point that Nicky may have interpreted as a transition-relevant place, although Nanette's continuation of her turn after the pause indicates that it may not have been intended that way. Nicky's overlap ends in a successful attempt to finish what Nanette was saying (lines *d* and *e*). One interpretation is that Nicky interrupted Nanette and *stole* the floor from her. However, Edelsky (1993) found that this type of overlapping may not be perceived by the group as an interruption, but rather as a single turn that has been collaboratively constructed by two or more speakers. In other words, Nanette and Nicky may be *sharing* the floor, thereby creating greater intersubjectivity by demonstrating that they are on the same wavelength.

Nicky's pauses after "just" and "really" (lines *e* and *f*) are a kind of hesitation. Both might be interpreted as uncertainty as to whether or not her audience has followed her train of thought. She restarts her message, repairing her turn by providing more background information ("because they were coming up with T") and then repeats and completes her turn (line *f*). When Nanette latches on to Nicky's turn at a transition-relevant place (lines *g-h*) she builds coherence and intersubjectivity by combining her own recycled phrases "you think" (from line *a*) and "didn't have a chance to" (from line *d*) with Nicky's "explain" (from line *e*).

In these few brief examples, it is clear that conversation analytic tools that enable the researcher to document subtle features of discourse such as pauses and overlapping speech can be quite powerful. In the next section, I explore how these tools have been employed in the study of instructional conversations.

CONVERSATION ANALYSIS AND THE STRUCTURE OF INSTRUCTIONAL CONVERSATIONS

The analytic tools and many of the empirical findings regarding general patterns of conversational language described by Schegloff and his colleagues (e.g., Schegloff & Sacks, 1973; Sacks, Shegloff, & Jefferson, 1974; Schegloff, Jefferson, & Sacks, 1977; Shegloff, 1987) are applicable in educational settings; however, there are also discourse patterns that are specific to instructional conversations. For instance, the turn-taking rules that regulate discourse in the classroom are not necessarily generalizable to other daily interactions, or vice-versa. Cazden (1988) sums up what makes classroom discourse unique as follows:

> In typical classrooms, the most important asymmetry in the rights and obligations of teacher and students is over control of the right to speak. In the bluntest terms, teachers have the right to speak at any time and to any person; they can fill any silence or interrupt any speaker; they can speak to a student anywhere in the room and in any volume or tone of voice. And no one has the right to object. But not all teachers assume such rights or live by such rules all the time. (p. 54)

Unlike most other kinds of daily conversations, in the managing turn-taking classroom is often a very explicit process conducted by the teacher. Looking back at Transcript A (Table 2.1), for example, we can see Lampert determining who will speak next (lines 2 and 5) and deciding when talk will stop (line 8). In Transcript B (Table 2.2), Nanette decides to listen to Gregg although Nicky had been speaking (lines 14-16); she then interrupts him, perhaps to make sure other students understand what he is saying (lines 18-19).

Throughout these transcripts, it is generally the case that the instructor asks a question, a learner responds, and the instructor makes a comment regarding the students' response. Sinclair and Coulthard (1975) laid the groundwork for the study of this sequential and hierarchical pattern in teacher–student interaction. They named the structure "initiation, response, feedback" (IRF). The teacher asks a question in order to *initiate* a turn sequence, a student *responds*, and the teacher provides *feedback* to the student regarding the correctness of the response and the cycle begins again. Mehan (1979) and Erickson and Schultz (1981) have also contributed to this body of research, providing an alternative cycle, IRE, in which the E stands for evaluation. Based on this pattern of interaction, Mehan transcribed classroom talk into a three-column table, with I, R, and E as the column headings. Using this basic model as a framework, Mehan considered various phases of a lesson, focusing on how the teacher's talk controlled the conversation. So lines 18-20 of Transcript B might look like those presented in Table 2.5.

Table 2.5. Mehanesque Version of Transcript B, lines 18-20

INITIATION (PROF. DEVELOPER)	RESPONSE (TEACHER)	EVALUATION (PROF. DEVELOPER)
Okay, so adding three to what?	To the . . . to whatever shape it was . . . whatever you started with.	Okay.

In looking at this Mehanesque transcript, it is important to recall that it is the researcher's theoretical frameworks and biases that lead to a particular transcription. The very structure of this transcript sets up the interactions to both begin and end with the teacher interaction, thereby emphasizing the teacher's role and power. Were it not theoretically driven, the transcript might just as well have begun and ended with a student's voice. Cazden (1988) boldly claims that this "three-part sequence of teacher initiation, student response, teacher evaluation (IRE) is the most common pattern of classroom discourse at all grade levels" (p. 29). The consistency and pervasiveness of this instructional pattern is striking but perhaps not surprising. Gee (1999) suggests a reason for this:

> Situations are never completely novel (indeed if they were, we wouldn't understand them). Rather, they are repeated, with more or less variation, over time (that is distinctive configurations or patterns of semiotic resources, activities, things, and political and sociocultural elements are repeated). Such repetition tends to "ritualize," "habitualize," or "freeze" situations to varying degrees, that is, to cause them to be repeated with less variation. Such repetition . . . is the life blood out of which *institutions*, such as schools, hospitals, businesses, . . . and so on and so forth through a nearly endless list, are created. (p. 83)

The IRE/F pattern has been the focus of much study and the transcripts of instructional conversations that I selected seem to follow this ubiquitous pattern. Just because these patterns are well documented, however, it is *not* reasonable to assume that all instructional conversations are like this. This is important for two reasons. First, questions about the discursive structure in PD have yet to be explored and it would be unwarranted to jump to any conclusions about the nature of teachers' discourse in PD based on the few moments of practice by one professional developer presented here. Second, and perhaps more important, not all conversations in classrooms do follow an IRE/F model. Despite her claims, Cazden (1988) herself suggested times when the IRE/F pattern seems to be broken in classroom conversations and times when the teacher is not directing the flow of discursive traffic (e.g., small-group work).

CONVERSATION ANALYSIS AND LEARNING

Cazden expanded on the study of classroom turn-taking in other ways as well. Her semantic analysis explored the differences in meaning that are entailed by IRE/F interactions. Her example, "what time is it, Sarah?" (Table 2.6) illustrates the how teachers' questions in classrooms and structurally identical questions in "normal conversations" have quite different, context-specific meanings.

Table 2.6. What Time Is It?

CONVERSATION	CLASSROOM TALK
What time is it, Sarah?	What time is it, Sarah?
Half-past two.	Half-past two.
Thanks.	Right.

Note. From Cazden (1988, p. 30).

In any other context, a response like "right" to such a question would seem odd. Why would someone waste another person's time by asking a question to which the answer was already known? But the "half-past two" provides different information in the two interactional contexts. In the former, the asker learns the time. In the latter, the asker learns that the student can tell time. Transcript A (Table 2.1) provides a good example of this. When Lampert asks Anthony what happens to the numbers (lines 1-2), she is not trying to find out about the numbers; she already knows about the numbers. She is trying to find out what *Anthony* is thinking about the numbers.

Cazden (1988) argues that the teacher "is the only native speaker in the classroom culture" (p. 44) and that students must learn a lot in order to demonstrate native competence in the classroom—what Gee (1999) calls pulling "off specific social activities and social identities" (p. 1). Not only must a student learn how to get recognized by the teacher in order to get the floor, he or she must also learn to correctly interpret what the teacher is trying to find out when the teacher asks a question like "What time is it?" or "What happens [to the numbers]?" Yet ironically, the teacher "has to depend on her 'immigrant' students for help in enacting a culturally defined activity" (Cazden, 1988, p. 44). The work of learning to "student" (Fenstermacher, 1986) is actually quite complicated, if we accept Cazden's theories of natives and immigrants in the classroom culture. Far from being a triviality of language, Lortie (1975) and Rosenholtz (1989) suggest that teachers depend on their students' successful studenting for their own sense of success and self-esteem.

Yet, clearly the discursive rules the teacher employs while speaking are not rules that students are to simply mimic as the ways of interacting in the classroom. Students must learn to interact, not as teachers, but as students in the presence of a teacher, and further, they must learn to student within school subjects that grow out of disciplines with distinct discursive practices. For examples of works within specific subject areas see Rex (2001) in literacy, Moschkovich (1999) and Brilliant-Mills (1994) in mathematics, Floriani (1994) in social studies, and Lemke (1989) in science.

FEATURES OF CLASSROOMS AND PROFESSIONAL DEVELOPMENT AS INSTRUCTIONAL CONTEXTS

Like classrooms, PD settings are crowded places in which "non-one-on-one" instructional conversations are the norm. The discursive patterns of classroom talk help mitigate the chaos that might ensue were 30 or more speakers to simultaneously vie for the floor. The patterns are possible, in part, because of the identities and roles the participants enact as teacher and students, adult and children. The same does not necessarily hold true in the PD context.

Frame, footing, and *alignment* are terms appropriated by Goffman (1981) in order to grapple with the ever-changing relationships between interactants in a conversation. How people perceive and position themselves and others during conversations impacts how each turn is constructed, and therefore, how the conversation flows. Although teacher–students and professional developer–teachers relationships share many characteristics, they also differ in fundamental ways. In terms of relative status, age, knowledge, experience, and ability teachers and their professional developers are far more alike than are students and their teachers. Students spend an extended period of time developing relationships with their teachers (approximately 500 hours in elementary classes and 100 hours in secondary classes per semester); whereas teachers may spend only a few hours with their professional developers and may have a different professional developer every time they meet. Teachers share a common knowledge of the local instructional context with their students, whereas the professional developer may work in or come from a very different instructional context than the teachers he or she teaches.

These relational differences may hold important keys for understanding the nature of instructional talk in the PD context. Because all of the participants are teachers themselves (and therefore "native speakers" of *teacher talk*), they may readily grasp the professional developer's pedagogical moves. But as learners in the PD context, teachers are positioned to enact talk that is more student-like. It seems reasonable that some teachers would be resistant to assuming this student-like identity. This line of inquiry may also lead to insights into why PD is often viewed as unsuccessful. That teacher learners are acting and interacting in student-like ways in their professional development raises significant questions about how teachers manage to "translate" that student-like discourse into teaching practices and teacher talk back in their own classrooms.

LIMITATIONS OF CONVERSATION ANALYSIS IN EDUCATIONAL SETTINGS

Conversation analysis of classroom interactions yields much about norms of talk in that setting. The patterns are instantly recognizable to anyone who has ever spent time in school (as students, teachers or researchers). But this body of work fails to substantively address a quintessential facet of educational research in both classroom and PD settings—learning. "The study of linguistic phenomena in school settings should seek to answer educational questions. We are interested in linguistic forms only insofar as through them we can gain insight into the social events of the classroom" (Barnes, cited in Cazden, 1988, p. 2). That is, the study of instructional discourse should be centrally about teaching and learning something, not just about patterns of speaking in educational contexts.

CA does provide some evidence of learning if we deduce that *de facto* children must have learned to follow the implicit conversational rules of the classroom such as IRE/F. However, as CA focuses only in micro-instantiations of talk within turn sequences, it does not provide the tools to investigate that learning given that we generally assume that such learning takes place over time. CA adds to our knowledge of how we manage to participate in and maintain conversation, but it does not help us get at issues of studying, learning, or making meaning of school content. Therefore, although it may take place in classrooms, CA is essentially linguistic research within an educational context, rather than educational research. As an analogy, both Schegloff (1987) and Tannen and Wallat (1993) used CA to study interactions between doctors and their patients. These studies were essentially linguistic research within a medical context rather than medical research. In other words, although their work may have implications for that field (just as CA might for education), it is not about healing and wellness. And just as medical studies *should be* primarily about healing and wellness, educational studies *should be* primarily about teaching and learning. Conversation–analytic research is primarily about language. Of course it may be trickier in the case of education, because, whereas in medicine, language is only one of the many media through which doctors and patients interact (others include medicine and surgery), language is the primary medium of interaction in education.

INTERACTIONAL ETHNOGRAPHY

Interactional ethnography, a method developed specifically for studying teaching and learning, takes a very different approach to the study of classroom discourse. With roots in linguistics, anthropology, and sociology, IE was created in and for educational research by Judith Green and her colleagues (Green & Dixon, 1993; Green & Meyer, 1991; Santa Barbara Classroom Discourse Group, 1992). Through IE, these scholars work to discover how students and teachers co-construct and negotiate local meanings through their discourse over time. A basic assumption of this work is that a classroom can be understood as a culture and as such may be researched through an ethnographic lens. Unlike Cazden's (1988) model in which the teacher is the only native in the classroom, from an IE perspective, all members of a community can be considered part of the local culture. Rather than viewing it as static, interactional ethnographers view culture as constantly building and rebuilding itself through the interactions of its members.

IE grows out of *ethnography of communication* (e.g., Hymes, 1972, 1974) and *interactional sociolinguistics* (e.g., Gumperz, 1986). Instead of focusing on the mechanisms of talk (as a conversational analyst does), an ethnographer of communication investigates "patterns of communication as part of cultural knowledge and behavior" recognizing "both the diversity of communicative possibilities and practices . . . and the fact that such practices are an integrated part of what we know and do as members of a particular culture" (Schiffrin, 1994, p. 137). Like CA, ethnography of communication seeks to understand how speakers demonstrate communicative competence, but it differs fundamentally by locating communicative competence within a group, rather than within an individual or pair of speakers. A major goal in this research tradition is to determine what "counts" within a cultural group or "speech community" (Hymes, 1974). Whereas CA seeks to discover the methods by which people create a sense of social order, the ethnography of communication seeks to study the social order itself.

Like its precursors, IE uses observation–participation over an extended period of time as a means of discovering what members of a culture make sense of and how they communicate their understandings. As such, IE is well suited to the study of instructional contexts given the assumption that learning takes place over time. IE is a constructivist methodology that relies on finding locally meaningful units of analysis. "The ethnography provides information for understanding the linguistic, social, and contextual presuppositions members of the group bring to an event from membership and participation in other groups" (Green & Meyer, 1981). "Underlying this view of classroom communication is the understanding that members of a group are insiders in a culture, and that as insiders, they understand the patterns of life in ways that visitors or outsiders may not" (Santa Barbara Classroom Discourse Group, 1992, p. 30).[4]

> The ethnographer is responsible to report, not a travelogue of life in the observed community, but a specification of what the members of that community must know in order to behave sensibly within it and to make sense of the behaviors of others. To this end, the fieldworker must find out not only what is going on in the community, but what the goings on mean to the participants, and what those participants must know in order to do what they do.
>
> Underlying the current use of ethnography in the study of teaching and learning is the assumption that an analogy exists between the school or classroom and culture. Given the claims of general ethnography, the particular claim of educational ethnography is that it discovers and describes the ways that members of the school communi-

---

[4]For more background on ethnography in education, see Green and Bloome's (1977) "Ethnography and Ethnographers of Education: A Situated Perspective"; and Zaharlick and Green's (1991) "Ethnographic Researcher." These articles echo Lesley Rex's (personal communication, February 1, 2001) forceful reminder that "an ethnographic approach [to studying classroom interactions] is not badly done ethnography!"

ty create and share meaning. Ethnographers are thus aiming to document the operating knowledge that enables educators and students to navigate everyday life in schools. In this light, teachers, who are perhaps the only enduring and native members of the classroom community become very important arbiters of the validity of educational research. (Florio, 1981, pp. 2-3)

It seems reasonable to think of a class as a culture. Although enrollment varies from grade to grade and transiency rates vary from school to school, on average the same 30 individuals occupy the same 30 x 30-foot space for an entire semester or more and attendance is compulsory. Florio (1981) makes it clear that it isn't just time spent together in a small space that makes that class a "culture"; it is that (as in other kinds of cultures) members of the class community create and share meaning. In his argument for why an ethnographic perspective can be helpful, Erickson (1992) uses the metaphor of the "black box" to describe what we don't know about classrooms. He writes that classrooms entail "the routine actions and sensemaking of participants . . . which, because they are habitual and local, may go unnoticed by practitioner and research alike" (p. 202).

AN ETHNOGRAPHIC LOOK AT THE INTERACTIONS IN CLASSROOMS AND PROFESSIONAL DEVELOPMENT

An ethnographic perspective provides the educational researcher opportunities for multifocal analysis that can lead to insights that are not available through microanalysis alone. As an example, Lampert's (2001) book contains a wealth of ethnographic detail about the participants, content, and context of the lesson we glimpsed through Transcript A (Table 2.1). That interchange took less than 1 minute in real time, one of the more than 6,000 minutes Lampert taught this group of fifth graders. This transcript is part of an extensive data set that includes more than 100 hours of transcribed video of Lampert teaching this class mathematics during the 1989–1990 school year. The data set also includes copies of all the students' math journals containing most of their work for an entire year, Lampert's teaching journal, videotaped interviews with individual students, assessments of students' understandings, and seating charts including who was present and absent for every day she taught.

These data can be used to provide background information about the context and content of the lesson in Transcript A, information about the participants, and background about how the class came to this point in their conversation. Donna Ruth, for example, is "a statuesque African American girl from Detroit whose social sophistication matched her adolescent appearance" (Lampert, 2001, p. 11). This was the fifth year

Lampert, a university-based researcher, taught math in this school. During the year this data was collected, she worked with Mr. Dye's fifth-grade class in order to study the practice of teaching mathematics with an insider's perspective. The conversation represented in Transcript A occurred in the last few minutes of math class on the September 28th.

The students were studying multiplicative groupings and coin problems and had been for a few weeks. Most days, when the students arrived in Lampert's math class they found "problems of the day" on the chalkboard. As usual, on this day students spent the first half of class working independently on the problems; the remaining time was devoted to a whole-class discussion of the problems that sometimes lasted beyond the time set aside for math class. Transcript A finds Lampert and her students at the end of a whole-class discussion of the following three problems of the day:

a. ☐ groups of 12 = 10 groups of 6
b. 30 groups of 2 = ☐ groups of 4
c. ☐ groups of 7 = ☐ groups of 21

The class is discussing problem c when Anthony says, "Three times all the time?" (line 3) in response to Lampert's "What happens?" (line 1). "Let's have the pens collected and have you put your notebooks in your desks please" (lines 8-9) is particularly meaningful in this classroom culture; Lampert's students work in special notebooks in black pen that prohibits erasing when error or changes in thinking occur. This is a very unusual practice in elementary math classes, but they do it because it facilitates Lampert's data collection (i.e., xeroxing *all* of the student work, including mistakes and false starts). Taking care of these materials, therefore, is a meaningful ritual for in this classroom culture.

Transcripts B and C come from a much smaller data set than Lampert's. It includes approximately 6 hours of video of PD, a variety of transcripts based on these videos, and instructional artifacts that were used in teaching these teachers. The smallness of the data set, however, does not preclude us from taking an ethnographic perspective. In fact, the relative size of the data set is directly related to the nature of PD in school and district-based endeavors. That is, teachers do not have the opportunity to meet for hundreds of hours during a school year to talk about one topic; rather, they meet only periodically, for relatively short periods of time often to discuss a variety of topics (Morris, 2003).

The elementary and middle school teachers who attended the PD seen in Transcripts B and C were teacher leaders from different schools in a mid-sized suburban school district. They came together a few hours monthly to study issues related to teaching mathematics. Nanette is a math teacher educator working to develop a series of video-based instructional case studies designed to foster the study of mathematics teaching and learning in professional development.[5] She is not the group's regular facilitator. She was invited to kick-off the new school year for the teacher leaders by sharing one of her video-based instructional cases—the "Cindy Case." The case features videotape of Cindy, a middle-school teacher, teaching the same lesson on linear functions to seventh graders in 2 consecutive years. The case also includes transcripts of Cindy's lessons, samples of her students' work, and lesson tables.

During their PD with Nanette, the teacher leaders began by working on the linear functions problem Cindy taught her students in the case. They worked to find a mathematic rule or formula for determining the perimeter of a figure made up of any number of regular equilateral hexagons arranged in a straight line. After working on the hexagon problem, they watched a video of Cindy using the same problem to teach her students and discussed the mathematics, students' opportunities to learn the mathematics, and Cindy's teaching. They then watched the video of Cindy teaching the lesson to a new group of students the following year and continued their discussions. Transcript B (Table 2.2) is derived from this session.

When Nanette met with the group in August, she did not plan to work with them again, but she did videotape the entire PD session because she was piloting the use of the Cindy Case. Nevertheless, Nanette was invited back to work with the teacher leaders when their regular facilitator was unable to attend the December meeting. Her second session with these teacher leaders began with the discussion of a book assigned by the regular facilitator. The group then viewed excerpts from the videotape of themselves from the August meeting, and reviewed excerpts of the video from the Cindy Case. Transcript (Table 2.3) C is taken from a whole-group discussion of the Cindy Case in December that focused on a specific interaction between Cindy and her student Lindsey.

"A PICTURE IS WORTH A THOUSAND WORDS"

As evident, narrative description of the contexts in which micro-analytic transcripts are located can become quite lengthy. Yet as detailed as they may be, they do not reveal all the relevant structures. Conversation maps (alternately referred to as structure maps, structuration maps, and event maps) are representational tools that help the researcher to navigate an

[5]Nanette is co-principal investigators with Judy Mumme in the Video Cases for Mathematics Professional Development (VCMPD) Project [NSF: ESI-9731339, 1998–2003]. For more information on their project, see Mumme and Seago (2002) and LeFevre (2002).

interactional space in multiple ways in order to trace socioculturally constructed relationships across time. When Green and Wallat (1981) introduced the process, they described conversational mapping as:

> a multistep analysis system designed to describe the flow of the
> instructional conversation, to identify conversationally and themati-
> cally tied conversational-instructional units of varying length, to pro-
> duce structural maps of the instructional conversation, and to pro-
> vide insights from the basic units for the identification of social action
> rules and conversational contexts. (p. 163)

This macro-analytic representation is, in fact, an important kind of
transcription in IE, quite distinct from the micro-analytic Jeffersonian-
style transcriptions. This form of transcription enabled interactional
ethnographers to address a quandary other educational researchers were
grappling with. Cazden (1988) writes:

> Mehan was originally motivated by some nagging problems to look
> for an intermediate unit of discourse structure between the IRE
> sequence and the lesson as a whole. If IRE's were the only structural
> component of a lesson, one could assemble them in any order; it is
> clear that, in terms of topic (or propositional content), that wasn't so.
> Moreover, we couldn't understand why the evaluation component
> was sometimes present and sometimes not. . . . Mehan's construct of
> Topically Related Sets solved both these problems. The basic and con-
> ditional sequences are ordered within each set, and evaluations
> always occur at the end of sets, but not necessarily after each student
> response within them. (pp. 36-37)

But the mappings that Mehan created were noticeably lacking in two features that are typically prominent in the maps of interactional ethnographers: *content* and *context*. Figure 2.1 presents one of Mehan's maps.

Interactional ethnographic mapping of conversations enables the
researcher to ask questions about patterns among the speech events in the
classroom. These questions lead to theorizing about "cycles of activities"
within a classroom over time (Green & Meyer, 1991). These cycles are recognizable specifically because some key features of the previous speech
events and activities are present in new ones. Green and Wallat began this
work because they found the terms event and lesson to be problematic—
their boundaries were illusive. The notion of a cycle allowed them to look
over time. "To be part of a cycle of activity, events must be 'tied' together
by a common task or serve a common purpose" (p. 150).

The conversation map in Fig. 2.2 provides an example of this kind of
macrotranscription. It helps us locate Transcripts B and C (see Tables 2.2

Event							
Lesson							
Phase							
Opening		Instructional				Closing	
Type of sequence							
Directive	Informative	Topical sets		Topical sets		Informative	Directive
		Elicit	Elicit	Elicit	Elicit		
Organization of sequences							
I-R-E	I-R($E_\varnothing$)	I-R-E	I-R-E	I-R-E	I-R-E	I-R($E_\varnothing$)	I-R-E
Participants							
T-S-T	T-S-T	T-S-T	T-S-T	T-S-T	T-S-T	T-S-T	T-S-T

—— Sequential Organization ——→

←—— Hierarchial Organization

FIGURE 2.1 The structure of classroom lessons. (From Mehan, 1979, p. 73)

Key: T = teacher; S = student; I-R-E = initiation-reply-evaluation sequence; ($E_\varnothing$) = evaluation optional in informative sequence.

57

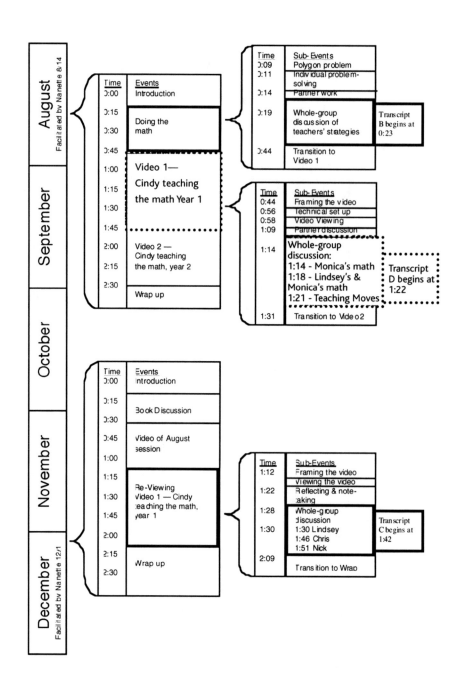

FIGURE 2.2: A conversation map of Transcripts B, C, and D.

and 2.3) and the forthcoming Transcript D (see Table 2.7) within the larger scope of five teacher leader meetings held during Fall 1998. Whereas in CA, one bit of data that captures two or more people talking might serve as well as any other for answering questions of communicative competence, in IE choosing a segment to present as a *telling case* (Agar, 1994) is pivotal phase of the research. This choice is inextricably tied to one's driving questions and the argument that is being constructed.

If, for example, the research question were, "How do teachers studying teaching practice make sense of and discuss teachers' knowledge of student thinking?" then Transcript D might provide more relevant evidence than Transcript B. Both Transcripts D (August) and C (December), are selected from whole-group discussions in which Nanette is asking the teachers to explain what they think Cindy, the teacher in the video case, might understand about her student Lindsey's thinking about the hexagon problem. Because these conversations occur 4 months apart, one might study whether the teachers interact similarly in both sessions or become more adept at engaging in this kind of inquiry into teaching practice over time.

Close inspection of the conversation map (Fig. 2.2) reveals other patterns as well. For example, both times Nanette provided professional development for this group of teachers, she engaged in a similar cycle of activity. At the event level, each session began with an introduction and concluded with a wrap up. In between these events, were three events,

Table 2.7. Transcript D

32	Nanette:	So what could possibly be going through Cindy's thinking, when
33		Lindsey says wouldn't it be plus four? What are some possible —
34	Missy:	We can identify a little bit more where the plus two is coming
35		from. Find out where she is getting her plus four.
36	Nanette:	So you think that could be possibly what's going through Cindy's
37		head. Are there any other possibilities?
38	Martha:	There are probably more kids out there that aren't clear on it. And
39		if one kid is willing to verbalize it, usually there are a few in the
40		background that match the scenario.
41	Nanette:	And what would she, what would Cindy do with each of those,
42		with each of those ways. So when she thought that there are kids
43		out there that have plus four, what did she do in this particular case
44		that actually could give evidence to what that is? Do you
45		understand what I'm asking?

Note. Data used with permission, VCMPD (NSF: ESI-9731339, 1998–2003).

and the second two involved video. The event need not be the finest analytic grain-size we considered, for each event can be divided into smaller units called subevents. At this grainsize, we can see that Transcripts B, C, and D each come from whole-group discussion subevents that were preceded by activities to prepare the teachers for participating in the whole-group discussion (either talking with a partner or writing reflections). Each was followed by a transition to the next event. The map also shows how subevents can be broken down further into phases of the conversation (e.g., phases of the whole-group discussion in which teacher address different students in Cindy's class in turn).

LINKING TEXTS AND CONTEXTS

These are not the only kinds of discursive patterns that IE can make visible. "Chains of interactional sequences that classroom members produce and regard as temporally, topically, and purposefully bound are cultural discourse events" (Rex, 2001, p. 297). Classroom speech events can be viewed as texts that are co-created by members of a classroom. Discussions from the August professional development sessions, for example, served as texts for the December session. Of course, when this kind of text is not captured on and re-viewed via video as it was in December, it may not be as obvious or easily recalled as it was for these teachers. But participants can and do create intertextual connections between event. Bloome's often quoted passage describes the nature of intertextuality:

> Whenever people engage in a language event, whether it is a conversation, the reading of a book, diary writing, etc., they are engaged in intertextuality. Various conversational and written texts are being juxtaposed. Intertextuality can occur at many levels and in many ways.
>
> Juxtaposing texts, at whatever level, is not in itself sufficient for intertextuality. Intertextuality is a social construction. The juxtaposition must be interactionally recognised, acknowledged and have social significance.
>
> In classrooms, teachers and students are continuously constructing intertextual relationships. The set of intertextual relationships they construct can be viewed as constituting a cultural ideology, a system for assigning meaning and significance to what is said and done and for socially defining participants. (Bloome, 1989, pp. 1-2, cited in Green & Meyer, 1991, p. 153 and SBCDG, 1992, pp. 133-134)

Researchers including the Santa Barbara Classroom Discourse Group (1992), Bloome and Egan-Robertson (1993), and Lin (1993) have used this concept to describe ways in which a teacher "consciously and systematically helped students construct a range of intertextual relationships among events that supported particular ways of engaging with texts, communicating with others, and constructing text" (Lin, 1993, p. 396). For example:

> The common pattern of life members constructed constituted a body of common knowledge about content and social life within the classroom. This knowledge marked an individual as an insider . . . this knowledge was not a given but was constructed over time. This body of knowledge included understandings of a variety of processes, events and positions including (a) intertextual relationships between one event and another, one type of task and another . . . and various types of written texts used in the classroom; and (b) roles and relationships among members and with academic content. Through such relationships and the patterns of interactions within an event and across events, the teachers and students constructed social and discursive practices that supported the academic and social processes of the classroom. (Lin, 1993, p. 403)

Context is another term that is of particular importance to the work of the interactional ethnographer, but as the following four descriptions of context reveal, it is nevertheless a problematic one:

> In order to know whatever they need to know to operate in a manner acceptable to others in society, children and adults must know what forms of verbal and nonverbal behavior are appropriate in which social contexts. This requires knowing what context one is in and when contexts change. . . . Contexts are not simply given in the physical setting (kitchen, living room, sidewalk in front of drug store) nor in combination of personnel (two brothers, husband and wife, firemen). Rather, contexts are constituted by what people are doing and where and when they are doing it. (Erickson & Schultz, 1981, p. 148)

> We defined what context meant using the classic definition proposed by Erickson and Shultz. . . . We considered what *context* meant by comparing the English version of our *text* with the Spanish one and realized that in Spanish there was an implied relationship if the work was read *con*(with)*texto*(text). This interpretation led to a series of questions for future work that are explored in this study: Who is with text and what does it mean "to be with text"? [*sic*]. (Floriani, 1994, p. 244)

> The context of an utterance (oral or written) is everything in the material, mental, personal, interactional, social, institutional, cultural, and historical situation in which the utterance was made. . . . Thus, context is nearly limitless. (Gee, 1999, p. 54)

The significance of any speaker's communicative action is doubly contextual in being both *context-shaped* and *context-renewing*. (Heritage, 1984, p. 242, cited in Schiffrin, 1994, p. 235)

Gee's (1999) advice that there is no one *right* way to do discourse analysis resonates; determining what should be part of the context of a study is depends on one's theoretical framework, assumptions, and of course, research question(s). "Once the contexts of the classroom instructional situation have been identified, the researcher can begin to ask questions about the nature of the classroom as a social system" (Green & Wallat, 1981, p. 183).

Floriani's (1994) work on *intercontextuality* has expanded notions of both text and context. Relying on her definition of context from the Spanish *contexto* as literally "to be with text" (see quote above), she explains:

By examining texts constructed by members of a group . . . across time . . . it is possible to examine how the interactional patterns observed in the preceding analysis are related to other patterns of life. Central to this view is the understanding that over time members are constructing patterned ways of negotiating, interpreting, interacting, and viewing what is socially and academically appropriate in this . . . group. . . . Thus, as members construct the patterns of everyday life, they are constructing social and academic conventions, social and academic texts, and social and academic practices that may be invoked as resources for interpreting and participating in the local context under construction. . . . The notion of intercontextuality builds on the concept of intertextuality as framed by Bloome (Bloome & Bailey, 1992; Bloome & Egan-Robertson, 1992), but goes beyond that notion of text to the view that contexts themselves can be juxtaposed and interactionally invoked by members. . . . These prior contexts, with their socially negotiated roles and relationships and texts and meanings, become resources for members to reexamine past events, to resolve differences in interpretation and understanding, and to lay the foundation for revising and modifying the present in light of the past and vice versa. (pp. 256-257)

INTERACTIONAL ETHNOGRAPHY
IN PROFESSIONAL DEVELOPMENT

As tools of inquiry developed through the study of teaching and learning, *cycle of activity, text, intertextuality, context,* and *intercontextuality* are well suited to the study of PD. The logic of intertextuality and intercontextuality are particularly valuable given that in PD teachers are expected to take conversational texts they have co-constructed within that context and apply these texts to their practice in their own classrooms. This intertextual and intercontextual leap from PD to the classroom is implicit in teachers' work in PD.

The teacher learning that results from studying teaching in PD consists of meanings that are situated in that particular context. Teachers are asked to take texts whose meaning has been constructed in one interactional space within one educational subculture and renegotiate them within an entirely different interactional space and discourse community—their own classroom. Intercontextuality has typically be used to investigate the relationships between two or more instructional contexts in which the participants roles as teachers and learners are stable. Brilliant-Mills (1994) alluded to this issue of whether situated meanings can travel beyond the context of the classroom communities in which they are co-constructed when she questions whether students carry their definitions and understandings of what it means to be a mathematician, scientist, and so on, "outside of the classroom" (p. 301). But using intertextuality and intercontextuality to explore the inherent leap between PD and the classroom, where teachers significantly shift their interactional role as they shift from learner to teacher has heretofore been unexplored in the research literature. In the PD context, questions of whether and how situated meaning that is co-constructed in the one context can transfer to a new context is of central importance.

IE provides a cache of tools of inquiry that plausibly supports researchers to shed much needed light on aspects of teacher learning and conventional professional development that are frequently criticized including knowledge transfer and teacher change (e.g., McLaughlin & Oberman, 1996; Wilson & Berne, 1999). Referring back again to Cazden's (1988) suggestion that teachers are the only natives in their classrooms, perhaps there is a way in which this concept applies when we think about reputedly poor transfer of conventional school- and district-based professional development back in the classroom. IE might provide some clues as to why. Although teachers work among colleagues, certain text and contexts are available as constructive resources for the future work, however, what they have created is "native" to the PD context not the classroom. This leads to unforeseen challenges as teachers attempt to re-construct socially constructed and situated understandings in the classroom. One goal for future research, then, might be to study and theorize the intertextual and intercontextual links between PD communities and classroom communities in order to support teachers by increasing their opportunity to transfer what they learn between the two contexts.

Because IE is grounded in theories of ethnography, and therefore culture, before proceeding with this kind of study of PD, we must establish that teachers in a school are actually part of a culture. Does it make sense to reason about teachers in a school as we reason about students in a classroom? Teachers do spend the same 1000+ hours per year within the boundaries of the school as students spend in their classes, but the patterns of interaction are certainly distinct. The cellular organizational structure of self-contained classrooms, aptly described by Lortie's (1975, p. 14) egg-crate metaphor, entails the physical, logistical, and intellectual separation between teachers during most of their hours in school. Certainly, there is far less time for interaction between teachers of different classes than there is between teachers and students within classes.

Typically required to arrive 15 minutes before school begins, teachers may drop in the teachers' lounge to touch base with peers and check their mail or they may go directly to their classroom to prepare. Some teachers may interact in teachers' lounge conversations whereas others may not. (See Ben-Peretz & Schonmann, 2000, for more details on the role the teachers' lounge plays in the school culture.) Once the bell rings, scheduling often limits teachers' contact with colleagues. In elementary schools, multiple schedules for recesses, lunch, and dismissal based on grade level are common; different prep periods, breaks, and lunch periods are common in secondary schools. Consequently, the faculty as a whole is constrained in its ability to interact freely, despite the fact that teachers work within 100 yards of most of their colleagues. At least within the United States, many teachers stay in their own classrooms after school to go over the day's work and prepare their lessons for the next day.[6]

A culture or speech community is not determined simply on the basis of time spent together. It is also based on shared norms, practices, and values. Certainly, the conservatism and continuity of professional practices (Lortie, 1975), the linguistic consistency of classroom discourse (e.g., Mehan, 1979; Sinclair & Coulthard, 1975), and the distinct patterns of discourse teachers employ in the teachers' lounge (Ben-Peretz & Schonmann, 2000) would suggest a deep-rooted and long-standing culture of teachers within their schools. Lave and Wenger (1991) use the term *community of practice* to describe a particular kind of culture that interacts around the work they do. Rosenholtz's (1989) in-depth study of more than 1,200 teachers in Tennessee makes it clear that teachers at a school site may share a *technical culture* based on shared values, goals,

---

[6]I observed a very different model at an elementary school in Tokyo in which all of the teachers had their desks in the same room. Consequently, at times when U.S. teachers might be isolated in their rooms preparing for upcoming teaching, these Japanese teachers were preparing communally, if not collaboratively. Catherine Lewis (personal communication, June 1999) indicated that it is the norm throughout Japan.

norms, and practices, or they may not. Drawing on substantial qualitative and quantitative evidence in her work, Rosenholtz finds that a technical culture is related to teachers' visions of successful teaching, their self-esteem, and their ability to offer and receive help with teaching.

The presence or absences of a technical culture is therefore also correlated with teachers' opportunities to grow as professionals. Where there is evidence of technical culture, teachers' opportunities for studying and learning teaching are enhanced; where minimal or no technical culture exists, they are diminished. Identifying a collection of teachers as a culture seems reasonable, however, if there is no evidence of a "technical culture" or "community of practice" (e.g., the absence of evidence that the teachers share values, goals, normative practices, etc.), a methodological approach such as IE, that by design investigates interactions within a community may not be appropriate or even justifiable.

CONCLUSIONS

Studying PD by examining the interactions of the participants provides an important opportunity for the researcher to disaggregate teachers' opportunities for learning from the implementation of new or improved practices in the classroom. By focusing on language in use, a researcher would be able to capture teachers studying practices and investigate opportunities for learning that are afforded through particular interactions (Tuyay, Jennings, & Dixon, 1995). This is not to say that how teachers *use* what they learn in PD is not important, but rather to say that if we are seeing consistent evidence that teachers are not implementing what they learn in PD, perhaps we need to step back and look more closely at the issue of whether they actually have the opportunity to learn. Many studies *ipso facto* connect PD and implementation, but it seems that until we understand more about the real opportunities for teacher learning in the former, we will continue to have a "Band-Aid approach" to fixing the latter.

Discourse analysis seems to provide a well-suited toolkit for carefully investigating what is available for teachers to learn in conventional school- and district-based PD. It may appear that I have structured this chapter to make a "straw man" of CA in order to strengthen the argument for the use of IE. Such is not the case. Rather, my intent was to build a case illustrating that each methodological approach has a role to play in the study of PD and that the two approaches can complement each other in addressing a myriad of important and unexplored questions. Like Gee, I hope my readers will borrow the tools of inquiry I have nominated and transform them, forging their own tools they begin to take on some of the fundamental questions in the field of professional development. There is much to discover and the theoretical frameworks and methods of conversation analysis and interactional ethnography, with their proven track records in other educational contexts, provide a means of facing the challenges ahead.

REFERENCES

Agar, M. (1994). *Language shock: Understanding the culture of conversation.* New York: Quill.

Atkinson, J., & Heritage, J. (1999). Jefferson's transcript notation. In A. Jaworski & N. Coupland (Eds.), *The discourse reader* (pp. 158-166). London: Routledge Press.

Baker, C. (1997). Transcription and representation in literacy research. In J. Flood, S. Brice-Heath, & D. Lapp (Eds.), *Handbook of teaching literacy through communicative and visual arts* (pp. 110-120). New York: Macmillan.

Ben-Peretz, M., & Schonmann, S. (2000). *Behind closed doors: Teachers and the role of the teachers' lounge.* Albany: State University of New York Press.

Bloome, D., & Bailey, F. (1992). Studying language and literacy through events, particularity, and intertextuality. In R. Beach et al., (Eds.) *Multidisciplinary perspectives on language and literacy research* (pp. 181–210). Urbana, IL: NCRE & NCTE.

Bloome, D., & Egan-Robertson, A. (1993). The social construction of intertextuality in classroom reading and writing lessons. *Reading Research Quarterly, 28,* 305-333.

Brilliant-Mills, H. (1994). Becoming a mathematician: Building a situated definition of mathematics. *Linguistics and Education, 5,* 301-334.

Cazden, C. (1988). *Classroom discourse: The language of teaching and learning.* Portsmouth, NH: Heinemann.

Cazden, C. (2001). *Classroom discourse: The language of teaching and learning* (2nd ed.). Portsmouth, NH: Heinemann.

Darling-Hammond, L., & Sykes, G. (1999). *Teaching as the learning profession: Handbook of policy and practice.* San Francisco, CA: Jossey-Bass.

Edelsky, C. (1993). Who's got the floor? In D. Tannen (Ed.), *Gender and conversational interaction* (pp. 189-226). New York: Oxford University Press.

Erickson, F. (1992). Ethnographic microanalysis of interaction. In M.D. LeCompte, W. L. Millroy, & J. Preissle (Eds.), *The handbook of qualitative research in education* (pp. 201-223). San Diego, CA: Academic Press.

Erickson F., & Schultz J. (1981). When is a context? Some issues and methods in the analysis of social competence. In J. Green & C. Wallat (Eds.), *Ethnography and language in educational settings* (pp. 147-160). Norwood, NJ: Ablex.

Fenstermacher, G. (1986). Philosophy of research on teaching: Three aspects. In M. Wittrock (Ed.), *The handbook of research on teaching* (3rd ed., pp. 37-49). New York: Macmillan.

Floriani, A. (1994). Negotiating what counts: Roles and relationships, texts and contexts, content and meaning. *Linguistics and Education, 5,* 241-274.

Florio, S. (1981). *Very special natives: The evolving role of teachers as informants in educational ethnography* (Occasional Paper, no. 42). East Lansing, MI: Institute for Research on Teaching.

Gee, J. P. (1999). *An introduction to discourse analysis: Theory and method*. New York: Routledge.

Goffman, E. (1981). *Forms of talk*. Philadelphia: University of Pennsylvania Press.

Green, J., & Bloome, D. (1997). Ethnography and ethnographers of and in education: A situated perspective. In J. Flood, S. Brice-Heath, & D. Lapp (Eds.), *Handbook of teaching literacy through communicative and visual arts* (pp. 181-202). New York: Macmillan.

Green, J., & Dixon, C. (1993). Introduction to talking knowledge into being: Discursive and social practices in classrooms. *Linguistics and Education, 5*, 231-240.

Green, J., Franquiz, M., & Dixon, C. (1997). The myth of the objective transcript. *TESOL Quarterly, 31*, 172-176.

Green, J., & Meyer, L. (1991). The embeddedness of reading in classroom life: Reading as a situated process. In C. Baker & A. Luke (Eds.), *Toward a critical sociology of reaching pedagogy* (pp. 159-174). Mahwah, NJ: Erlbaum.

Green, J., & Wallat, C. (1981). Mapping instructional conversations: A sociolinguistic ethnography. In J. Green & C. Wallat (Eds.), *Ethnography and language in educational settings* (pp. 161-205). Norwood, NJ: Ablex.

Gumperz, J. (1986). Interactional sociolinguistics on the study of schooling. In J. Cook-Gumperz (Ed.), *The social construction of literacy* (pp. 45-68) New York: Cambridge University Press.

Hymes, D. (1972). Models of the interaction of language and social life. In J. Gumperz & D. Hymes (Eds.), *Directions in sociolinguistics: The ethnography of communication* (pp. 35-71). New York: Holt, Rinehart and Winston.

Hymes, D. (1974). *Foundations in sociolinguistics: An ethnographic approach*. Philadelphia: University of Pennsylvania Press.

Jackson, P. W. (1968). *Life in classrooms*. New York: Teachers College Press

Lampert, M. (2001). *Teaching problems and the problems of teaching*. New Haven, CT: Yale University Press.

Lave J., & Wenger, E. (1991). *Situated learning: Legitimate peripheral participation*. New York: Cambridge University Press.

LeFevre, D. (2002). *Developing curriculum: The design of video-based multimedia tools for learning teaching*. Unpublished doctoral dissertation, University of Michigan, Ann Arbor.

Lemke, J. L. (1989). The language of science teaching. In C. Emihovich (Ed.), *Locating learning: Ethnographic perspectives on classroom research* (pp. 216-239). Norwood NJ: Ablex.

Lin, L. (1993). Language of and in the classroom: Constructing the patterns of social life. *Linguistics and Education, 5*, 367-410.

Lortie D. (1975). *Schoolteacher: A sociological study*. Chicago: University of Chicago Press.

McLaughlin, M., & Oberman, I. (1996). *Teacher learning: New policies, new practices*. New York: Teachers College Press.

Mehan, H. (1979). The structure of classroom lessons. In ed. home for Mehan *Learning lessons: Social organization in the classroom* (pp. 35-80). Cambridge, MA: Harvard University Press.

Morris, K. (2003). *Elementary teachers' opportunities for learning: An ethnographic study of professional development.* Unpublished doctoral dissertation, University of Michigan, Ann Arbor.

Moschkovich, J. (1999). Supporting the participation of English language learners in mathematical discussions. *For the Learning of Mathematics, 19*(1) 11-19.

Mumme, J., & Seago, N. (2002, April). *Issues and challenges in facilitating video cases for mathematics professional development.* Paper presented at the annual meeting of the American Educational Research Association, New Orleans, LA.

Ochs, E. (1979). Transcription as theory. In E. Ochs & B. Schieffelin (Eds.), *Developmental pragmatics* (pp. 43-72). New York: Academic Press.

Psathas, G., & Anderson, T. (1990). The "practice" of transcription in conversation analysis. *Semiotica, 78*(12), 75-99.

Rex, L. (2001). Remaking of a high school reader. *Reading Research Quarterly, 36,* 288-314.

Rosenholtz, S. (1989). *Teachers' workplace: The social organization of schools.* New York: Teachers College Press.

Sacks H., Schegloff, E., & Jefferson, G. (1974). A simplest systematics for the organization of turn-taking for conversation. *Language, 50,* 696-735.

Santa Barbara Classroom Discourse Group. (1992). Do you see what we see? The referential and intertextual nature of classroom life. *Journal of Classroom Interaction, 27*(2), 29-36.

Schegloff, E. (1987). Recycle turn beginnings: A precise repair mechanism in conversation's turn-taking organisation. In G. Button & J. R.E. Lee (Eds.), *Talk and social organization* (pp. 70-85). Clevedon, England: Multilingual Matters.

Schegloff, E., Jefferson, G., & Sacks, H. (1977). The preference for self-correction in the organisation of repair in conversation. *Language, 53,* 361-382.

Schegloff, E., & Sacks, H. (1973). Opening up closings. *Semiotica, 7*(3/4), 289-327.

Schiffrin, D. (1994). *Approaches to discourse.* Cambridge, MA: Blackwell.

Sinclair J., & Coulthard R. (1975). *Toward an analysis of discourse: The English used by teachers and pupils.* London: Oxford University Press.

Tannen, D., & Wallat, C. (1993). Interactive frames and knowledge schemas in interaction: Examples from a medical examination/interview. In D. Tannen (Ed.), *Framing in discourse* (pp. 57-76). New York: Oxford University Press.

Titscher, S., Meyer, M., Wodak, R., & Vetter, E. (2000). *Methods of text and discourse analysis.* London: Sage.

Tuyay, S., Jennings, L., & Dixon C. (1995). Classroom discourse and opportunities to learn: An ethnographic study of knowledge construction in a bilingual third-grade classroom. *Discourse Processes, 19*(1), 75-110.

West, C. (1996). Ethnography and orthography: A (modest) methodological proposal. *Journal of Contemporary Ethnography, 25,* 327-352.

Wilson S., & Berne, J. (1999). Teacher learning and the acquisition of professional knowledge: An examination of research on contemporary professional development. *Review of Research in Education, 24,* 173-209.

Zaharlick A., & Green, J. (1991) Ethnographic research. In J. Flood, J. Jensen, D. Lapp, & J. Squire (Eds.), *Handbook of research on teaching the English language arts* (pp. 205-225). New York: Macmillan.

PART I

Assessing the Opportunities for Learning Made Available for Students

Alexandra Miletta

Mary Yonker

Carol Connor

Each of us came to interactional ethnography (IE) with experiences in both quantitative and qualitative research methods, and with some degree of dissatisfaction with methods that could not adequately answer the questions in which we were interested. These were questions about the sociocultural contexts of classrooms, student and teacher interactions, and opportunities for learning. For Mary, who chose an after-school program for Spanish-speaking immigrant children, consisting of undergraduate students tutoring children in reading, IE provided tools for examining how the children, the tutors, and the directors established reading practices. Alexandra was able to identify both teaching and learning opportunities, as well as student take up of the intentions of the elementary teacher, who collaborated on the study with Alexandra, to understand how morally acceptable behavior was being socially constructed in the classroom. Carol, for her study, used IE to verify language-and-reading-assessment results for proficient and struggling readers. She wanted to examine whether these results were stable from kindergarten through third-grade, as well as to observe how the students' reading skills affected their role in their third grade classroom. She and Lesley recognized the potential of deliberately using both a sociocultural lens and a cognitive/developmental lens and decided to rewrite her study into an article that has become Chapter 5.

Nevertheless, we encountered common challenges while we were engaged in using interactional ethnographic methods in our studies. These included the time-consuming, intellectually challenging, and patience taxing process of refining our research questions, managing large amounts of data, confronting the issue of how much data analysis was needed to support our claims, and combining conceptual lenses. Mary, for example, found that as she observed the reading practices in the after-school program, several interesting aspects of the group's interaction would have been worth pursuing and there were multiple questions the data set could have addressed. She kept changing her research question until she found the focus that she wanted to follow. This meant she tried out the logic of a number of questions to the point of selecting data for analysis and then mapping and transcribing it, until, after a number of practice methodologies she found the one she thought would yield the most robust results. Because Lesley and Carol were applying two lenses, they had to create a guiding question, which was, "Can we use these two very different paradigms to draw a more complete picture of the challenges facing struggling readers, which will, in turn, lead to more effective classroom-based assessment and intervention?" In having to sort out for each other what they meant as they co-wrote the article, they learned that the answer to their question was definitely "yes." However, their struggle to come to a common understanding illuminated the important differences between the two lenses and why miscommunications between sociocultural and developmental/cognitive perspectives can be pervasive and seemingly intractable. As they wrote, and rewrote, they also confronted clashes between the different conventions for writing reports of research. Alexandra's challenge was to combine IE with the concept of manner in teaching, where manner was defined as human conduct that is consistent with a relatively stable disposition or character trait. This meant she had to work with data that had been collected to observe a discrete phenomenon and devise a research question and methodology that could observe it as fluid interactional activity. Alexandra solved that dilemma by sorting out the specific purpose of her study in terms of the theoretical constructs of IE. She wanted to understand how the teacher's manner and social situations with students were interacting to construct meaning.

For each of us, collaboration with our peers in Lesley's course constructed our dilemmas, by challenging us to think and perform in ways that we hadn't ever experienced, and then helped us solve them. Along the way to creating successful studies, our dialogue about our research questions, methods, combining theoretical frameworks, and data analysis created a more complete understanding of IE. At the same time, we gained new insights and perspectives into our own work and how to do it by hearing each other's interpretations of our research projects, reading and analyzing other studies for their rhetorical structure, logic, and flow, as well as guiding each other through the challenges and complexities of analyzing discourse.

3

Establishing a Positive Classroom Climate: An Experienced Teacher in a New School Setting

Alexandra Miletta

What makes teaching a moral endeavor is that it is, quite centrally, human action undertaken in regard to other human beings. Thus, matters of what is fair, right, just, and virtuous are always present. . . . The teacher's conduct at all times and in all ways, is a moral matter.

—Fenstermacher (1990, p. 133)

Teaching as an activity can be described as moral because, in very general terms, it presupposes notions of better and worse, of good and bad. As typically understood, teaching reflects the intentional effort to influence another human being for the good rather than for the bad.

—Hansen (2001, p. 828)

That teaching has moral implications may seem self-evident, yet there is nevertheless a great need for research in the area of teachers' beliefs and practices with regard to the moral dimensions of teaching, and the ways in which the cultivation of moral and intellectual virtues are intertwined in teaching practices. David Hansen (2001) states:

> Perhaps there has never been a greater need for research that seeks to spotlight enduring aspects of educational work, those that constitute the very reasons for performing such work in the first place. As we have seen, the idea of teaching as a moral activity captures many of these aspects. Keeping the idea in view in a sharp and lucid manner remains an important task of both research and practice. (p. 855)

Like Hansen, I too believe that "the moral meaning of teaching can be derived from the basic terms of the work itself. . . . Teaching means attending to students, listening to them, speaking with them in intellectually serious ways, identifying their strengths and weaknesses with an eye on supporting the former and overcoming the latter, and more" (Hansen, 1998, pp. 652-653). Furthermore, I believe a careful and close analysis of classroom life, with a particular focus on seeking a better understanding of pedagogical beliefs and practices that are influential in the moral and intellectual development of students, can lead to improving the ways in which we engage teachers and students in thinking about these moral dimensions of teaching and learning. The discourse, beliefs, and behaviors of students should also be carefully examined if the influences of the teacher are to be fully explored.

The questions for this study are as follows:

- How does an elementary teacher together with her students construct what counts as morally acceptable behavior through verbal, non-verbal, and written communication in order to establish the climate of this classroom?
- In particular, how does the teacher take advantage of the interactional moment and use it as a teaching and learning "opportunity," and what is the evidence for student "take up" of the intended lessons?
- Does the teacher perceive certain student characteristics that differ across two school contexts, and what noticeable effect do such differences have on the ways in which the teacher perceives the co-construction of the classroom climate?

The final question emerged when Darlene, the elementary teacher who is the focus of this study, moved to another school after the second year of the study. This change provided a unique opportunity to begin to explore how differences in schools may have an effect on moral dimensions of teaching.

The second question relates to a study from the Santa Barbara Classroom Discourse Group (SBCDG; Tuyay, Jennings, & Dixon, 1995) that showed how opportunities for learning become visible through discourse interactions. They define an opportunity to learn as "one that offers the student a chance to interact with information and to make sense of it" (p. 76). "Take up" is illustrated through sociolinguistic analysis by examining "how, through talk, members negotiated and constructed situated definitions" (p. 92). My goal in this study has been to gain a holistic view of the classroom community, and to co-construct with the teacher an interpretation of the emic moral meanings that the students and their teacher reveal in everyday actions and discourse. I have sought to understand the "customary actions, beliefs, knowledge, and attitudes of a social group as reflected in the ways of engaging in everyday life" (Zaharlick & Green, 1991, p. 207).

One of the ways in which Darlene takes advantage of an interactional moment during instruction to construct understandings of morally acceptable behavior with her students can be seen in the vignette (see Table 3.1) transcribed from a videotape of a lesson (Jordan Elementary, second year of study, 10/22/98). Darlene is in the middle of a brainstorming session with the whole class of third and fourth graders when she notices that Justin has gotten out of his seat and has walked to the back of the room, out of the camera's range. However, there is a clear view of Stephanie, who follows the exchange with great interest.

What is morally significant about this episode? Darlene interrupts the lesson to ask Justin about his behavior (lines 8-18), and to help him remind himself of his responsibility as a student in her classroom. She then provides him with a clear rationale as to why she is telling him he shouldn't get up out of his seat (lines 21, 24). Furthermore, this example provides evidence that another student in the class is taking up her teacher's lesson on morally acceptable behavior because Stephanie shakes and nods her head in response to Darlene's questions and statements.

The purpose of this chapter is to explore more thoroughly and systematically what Darlene is attempting to teach and what her students are taking up by examining a few segments of everyday classroom life in each of the two school settings in order to understand how Darlene takes advantage of the interactional moment. This analysis is complemented by student and teacher interview excerpts, and by a comparison of student remarks during a community circle classroom meeting that was structured in similar ways in both schools at about the same time of year.

Table 3.1. Justin

LINE	TEACHER'S TALK	GESTURES
006	Now	Darlene turns off overhead,
007	I'm a little confused	caps pen, watches Justin, then frowns
008	Justin	
009	what's happening here?	
		Stephanie follows Justin's path with her eyes
010	wuh wait wait wait	
011	right there	
012	wait stop	Darlene puts her hand out
013	stop	nods her head
014	can you answer me please?	Darlene looks straight at Justin
015	What's happening?	
		Stephanie looks at Darlene
016	Are you learning right now?	
		Stephanie shakes her head
017	Am I teaching right now?	Darlene points at herself
		Stephanie nods her head
018	So what's your responsibility?	
		Stephanie looks back at Justin
019	Yes will you go back to your position please your learning position	Darlene remains in the same position, watching Justin
020	Quickly!	
		Justin goes back to his seat, then away again off camera
021	You stopped our teaching time	
022	Thank you	
023	Don't do that anymore okay	
		Stephanie shakes her head
024	'cause it stops my teaching and makes me angry	
025	Right?	
		Stephanie nods her head
026	Okay	Darlene turns from Justin

CONCEPTUALLY FRAMING THE STUDY

Looking at the classroom as a culture (see Gallego, Cole, & The Laboratory of Comparative Human Cognition, 2001) is essential to this inquiry into moral dimensions of teaching. For my purposes, the following working definition of culture (Peacock, 1986) is a succinct and appropriate one: "The taken-for-granted but powerfully influential understandings and codes that are learned and shared by members of a group" (cited in Egan-Robertson & Willett, 1998, p. 8). In all classrooms, words spoken and patterns of action converge in ways that help members of that classroom understand what is and is not morally acceptable. Robert Boostrom (1991) has said of rules, "They are structures of meaning we use to make sense of the world around us" (p. 194). In the classroom I have chosen to study what counts as morally acceptable behavior is taught very purposefully, with a specific vocabulary and using consciously chosen strategies.

Three conceptual lenses that are used for this study are the concept of manner in teaching (Fenstermacher, 1992; Richardson & Fenstermacher, 2001), which helps clarify why teaching is an inherently moral activity; an ethnographic approach; and a discourse microanalysis of interactions. Each of these enables a particular view into the moral dimensions of teaching of concern in this study. The convergence of views is meant to add to theories about how classroom moral climates are established, by showing both *what* moral understandings are constructed over time, and *how* these understandings are constructed by members of the classrooms through language. Each is presented in the following sections, followed by a brief discussion of a related study.

The Concept of Manner

For 2 years, I was a member of the Manner in Teaching Project at the University of Michigan. The project was a 3-year study funded by the Spencer Foundation. *Manner* in this context was defined as human conduct that expresses moral and intellectual virtue and is consistent with a relatively stable disposition or character trait (Fenstermacher, 1992; Richardson & Fenstermacher, 2001). Manner was initially conceived as distinct from a teacher's *style*, which reflects personality, and *method*, which refers to what the teacher does to convey content to students. In the words of the Manner Project proposal (Fenstermacher & Richardson, 1997): "The purposes of this study are to further develop the concept of manner in teaching, and to address the question of whether and with what means teachers can undertake the reflective study of their own manner, attending to it in ways that permit its thoughtful connection to instructional method and to their intended results for student learning" (p. 5). This study was somewhat unique in that it combined a philosophical inquiry and analysis, led by co-principal investigator Gary Fenstermacher, and a qualitative empirical study, led by co-principal investigator Virginia Richardson. In collaboration with the 11 teachers in two schools involved in the project, we attempted to better understand the nature of manner in teaching and the ways in which teachers strive to construct a virtuous classroom community (Richardson & Fenstermacher, 2001).

Insights gained from both the empirical research and the philosophical inquiries led to some significant findings. First of all, we discovered that one philosophical theory, rooted in the Aristotelian notion that students become virtuous by having a virtuous teacher to model and guide them in the development of their moral character, was insufficient to explain the moral complexity of what teachers were doing to foster moral agency in their students (Sanger & Fenstermacher, 2000). Second, we discovered that method and style were as vital to the moral work of teachers as manner. Six methods were identified as ways that teachers seek to convey virtues, enhance moral relationships, and develop intellectual dispositions in their classrooms: constructing classroom community, didactic instruction, designing and executing academic task structures, calling out for a particular conduct, and showcasing specific students (Fenstermacher, 2001). Call-outs are especially relevant to this study, as we see multiple examples of this approach in the segments of videotape analyzed. As Fenstermacher explains: "At least in the case of the teachers participating in our study, the call-outs were, in the main, far from simple demands for compliance or order, but the expression of a very genuine interest in helping the student to become a good person" (p. 646). Finally, the relationship between the school context and the moral climate in classrooms was found to be salient (Chow-Hoy, 2001) in that both the school mission and the leadership style of the principal had an effect on the manner and methods of teachers. This study attempts to expand on the notion that the nature of the place where teachers work may have an effect on the moral aspects of their teaching.

Discourse Analysis and Adopting an Ethnographic Approach

Ethnographers set out to describe and compare the cultures of the people they study by observing closely the activities, discourse, and patterns of everyday life. Frederick Erickson (1986) said: "Interpretive, participant observational fieldwork research, in addition to a central concern with mind and with subjective meaning, is concerned with the relations between meaning-perspectives of actors and the ecological circumstances of action in which they find themselves" (p. 127). Elsewhere, Erickson used the analogy of ethnography in educational research as useful for revealing what is inside the "black boxes" of daily life in classrooms by documenting processes that "consist of the routine actions and sense-making of participants in educational settings, which, because they are habitual and local, may go unnoticed by practitioners and researchers alike" (Erickson, 1992, p. 202). James Gee and Judith Green (1998) explain what is meant by an ethnographic perspective that guides the analysis of discourse by citing the definition by George and Louise Spindler (1987) which states that a "culturally constructed dialogue" expressed in action, words, and symbols is constructed by social actors in a social scene and setting. Discourse, then, is language as social action and behavior. Gee and Green (1998) provide a succinct summary of how the microanalysis of discourse interactions, including talk and gestures, coupled with an ethnographic approach is useful for this study:

> Discourse analysis, then, when guided by an ethnographic perspec-
> tive, forms a basis for identifying what members of a social group
> (e.g. a classroom or other educational setting) need to know, produce,
> predict, interpret, and evaluate in a given setting or social group to
> participate appropriately (Heath, 1982) and, through that participa-
> tion, learn (i.e. acquire and construct the cultural knowledge of the
> group). Thus, an ethnographic perspective provides a conceptual
> approach for analyzing discourse data (oral or written) from an emic
> (insider's) perspective and for examining how discourse shapes both
> what is available to be learned and what is, in fact, learned. (p. 126)

It is worth noting that these theoretical lenses are not in conflict, but rather complement each other. The concept of manner as I interpret it in this chapter does not imply that manner is located only in the minds of individuals, neither that manner is the same for all teachers in all class-rooms, or that having good or appropriate manner is necessarily a state of being one seeks to achieve. An important understanding gained from the Manner Project was that within the range of identifiable virtues teach-ers were seeking to foster in students, even those with common labels looked somewhat different in each teacher's classroom (Sanger, 2001). Understanding manner entails examining the dynamic processes of social interactions in classrooms that reveal what moral and intellectual virtues are valued and what they mean to individuals as they gain mem-bership in a group, in this case, a classroom. Perhaps it is best to speak of *manners* in the classroom (not to be confused with polite behaviors) for both the manner of the teacher and the manner of the students interact to constitute what counts as morally acceptable behavior and discourse (for a discussion of literacy and literacies as a parallel argument see Castanheira, Crawford, Dixon, & Green, 2001).

A Related Study

Richardson and Fallona (2001) examined how classroom management brings together experienced teachers' manner and method, by comparing two teachers involved in the Manner Project, one of whom is Darlene, the teacher who is a co-researcher in this study. "We are looking at classroom management, manner, beliefs about classroom life and moral and intellectual goals for students, and classroom behavior that directly informs students of expectations for virtuous conduct" (p. 707). Their findings suggest that "the degree of authenticity-coherence in which he or she [the teacher] expresses his or her beliefs, goals, manner and methods" (p. 724) can help enhance our understanding of effective classroom management and teacher expertise. There are also significant implications for teacher education. Preservice teachers "should be asked to reflect upon their beliefs about teaching and the attributes of their style that may be indicative of their manner" (p. 725), as this has everything to do with how they will interact with their students and establish the classroom environment.

CONTEXTUALIZING THE STUDY

Profile of Darlene

Darlene is a White female in her late 40s who has been teaching elementary school students for 15 years. She has also worked for several years as a staff developer for an early reading program. During the years of the study's data collection, she was teaching a multi-age class of third and fourth graders, and she was team-teaching with two other teachers who also teach in third-and fourth-grade multi-age classrooms at her previous school. One of the team teachers had also been involved in the Manner Project, and she and Darlene had adjacent rooms so students could move easily from one to the other when necessary. Darlene has a ready smile, and greets her students each day at the door with a hug, handshake, or a high-five. A peaceful calm characterizes the atmosphere in her classroom. Things run very smoothly, and students move purposefully around the room when appropriate during activities and during transitions. Darlene is a very self-reflective teacher who expressed keen interest in research and in furthering her understanding of manner and the issues we were exploring together in the Manner Project. She is very purposeful in selecting strategies for eliciting morally virtuous conduct from her students, and she is adept at analyzing her own communication in the classroom. She was willing to devote extra time to analysis of videotapes, and she developed her own system of coding certain teacher moves in selected portions of her videotapes. Furthermore, four of her students who were interviewed in early February 1999 were able to articulate some of Darlene's strategies and their purposes in surprising and revealing ways.

Darlene's students describe her as nice, funny, caring, loving, and likeable. She is "strict when she needs to be" and has a good sense of humor. "She always makes these little mistakes that we laugh about it with her," explains Darcy. She's a good teacher, they say, because "she like learns like how one kid learns . . . she adapts to their learning" and because "she gives you time to think." Lisa said Darlene is a good teacher "because I have a kind of problem reading and she helps me read and I'm getting better at it." Darlene's team teacher, Margaret, wrote about her in a journal entry from late October 1998:

> Darlene is one of the best teachers I have ever seen! She is so good at getting children to work to their potential . . . she is a pro. Darlene is so good at breaking the very complex down so that it becomes diges- tive for students. They will easily learn the concept. She is so good at putting it all back together so that students see the real life issues. She hardly ever raises her voice or snaps at a child. I am simply amazed how she can stay so calm in a crisis. I really respect her patience.

When asked to describe herself, Darlene said, "I think I'm loving . . . inclusive. I see myself as relating to kids in a caring way . . . personable. . . . I have high expectations and yet there's a leniency about getting them there at their own time within certain parameters" (4/27/98).

The Schools

The school site where Darlene was previously teaching is Jordan Elementary in the Riverton School District (pseudonyms are being used to protect the participants' privacy). It is a relatively small neighborhood K–5 school with approximately 280 students and 13 certified classroom teachers. Slightly more than half of the student population is Euro- American, about 33% is African American, and nearly 40% of the students receive free or reduced lunch. The school's vision is driven by the Together Everyone Achieves More (T.E.A.M.) concept and a warm, invit- ing atmosphere is felt throughout the school.

Darlene's current school, Woodcreek Elementary, is on the opposite side of town, but is part of the same district. Woodcreek is larger than

Jordan with an enrollment of about 350 students, 84% of whom are Euro-American. There are 15 certified classroom teachers. In comparison to Jordan, only about 12% of students receive free or reduced lunch. The school's mission is to "nurture within each student the joy of lifelong learning through academic preparation, building positive self-esteem, and developing social responsibility."

Many schools in the Riverton School District have adopted the language of the "life skills" (Kovalik, 1997), which seeks to teach the importance of integrity, patience, effort, cooperation, responsibility, and so forth, and these are prominently used at both Jordan and Woodcreek and in Darlene's classroom. Behavior guides known as Lifelong Guidelines (trustworthiness, truthfulness, active listening, no put-downs, personal best) are also posted throughout the two schools. At Woodcreek, where the life skills have been used for a longer time, and by more teachers than at Jordan, the parents and students sign an agreement "to work together to model the Lifelong Guidelines and life skills every day." Treating people with respect and dignity, as well as making others feel they belong and are cared for and are important to the community are all messages that the schools work hard to convey to students, parents, and teachers.

METHODS AND METHODOLOGY

Primary data for this study was selected by the researcher and teacher from two videotapes of classroom lessons, one in each school, as well as two videotapes of a community circle class meeting in each school with a similar purpose and at the same time of year. In addition, four of the students from Jordan Elementary were interviewed. The teacher herself interviewed three students from Woodcreek Elementary. The teacher was interviewed six times, and three of the teacher interviews were structured around viewing videotapes of classroom lessons. In addition, various artifacts such as the teacher's reflections and journal entries were collected and analyzed (see Appendix A for a data collection map).

Data analyzed for this study includes the following:

- Selections of three school years of classroom videotapes from 2/4/98, 10/22/98, and 2/15/99 (Jordan Elementary) and 1/28/00 and 2/16/00 (Woodcreek Elementary)
- Teacher interviews from 10/20/97, 4/27/98, 2/18/99, 11/29/99, 12/2/99, 3/3/00
- Teacher's analysis of selected video segments
- Four Jordan Elementary student interviews from 2/1/99 and 2/12/99 (for interview schedule, see Appendix B)

- Three Woodcreek Elementary student interviews by the teacher from 3/17/00 and 3/23/00
- Fieldnotes from Years 2 and 3 of the study, and context notes for videotapes and interviews
- Various text artifacts including classroom assignments, teachers' journal entries, and e-mail communications

The videotaped data chosen for analysis is meant to be a representative slice of life in the classroom. However, rather than argue for typicality, the intent is to see each episode as a telling case (Mitchell, 1984) "in which the particular circumstances surrounding a case serve to make previously obscure theoretical relationships suddenly apparent" (p. 239). The teacher selected some episodes, the researcher others, and some were chosen together, and then they were narrowed down to the cases analyzed in this chapter. The episodes analyzed at each school were taken from a lesson in mathematics at Jordan and in reading at Woodcreek, and from a community circle meeting at both schools.

Working closely with Darlene on the analysis of the data was essential and we are continuing to push for deeper understandings. It is important to note that these interpretations are evolving. Like Kyratzis and Green (1997), we view "the research narrative as a theoretical exposition of how narrative can be understood as a joint construction and as 'a' not 'the' representation of the ways in which members of a group inscribe a social world, identity, knowledge, and practice" (p. 17).

The transcripts of the videotaped classroom lessons are also jointly constructed representations. As Carolyn Baker (1997) said:

> Transcription (the process) is a method of inquiry, involving analysis from the beginning. The transcript (the product) reflects that inquiry. As a number of researchers have observed, transcription is more than a merely technical matter; the transcription process and its outcomes are by no means neutral. (p. 110)

I have chosen to use "message units" of talk (see Green & Harker, 1988; Green & Wallat, 1981) to show and analyze the actions and interactions of members of the classroom as accurately as possible in the transcription from videotape so as to place nonverbal and other contextual data in the precise moments in which they occurred. This was necessary to reveal indications of student take up (Putney, Green, Dixon, & Kelly, 1999; Tuyay et al., 1995), as in the episode presented in Table 3.1 with Justin and Stephanie. In the longer transcripts, interpretative commentary was added to assist the reader in understanding the related meaning of both talk and gestures constructed in the interactions.

RESULTS: JORDAN ELEMENTARY

The first data chosen for analysis from Jordan Elementary represents a slice of classroom life, as taken from a videotape of a whole class lesson on February 4, 1998, in the first year of the study. It is a 6-minute excerpt in which Darlene is giving instructions for writing math story problems with a partner. We have chosen five short episodes from the 6 minutes, three of which are explained in detail, because Darlene and I felt that they represented morally salient classroom management dilemmas. A careful look at the language and action in each episode helps to illustrate how morally acceptable behavior is constructed in this classroom by the teacher and the students. Supplemental data from interviews and from a community circle class meeting are analyzed as well in order to demonstrate further student take up of these ideas.

Larry and Max

The first episode involves two boys, Larry and Max, who are sitting adjacent to each other in a trio of individual desks. When Larry claims that Max pushed his desk, Darlene chooses a stance with Max that avoids accusing him and gives him the responsibility for fixing the situation. (In the transcript shown in Table 3.2, emphasis in indicated by **bold** type; an equal [=] symbol is used for overlapping talk.)

When Larry explains why he pushed his desk forward and said, "Quit it!" to Max, Darlene accepts his explanation that Max had violated his right to his personal space. Rather than reprimanding Max, or just telling him what to do, she asks him if he needs to pull back, giving him the responsibility for righting a wrong. When she finally does tell him to adjust his desk, requesting a particular conduct, she gives him a rationale for her directions. He responds to her request by nodding and then moving his desk and chair back away from Larry. Darlene explained in an interview about this episode that "he [Max] can be very oppositional and to avoid the immediate defensiveness that he would have had, even though he was the instigator, I phrase it in the way in which I do to kind of encourage him to decide to take responsibility." This implies that Darlene has learned to use this approach with Max from past experiences, when perhaps other approaches made him defensive and oppositional. Max's acknowledgment is important to Darlene, and she goes on to say, "I have to get something, so I get a nod and I accept that, and then if I leave him alone he generally will do it because he decided to do it and that makes it okay." So Darlene is very intentional about enhancing moral relationships by empowering Max to take responsibility, because she has learned from experience that when he feels in charge of his decisions, "he can still learn. Otherwise, he's oppositional and he's ticked to the hilt and he will not learn" (12/2/99).

Justin

Immediately following this episode, Darlene notices that Justin is having problems focusing on her. She has noted that he needs frequent behavioral redirection. As Darlene describes Justin, "if he ever has the chance to wander, that's what he does" (4/27/98). In fact, as seen in Table 3.1, Justin sometimes has trouble staying in his seat when he is supposed to be listening and learning, an intellectual disposition that Darlene values. Body language and eye contact are important signals that students are engaged, and Darlene is explicit about what "active listening" looks like.

In the episode presented in Table 3.3, Darlene is emphasizing the importance of listening to directions, and implies to Justin that sustained eye contact will show her that he is listening. As with Max, she awaits acknowledgment that Justin "got it" before she continues with her explanations. She explained her approach as "with Justin you have to say it sternly or it doesn't, it's like it doesn't get past this first barrier, the one that is this inattention thing" (12/2/99). Justin shows that he is taking up her lesson when he turns to a peer and says, "Got it." Furthermore, Justin talked several times in an interview about the importance of paying attention to the teacher. When asked how he shows the teacher that he likes to learn he replied, "Pay attention when she's teaching," and when asked more generally what someone should do in that classroom to be a good student he said, "When it's teaching time you don't sharpen your pencil and you don't get up from your seat unless it's an emergency." He also elaborated that following directions, keeping your hands to yourself, and not tipping back in your chair were important aspects of being a good student. Justin is also aware of the role that Darlene plays in his learning these lessons. When asked, "What is your teacher doing to help you be a better student?" he answered, "To stay on task." When probed as to how she did that, he said she only gives him one reminder (2/12/99). Justin's comments show that Darlene's strategies of calling out for a particular conduct in order to develop certain behaviors and dispositions toward learning, and showcasing Justin by incorporating him into her example, are not only explicit but effective.

Table 3.2. Larry and Max

LINE	SPEAKER	TALK	GESTURES	ANALYST'S COMMENTARY
001	Darlene	you're going to be really excited to be able to do these difficult problems	Darlene stands in front of cluster of three desks; Larry	
002		I was so impressed with the ones you wrote last week	adjusts his desk that appears to have been shifted by Max's	
003		I thought you were ready for this challenge	legs, then moves his chair	
004		now		
005		what I hope to do=		
006	Larry	=quit it	Pushes his desk forward again, Darlene notices	
007	Darlene	is to have you	Darlene looks down at Larry and Max	Darlene can see what is happening, even though Max's legs are hidden under the desk.
008	Larry	he pushed my desk into me	Larry looks at Max	
009	Darlene	Max	Turns to look at Max directly, makes eye contact	Darlene acknowledges Larry's claim that Max has caused a problem, but puts the responsibility for remedying the situation in Max's hands with her question to him.
010		do you need to pull back?		

Table 3.2. Larry and Max (*continued*)

LINE	SPEAKER	TALK	GESTURES	ANALYST'S COMMENTARY
011	Max	huh?	Max has his hands on his head, is leaning back slightly, his legs are still extended under desks	She waits a moment before repeating the question, giving Max another chance to respond even though he shows little or no reaction.
012	Darlene	do you need to move back?	Still looking at Max	Now she gives directions but also a
013		well do so if it's going to irritate others		
014		okay?		rationale. She checks with Max to make
015		okay?	Max nods slightly	sure he understands and accepts her
016		okay good	Darlene looks out at class	thinking. Max nods and moments later
017		um I hope at the end of this lesson that you will be able to trade your story problems with somebody from another pride		moves his desk away from Larry's desk, and adjusts his chair.
018		to challenge them		

87

Table 3.3. Justin

LINE	SPEAKER	TALK	GESTURES	ANALYST'S COMMENTARY
021	Darlene	you need to be the expert on your story problem Justin so if	Darlene notices that Justin is turned away from her; when he	Darlene says Justin's name and Justin doesn't stay focused on her. Then she showcases him
022		for instance	hears his name he	and makes him the focus of her
023		Travis can't figure out your story	turns his head to her	explanation, with Travis as an
024		problem you have to be able to	then back away again.	example of his potential partner for the activity.
025		Justin	Justin continues to	
026		I'm talking to you sweetheart	face away from	
027		if Travis can't figure out your story problem	Darlene.	
028		you have to be the expert that teaches him how	He turns around to look at Darlene, they	
029		so you can't just write a ridiculous one that nobody can	make and sustain eye contact.	
030		figure out		
031		you want it to be challenging	Darlene points at Justin	
032		but you want to know how to teach it in case they can't do it	Darlene points for	

Table 3.3. Justin (*continued*)

LINE	SPEAKER	TALK	GESTURES	ANALYST'S COMMENTARY
033		got it?	emphasis. Darlene is still pointing right at Justin	
			Justin turns around away from Darlene and mouths "got it" to girl to his left while nodding his head up and down and smiling at Laura, sitting diagonally across from him. Then he turns back to look at Darlene.	Justin acknowledges Darlene's question by repeating it as a statement, signaling his understanding of what she expected of him.

Travis and Laura

In the next two episodes, we see similar examples of calling for appropriate behavior when Travis doesn't hide his displeasure regarding the partner he will have to work with, and Laura is repeatedly distracted. When Darlene explains that the students will be working in pairs for this assignment with the person sitting across from them, Travis, who is sitting opposite a girl off camera, reacts by turning away from her and shielding his face from her with his left hand. Darlene asks him twice if he is worried about this lesson, or if he's just being silly, and then asks him to stop the silliness as "this is learning time." Travis then decides the best way to handle his discomfort about his partner is to look up instead of across his desk to avoid further silliness. Once again, in this episode we see that Darlene provides a rationale when she calls out for certain behaviors. Darlene describes Travis as someone who "spends a lot of time pointing fingers at everybody else and cannot admit fault." She does find that in talking with him he has begun to change his behavior of putting others down. "Every time we talk, he can admit it, but we've got to go through this little game of, 'How are you going to grow if you don't be honest. You can't make the change. And everybody else here is able to say, this is what I did wrong . . . now we need to hear it from you. What did Travis do wrong?' And he could always do it, but you have to go through the game. Now, he's just beginning to change that" (4/27/98). Darlene has developed an interactional style that is helping Travis to change his behavior of blaming others and not admitting when he has been wrong. As with the other examples, Darlene is conscious of teaching her students to be responsible for their behavior and their learning, and she is keenly aware of the progress they are making in that regard. Learning over time from trial and error the approaches that work with each individual student, Darlene is able to promote understandings of morally acceptable social behavior in her classroom. Justin, Max, and Travis show in their response to Darlene's requests that they are taking up her attempts to teach them in each of these interactional moments.

Although these examples involved boys, Darlene calls out for certain behaviors in similar ways with the girls. Her approach with each student is slightly different depending on the interactional style that she has found to be most effective in each case. In the episode with Laura, who is sitting diagonally across from Justin, Darlene asks her to move to another table because "you need to be where you can listen." Darlene provided an explanation for her direct approach with Laura. "There was a new little friendship developing there, it was the thing between Laura and Justin that kept going on." She described it as a kind of "parallel play" and added that "some people would think they were both off task but if you really know the kids you know they're doing it for each other. . . . It was a constant daily problem all day, and you work with them and work with them. . . . We ultimately had to separate them, they couldn't work in the pride [table group] together because she just became a whole different person in his presence, which was not helpful to her." Unlike her approach with Max and Travis, Darlene doesn't ask Laura a question about her behavior. As she explains her reasoning, "You can't ask her questions because she doesn't integrate and process the language well enough to make the connection with what's going on. You just have to tell her. And she's just so kind hearted and wonderful and just tickled pink to have your attention whether it's positive or negative, and [she's] very compliant and she'll be fine, so see, it's really okay with her" (12/2/99). Darlene is intentionally teaching Laura about acceptable behavior in a slightly different way based on her assessment of Laura's learning style and needs.

Adam

In the last episode (see Table 3.4), Adam, who has had his hand raised since the Travis episode, demonstrates that he has taken up Darlene's lessons about appropriate norms for participation. But there is something more sophisticated at work in this episode than in the previous ones. Here, we can glimpse a moment that helps shed light on how Darlene enhances a moral relationship with a student through discourse. It is also significant because Darlene is learning from the student, and she explicitly acknowledges it and thanks him for it.

Darlene described Adam as a "high-level thinker" even though when he initially came to Jordan Elementary as a third grader, he "couldn't read anything, couldn't spell anything, couldn't put letters on the line." It pleased her greatly that he had the confidence to share his "joking little comment with the teacher in front of the class" as demonstrated by the length of time that his hand was raised, and his patience in waiting to be called on. "He was being literal," Darlene explained, "it's not a question it's a comment and then he asked it as a question and I thought, well, he does have some language learning problems so I'll just take this little second to train him that it is a question, so you could have asked it, and you didn't know the difference between a question and comment so that this doesn't have to happen again. Or else you need to be able to say, no, it's not a question, but I have a comment." Adam's thinking, she added, was "that's the rule, you don't ask that, you don't make a comment now she said is it a question, so I'll just hold it, but I don't want to lose it so I'll get my hand up there keeping my brain holding on to that." Darlene said this is a typical comment for Adam, that he has a great sense of humor and "can catch double meanings when you say something and laugh because you mean for it to be funny." Adam likes to reciprocate with his own wit, Darlene said, although usually it happens privately. "He'll often come up after and say, well, Mrs. Danielson, you know, and he'll do this little thing like he did, like take this to another level" (12/2/99). Darlene's own sense of humor is evident in her response to his comment, and she not only laughs out loud, she praises him for his "good thinking" and lets him know that his idea is worth putting into practice.

Each of these episodes gives some insight into *how* Darlene and these students are building understandings about what is acceptable and what is not in the classroom. Clearly, Darlene has developed relationships with each of these students that enable her to handle the disruptions in the ways that she does. Each relationship is unique and entails in-depth knowledge of the student and the interactional style or stance that is most effective with that student in different classroom scenarios, both public and private. This is developed over time from multiple close observations of students, and from trial and error in using different styles in order to test hypotheses about which ones are most effective. To better understand exactly what Darlene has accomplished in terms of developing her students' understanding of morally acceptable behavior, it is worth looking at other evidence that students understand what Darlene is attempting to teach them in a different classroom context. This will also help to show how resilient this learning is and how students are able to apply the concepts in a more abstract example.

Table 3.4. Adam

LINE	SPEAKER	TALK	GESTURES	ANALYST'S COMMENTARY
132	Darlene	any other questions about your assignment?	Darlene points toward Adam, who still has his	
133		is that a question?	hand on his head	
			Adam nods	
134	Darlene	Adam?		Adam has a comment, not a question,
135		no?	Adam shakes his head	but he doesn't say that to Darlene yet
136	Darlene	well put your hand down	Darlene motions down	
137		I'll think you have a question	with her hand and her	
138		okay	tone is playful.	
139		alright		
140		would you please begin with the		
		person across from you		
		or		
141		in the case of uh		
142		Tim and Joe		
143		beside you or in the case of three people		
144		okay you may begin	Adam shoots his	Adam changes his mind.
			hand up in the air	

93

Table 3.4. Adam (continued)

LINE	SPEAKER	TALK	GESTURES	ANALYST'S COMMENTARY
145	Darlene	don't do that unless you have a question	Darlene shakes her head and moves toward Adam	
146	Adam	[...]	Adam puts his hand down	Adam obeys the teacher's direction, and puts his hand down because, it later turns out, what he wants to say is not in the form of a question.
147	Darlene	then don't do that	Darlene starts to turn away from Adam	Darlene means he shouldn't raise his hand if he doesn't have a question.
148	Adam	[...]		Adam explains something to Darlene.
149	Darlene	oh well why didn't you say that?	Darlene moves back toward Adam	
150	Girl	[...]	Stops Darlene to ask her a question	
151	Darlene	absolu oh	The girl shakes her head no and points	
152		you gotta go next door?	Adam taps on Darlene's arm	He wants to get her attention back.
153	Darlene	out there?	Darlene asks the girl.	
154		yes	She turns to face Adam	

Table 3.4. Adam *(continued)*

LINE	SPEAKER	TALK	GESTURES	ANALYST'S COMMENTARY
155	Adam	why do we gotta do this for you?	Adam looks up at Darlene, who is bending down so they are face to face	Adam frames his comment as a question.
L156	Darlene	that's a question		Darlene doesn't answer his question; she makes a comment.
157	Adam	so		He quickly reframes his question as a comment, because he doesn't want to know the answer to his question, he wants to make his clever comment.
158	Darlene	that's not a comment		
159	Adam	this	Adam points his pencil for emphasis	Adam's tone is playful.
160		we gotta do this for you because you don't want to do it		
161	Darlene	'cause I don't want to do it?	Darlene is looking right at Adam as she asks him the question.	Darlene contemplates his statement for a moment. Then she shows she understands, and shows Adam she finds his comment funny, but she also praises him for being clever.
		Ah ha ha ha	Then, she stands back up and throws her head back, laughing.	
162		that's good thinking		
163		I hadn't thought about it but I'll have to use that now that you gave me the idea		
164				
165		thanks	She taps his shoulder. Then she points at Adam and is smiling at him, then chuckling to herself as she walks away.	Adam shows Darlene he is pleased, and then he turns to smile at his neighbor as Darlene walks away.

Community Circle

Further evidence that students are taking up Darlene's lessons about responsibility and what good student behavior entails can be found in a classroom meeting (known as "community circle"), which was video-taped on February 15, 1999 in the second year of the study. Community circle meetings occurred frequently, sometimes several times a week, and served different purposes. Darlene describes why she planned this particular activity:

> We had dealt with a concern about the "crabbiness" of the computer teacher and decided that, if we changed our action during class, she would change hers. We created a graph on which a student would write the name of another student who helped them remember our commitment to good behavior. We sent a letter to the computer teacher telling her we were committed to improving our behavior and asking for her help in using the chart. It worked! Our behavior improved and she is nicer to us. So I thought we were ready to take this a step further. On the whole, cruelty was on the rise. Students' ability to see another point of view during conflict management was hampered by apparent lack of understanding and care regarding the full impact of their actions. Comments like "I was only kidding" and "It's not that big a deal" helped to prove my concern. Somehow I had to make the point that everything we do or don't do affects everyone whose lives we touch. I would set up a chain storytelling experience in which the children had a right to pass. We would reflect on the experience with every child contributing thoughts and feelings. I would make the reason for the activity clear: everything you do or say affects every member of this community. I would make the connections between this activity, the computer lab experience, and our lives in and out of the classroom.

After an introduction in which Darlene explained the purpose of the community circle meeting that day to the students, they created the chain story, and then were asked to reflect on a list of questions written up on the board. These were as follows:

1. Why is creating a story fun?
2. How is it different if one person creates the whole story?
3. How can we improve the way we work together?
4. How does your part of the story affect everyone else?
5. How does it affect us when one person doesn't listen?
6. How does it affect us when one person doesn't participate?

After students had a chance to reflect, they went around the circle and those that wanted to share their reflections with the group did so. Three girls who picked Question 5 said the following:

> Okay um, mine is number five, how does it affect us when a person doesn't listen? It affects us because if a person doesn't listen we have to wait and wait and wait and so, and then when the person doesn't listen, um, we have to wait and wait and wait and wait and wait and then we get really mad if a person doesn't listen. And then they'll be going huh? uh? What did you say? Huh? Huh? And then they'll be like puzzled why they why, why they weren't, what they were supposed to be doing. So it really affects us because when a person doesn't listen and we have to say it all over again. (Sarah)

> I picked number five um, how does it affect us when one person doesn't listen to us. Um, if the teacher is teaching it takes up the teacher's teaching time and it takes our learning time. It takes up our learning time. (Jenny)

> I picked five, how does it affect us when one person doesn't listen. I think, I think the teachers get really mad because then they have to say what they just said again and we have to wait and start over again. (Katie)

Sarah and Katie have picked up on Darlene's rationale from the episode with Justin in the introduction: "don't do that anymore 'cause it stops my teaching and makes me angry." They also express that consequences of not listening are both for the individual, who won't know what he or she is supposed to be doing, and for the group, which has to wait while directions are given again. Jenny's language echoes Darlene's "you stopped our teaching time" from the same episode with Justin, and "this is learning time" from the episode with Travis. Lisa, in an interview (2/1/99), said of Darlene, "just sometimes when people start talking a lot, she kind of gets angry." She explained that a good student "is somebody who follows directions . . . and who doesn't talk that much. I mean, you can talk, but doesn't do like too much talking." Dan, like Justin, echoed this in his interview (2/1/99) when asked what it takes to be successful in Mrs. Danielson's classroom. "Don't play around while she's teaching, don't interrupt while she's talking, um, do your work and don't talk to neighbors. And follow instructions, if she's giving them out for something." Some students have taken up Darlene's rationale for why paying attention is important, for example in Darcy's interview (2/1/99) she states:

> Well, Mrs. Danielson is like . . . she like says, "Who is responsible for your learning?" And like we, if we say her, she knows that we weren't like, we're not really knowing everything about what they need to know . . . and then we always say like, "We are!" . . . so, really we're responsible to learn and we could be like drifting off in space and stuff and pretending to listen, but really we're in control of learning. We just got to like listen.

Another comment demonstrates that the message Darlene is trying to convey about the importance of community, that "everything you do or say affects every member of this community" has been taken up by Melissa, who says:

> I picked number six, how does it affect us when one person doesn't participate. Well, I wonder like Mrs. Danielson said, um, what they have to say, but it also feels to me like a piece of our community is missing. Like we're a pie and somebody ate half of it.

Now we turn to Darlene's current school setting for some other examples of significant interactional moments. Although there are many similarities, there are also some differences that Darlene has become aware of, and that she articulated in interviews. These will help to show to some extent both change and continuity in Darlene's teaching of morally acceptable social behavior in two different school contexts. The similar community circle meetings also provided an interesting point of comparison between the two school contexts, given that the lesson was designed in the same way both times. In Darlene's new school, we also made a decision to probe more thoroughly into the cultivation of intellectual virtues, and the reading comprehension lesson that was chosen for analysis proved to be a rich source of data in which students and teacher negotiated meanings related to working with the coding of informational text.

RESULTS: WOODCREEK ELEMENTARY

The February 16, 2000 lesson analyzed in the next section was a whole-class reading comprehension exercise that entailed coding an expository text about zebras with categories such as "What does it look like?" and "How does it behave?" Darlene sat at the overhead projector during most of the lesson, and students were seated in four long rows of desks. Initially, students read through the text to identify places where the word zebra or an equivalent word such as "it" appeared in the text. They were instructed to circle with their finger, not their pencil, and to say aloud "beep" each time such a word was encountered. There was also a discussion about the title and its relationship to the subject of the text. After the first 10 minutes of the lesson, coding of the text was completed one sentence at a time as students volunteered to read aloud and to offer a code. In the following episodes, it is possible to identify ways in which Darlene makes use of these interactional moments with students to develop understandings of what she considers desirable moral and intellectual virtues.

Mark

In this episode (see Table 3.5) we see Darlene is calling for students to show readiness for learning in their body language. But there is also an interesting moment with a student who isn't following Darlene's directions. Mark is sitting at the end of the first row, just to Darlene's left. They are about to begin coding the text when Darlene notices that Mark has been circling words with his pencil.

Darlene gets the attention of students by mentioning specific names, as she did in the Justin episode at Jordan, and by inviting their cooperation and participation. When she requests that Alex raise his head from being slumped on his desk, she provides the rationale, "we're learning." Especially noteworthy is the way in which she lets Mark know he does-

Table 3.5. Mark

LINE	SPEAKER	TALK	GESTURES	ANALYST'S COMMENTARY
001	Darlene	is it coming back now?		
002		let's see if we can get Alex and Courtney and uh Mark	Darlene looks at the students as she says their name.	
003		to cooperate here		
004		head up please we're learning		Alex raises his head.
005		thank you		
006		ready Mark?		Darlene is assuming and stating a reason for Mark's failure to
007		you probably didn't hear me say we're not going to circle with our pencil	Darlene waves her hand.	follow her directions.
008		so you can stop now		
009		you're ready?		

n't need to be circling words with his pencil. She doesn't repeat the earlier rationale for these instructions, but assumes that Mark didn't hear
them. In an interview, Darlene elaborated on her decision to phrase it in
this way:

> When he was circling with the pencil and we had made an elaborate
> thing about we don't need to do that anymore and if you really
> absolutely have to, then use your pencil eraser so it doesn't . . . ,
> because you've got too much to look at there. And so he goes through
> the whole lesson doing that and of course I didn't catch him and I
> didn't stop him (and/or I don't remember which it was) but when I
> did catch him to just say "you didn't hear me" not that you're a bad
> child or you're doing it anyway or you're being obstinate or anything
> like that, "you didn't hear me," so now you know you don't need to
> do that anymore.

She goes on to explain why this sort of approach is needed more often
than it was at Jordan:

> Those kinds of things are really essential with this population, where
> with the past population it was nice, it kept them from feeling it was
> a put down, and therefore they could continue to learn. With this
> population it's essential. They will, they recognize put downs where
> they aren't even there. Sometimes they're just so alert and aware, the
> antennae of watching for anybody who might challenge them
> because they're so secure in their own thinking and they think that
> (well, there must be an insecurity or they wouldn't be doing that, but,
> just by virtue of their age), but they are so secure in understanding
> that they are important in this universe, that they don't allow that. So
> they go down deeper and they stay down and they're angry at you
> because you did it. So it's really important with this population to
> make sure that those are in place, those ways of accepting the respon-
> sibility myself, "Oh, I didn't make it clear" not "If you had paid atten-
> tion!" which is what you want to say, you know? (3/3/00)

The "security in their own thinking" that Darlene refers to is evident
in a second episode involving Mark that followed a discussion of the distinction between the code for "Where does it live?" and "Where is it
found?" Here the academic task structure is such that students negotiate,
through discussion, the code for each sentence. Darlene is developing an
intellectual disposition toward reading comprehension that makes
explicit what one thinks as one reads. In this episode (see Table 3.6),
Darlene showcases Mark's thinking as important not only for his classmates, but for teachers as well.

Table 3.6. Mark

LINE	SPEAKER	TALK	GESTURES	ANALYST'S COMMENTARY
050	Mark	most animals are not found where they live	Darlene has just called on Mark. His hand had been raised for several minutes.	Mark is offering a new distinction on found vs. live.
051		like hyenas are found in plains but they live in burrows		
052	Darlene	okay okay	She turns to look at him and nods.	
053	Mark	like lions are found in grassy areas but they don't live in they live in plains		Mark offers a new example.
054				
055	Darlene	oh Mark	Darlene extends her hand out to Mark.	Darlene acknowledges Mark's good contribution and makes sure others have heard and are learning from him
056		now say that again 'cause I'll bet Kay's going to be thinking yeah yeah		
057		say that again this is a good explanation	She turns to Trevor.	
058		you got this Trevor?		
059		listen to Mark		
060	Mark	most animals are not found where they live	Darlene turns back to Mark, then out to class as she is nodding.	Mark repeats his examples, and adds additional information about lions.
061		because hyenas are found in plains but they live in burrows		
062		and lions are found in grassy areas		

Table 3.6. Mark *(Continued)*

LINE	SPEAKER	TALK	GESTURES	ANALYST'S COMMENTARY
063		but they live in plains the only reason lions are found in grassy areas is because of they are predators and they have to hunt	Darlene turns to Mark again.	
064	Darlene	that is so cool I'm going to have you write that down have you done your thinking	Darlene wants Mark to record his thoughts so	
065		log entry today?	Mark shakes his head no1.	she will remember it too.
066		would you write that in your thinking log please for me because=	Darlene nods her head.	
067	Mark	=I've got,		Mark cuts Darlene off again.
068		I've got fifty major things to write down		
069	Darlene	well write that statement down	Darlene points at Mark for emphasis.	Darlene shows Mark his ideas are important to
070		because that I am going to photocopy that and take that to teacher training		teachers as well as students.
071		because teachers have the same	She gestures with a pointing finger out at	
072		problem you're having trying to figure out what's the difference	the class and then turns back to the overhead.	Darlene is signaling to Mark that she is ready to move on.
073	Mark	that was an excellent explanation so now= all I did was watch the Discovery Channel!		Mark cuts Darlene off again.
074	Darlene	OKAY WELL I'LL GIVE THEM THAT SUGGESTION TOO	DARLENE TURNS BACK TO HIM AGAIN.	SHE OFFERS HIM THE CHANCE TO PROVIDE

102

Table 3.6. Mark *(Continued)*

LINE	SPEAKER	TALK	GESTURES	ANALYST'S COMMENTARY
075		so then could we agree by that definition that this is where they live?		closure to their exchange.
076	Mark	yeah that's pretty much where they live	Mark nods.	
077	Darlene	they don't get to burrow		Darlene is offering a non-example.
078	Mark	they're like the one third of the animal population that lives where it's found because zebras are not going to be	Mark gestures with his hand, looking at Darlene. He uses both hands on "hey lions!"	Mark wants to continue to hold the floor and provides additional information about zebras and lions.
079		seen walking around going "hey lions come and attack me" because lions are much faster than zebras so they're gonna be=		
080				
081	Darlene	=and they don't get to burrow and they don't get to nest so they just sort of wander	Darlene is still looking at Mark.	Darlene offers another non-example.
082	Mark	yeah because zebras don't live in grassy areas they eat there but they don't live there		
083		so if they don't live there lions are going to have a hard time attacking	Darlene turns back to the overhead.	Now Darlene is signaling again that she is ready to move on.
084		them because the lions can't hide anywhere		
085	Darlene	Okay	She looks at the class.	

Table 3.6. Mark (CONTINUED)

LINE	SPEAKER	TALK	GESTURES	ANALYST'S COMMENTARY
086	Mark	unless they live right next to the tree		Mark has to finish his last thought.
087	Darlene	alright I think we got that cleared up and you can probably speed through some of the rest of this?		Darlene provides the closure while honoring Mark's contribution to
088		yes?		clarifying the live vs. found distinction and
089		we're ready to go?		then asks if they can
090		do you have another comment?		She waits when she sees Alex's hand up.

Mark has the confidence to share his examples of the distinction between *found* and *live* as well as his additional knowledge of zebras and lions with the class. So great is his enthusiasm that he is unwilling to give up the floor when Darlene attempts to signal through body and verbal language that it is time to move on. Darlene noted in an interview that this was a difference she had begun to notice between the different school populations:

> I mean they [Jordan students] would feel secure to share that information, and the Discovery Channel was one of the things that a few kids in particular really enjoyed and they would share information like that, but once it was done, or their teacher indicated it was done, it was done. Yeah. That's that, I call it a security, it's a, there's a self-esteem thing. Kids, parents have done a wonderful job in this community [Woodcreek] of making kids feel that they are very important. Their point of view is important and they should speak up and share it. It's a different population. (3/3/00)

Darlene contributes to Mark's confidence in his ideas not only by allowing him to share all that he has to say, but also by publicly commenting that his insights will help teachers as well as students. She shows she respects Mark's contributions, and by having him record them in his thinking log, provides an opportunity for him to take responsibility for remembering them. In fact, Mark says he has "50 major things to write down" in his thinking log, signaling that he is aware of other important thoughts that are worth recording and preserving. Mark was also able to articulate how important this recognition and respect is to him in his interview with Darlene. "You're pretty much always demonstrating respect for students," he told her, "including me. It's like one of your special abilities" (3/24/00). Showcasing students publicly is one way that Darlene builds mutual respect in her classroom community, at the same time developing an intellectual disposition toward sharing knowledge for the betterment of others' learning.

Alex

In the following two episodes (see Tables 3.7 and 3.8), we see how differences of opinion are negotiated through discussion as Darlene works to clarify both her thinking and that of her students. They have just finished establishing that the text is about zebras, and are discussing the title, "A Horse in Striped Pajamas."

Table 3.7. Alex

LINE	SPEAKER	TALK	GESTURES	ANALYST'S COMMENTARY
010	Darlene	it says zebras or all about zebras	Darlene is at the overhead screen	
011	Alex	it's a twist		
012	Darlene	or something about zebras		Darlene realizes Alex has a point to share
013		oh		that's different from
014		you think it's a direct statement with a twist?	Darlene pantomimes twisting a key with her hand	where she was going
015		what makes you=		
016	Alex	='cause you think there'd be a zebra under the [. . .]		
017	Mark	how would you know it's in the horse family?		Mark calls out, but doesn't interrupt Alex
018	Darlene	ah it's assuming that we know that		
019		yeah I can see what you're thinking		
020		if	Darlene nods	
021		if your audience=	She leans in	
022	Mark	=if it's a twist I would think it's a double twist	Mark looks at Darlene	Mark cuts Darlene off.
023	Darlene	I'm sorry let me finish hearing this	Puts her hand out to Mark but looks at Alex. Mark turns to look at Alex.	She lets Mark know that Alex still has the floor. He shows he understands by turning to Alex.

106

Table 3.7. Alex *(Continued)*

LINE	SPEAKER	TALK	GESTURES	ANALYST'S COMMENTARY
024	Alex	if you were like shining a light on them	Alex points with his hand to indicate the zebra and horse	
025		like a zebra and a horse		
026		and you look at their shadow you'd think they were the same		
027	Darlene	so you're assuming that your readers all know that the zebra is in the same family as the horse	Darlene points to the text on the screen.	Darlene is trying to clarify Alex's underlying assumption.
028	Alex	no I didn't mean all of [...]		
029	Darlene	ah so then it probably wouldn't be a twist	Darlene uses the twisting key gesture again. Alex shrugs then looks at Darlene. She uses her fingers in quotes for "special feature."	Alex seems unwilling to give up on his idea that it's a twist, so Darlene tries to find a way to compromise between his opinion and hers.
030		a direct statement with a twist		
031		yeah so for some people it would be for others it would be a special		
032		feature		
033		so we're probably safe to say special feature for everyone		
034		and that some readers who know the family		
		would be able to recognize it as a twist	Alex looks at his paper.	
035		okay?		
036		good		
037				

107

Table 3.8. Alex

LINE	SPEAKER	TALK	GESTURES	ANALYST'S COMMENTARY
038	Darlene	Alex?	Alex raises his hand	
039	Alex	I think like when they say stripes it could also be the special category because most animals don't have that	Alex points to the text for emphasis.	Darlene had established it was the "looks like" category.
040	Darlene	hmm most don't	Darlene gestures with her hands for emphasis.	Darlene is reminding him of her previous rationale for using the special category only when no other category fits.
041		but if we can fit it in another category		
042		that other category=		
043	Alex	[...] also	He points again	Most of Alex's comment is incomprehensible
044	Darlene	good		Darlene continues her explanation and asks if Alex understands the point she is making.
045		I just want to make sure you understand that we won't pick the special category if it could possibly fit somewhere else is that really clear?		
046	Alex	Yeah	He nods.	
047		okay good	Moves closer to Alex and moves her hand back and forth.	
048	Darlene	we were saying the same thing I think		
049		I just wanted to clarify		

Darlene said in an interview that this sort of negotiation occurs a lot at Woodcreek. Ultimately what matters to her is that students come to understand the point of view that differs from their own, and she sees herself as negotiating for clarity, not necessarily for conversion to another's point of view. "I really do believe that as long as they understand, I don't really care which one they take." At Jordan, she said these types of exchanges were different. "I'd say this is what I'm taking and this is why I'm taking it. But I want you to feel powerful enough to say that this is what I'm taking and this is why I'm taking it. As long as you can tell me that and it's not a wrong answer, then I can accept multiple right answers. I had to teach them how to do that. These kids [Woodcreek] come with that. That power, it's my way, and this is why. . . . Everybody's got a comment about everything. Like Alex and his twist" (3/3/00). Alex and Darlene negotiate another difference of opinion about the coding categories shortly after the previous exchange.

Darlene provides Alex with a rationale for their exchange about the use of the special category by saying she wanted to "clarify." Once again she is modeling how discussion helps everyone to see different points of view as well as learn the academic content. Her design and execution of this particular academic task structure enabled her to weave moral and intellectual instruction together. These interactions show that she values students' contributions and respects their points of view, and that she expects other students to value them as well.

Eve

Negotiations of meaning such as these occur in similar ways with girls. In the next episode (see Table 3.9), Eve, like Alex, wants to use the special category to code a sentence that relates to what the zebra looks like. When Darlene realizes that Eve is not convinced after her initial attempt at negotiation, she tries additional examples and strategies. Here we see Darlene's trial-and-error process in action.

Darlene is attempting to develop flexibility as an intellectual disposition in this episode by explaining to Eve that inflexible thinkers make this kind of process more difficult for themselves. Darlene's explanation of dotted rather than solid lines is quite sophisticated, and Eve shows she recognizes herself as the kind of thinker that has to see things as black or white by nodding her head. Although she shows she is not entirely convinced in this episode, in a later one from the same lesson she and Darlene come to a mutual understanding that ends in a shared smile.

Table 3.9. Eve

LINE	SPEAKER	TALK	GESTURES	ANALYST'S COMMENTARY
103	Darlene	look like LL		
104		do you agree with that Devin?		
105		that's kind of a cool look I think too isn't it=		
106	Eve	=I don't really agree with that		Eve cuts Darlene off.
107	Darlene	you don't		
108		what are you thinking?		
109	Eve	it's just saying something on how it looks it's not saying what it looks like		Eve is attempting to argue for a distinction between how and what.
110	Darlene	close enough	Darlene nods her head as she looks at Eve.	Darlene starts to close the exchange with her statement,
111		we'll call that the same category		but then poses a question to Eve.
112		do you see a category that fits it better?		
113	Eve	what's special about it		
114	Darlene	Hmm		
115		[several kids talk at once]		Eve's comment sets off many reactions.
116	Jeff	if you put it in but it doesn't make too much sense but you can still fit it in		
117	Darlene	good I like that thinking		
118		what Cameron?		
119	Cameron	if it could be LL it should be		

110

Table 3.9. Eve *(CONTINUED)*

Line	Speaker	Talk	Gestures	Analyst's Commentary
120	Darlene	if it could be LL it should be LL		Darlene repeats his statement for emphasis, since he is using the argument she used in her earlier explanations.
121	Alex	but what if it could be let's say L? Or B?		Alex's question is meant to clarify the use of multiple categories.
122				
123	Darlene	what do you think?	Darlene looks at Alex.	
124	Alex	what about when we should use special if it doesn't fit anywhere else?		Now he is trying to clarify the use of the special category.
125	Darlene	then we'll duke it out when that happens okay?	Darlene nods at Alex. He tilts his head, then shakes it no.	
126		duke it out you know what that means?	Alex looks down.	
127		We'll have a controversy and we'll make a decision	Darlene turns back to Eve.	
128		but that's not happening here one of		
129		the things you have to be real careful about Eve and I'm glad you brought this up because this is typical for	Darlene nods. She points her finger to her palm.	Darlene is going to try a different approach to help Eve see why the special category
130		some thinkers		shouldn't be used in this
131		some people are so good at being specific that they make the whole process difficult for themselves		case.

111

Table 3.9. Eve *(continued)*

LINE	SPEAKER	TALK	GESTURES	ANALYST'S COMMENTARY
132		if you are that kind of thinker you have to let go a little bit	Eve nods.	Eve is acknowledging to Darlene that she is that kind of thinker.
133		think of these categories as having no lines on the boxes just kind of like dotted lines	Darlene opens her arms, then holds up the paper to point.	
134		so some of the ideas can overflow into other categories		
135		that might help you a little bit		Darlene continues with her explanation and reminds students of the rationale for coding the sentences in the first place, which is to help them with comprehension and with their own writing of animal reports. Eve doesn't seem entirely convinced.
136		the whole reason for collecting them in a certain category is to help you see	Darlene opens her hands, then punches her fist in her palm on "facts"	
137		which facts should belong in this paragraph and which facts should belong in this paragraph	She shapes her hands in a ball to represent the paragraphs.	
138		so that you're not putting lots of different kinds of things all in one paragraph		
139		does that make some sense? when we get to the writing stage I think it will make more sense hopefully	Eve makes a so-so gesture with her hand out.	
140				
141		it always has in the past if that gives you any comfort okay?	Darlene looks at the overhead.	Darlene is sharing her knowledge from previous teaching experiences to persuade Eve that the process of coding will help with writing later on.

Cameron

Darlene negotiates the use of the proper codes in the following episode (Table 3.10) as well, but this time with another male student, Cameron, who, she says, "cannot understand flexibility. He cannot understand gray. It's black or it's white and it does not fit if it doesn't fit into a black or a white category" (3/3/00). In this example, students had been discussing using two codes for one sentence.

Table 3.10. Cameron

Line	Speaker	Talk	Gestures	Analyst's Commentary
142	Darlene	does that fit under what they eat or how they behave?		Darlene is trying to clarify the debate over whether the sentences should be coded for both behavior and what it eats.
143		that's the dilemma		
144	Cameron	It's how they eat		
145	Darlene	you think that's how they eat but this category	Darlene nods, then points to the paper.	
146		says what does it eat		
147		that's the dilemma we're having		
148		you see what we're saying?	She nods.	Darlene is trying to clarify the issue.
149	Cameron	it eats grass		He is trying to clarify the issue of what it eats.
150	Darlene	yes it does		Darlene refers back to the text to further illustrate her point that it also refers to the zebra's behavior.
151		and this says its lips snatch the grass while the strong teeth bite it off and we're thinking=		
152	Cameron	=it eats [. . .]		
153	Darlene	although it's about their eating it doesn't tell us what they eat it tells us	Darlene points to the paper.	
154		how it eats		

Table 3.10 (continued)

Line	Speaker	Talk	Gestures	Analyst's Commentary
155		that's why we're having to put the behavior thing in with the eating thing	She moves her hand to show they go together.	Darlene is trying to clarify the use of two codes.
156		does that make sense?		
157	Cameron	yeah	Cameron shrugs.	His body language suggests he is not convinced.
158	Darlene	just because they were so specific about this	Darlene points to the paper again.	Darlene provides additional reasons for using both codes in her effort to persuade him of her reasons for using both codes.
159		they didn't say eating	She gestures with both hands together.	
160		then we could just put E couldn't we		
161		but they said what does it eat so that's the only reason we're putting in both categories		
162		does that make sense?		
163	Cameron	Well	Cameron shrugs.	He still seems unconvinced.
164	Darlene	you don't have to agree just as long as you understand	Cameron looks down, then up again.	Darlene's goal is clarification and understanding.
165		okay?		
166	Cameron	alright		

When Darlene senses from Cameron's comments and gestures that he is not convinced that the codes for what it eats and for behavior should be used together for one sentence, she tries giving multiple examples to clarify for Cameron the collective thinking of the class. Her closing comment (line 164) states explicitly what was implied in previous negotiations, that what matters is clarification of ideas and points of view, not agreement on a single right answer. In an interview with Cameron, Darlene asked him about the role of explanations in these kinds of negotiations.

Darlene: Do you think that children want to know why?
Cameron: Yeah, because if they don't really know why then later on, they might get like, if they have fractions then they'll get stuck on it. (3/17/00)

Before turning to the community circle meeting at Woodcreek that was very similar to the one at Jordan, it is useful to hear in Darlene's own words what she was attempting to get across to her students in the types of interactions examined at Woodcreek. "One thing I want for children," she said in an e-mail (4/5/00), "is that they assert that authority while, at the same time, remaining open to opportunities to learn and grow and try on new things."

Finally, Darlene noted that the biggest difference between the students at Jordan and those at Woodcreek was that teaching the students in her new school felt like moving two grades up, even though she was still teaching a mixed group of third and fourth graders. Yet, the students at Jordan couldn't sustain attention for very long compared to the students at Woodcreek.

> That was the biggest difference right there. The level of maturity and understanding, and cognition, and world experience. Two levels above the other kids, but their attention and their, um, ability to sustain themselves in any learning situation was one third. (3/3/00)

Darlene's theory about this difference was that the students at Woodcreek had very structured lives in after school extracurricular activities, and therefore needed recess and unstructured time more than the students at Jordan, who thrived in a structured environment. Other evidence about differences between the student populations at both schools emerged when we analyzed the comments made by students during the community circle meeting.

Community Circle

Because some of the problems with her class at Woodcreek were similar to those that had been going on at Jordan around the same time of year, Darlene decided to try the same activity (1/28/00) she had done the year before, and we decided to tape it so we could compare the discussions. The students would create a chain story in community circle and Darlene would ask them to reflect on some questions that were meant to help them make a connection between the storytelling experience and the way their actions in the classroom affect everyone else in the classroom. Unlike the meeting at Jordan, Darlene did not explain the purpose of the activity ahead of time, that "everything you say or do affects every member of this community," but Evan predicted the purpose. "I think this is about, is like the questions about like how one thing um affects other things? Like if one person starts this story it affects um the way the, if someone, the next person has to uh, has to like make the story connecting? So then if what one person says affects what another person is going to say." Darlene praised him for this prediction before beginning the story. When students went around the circle, many chose to pass instead of to participate, making the story shorter. Some noted in their reflections that less participation made it less fun. Some explained why creating a story together was more fun than doing it alone:

> When more than one person creates the story it's funner because not only do you get to participate, but when at the end, when you're listening to it you get everyone's mind in it and when you do it by yourself you only get one imagination. (Carrie)

> I thought that when one person does the whole story sometimes it can be hard for that person, so sometimes it takes more than one mind to make a story but sometimes it's harder to do that 'cause people don't participate on the story, and they get lost in jokes and things when they're really supposed to be doing the story. But when you use more than one person another person doesn't feel left out and it sort of makes it more fun of a story. (Mindy)

> If one person is thinking of an idea for a story and they can't think of another? If you have another person in it that's two minds combined. So that means that there's more ideas that could come out of your brain and stuff? And it's kind of like, uh, if you're writing a story by yourself, and you're stuck on one thing and you ask your friend for help and they give you a little idea, it's a good thing. (Eve)

A few students chose to answer the question, "How does it affect us when one person doesn't listen?" They were candid about how this can generate bad feelings:

> It affects the rest of the class when a person doesn't listen. The class would feel bad and that person will not know what to do and it would take a really long time for him to think about it. (Andrew)

> If one person doesn't listen and then the person talking feels bad they weren't listened to, then they feel upset and are thinking about how they feel and forget to listen, and then you have two people not listening and it could keep going. (Evan)

Darlene noted the references to bad feelings when she compared the tapes of the two community circle meetings. "They were saying this is a good place to let you all know how I feel when you don't pay attention to me, because it didn't happen here [in this community circle] so they're harking back to something else" (3/3/00). Although the student comments at Woodcreek were not as explicitly related to the language Darlene uses about why it is important to listen and participate in the classroom community, it is clear that the students understand the positive and negative consequences of listening and participating versus not doing so. This understanding is sometimes fragile, and in an interview Darlene elaborated on why community circle plays an important role in helping students with morally acceptable social behavior:

> I know when I haven't touched it recently because things start to fall apart. Kids start to act differently around kids. We get more call outs. We get more negative comments. We get more kids coming in from recess and saying, "He did this, she did that." And I just have to back off, put everything academic on the shelf, get up here in community circle and we have to go back. Not just deal with the issues, but go back to community development. (11/29/99)

Darlene used the storytelling experience as a metaphor for other kinds of classroom interactions, but what is especially significant about her pedagogical choices in this example is her recognition of the need to set aside time for discussing with students the process of improving the classroom climate so that it is inclusive, fun, and enhances positive relationships.

DISCUSSION AND IMPLICATIONS

This analysis shows that Darlene is consciously and purposefully working together with her students to construct understandings about what it means to be a good student and to behave in morally acceptable ways in the classroom community. The micro-analysis of classroom interactions shows how Darlene and her students accomplish this co-constructed understanding. Moreover, students' actions and discourse indicate that they are taking up and internalizing these lessons. In their study of classroom management, Richardson and Fallona (2001) found that one aspect of effective classroom managers "derives from the seamlessness among beliefs, manner and method" (p. 724). Another aspect of effectiveness that is shown in this study is the degree to which students are taking up what it is the teacher is seeking to impart to them. As Boostrom (1991) said, "When we think about a successful classroom, we imagine that the students' inclinations and the teacher's plan are so united that the statement of classroom rules seems superfluous" (p. 203). He later added:

The way we think about rules is very important. It is not just a philosophical point, but a practical one, because when teachers forget the
significance of their own rules, a chasm begins to open between what
they are doing and why they are doing it. The results can be both a
mechanical classroom and an uncertain teacher. . . . Avoiding the
mechanical in the classroom is not a matter of letting up on rules but
of seeing them for what they are—a moral ordering of the world for
which the teacher is accountable just as the students are to be obedi-
ent. (pp. 212-213)

Therefore, classroom management should be reconsidered as not just a
mechanical series of strategies for running a smooth and orderly classroom, but also as a significant aspect of developing morally acceptable
social behavior in students that will construct a positive classroom
climate.

This analysis also shows that the ways in which Darlene is helping
her students to have common understandings of what it means to be a
good student in her classroom is a construction of language. She uses
even the smallest of classroom disruptions as learning opportunities for
understanding morally acceptable behavior. Through careful choice of
words and by using the appropriate interactional style, Darlene is able to
make students feel and want to be responsible for their learning, as we
have seen in some of their interviews and comments during community
circle. As Darlene states in an interview:

The only way you can continue to learn in the world outside is to recognize that you have to have the courage, you have to demonstrate
the curiosity, you have to do the problem-solving, you have to be
responsible for your own learning, and in order to be responsible for
your own learning you have to plug into it, dig right in and ask the
questions, and you have to wonder what you wonder right out loud,
and low and behold you help someone else when you do that. Once
you learn how to do that in one setting, you can do it in another setting. This is such a huge notion, that we're training children to be
learners. And moral development and community building is a big
piece of that. I tell them that all the time. You're gonna hark back to
what you learned in third and fourth grade. All of the moral stuff is
wrapped up in learning and taking that learning into life. And you
can't separate them. And every time you do—and this is what I keep
learning, I keep getting slapped in the face—every time I let the
moral issues, the moral development of the children slip to the side
or stand in the sidelines, it starts to fall apart academically. It starts to
fall apart academically because the kids stop caring as much about
each other. (11/29/99)

The implications of this are reflected in the following quote from Douglas Barnes (1995) regarding the influence of Mikhail Bakhtin's (1986) concepts of dialogue:

> Bakhtin's line of thought carries with it two important corollaries for education. First, talk is not just an individual creation, but arises from previous participation in many dialogues. Second, much of our most important learning depends upon building networks of connections with other "voices" that have made up our lives. If this is how the culture is maintained and how we become participants in it, then every member of society, including school students, is inevitably involved in the maintenance and recreation of the complex patterns of meaning, intentions, and action that make up our lives. One implication of this is that students should be given as much responsibility as they can bear for the management of their learning. (p. 6)

Darlene articulated her feelings about this notion of students' responsibility for their learning in another, earlier interview:

> The immediate reaction from me generally is how can I get them to take care of this thing and still learn. But the higher good is exactly what we said. Ultimately you want them to feel responsible and want to be responsible and want to be compliant in order to help everybody learn that. And you're not going to get there in one day. . . . You just have to make sure that you get to the place where they give you permission to have authority over them, and that comes only when they respect you and they know you respect them. (12/2/99)

We have seen how concepts such as mutual respect and personal responsibility are not just empty words in Darlene's classroom. Fenstermacher's (2001) ways in which manner is made visible are plainly evident in Darlene's teaching. Through her calling out for particular conduct, while at the same time providing students with a rationale for her requests, Darlene is able to develop certain behaviors and dispositions toward learning that are both explicit and effective. We have also seen how showcasing students and publicly thanking them for contributing to the learning of others is an important aspect of developing a classroom climate of mutual respect. She also uses didactic instruction with specific language from the life skills to teach students. She designs academic task structures so as to facilitate discussion and debate, negotiating differences of opinion and clarifying students' confusion, so that they learn from each other as well as from her. She uses other classroom participation structures such as community circle to develop common understandings of what a healthy classroom community should look and sound like.

Finally, two other claims that can be made about Darlene echo findings from Richardson and Fallona's study (2001). Using Fallona's (1998) interpretation of Aristotelian moral virtues, they described those that were most strongly expressed by Darlene in her teaching. These included "friendliness—showing care and respect for children" and "justice—fairness in the application of both rules and norms to individual children" (pp. 10-11). This analysis also shows that Darlene is a caring teacher. In Darcy's interview she was asked, "What is it that she [Darlene] does to let you know that she cares?" and the student's reply was, "She like . . . sometimes when she, like, we help and stuff or do something while she's gone, she says like, 'Oh, I love you guys!' and she's always like really nice to us." The interviewer went on to ask, "So you can tell she cares from that?" and Darcy added, "And she always like . . . at the end of the day she usually makes us give a, one of the three Hs—a high five, a handshake, or a hug. And then she got this sign that says, Free hugs! One size fits all!" (2/1/99). Darlene described herself as "relating to kids in a caring way. I have the time for you, but if I don't I'll say, 'I really want to hear this. Can I check it out at recess? Can I ask you after spelling?' That kind of thing. . . . If they're talking to me and I'm talking to somebody else, I put a hand on theirs and just keep my attention here so that they know. And if they keep, 'Mrs. Danielson, Mrs. Danielson" then I'll say, 'In a moment please, I'm talking,' and I make it real clear that that was inappropriate without stopping too long to do that. So what is that? I think that still shows caring" (4/27/98).

Furthermore, Darlene is clear about her differential treatment of individual students based on their personality, learning style, and needs. She takes her responsibility to understand these aspects of each student very seriously, and works hard at developing relationships with all students that are based on mutual respect and understanding. This entails an in-depth knowledge of each student that is developed over time from close observation, and from reflection on success and failure as hypotheses about students are tested and tried out. Darlene is conscious of using this knowledge of each student during in-the-moment decisions about which interactional stance to take or what choice of words to use when promoting morally acceptable social behavior.

This study has important implications for teacher education. If teachers are made aware of their beliefs about teaching and their personal style as aspects of their manner, they can become more conscious of the ways in which they are helping to establish a positive classroom environment. Darlene expressed the hope that research in the moral dimensions of teaching might mean "that teachers-in-training are going to be understanding, fully understanding their responsibility in coming into this field . . . [they] will know that that is an important piece" (11/29/99). One way in which they can begin a process of reflection is to carefully analyze their discourse and their interactional style with individual students. It is also probable that an important part of this kind of learning is experimenting through trial and error and experiencing success and failure over time. Darlene seems to find that a significant outcome of such experimentation on her part is a much more in-depth knowledge of each student. Darlene described how her involvement with this research has had an effect on her:

> You made me really look at what I do and how I do it. Not as if you wanted me to change it, but as if you wanted me to understand it. And um, therefore, I do understand it more. I look at why I do what I do. And I've made some changes . . . so now I look more at, look at the children, at their upbringing, and what do they need . . . So I kind of fine tune, change, alter things um, from the way I did because of this experience of having to look at it, but also I now look more carefully at how it's affecting the children, and who it's affecting, and in what way, and who's coming along easily and who isn't coming along easily, and why, and then I have to change it again to meet that child's needs, and I know that it isn't the same for every child . . . It's got to be kind of a spiral approach to moral development. . . . You have to continue to teach it. (11/29/99)

Such awareness does bring change and growth for the teacher, and consequently, for the students as well. There are also implications for classroom management, which continues to be a puzzle for many beginning teachers. Helping them understand the importance of examining their own beliefs and actions with regard to the moral dimensions of teaching should be a prominent feature of their professional development.

This chapter raises several questions for future research. What, for example, are the influences of constructing the classroom climate at the school level? In this chapter, I have only explored some initial impressions of Darlene's experiences in two schools. What are some factors that are influential beyond those directly related to classroom interactions? Do the characteristics of the parent community have an influence, and to what degree? Is there evidence of student take-up outside of the classroom, for example in the lunchroom, playground, and at home? Are there gender and racial differences in how students take up these understandings? These questions merit further study if this kind of research is going to help teachers understand how classroom climate is constructed through language both in momentary occurrences and in sustained ways over time. What is at stake is nothing less than the welfare of the young people who are striving to become contributing citizens in a pluralistic and democratic society.

APPENDIX A:
DATA COLLECTION MAP

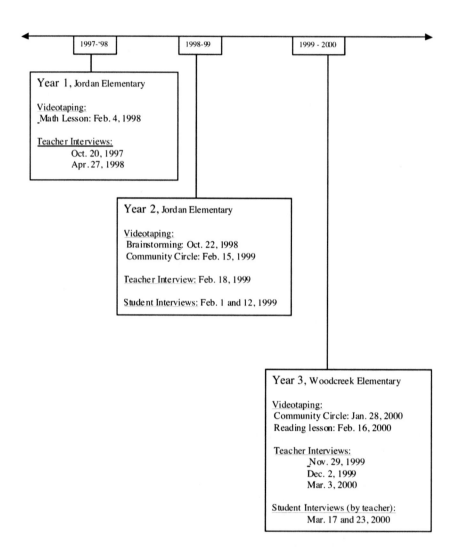

APPENDIX B:
INTERVIEW SCHEDULE FOR STUDENT INTERVIEWS

Student Interview Questions (K–3)

General questions that help to focus the attention of the interview on the teacher and the student's perception of teaching:

1. What is a teacher? What does a teacher do?
2. Do you live at home with your mother or grandmother? How is a teacher different from your mother? Or your grandmother?
3. How do you know your teacher cares about you?
4. How would you describe your teacher?

Communication about teaching—Student perceptions of what happens in the classroom:

5. Pretend that I am a new student. What kind of things would you tell me to help me do well in your class? Are there rules I should know about? How are you supposed to behave or "be good" in your classroom?
6. What makes your teacher happy or proud of you?

Student feelings about learning—shift focus from teaching to student learning:

7. Do you like to learn different things in school? What kinds of things are you being asked to learn?
8. Tell me something interesting or cool that you have learned about in school. Did you talk to people at home about it?
9. Would you say that you really like to learn? How do you show this? Does your teacher like to learn? How does your teacher show this?

Achievement—Student-assessed teacher perceptions of student learning:

10. How are you doing in school?
11. What is your teacher doing to help you become a better student?
12. If your teacher were making an example of someone who was a good student, what kinds of things would she say about him or her?

Differences and perceptions—Student feelings of individual treatment by teachers:

13. Does your teacher treat different kids differently? Explain.
14. How well does you teacher know you?

School-level questions—broader student/school relationship:

15. What is it like being a student at this school?
16. How would you describe your school?

ACKNOWLEDGMENTS

This research was supported by funding from the Spencer Foundation.

REFERENCES

Baker, C. (1997). Transcription and representation in literacy research. In J. Flood (Ed.), *Handbook of teaching literacy through the communicative and visual arts* (pp. 110-120). New York: Simon & Schuster Macmillan.

Bakhtin., M. (1986). *Speech genres and other late essays.* Austin: University of Texas Press.

Barnes, D. (1995). Talking and learning in classrooms: An introduction. *Primary Voices K-6, 3*(1), 2-7.

Boostrom, R. (1991). The nature and functions of classroom rules. *Curriculum Inquiry, 21*(2), 193-216.

Castanheira, M. L., Crawford, T., Dixon, C., & Green, J. (2001). Interactional ethnography: An approach to studying the social construction of literate practices. *Linguistics and Education, 11*(4), 353-400.

Chow-Hoy, T. K. (2001). An inquiry into school context and the teaching of the virtues. *Journal of Curriculum Studies, 33*(6), 655-682.

Egan-Robertson, A., & Willett, J. (1998). Students as ethnographers, thinking and doing ethnography: A bibliographic essay. In A. Egan-Robertson & D. Bloome (Eds.), *Students as researchers of culture and language in their own communities* (pp. 1-32). Cresskill, NJ: Hampton Press.

Erickson, F. (1986). Qualitative methods in research on teaching. In M. C. Wittrock (Ed.), *Handbook of research on teaching* (3rd ed., pp. 119-161). New York: Macmillan.

Erickson, F. (1992). Ethnographic microanalysis of interaction. In M. D. LeCompte, W. L. Millroy, & J. Preissle (Eds.), *The handbook of qualitative research in education* (pp. 201-225). San Diego, CA: Academic Press.

Fallona, C. (1998). *Manner in teaching: A study in moral virtue.* Unpublished dissertation. Tucson: University of Arizona.

Fenstermacher, G. D. (1990). Some moral considerations on teaching as a profession. In J. I. Goodlad, R. Soder, & K. A. Sirotnik (Eds.), *The moral dimensions of teaching* (pp. 130-151). San Francisco, CA: Jossey-Bass.

Fenstermacher, G. D. (1992). The concepts of method and manner in teaching. In F. K. Oser, A. Dick, & J.-L. Patry (Eds.), *Effective and responsible teaching: the new synthesis* (1st ed., pp. 95-108). San Francisco, CA: Jossey-Bass.

Fenstermacher, G. D. (2001). On the concept of manner and its visibility in teaching practice. *Journal of Curriculum Studies, 33*(6), 639-653.

Fenstermacher, G. D., & Richardson, V. (1997). *Manner in teaching: Proposal to the Spencer Foundation.* Ann Arbor: University of Michigan.

Gallego, M. A., Cole, M., & The Laboratory of Comparative Human Cognition. (2001). Classroom cultures and cultures in the classroom. In V. Richardson (Ed.), *Handbook of research on teaching* (4th ed., pp. 951-997). Washington, DC: American Educational Research Association.

Gee, J., & Green, J. (1998). Discourse analysis, learning, and social practice: A methodological study. *Review of Research in Education, 23,* 119-169.

Green, J., & Harker, J. (1988). *Multiple perspective analyses of classroom discourse.* Norwood, NJ: Ablex.

Green, J., & Wallat, C. (1981). *Ethnography and language in educational settings.* Norwood, NJ: Ablex.

Hansen, D. T. (1998). The moral is in the practice. *Teaching and Teacher Education, 14*(6), 643-655.

Hansen, D. T. (2001). Teaching as a moral activity. In V. Richardson (Ed.), *Handbook of research on teaching* (4th ed., pp. 826-857). Washington DC: American Educational Research Association.

Heath, S. B. (1982). Ethnography in education: Defining the essentials. In P. Gilmore & A. Glatthorn (Eds.), *Children in and out of school* (pp. 33-58). Washington, DC: Center for Applied Linguistics.

Kovalik, S. (1997). *Integrated thematic instruction: The model* (3rd ed.). Kent, WA: Susan Kovalik & Associates.

Kyratzis, A., & Green, J. (1997). Jointly constructed narratives in classrooms: Co-construction of friendship and community through language. *Teaching and Teacher Education, 13*(1), 17-37.

Mitchell, C. J. (1984). Typicality and the case study. In R. F. Ellens (Ed.), *Ethnographic research: A guide to general conduct* (pp. 238-241). New York: Academic Press.

Peacock, J. L. (1986). *The anthropological lens: Harsh light, soft focus.* New York: Cambridge University Press.

Putney, L. G., Green, J. L., Dixon, C. N., & Kelly, G. J. (1999). Evolution of qualitative research methodology: Looking beyond defense to possibilities. *Reading Research Quarterly, 34*(3), 368-377.

Richardson, V., & Fallona, C. (2001). Classroom management as method and manner. *Journal of Curriculum Studies, 33*(6), 705-728.

Richardson, V., & Fenstermacher, G. D. (2001). Manner in teaching: The study in four parts. *Journal of Curriculum Studies, 33*(6), 631-637.

Sanger, M. G. (2001). Talking to teachers and looking at practice in understanding the moral dimensions of teaching. *Journal of Curriculum Studies, 33*(6), 683-704.

Sanger, M. G., & Fenstermacher, G. D. (2000). *Aristotle's terrific, but is he enough? Expanding the philosophical ground for the moral conduct of teachers.* Paper presented at the American Educational Research Association Annual Meeting, New Orleans, LA.

Spindler, G. D., & Spindler, L. S. (1987). *Interpretive ethnography of education: At home and abroad*. Hillsdale, NJ: Erlbaum.

Tuyay, S., Jennings, L., & Dixon, C. (1995). Classroom discourse and opportunities to learn: An ethnographic study of knowledge construction in a bilingual third-grade classroom. *Discourse Processes, 19*(1), 75-110.

Zaharlick, A., & Green, J. (1991). Ethnographic research. In J. Flood, M. J. Jensen, D. Lapp & R. J. Squire (Eds.), *Handbook of research on teaching the English language Arts*. New York: Macmillan.

4

Mentoring Non-Latino Tutors in a Biliteracy Latino After-School Program

Mary M. Yonker

Across the United States, communities are recognizing the need for school support programs to assist children from diverse backgrounds (Osher & Mejia, 1999). Latino communities in particular are establishing grassroots literacy tutoring programs from Florida to California in order to support their children (Aspiazu, Bauer, & Spillett, 1998; Marsh, 1995; Osher & Mejia, 1999). According to Fox (1996), Latino children in general have not succeeded in the public school system because they suffer from social, educational, and economic disadvantages. They are the most undereducated segment of the U.S. population and the largest minority group in the schools (National Center for Education Statistics, 1998b). They have demonstrated lower levels of literacy development in comparison to students from mainstream backgrounds (National Center for Education Statistics, 1998a). In order to combat these problems, Latino communities have developed after-school programs to support their children (Marsh, 1995; Osher & Mejia, 1999).

This study investigates one of these grassroots after-school programs, organized by a nonprofit organization called VIVA (the name of the after-school program and the participants are pseudonyms). Its primary purpose was to support Latino families in a small midwestern city. One of its functions was to provide for and sustain the biliteracy development of Latino students in the organization. This chapter focuses on "circle time," the beginning activity of this after-school program. This activity created an environment in which novice non-Latino students were mentored to assume the teacher's role. The teacher mentored the tutors by telling them what to do and by modeling how to do it. This circle-time activity was introduced during the first month of the volunteers' entry into the VIVA community. Before this activity, there was very little interaction between the volunteer tutors, children, and teacher as a group.

Here, I use Gee's (1999) concept of *D/discourse* in order to define community. According to his definition, a community is based on a common discourse among people. Gee (1999) defines two types of discourses, big D and little d, which are interconnected. Little d, discourse, "is how language is used 'on a site' to enact activities and identities" (p. 7). Big D, Discourse, is a "way one acts, interacts, feels, believe, value, together with other people and with various sorts of characteristic objectives, symbols, tools and technologies" (p. 7). Therefore, a person is accepted into a community through common "ways of using language, of thinking and of acting, which can be used to identify oneself as a member of a socially meaningful group or social network" (Gee, 1991, p. 3).

I chose circle time as the focal point of my research investigation for three reasons. First, it provided an environment where the teacher could mentor the tutors by immersing them in a teaching situation. Second, once established, it was the most regularly occurring reading activity in the after-school program and it was the only available time during which children, volunteer tutors, and teachers could possibly gather as group. Finally, circle time created the possibility for the tutors' incorporation as members into this Latino community. Before this activity, the tutors tutored the children one on one, and rarely interacted with the rest of the members of the organization. After 3 weeks, circle-time members began to co-construct and negotiate biliteracy practices and formed a community between all the members.

By this point, my observations had led me to my main questions: How did the tutors become teaching members of circle time? Specifically, what were the bilingual reading practices through which the teacher, novice tutors, and students co-constructed? What did the teacher and tutors teach as reading practices, and how did the students enact those practices? Finally, how did these reading practices promote community-building between the teacher, novice tutors, and students?

I begin by describing the immersion process of mentoring the tutors in a biliteracy environment. Through this mentoring, I illustrate how the tutors, the teacher, and the children created an environment that promoted community within the VIVA organization. Finally, I call attention to ways in which the members supported Beatriz (a tutor) and Pedro (a child) when they directed circle time by taking up the teacher's role.

LITERATURE REVIEW

There is a considerable amount of research describing the training of college-age tutors in early reading intervention programs in schools (Meyer
& Keefe, 1998; Reisner, Petry, & Armitage, 1990; Wasik, 1998). According
to Wasik, a successful tutoring program provides support to the tutors by
promoting the following seven conditions:

1. The tutors need to have ongoing training and feedback by a reading specialist.
2. Tutoring sessions should be structured and should contain basic
   elements like re-reading a familiar book, word analysis, and writing.
3. Tutors need to tutor the same child over a period of time.
4. Tutors should have access to quality materials to facilitate the
   tutoring.
5. Assessment of the tutee should be ongoing.
6. Schools must ensure that tutors will attend regularly.
7. The tutoring should be coordinated with classroom instruction.

In addition, Meyer and Keefe (1998) state that the trainers of the tutors
should model the reading strategy for the tutors to understand how to
implement it and give them ample practice in using it before they begin
tutoring children. Furthermore, if the tutors receive supervisory support
and training, they can provide the kind of critical instruction that could
enable the tutees to succeed in school (Vadasy, Jenkins, & Pool, 2000).
These research studies suggest that the tutor should be trained outside of
the tutoring environment and then assigned a tutee after the training
(Meyer & Keefe, 1998; Reisner et al., 1990; Vadasy et al., 2000; Wasik, 1998).

Researchers (Snow, Burns, & Griffin, 1998; Wasik, 1998) warn that if
tutors are not properly supervised and trained, they may cause problems
for the tutees. Wasik (1998) states that an inexperienced or poorly trained
tutor may "discourage struggling readers and even harm them by their
inexperience" (p. 569). In addition, tutors should not provide reading
instruction but rather they should provide "a valuable practice and motivation support for the children" (Snow et al., 1998, p. 12).

Several grassroots organizations have developed to provide academic support to school age children by recruiting volunteer tutors (Aspiazu
et al., 1998; Osher & Mejia, 1999). In particular, Latino populations are
developing after-school programs to support their youth (Aspiazu et al.,
1998; Osher & Mejia, 1999). These programs began because the Latino
population believes schools are not providing adequate support for their
children (Quintero & Huerta-Macias, 1990).

Moll (1992) found that Latino families provide support to each other by creating networks within their family members and extending them to outside households. In this way, they have the necessary *funds of knowledge* to succeed in the community. Moll (1992) defines funds of knowledge as a "historically accumulated and culturally developed bodies of knowledge and skills essential for household or individual functioning and well-being" (p. 133). For example, if a family member has not learned how to read, then the family seeks support within the family or within their network communities. The networks established outside the household are based on *confianza* (mutual trust) between family and individual (Moll, 1992).

Some Latino after-school programs focus on maintaining students' cultural identity (Aspiazu et al., 1998). Cultural identity is maintaining an "image of the behaviors, beliefs, values, and norms appropriate to members of the ethnic group(s) to which one belongs" (Ferdman, 1990, p. 183). Therefore, Latino after-school programs promote bilingualism, which entails biliteracy. Volunteer tutors do not have structured literacy training, although they are trained by the community members of the organization (Aspiazu et al., 1998). Quintero and Huerta-Macias (1990) maintain that literacy and biliteracy skills are more effectively taught through whole-language instruction. They indicate that the "whole language approach to language learning emphasizes that language be taught naturally as it occurs within any social environment instead of segmenting it into bits and pieces" (p. 10). Therefore, the acquisition of literacy should be focused on the interests of the students rather than of the educators (Freire & Macedo, 1987). There is a limited amount of research on training volunteer tutors in Latino after-school programs (Aspiazu et al., 1998). This chapter adds to this strand of research by describing how non-Latino tutors were mentored in a biliteracy setting and how they were incorporated into an after-school community.

THEORETICAL FRAMEWORK

This study was conducted using a combined sociocultural and sociolinguistic theoretical lens. These lens encompasses the concepts of *literacy as a situated practice* (Castanheira, Crawford, Dixon, & Green, 1998; Crawford, Castanheira, Dixon, & Green, 2001; Green et al., 1992; Green & Dixon, 1993; Green, Dixon, & Zaharlick, 2001), *socioculturally situated identity* (Gee, 1999), *opportunities to learn* (Tuyay, Jennings, & Dixon, 1995), and *intercontextuality* (Floriani, 1993). Although most of these concepts were defined and identified in a classroom environment (Castanheira et al., 1998; Crawford et al., 2001; Floriani, 1993; Gee, 1999; Green et al., 1992; Green & Dixon, 1993; Green et al., 2001), they are applicable to the circle-time activity, because it resembled a classroom situation. I am not using these concepts as individual ideas but instead combining them in order to understand and explain the VIVA community in circle-time.

I view literacy as a situated practice (Castanheira et al., 1998; Crawford et al., 2001; Green et al., 1992; Green & Dixon, 1993; Green et al., 2001), which is developed through a particular activity (Gee, 1999) that is intercontextualized (Floriani, 1993) within a community. Ethnographic researchers of reading instruction (Castanheira et al., 1998; Crawford et al., 2001; Green & Dixon, 1993; Green et al., 2001; Green & Meyer, 1991) claim that reading is a situated practice. It is defined by the members of the classroom through interactions and actions about, with, and through the text (Green et al., 1992). Through these daily interactions, patterns of behavior emerge and reading practices are established over a period of time. In other words, the reading practices are constructed and co-constructed within the learning environment (Castanheira et al., 1998) and are constantly being changed or redefined by the members of the classroom (Green et al., 1992). *What counts as reading* is created and is incorporated into the teachers', tutors', and students' knowledge of the circle-time culture, and it becomes part of their beliefs; therefore, the members know how to act within that environment (Green & Meyer, 1991) and develop a sense of community. This is in accordance with Gee's (1999) concept of socioculturally situated identity, which states that the members are "using cues or clues to assemble situated meaning about what identities and relationships are relevant to the interaction, with their concomitant attitudes, values, ways of feeling, ways of knowing and believing, as well as ways of acting and interacting" (p. 86). Therefore, the circle-time culture is where "students have to use language, act, and produce artifacts that reflect the dominant ways of thinking, feeling, believing and acting" (Rex, 2000, pp. 318-319). As members of the activity they understand, construct, engage, and hold each other accountable during the reading instruction, which is defined by the classroom culture (Castanheira et al., 1998; Crawford et al., 2001). Finally, what counts as reading is developed over time to serve the reading purposes and goals of the members of the learning environment (Crawford et al., 2001). In this way, the VIVA community established "what counts as reading" in circle time.

Through the process of establishing what counts as reading, the teacher, tutors, and students reinforce the reading practices by taking up opportunities to learn. According to Tuyay et al. (1995), opportunities to learn are the negotiation and renegotiations between members of a classroom to establish knowledge, understanding, and incorporate new concepts into the reading tasks. It is an interactional phenomenon between two members of the classroom, which can only be identified after one of the members verbally or nonverbally indicates that he or she has learned and understood the new information. The student or tutor incorporates the new information to his or her prior knowledge if he or she takes the opportunity to learn. Through these interactions, patterns of everyday classroom life are constructed and reconstructed thus defining what counts as reading (Tuyay et al., 1995).

To advance this concept further, I include intercontextualization as a part of opportunities to learn. Intercontextualization, according to Floriani (1993), extends the given context that is constructed and negotiated in a social situation from a moment to a period of time. During circle time, the members construct discrete patterns in their interactions that are maintained from one circle time to another. If a member does not take the opportunity to learn about the reading practices in circle time, then he or she will not be seen as a capable member of the group. In order for a member to become a full participant, he or she actively builds and incorporates previous experiences with the emergent reading culture. The active co-construction of the literacy practices over time make it possible for the members to have interactive relationships with each other through social identity, knowledge construction, and group expectations (Rex, 2001). In conclusion, using these different concepts together provides a lens with which to describe the circle-time activity.

CONTEXTUALIZING THE STUDY

The VIVA organization is a grassroots, nonprofit program to help immigrant Latino families. VIVA, an after-school program, began in 1999. The members met twice a week for 2 to 3 hours in order to support their children. The meetings helped the children maintain their native language and heritage while promoting their schoolwork and understanding of American culture.

Seven families participated in the after-school program. These families reflected Moll's (1992) notion of Latino family networks because all of them were related, with the exception of two. The majority of the families came from disadvantaged social, educational, and economic environments. Two of the students were born in the United States, but their parents were from Puerto Rico and Costa Rica. At the time I started the research project, seven children had lived in the United States for 3 years and 1 child for 1 year. These children had emigrated from Mexico. Two children, from Honduras, had lived in the United States for 3 months.

During the month of September, the after-school program implemented circle time for the first time. The participants of circle time were Patricia, the teacher; 12 children (ages 3 to 10; 11 undergraduate volunteer tutors; and myself, the researcher.

Nine of the undergraduate tutors were part of a Spanish-language immersion program at a midwestern university. They took a course taught by Patricia. The novice tutors volunteered and did not receive class credit or salary. The tutors received minimal mentoring from Patricia in biliteracy practices during circle time. The remaining three tutors participated in the Americareads Challenge program. These tutors had formal and extensive mentoring to support the literacy practice of young English-speaking children. The role of the three Americareads tutors in circle time was limited due to their lack of Spanish fluency.

The focal points of this investigation were Patricia, the teacher; Beatriz, a novice tutor who was part of the Spanish immersion program; and Pedro, a 10-year-old child. At one time or another, they all directed circle time during the data-collection phase.

Profile of Patricia

Patricia, a Latina in her mid-30s, is originally from Puerto Rico but lives in the United States sporadically. She is a graduate student enrolled in a dual doctoral program in anthropology and social work at a large midwestern university. During the investigation, she was a graduate student instructor of the Spanish immersion program at the same university. She did not have formal training in the education field but had been teaching undergraduate students Spanish for the previous 8 years. Her first contact in teaching younger children was through this after-school program.

Patricia founded the after-school program, VIVA. She contacted Latino families in the area and offered her services, which included helping their children with their schoolwork and teaching them English. During the first year of the program, Patricia had limited help in providing a structured program for the families. Therefore, at the beginning of the second year she recruited novice tutors from her undergraduate Spanish class and Americareads tutors to help her. Patricia felt there was a need to develop a beginning activity, circle time, that would provide a set routine for the children. Patricia developed the lessons for this activity. During circle time, she mentored the tutors and monitored the children's progress.

Profile of Beatriz

Beatriz, a white woman in her early 20s was a sophomore at the midwestern university and a resident of the state in which the university is located. She had not traveled to a Spanish-speaking country, although she was part of the Spanish immersion program and attended Patricia's class. VIVA was the first experience she had teaching young children. She did not plan to enter the field of education. Despite this fact, she was one of the tutors that consistently attended VIVA. Out of the 12 sessions of observation, Beatriz attended 4 and directed 2. She participated in the direct instruction on how to run circle time and observed Patricia several times during this activity.

Profile of Pedro

Pedro, originally from Mexico, had lived in the United States for 3 years when I began the investigation. He was 10 years old and was one of the oldest children participating in circle time. He was related to seven of the other members. He had a younger sister, Ingrid, who was 5 years old, who also participated in the after-school program. Pedro was in fourth grade but read at a third-grade level, according to the Qualitative Reading Inventory-II (Leslie & Caldwell, 1995). His Spanish reading level was also at a third-grade level based on running records. Pedro attended 11 of the 12 sessions. He was the only child who directed circle time on his own because he asked to. Children were not expected to direct circle time.

Role of the Researcher

I had been a member of the VIVA organization for 6 months before beginning the investigation. I served as the educational consultant and tutor to the students who needed the most help. Once I began the investigation, I became a participant-observer. My role changed to observing the interaction during circle time instead of leading the activity with Patricia.

Circle Time

Patricia introduced circle time to the after-school program in order to provide an organizing beginning activity. The children usually played as they waited for instruction or for their tutors to arrive. It frequently took 20 minutes for them to settle down and start working. However, once a routine was established with circle time, the progression to one-on-one tutoring occurred more rapidly.

Patricia created the circle-time activity after observing a Montessori teacher read to her students. The teacher and the students were sitting on the floor in a circle formation. Patricia was impressed with the way the Montessori students participated and behaved during the storybook reading.

Circle time began when Patricia, the children, and tutors sat in a circle. They began the activity by singing a welcoming song in Spanish.

During this song, the children, Patricia, and the tutors shook hands greeting each other. After the song, members of the circle began to ask one another about his or her day. In Pedro's interview, he reported that these activities created a safe space for the children to express their success and worries. After each person in the circle expressed how his or her day went, a book was read to the children. Sometimes the children participated in reading the book, although Patricia or the tutors were usually the main readers. The books were predominantly in Spanish, but English books were read occasionally. During the data collection, I observed nine circle times with Spanish books, and five with English books. At the conclusion of the reading, Patricia handed out Spanish material for the children to read aloud. The children took turns reading sections of the Spanish material although on some occasions, they read the section at the same time. Then the students and tutors left the circle to begin their individual tutoring sessions, which focused on English/Spanish reading, writing, and mathematics.

DATA COLLECTION AND METHODS OF ANALYSIS

The methods I used were an ethnographic and discourse-analytic approach known as interactional ethnography(IE). According to Green et al. (2001), ethnographic research "focuses on understanding what members need to know, do, predict, and interpret in order to participate in the construction of ongoing events of life within a social group, where cultural knowledge is developed" (p. 3). Cultural knowledge is defined and constructed by the members of a community (Spencer, 1994). My purpose was to uncover and describe the way the novice tutors were mentored to assume the teaching role in circle time and how they were incorporated into the VIVA community. In addition, I investigated how the members' actions and interactions co-constructed a biliteracy setting in order to create a learning environment and therefore establish a VIVA culture. In order to do so, I became a participant-observer and interacted with the VIVA members. This allowed analysis of the data using a holistic perspective, which has been described by Green et al. (2001).

I collected data for 12 consecutive sessions of the after-school program using field-notes, interviewing the participants, and videotaping the circle-time activity. During the videotaping and writing of the field-notes, I would informally interview the participants. The videotaped segments provide access to members' observable behavior during circle time. The data were transcribed on ongoing bases throughout the investigation. I transcribed the videotapes by identifying the different phases within the circle-time cycle of activity (Green & Dixon, 1993). The interviews were also transcribed to identify common themes and perceptions held by informants. Through these transcriptions, I identified and compared seven "rich" points in this community (Green et al., 2001). Rich points were events that demonstrate portions of the culture being studied which were later compared or contrasted with other rich points (Agar, 1994).

The rich points were as follows:

1. Patricia giving explicit instruction to the tutors on how to read the book in circle time.
2. Patricia's interview when she talked about the objective and reading practices she expected in circle time.
3. Patricia modeling the reading practices and the students' response to her instruction.
4. Beatriz's interpretation of the reading practices when she directed circle time and the students' response to her instruction.
5. Beatriz's interview as she talked about circle time.
6. Pedro's interpretation of the reading practices when he directed circle time and the student's response to his instruction.
7. Pedro's interview as he talked about circle time.

I then analyzed the rich points by using discourse analysis. Hicks (1995) defines *discourse* as "communication that is socially situated and that sustains social 'positioning': relations between participants in face-to-face interactions or between author and reader in written texts" (p. 49). Discourse is socially constructed; therefore it "reflects ideologies, systems of values, beliefs and social practices" (p. 53) which could mirror the culture of the members of VIVA. I analyzed what was said in particular circle-time events in order to understand how biliterate reading practices were established. Finally, I used the interpretive method (Erickson, 1986) to triangulate the data. This consisted of comparing and contrasting the circle time observation of Patricia, Beatriz, and Pedro when they directed circle-time, with Patricia's, Beatriz's, and Pedro's interviews when they talked about circle time. This comparison of the rich points in circle time provided confirming and disconfirming evidence of each phase of activity and interview. Through this triangulation, I describe how the novice tutors were mentored, and how the members established biliteracy practices. In addition, I describe how Beatriz and students assumed the teacher's role during the activity.

RESULTS

This analysis describes how Patricia, Beatriz, and Pedro directed circle time. It is divided into three parts. The first part describes Patricia's biliteracy practices and mentoring process. The second part illustrates Beatriz's biliteracy practice when she assumed the teacher's role incorporating Patricia's teaching methods. The final section describes Pedro's biliteracy practice when he directed circle time. These three analyses reflect the particular biliteracy practices as they interface with community-building during circle time.

Patricia's Biliteracy Practices and Mentoring

This section demonstrates why and how Patricia provided an environment where the non-Latino tutors were incorporated in the circle-time activity, and how she mentored the tutors by introducing them and the children to her biliteracy practices. These practices began to establish what the group considered what counted as reading (Castanheira et al., 1998; Crawford et al., 2001; Green & Dixon, 1993; Green et al., 2001; Green & Meyer, 1991).

Patricia possessed set ideas about the different roles of the tutors in circle time. She wanted the tutors to run the activity for several reasons. First, she felt that it would improve their language skills in Spanish. Second, if the tutors improved their language skills, then the children would respect them as authority figures. As she commented:

> I think it was important too, as much as we can give the tutor opportunities to read, because they will learn the skill. They need to learn [Spanish], and I think they gain the children's respect also that way.

Third, she believed that this would help to incorporate the non-Latino tutors into the VIVA community. Finally, she indicated that having non-Latino tutors wanting to learn the language sent a message to the students that their native language was valuable not only in their community but to a larger spectrum in society. As she stated:

> They [tutors] are not going to be our permanent readers but we do want to create a sense of community, and we also want to get the children use to the fact that there are other authority figures, and that they are sharing also with people that are not Latino. So that they can see that non-Latinos are interested in what they are doing and in learning Spanish. From my perspective . . . I am trying to find many different venues through which the children can understand that what they have is valuable. Having North Americans coming here to learn Spanish is one powerful way, and having them being college students [sic].

Patricia indicated that the overall purpose for tutors was not to learn how to become reading teachers but to be respected by the children, become part of the community, and to improve their language skills.

The mentoring of the tutors in VIVA was unconventional compared to the other programs (Meyer & Keefe, 1998; Reisner et al., 1990; Wasik, 1998) because tutors did not receive formal training. Rather, Patricia gave them explicit instructions about how to read the book minutes before circle time began and modeled how circle time should be conducted throughout the activity. Her elements of circle time reading included reading comprehension, vocabulary building, active participation, behavior norms, and language skills.

The mentoring of the tutors began before circle-time started, Patricia chose a tutor to read a book to the group. She then proceeded to tell him or her how to read it to the children. She gave these instructions in front of the group, which permitted the other tutors and the children to listen to the conversation. She told them how to read and hold the book. During this brief explanation, she explained to the tutor that she or he should stop periodically to ask the children comprehension questions to make sure they were listening and understanding the content of the story (see Table 4.1).

As Patricia talked to her, Catalina (one of the tutors) skimmed through the book because this was the first time she had seen it. Afterwards, Patricia did not ask Catalina if she understood what she needed to do. That was not part of the training. Patricia assumed that the tutors would follow her instructions, although they did not have prior teaching experience.

After Patricia gave the instructions to the tutor, she asked the children and the tutors about their day. Then she indicated to the tutor to begin reading the book. As the tutor read, Patricia interrupted her or him in order to model how to ask reading comprehension questions and the meaning of vocabulary words. Through these interactions, she emphasized the importance of language use as she maintained the behavioral norms of circle time.

For instance, the same day Patricia explicitly told Catalina how to read the book, she taught her how to ask reading comprehension questions and vocabulary words by modeling the conventional initiation, reply, evaluation(IRE) elicitation sequences (Mehan, 1979). She interrupted Catalina's reading of *El Gran Oso Gris* [*The Big Gray Bear*] by initiating the question, the students replied, and she evaluated whether the responses were correct. She followed this pattern of elicitation when asking information from the students about a particular event in the book or the meaning of a word.

Table 4.1.   Patricia Explaining How to Read a Book

SEQUENCE/INTERACTIONS	TRANSLATION	COMMENTS
3-Anna: What's that?		The students and tutors are sitting in a circle.
Catalina: A video camera		
3-Anna: No		
Catalina: Yeah		
Patricia: Okay, listos . . . entonces, Catalina,	Patricia: Okay, ready . . . then Catalina,	Patricia interrupts the conversation.
Catalina: Yeah		
3-Anna: no		
Patricia: Catalina cuando estes leyendo el libro enseña las fotos, en vez en cuando no tiene que ser con cada dibujo hazles preguntas a los niños sobre que es lo que ven (catalina looks at the book), que es lo que oyen, como asocian lo que han dicho con la foto. Osea para ayudarlos analizar lo que esta ocurriendo en el libro. Okay.	Patricia: Catalina when you are reading the book, show the pictures. Once in awhile, it does not have to be every page, ask the children questions about what they see and hear (Catalina looks at the book), so they can associate what they have said with the picture. In other words, so you can help them analyze what is happening in the book. Okay.	Catalina is holding the book towards her while she is talking to Patricia. The students and tutors are listening to the conversation. As Catalina is looking at the book, 3-Anna gets up and walks towards Patricia. 7-Albert and 8-Samuel, arrives at the meeting. Patricia asks Ann to sit down. Patricia asks 7-Albert and 8-Samuel to sit down.
10-Carlos: Hola Samuel		
Patricia: Sientese, wow, Alberto		
10-Carlos: We're making a movie	10-Carlos: Hi Samuel	
Patricia: Wow, we're growing, sientense. Vamos	Patricia: Sit down, wow Albert 10-Carlos: We're making a movie Patricia: Wow, we growing, sit Down, lets go	

Note. (.) = short pause; numbers next to names = the age of the children.

As Table 4.2 demonstrates, Patricia interrupted Catalina's reading to ask a comprehension question. First, she asked the children, "what do bears eat?" (This was a fictional story, so the food that bears ate in the book were small cookies called honey bear.) The students first responded by telling Patricia what real bears ate, and through a series of IRE inter-

Table 4.2. Patricia Modeling Comprehension Question

PHASE	SEQUENCE/ INTERACTIONS	TRANSLATION	COMMENTS
Catalina reading the text	Catalina: ... (reading) "¿Qué comen los Osos?", pregunto pequeño Oso gris. El pensó un momento antes de contestar el dijo, "Ositos de miel por su puesto."	Catalina: ... (reading) What do the bears eat?, asked the little gray bear. He thought for a moment before he answered and said, "honey bears of course."	Catalina reads and shows the pictures at the same time. All the students pay attention.
Comp. Question about the text	Patricia: ¿Qué comen, que comen los osos? (she leans forward) 10-Pedro: Ositos de miel (.), NOOO (shakes his head) se comen espagueti (.) 4-Lulu: /Noo, si comen, comen/ 10-Pedro: Pescados Patricia:Pescado, (She signaled to the book) ¿qué paso? 10-Carlos: Miel Patricia: Miel, pescado, (.)¿ Pero que dijo el que come? (She signaled to the book) 10-Pedro: Ositos de miel Patricia: Hmmmmm (she leaned back)	Patricia: What do bears eat? (She Leans forward) 10-Pedro: Honey bears (.), NOOO (shakes his head) spaghetti (.) 4-Lulu: /Noo, yes they eat, they eat/ 10-Pedro: Fish Patricia: Fish, (She signaled to the book) what happened? 10-Carlos: Honey Patricia:Honey, fish,(.) but what did he say that it ate? (She signaled to the book) 10-Pedro: Honey bears Patricia: Hmmmmm (She leaned back.)	*4-Anna looks at the camera. 10-Pedro, 10-Carlos, 6-Daleo, turns to look at Patricia. *10-Pedro criticizes the text by stating that bears do not eat honey bear. *Patricia wants the answer that the text give, which is bears eat honey bears.

Note. / = interruptions; (.) = short pause; CAPITAL LETTERS = increased volume of voice; numbers next to names = the age of the children. The Volunteer Tutor, Catalina, is reading to the students El Gran Oso Gris (The great big Bear).

actions, the students' eventually gave the response Patricia wanted. The reading comprehension questions generally consisted of asking the children questions that could be answered by the text with only one correct answer.

Patricia also interrupted the readings when she thought the students do not understand a word or words that the students use incorrectly. She would model the same series of IRE interactions when she clarified a vocabulary word.

For example, she interrupted the reading when a student misunderstood the word "sheep" for "bees" (see Table 4.3). Both of these words sound alike in Spanish and some students confuse them. During the interaction between Patricia and the students, the tutor attempted to continue reading. Patricia looked at her and she stopped. Once Patricia was sure that all the students knew the difference between sheep and bees, she indicated to Catalina to continue reading.

Another element of Patricia's reading practices was active participation. Patricia asked the students to act out portions of the book. She believed that if the students interpreted the text through action it would aid their understanding of the story and/or vocabulary words. Patricia also briefly interrupted the tutor's readings to request that students act out a segment from the book, although not as often as she interrupted with comprehension questions and/or vocabulary words. For example, during circle time in English, while Olga, another tutor, was reading *Curious George Takes a Job* Patricia interrupted her in order to have the students pretend to smell. As happened each time that Patricia made a request, the students complied. There was no discussion, and the tutor continued to read as if she was not interrupted. According to Patricia, these brief interactions allowed the students to react to the text and kept them interested in the story.

Throughout the reading comprehension, vocabulary questions and active participation, Patricia constantly maintained behavioral norms within the circle.

Table 4.4 demonstrates an example of her actions to maintain a behavioral norm. Brent and Albert had moved to the center of the circle so that they could see the pictures of the book better. Patricia noticed this while asking a vocabulary question. She stopped her inquiry and told the boys that she would not continue circle time until they formed a circle. Brent protested when he was asked to move. He stated that he could not see the pictures. Patricia explained to him that other children could not see the pictures because he was now blocking them. She told him that if

Table 4.3. Patricia Modeling Vocabulary Question

PHASE	SEQUENCE/ INTERACTIONS	TRANSLATION	COMMENTS
Catalina reading the text	Catalina: (reading) Excelente dijo el oso gris...	Catalina: (reading) Excellent said the gray bear....	6-Daleo raises his hand, and looks at Patricia. Patricia points at him. He interrupts the reading
Vocabulary lesson	6-Daleo: Ellos comen, pueden comer abejas como hacen BRIIIII (he acted like a bee stung him) Patricia: ¿Abejas? 6-Daleo: No 10-Carlos: /No, pero no,/ Patricia: Comen 10-Carlos: /Comen miel/	6-Daleo: They eat, they can eat bees that go BRIIIII (he acted like a bee stung him) Patricia: Bees? 6-Daleo: No 10-Carlos: /No, but no/ Patricia: They eat 10-Carlos: /they eat honey/	*10-Pedro, 7-Beto, 10-Carlos turn to look at Patricia.
	Patricia: Eso es importante, (.)(She leaned back), comen miel ¿Comen abejas o comen ovejas? 10-Carlos: Ovejas 10-Pedro: Ovejas 6-Daleo: Abejas Patricia: ¿Comen ovejas, ovejas, baa, baa, comen ovejas? 10-Pedro: No ovejas 10-Carlos: No abejas Patricia:¿Cómo hacen las abejas? Students: Bzzzzzz	Patricia:That is important, (.)(She leaned back), they eat honey, they eat bees o sheep? 10-Carlos: Sheep 10-Pedro: Sheep 6-Daleo: Bees Patricia: They eat sheep, sheep, baa, baa, they eat sheep? 10-Pedro: No ovejas Carlos: No bees Patricia: What sound do the bees make? Students: Bzzzzzz	*Catalina tries to continue to read the book during this conversation.

Note. /= interruptions; (.) = short pause; CAPITAL LETTERS = increased volume of voice; {} = talking at the same time; numbers next to names = the age of the children. The Volunteer Tutor, Catalina, is reading to the students *El Gran Oso Gris* [*The Great Big Bear*].

he could not see the pictures, he needed to ask the tutor to show them to him. It is interesting to note that Patricia did not tell the tutor to make sure she showed the pictures to the group as she read. Instead, she gave the power to the child to interrupt the tutor by requesting her to show him the pictures. In this instance, Patricia indicated to Brent that he could assume the teacher's role by asking the tutor to hold the book higher so that he could see the pictures. This sent a message to the tutors that the children also had a voice mentoring them in circle-time activity.

Table 4.4. Patricia Maintaining the Norms of Circle Time

INTERACTION SEQUENCE	TRANSLATION	COMMENTS
Olga: (reading) Don't let him get away. George headed for the fire escape. George reached out. Patricia: {What's a fire escape? 10-Carlos: {Ohhhh, Ohhhh, Ohhhh Patricia: {Brent and Alberto, Brent, we cannot continue until Brent and Albert make a circle. 10-Carlos: {Ohhhh, Ohhhh, Patricia: Brent, Brent get in the circle. 7-Brent: But I cannot see. Patricia: Just ask Olga so she can show you the pictures 10-Carlos: {Ohhhh, ohhhh, ohhhh Patricia: The thing is, if we don't make a circle, Alberto entonces otragente no puede ver. Patricia: What is a fire escape?	Patricia: .... Then other people cannot see.	*Olga is holding the book so everybody can see the picture. *Several children raise their hands. Carlos is waving his hand. *Brent and Albert are sitting in the middle of the circle. *Carlos is waving his hand. *Alberto enters the circle again. *Brent enters the circle too. *Carlos lowers his hand.

Note. { } = talking at the same time; numbers next to names = the age of the children. The Volunteer Tutor, Olga, is reading to the students *Curious George Takes a Job*.

When Patricia taught reading, vocabulary, and behavior norms, she also talked about the importance of language. During the reading of *Curious George Takes a Job*, Carlos asked her to stop speaking Spanish. Patricia was translating part of the book because some members did not speak English very well. Carlos was concerned because he brought a friend who did not speak Spanish to join him in the after-school program. Patricia indicated to him that his friend came to learn Spanish, and that Carlos was there to learn both, Spanish and English. In this instance, Carlos attempted to assume the teacher's role by requesting that Patricia stop speaking Spanish. Patricia listened to Carlos and explained to him why she would continue speaking both languages during that circle-time activity. He was not reprimanded for requesting a change of behavior from Patricia. This interaction also suggested to the tutor that the children's voice should be respected during this activity.

Although Patricia placed the tutors in a situation, where she gave them the opportunity to assume the teacher's role with her guidance the majority of the tutors did not do it. Instead, they just read the book while Patricia interacted with the children. This may have positioned the tutors in compromising ways, which was why they did not interact with the children as they read. When I asked Catalina why she did not ask any questions but just read the book, she stated that she did not feel comfortable doing it, because it was the first time she read a book to the group. She also indicated that she did not have the chance to preview the book ahead of time and was not prepared to ask questions. The other tutors had the same experience. In addition, she felt that her Spanish needed to improve before she could interact with the children the way Patricia wanted her to do.

Furthermore, Patricia created a space for the children to assume the teacher's role as the tutor was reading the book, which the children did. They voiced their opinion by informing Patricia and the tutors what they thought needed to happen in the activity. Their opinions were always heard but not always acted on, as indicated in the interaction with Carlos and Patricia about which language to use in circle time. This might have intimidated the tutors, especially when they directed circle time for the first time.

Despite this, Patricia began establishing what counted as reading in the circle-time activity. She did this by mentoring the tutors with brief explicit instruction, and modeling reading practices she believed would be beneficial to the children. She also interrupted and directed them as they read. Through these practices, she exposed the children and the tutors to key elements of the reading practices she thought were important. These elements of storybook reading were constantly being negotiated and renegotiated to establish what counted as reading by the members of circle time. These interactions provided an environment where the tutors became particular members of the community during the training process. This enabled the students to develop confianza with the tutors, which provided the children a safe place to express their ideas and thoughts.

Beatriz's Biliteracy Practices

The following analysis illustrates how Beatriz, one of the tutors, responded to Patricia's mentoring approach. Patricia asked Beatriz to direct circle time by herself because she had to talk to parents, and Beatriz was the first tutor to arrive that day. Beatriz had participated in circle time before directing it herself. During the mentoring, she did not assume the teacher's role or interact with the children or read a book to the group when Patricia was part of the circle. However, she did hear Patricia's instruction and saw her model the reading practices. When Beatriz was asked to direct circle time, she did assume the teacher's role and was able to incorporate some of the main themes that Patricia modeled with the help of the children and the other tutors. Together they negotiated comprehension questions, addressed language use, and maintained the behavioral norms of circle time.

Beatriz followed Patricia's format in asking comprehension questions using the conventional IRE elicitation sequences (Mehan, 1979), as she read *Buzz Lightyear*. Beatriz read the text, stopped at the end of the page and asked a question. As Beatriz asked comprehension questions she established the behavioral norms and addressed language use with the aid of the children and other tutors.

Table 4.5 depicts the interactions following the comprehension question, "¿Quienes son las fuerzas del mal?" (Who are the forces of evil?). The students responded to it, although they talked at the same time. Therefore, Beatriz stopped the conversation until only one child spoke at a time.

These interactions following the comprehension question depicted the children's recognition of Beatriz as a teaching figure because they actively participated in answering the question. Beatriz requested a response from the students, and she continued asking the same question until she heard the response from several children. At the end of each response, she evaluated it by commenting on it. The difference between Beatriz's and Patricia's inquiry was that Patricia stopped asking the question once she heard the correct response. Beatriz permitted several children to answer it, although they each gave an appropriate answer.

Despite the fact that Beatriz was seen as an authority figure in this circle-time, she shared that responsibility with Beto, another tutor, and

Table 4.5. Beatriz Asking a Comprehension Question

PHASE	INTERACTION/ SEQUENCE	TRANSLATION	COMMENTS
Com. Quest.	Beatriz: (reading) Tenía de cumplir una misión pelegrosa otra vez, salvar al universo de las fuerzas del mal. (Stops reading) ¿Quiénes son las fuerzas del mal? 10-Pedro: Unos malos y unos que quieren matar a Buzz Lightyear= Beatriz: No me digas, No me digas 8-Samuel: Yo ya se quien quiere matar a Buzz	Beatriz: (reading) He had to complete another dangerous mission, he needed to save the universe from the forces of evil.(stop reading). Who are the forces of evil? 10-Pedro: Some bad persons, and some want to kill Buzz Lightyear= Beatriz: really, really 8-Samuel: I know who is going to kill Buzz Lightyear	*Carlos, Samuel, Pedro, y Emilio, raise their hands. *Beatriz points to Pedro *Samuel, Emmanuel, Carlos, Alberto have their hands raised. *Beatriz points to Samuel
Norms	Lightyear Beatriz: Oh {4-Lulu, 10-Carlos, 10-Pedro, 8-Samuel talk at the same time. (.08) (unintelligible) Beatriz:{ Okay Brent what do you want to say?	Beatriz: Oh,{4-Lulu, 10-Carlos, 10-Pedro, 8-Samuel, are talking at the same time. (.08) (unintelligible) Beatriz:........................	*Lulu begins the interruption, she stands up and walks to Beatriz. Carlos and Samuel are arguing, *Every body quiets down
Lang. Norms Comp. Quest.	Lets listen to Brent. Escuchen a Brent. 7-Brent: Hum, (.2) I don't know Beatriz: ¿Quiénes son las personas? 7-Brent: I was going to say= Beto: {En Español Beatriz: Can you sit in a circle? 7-Brent: Ese malo quiere matar a buz light year. Beatriz: Si es muy malo	....Listen to Brent Beatriz: Who are the people Beto: In Spanish 7-Brent: The bad person wants to kill Buzz Lightyear Beatriz: Yes he is a very bad person	*Brent moves to the center of the circle *Brent enters the circle Carlos hand is still up

Note. (.) = short pause; CAPITAL LETTERS = increased volume of voice; {} = talking at the same time; = = adjacent pairs; numbers next to names = the age of the children. The Volunteer Tutor, Beatriz, is reading to the students *Buzz Lightyear*.

Carlos, a 10-year-old student. During this activity, Beto indicated to the group that code-switching between both languages was not acceptable and the group complied. Table 4.5 illustrates how Beto reminded Beatriz and the children to speak in Spanish. They responded by reverting from speaking English to Spanish.

In addition, Carlos at the beginning of the circle-time activity helped Beatriz establish a behavioral norm; the children needed to raise their hands before speaking. When circle time began, Carlos was not pleased when his peers shouted out the answer to Beatriz's first question. After that incident, he informed the children that they had to raise their hands before speaking. The children recognized Carlos' authority because for the most part, they raised their hands in order to answer a question. Nevertheless, sometimes they would continue to shout out the answer at the same time that their hand was up in the air, as indicated in Table 4.5.

Despite of the fact that Beto and Carlos assumed the teaching role with Beatriz, she was the primary teacher. Through a combination of Patricia's interactive mentoring and the active assistance of her peer tutors and the children, Beatriz could perform appropriately in the teacher's role, although she had only participated in circle time twice before. She negotiated the literacy practices with the other members in order to teach reading comprehension, behavioral norms, and language use. The lesson established by Beatriz with the aid of the members was consistent with the main elements that Patricia modeled and instructed. This indicated that the group as a whole worked together to maintain the reading practices from the previous circle-time interactions to this one. Therefore, there was a consistency between the past experiences and this one.

Beatriz did not mind that the other tutors and children helped her during her storybook reading. She indicated that she viewed "circle time as a combination between a social and reading activity." She added that it gave the students a chance to be "comfortable in both languages." In addition, she valued the fact that the students had a safe place to demonstrate publicly what they knew.

Nevertheless, this circle-time activity illustrated the complexity of this group when Patricia was not around because the teaching role was shared between three members—Beatriz, Beto, and Carlos. It is interesting to note that when Patricia was in the circle, the tutors did not assume the teacher's role. The tutors only assumed the role when they were left alone. However, the children assumed the teacher's role regardless who was in the circle. This may indicate that circle time prompted an atmosphere of community and confianza where the children felt comfortable in expressing their opinion in front of the tutors.

Pedro's Biliteracy Practices

This section focuses on how Pedro, a 10-year-old student, interpreted the reading practices by assuming the teacher's role. This activity was not designed for the student to direct without adult supervision. Nevertheless, Pedro assumed the teaching role one afternoon when Patricia decided to cancel circle time because of time constraints. Pedro's individual tutor arrived late that day, so Pedro asked me if he could run circle time. I indicated to him that he could, but that he would have to find members in the community to sit in his circle. He proceeded to call the younger members of the community to read to them *One Fish, Two Fish, Red Fish, Blue Fish*. He chose this book because it was the only one lying on the table next to him when he asked me if he could read.

Pedro indicated that he wanted to direct circle time because he wanted to become a tutor. He stated that he wanted to teach the younger children how to read as the tutors were teaching him. He saw this as an opportunity to imitate the tutors and Patricia. This was noticeable because Pedro usually did not assume the teacher's role when he participated in the circle-time activity when Patricia or other tutors directed it. This may indicate that Pedro perceived the tutors as role models because he wanted to imitate them, which could mean that Patricia's objective in having tutors in the after-school program to serve as role models was successful.

This was a unique situation because Pedro and the members of his circle demonstrated what they had internalized as circle time. They renegotiated and reconstructed the literacy practices as a limited version compared to the previous circle-time activities in VIVA. Nevertheless, Pedro brought to this activity his past experience with storybook reading. He held the book in the same manner that Patricia and Beatriz did but, in addition, he pointed to every word that he read. I asked him about this practice. He stated that the librarian in his school read the book using that method. As he read, it seemed that he was only concentrating on reading the book aloud. He read it slowly and clearly, pronouncing each word. The only interruptions during his reading were by the other members for him to maintain the behavioral norms of the circle (see Table 4.6).

The other members of the circle time attempted to assume the teacher's role by maintaining the behavioral norms. Pedro's sister, Ingrid, who was 5, and Lulu, Pedro's cousin, who was 4, kept telling the other members how to behave appropriately. Unfortunately, the other members did not accept their authority and continued to misbehave. In particular, 6-year-old Brent, Pedro's and Lulu's cousin, kept touching the microphone and making noises. Brent did not accept the younger children's authority during this activity. Ingrid noticed this and she changed

Table 4.6. Pedro Maintaining the Norms of Circle Time

INTERACTION/SEQUENCE	TRANSLATION	COMMENTS
10-Pedro: (reading) ... What does one jump 6-Ingrid: Mira Pedro 4-Lulu: No lo garres, no lo garres 10-Pedro: Calladitos, calladitos, mira por favor no toques esto (microphone). Así, nade lo toque, ponlo así. 10-Pedro: (reading) We know a man called Mr. Dunn...	6-Ingrid: Look, Pedro 4-Lulu: Don't touch it, don't touch it 10-Pedro: Be quiet, be quite, look, please do not touch it. (microphone). This way nobody will touch it, put it here.	*Brent is touching the microphone *Pedro takes the microphone away from Brent and places it at another location.

Note. Numbers next to names = the age of the children. The Volunteer Tutor, Pedro, is reading to the students *One Fish, Two Fish, Red Fish, Blue Fish*.

her strategy. Instead of telling Brent to stop, she indicated to her brother to stop reading to maintain order, which he did. Brent listened to Pedro and stopped his misbehavior. It is interesting to note that when Pedro maintained order he code-switched between languages. He was reading in English but when he spoke to the group, he did so in Spanish, thus indicating that he felt more comfortable speaking Spanish to the group then speaking in English.

This circle-time activity directed by Pedro indicated common features that the children internalized about the reading practices in this activity (how to hold the book and how to behave). It is concerning that Pedro did not demonstrate any of the strategies that Patricia and the tutors taught him about reading a book and that the children in the circle did not remind him about them. There could be several reasons why Pedro did not ask comprehension and vocabulary questions. For instance, all the members in this circle were related to each other. The family dynamics might have influenced the reading practices during this activity. Also, Pedro might have been self-conscious about his reading because he was being filmed. In addition, he was a struggling reader, so it seemed that he kept his full attention in just decoding the words as he read.

Despite this, it was interesting to see the younger children becoming assertive by attempting to assume the teacher's role. This could indicate that the circle-time environment prompted children to want to become the teacher, and have a voice during the activity. In the circle time directed by Patricia and the tutors, in general the younger children's voices were seldom heard. In other words, they usually did not attempt to assume the teacher's role. They did interact with the group, but they did not tell the members what to do as they did when Pedro directed the circle. They might have become more assertive because the members of this circle consisted of only the younger members of the organization.

The act of Pedro requesting to direct circle time was a clear indication that he admired the tutors whom participated in after-school program. He stated in his interview that he wanted to be like them. This could show that the non-Latino tutors have been incorporated into the community and were considered as full members of the VIVA organization.

DISCUSSION AND IMPLICATIONS

This study describes how Patricia introduced an activity, circle time, which helped the Latino children and the non-Latino tutors become a community of learning through biliteracy practices. This activity established a set routine for the after-school program, which created a space for Patricia, the tutors, and the children to congregate before the one-on-one tutoring. It allowed Patricia to mentor the tutors in literacy practices, which allowed the tutors and the children to interact as a group and learn from each other.

In the examples described in this chapter, Patricia, the tutors, and the children appeared to benefit from this activity. Patricia benefited by providing an environment where she could accomplish several of her objectives regarding the tutors and the children. She exposed the member to the biliteracy practices she believed would help the children, which established what counted as reading (Castanheira et al., 1998; Green et al., 1992; Green & Meyer, 1991). In addition, through modeling these biliteracy practices she mentored the tutors and established a set routine for the circle time activity thus allowing the tutors and the children to assume the teacher's role and learn from each other. In order for the children and tutors to participate in these practices, they had to develop confianza (Moll, 1992). Patricia created the environment she had envisioned.

The tutors benefited in several ways by being trained at the site. They received immediate support from Patricia if they had difficulty during the circle-time activity. In addition, the immersion of the tutors in the Spanish language and culture gave them a greater understanding of the children they were tutoring. Furthermore, the tutors were incorporated into the community and felt that they were members of the VIVA organization. They were invited to and attended special activities, such as birthday parties that were organized by the families. Through this community-building, the tutors who directed circle time were aided by the other tutors and children as they assumed the teacher's role. The other members provided support in order for reading practices to remain consistent with previous activities.

The children also benefited in having the tutors trained during the circle-time activity. They were exposed to non-Latinos who were interested in their culture and language. The children saw how the tutors struggled with the Spanish language, as they have struggled with the academic environment in their schools. This promoted an interesting dynamic. The tutors were experts in the academic situation, whereas the children were experts in the Spanish language. This enabled children and tutors to share leadership. In addition, the children observed and were involved in the training process of the tutors. They had the opportunity to assume the teacher's role during circle time and knew that their voices would be heard. In this respect, they had an equal standing with the tutors. Through participation in circle time, the children developed bonds with the tutors and some even considered them as role models, which strengthened the community-building in VIVA.

There were also some risks in mentoring the tutors in an immersion environment. These included (a) the organization of the circle time activity; (b) limited input tutors had about the tutoring practices, and (c) the nature of reading practices taught to the children. First, circle time did not have an established curriculum. Patricia developed the lesson minutes before the after-school program started. She then supplied the tutors with the materials they were going to use in the circle time before it began, but this did not allow the tutor to prepare a lesson about the book or to organize vocabulary or comprehension questions. In fact, the tutors were not required to write lesson plans; they were mentored to teach in the moment. This established a teaching environment where the tutors could perform poorly in front of the group of children. The circle time Patricia directed explicitly told the tutors what was expected from them. Most of the tutors did not do what Patricia said and failed to assume the teacher's role. This may account for the fact that most of the tutors came to the tutoring session erratically. It also placed the tutors in a stressful situation, although this notion of thinking on their feet as they taught did create a supportive environment between the tutors and the children.

Second, it did not provide a space for the tutors to reflect on their tutoring practices. Lubeck (1996) states that it is important for teachers to think critically and interrogate their assumptions about teaching and learning. Although she refers to teachers, I argue that it is equally important for tutors to reflect on their own practice. Tutors did not have an opportunity to discuss their successes or worries about how they directed circle time with each other or with Patricia.

Finally, the reading practices that were negotiated by the members of the group need to be analyzed further to understand the extent to which they are beneficial for the children. The reading strategies focusing on comprehension, vocabulary learning and active participation may hinder the children from developing critical thinking skills about the texts, because the majority of the responses were based on the text. Most of the questions did not require the students to consider information that was implicit. Furthermore, themes were not developed during these reading practices, so the information the student learned was erratic. There was no continuity from one lesson to another. Moreover, it is not known whether these reading practices transferred to the reading practices in the one-on-one tutoring sessions.

This study suggests questions that could be researched further. In particular, the formation of a group dynamic that focuses on children assuming the teaching role; the effects of the organization of circle time on the tutors and children; and the benefits and limitations of the reading practices in circle time. Circle time had a role in developing a particular dynamic between tutors and children, but there is a need to investigate how it came to be established. The organization of circle time provided an atmosphere where the tutors learned to accept instruction from the teacher and the children. In addition, it promoted collaboration between the tutors and the children who helped each other to establish and maintain the reading practices. Further research is needed to describe the limitations and benefits of this "mentoring" practice. Finally, it is important to identify the reading skills the children are acquiring through circle time. Specifically, are these skills helping the children in schools and at home when they are expected to read a new book?

Circle time became a mentoring platform for the non-Latino tutors to learn about the reading practices and the culture of the VIVA community. The original purpose of this activity was not to mentor the tutors in becoming reading "teachers" in circle time, but to provide a venue for teaching the tutors how to conduct circle time and become incorporated into the community. Judging these practices by the criteria of Wasik (1998), this program would not be considered successful. Yet, one might argue that this program was successful in providing the opportunity for non-Latino tutors and children to interact and establish a community. Both of these groups were able to assume the teacher's role through negotiation and mutual support, in order to maintain VIVA's reading practices in circle time.

REFERENCES

Agar, M. (1994). *Understanding the culture of conversation.* New York: Quill.

Aspiazu, G. G., Bauer, S. C., & Spillett, M. D. (1998). Improving the academic performance of Hispanic youth: A community education model. *Bilingual Research Journal, 22*(2-4), 127-147.

Castanheira, M., Crawford, T., Dixon, C., & Green, J. (1998). Interactional ethnography: An approach to studying the social construction of literate practices. In J. J. Cummings, C. M. Wyatt-Smith, J. Ryan, & S. M. Doig (Eds.), *Literacy–curriculum connections: Implications for theory and practice. Commission paper to the Literacy Curriculum Interface: The literacy Demands of the Curriculum in Post-Compulsory Schooling Project.* Washington, DC: Department of Employment, Education, Training, and Youth Affairs and Griffith University.

Crawford, T., Castanheira, M., Dixon, C., & Green, J. (2001). What counts as literacy: An interactional ethnographic perspective. In J. J. Cummings & C. M. Wyatt-Smith (Eds.), *Literacy and the curriculum: Success in senior secondary schooling.* Sidney: The Australian Council for Educational Research Ltd.

Erickson, F. (1986). Qualitative methods in research on teaching. In M. Wittrock (Ed.), *Handbook of research on teaching* (pp. 119-161). New York: MacMillan.

Ferdman, B. M. (1990). Literacy and cultural identity. *Harvard Educational Review, 60*(2), 181-204.

Floriani, A. (1993). Negotiating what counts: Roles and relationships, texts and contexts, content and meaning. *Linguistics and Education, 5,* 241-274.

Fox, G. E. (1996). *Hispanic nation: Culture, politics and the constructing of identity.* New York: Birch Lane Press.

Freire, P., & Macedo, D. (1987). *Literacy: Reading the word and the world.* Westport, CT: Bergin & Garvey.

Gee, J. P. (1991). What is literacy? In C. Mitchell & K. Weiler (Eds.), *Rewriting literacy: Culture and the discourse of the others* (pp. 3-12). New York: Bergin & Garvey.

Gee, J. P. (1999). *An introduction to discourse analysis: Theory and method.* London: Routledge.

Green, J., Dixon, C., Lin, L., Floriani, A., Bradley, M., Paxton, S., Mattern, C., & Bergamo, H. (1992). Constructing literacy in classrooms: Literacy action as social accomplishment. In H. H. Marshall (Ed.), *Redefining student learning* (pp. 119-150). Norwood, NJ: Ablex.

Green, J. L., & Dixon, C. A. (1993). Introduction to talking knowledge into being: Discursive and social practices in classrooms. *Linguistics and Education, 5* (3&4), 231-240.

Green, J. L., Dixon, C. N., & Zaharlick, A. (2001). Ethnography as a logic of inquiry. In J. Flood, M. J. Jensen, D. Lapp, & R. J. Squire (Eds.), *The handbook for research in the teaching of the english language* (pp. 201-224). Mahwah, NJ: Erlbaum.

Green, J. L., & Meyer, L. A. (1991). The embeddedness of reading in classroom life: Reading as a situated process. In C. Baker & A. Luke (Eds.), *Toward a critical sociology of reading pedagogy* (pp. 141-160). Philadelphia: John Benjamins.

Hicks, D. (1995). Discourse, learning and teaching. In M. Apple (Ed.), *Review of research in education* (Vol. 21, pp. 49-95). Washington, DC: AERA.

Leslie, L., & Caldwell, J. (1995). *Qualitative reading inventory-II*. New York: HarperCollins College Publishers.

Lubeck, S. (1996). Deconstructing "child development knowledge" and "teacher preparation." *Early Childhood Research Quarterly, 11*, 147-167.

Marsh, L. (1995). A Spanish dual literacy program: Teaching to the whole student. *The Bilingual Research Journal, 19*(3-4), 409-428.

Mehan, H. (1979). "What time is it, Denise?": Asking known information questions in classroom discourse. *Theory into Practice, 18*(4), 285-294.

Meyer, V., & Keefe, D. (1998). Supporting volunteer tutors: Five strategies. *Adult Basic Education, 8*(2), 59-67.

Moll, L. C. (1992). Funds of knowledge for teaching: Using a qualitative approach to connect homes and classrooms. *Theory Into Practice, 31*(2), 132-141.

National Center for Education Statistics. (1998a). *Mini-digest of education statistics 1997*. Washington DC: U. S. Department of Education.

National Center for Education Statistics. (1998b). *Report in brief. NAEP 1996 trends in academic progress*. Washington DC: U.S. Department of Education.

Osher, D., & Mejia, B. (1999). Overcoming barriers to intercultural relationships. *Reaching Today's Youth, 2*, 48-52.

Quintero, E., & Huerta-Macias, A. (1990). All in the family: Bilingualism and biliteracy. *The Reading Teacher, 44*(4), 306-312.

Reisner, E. R., Petry, C. A., & Armitage, M. (1990). *A review of programs involving college students as tutors or mentors in grades K-12* (Vol. 1). Washington, DC: Policy Studies Associates.

Rex, L. A. (2000). Judy constructs a genuine question: A case of interactional inclusion. *Teaching and Teacher Education, 16*, 315-333.

Rex, L. A. (2001). The remaking of a high school reader. *Reading Research Quarterly, 36*(3), 288-314.

Snow, C. E., Burns, M. S., & Griffin, P. (Eds.). (1998). *Preventing reading difficulties in young children*. Washington, DC: National Academy Press.

Spencer, J. W. (1994). Mutual relevance of ethnography and discourse. *Journal of Contemporary Ethnography, 23*(3), 267-279.

Tuyay, S., Jennings, L., & Dixon, C. (1995). Classroom discourse and opportunities to learn: An ethnographic study of knowledge construction in a bilingual third grade classroom. *Discourse Processes, 19*(1), 75-110.

Vadasy, P. F., Jenkins, J. R., & Pool, K. (2000). Effects of tutoring in phonological and early reading skills on students at risk for reading disabilities. *Journal of Learning Disabilities, 33*(4), 579-590.

Wasik, B. A. (1998). Using volunteers as reading tutors: Guidelines for successful practices. *The Reading Teacher, 51*(7), 562-570.

5

Using Sociocultural and Developmental/Cognitive Lenses to Inform Classroom-Based Assessments of Children's Reading

Carol McDonald Connor

Lesley A. Rex

The 1997 reauthorization of the Individuals with Disabilities Act (IDEA), recent policy changes (Act, 2002; Neuman, 2002), and standards-based reform, including the No Child Left Behind Act (www.ed.gov/nclb), have significantly changed the role of the speech-language pathologist and reading specialist toward one of classroom-based assessment and services, collaborative consultation with teachers, and curriculum-based intervention (Whitmire, 2000). Standards-based reform has mandated that all students, including those with special needs, be evaluated in terms of performance standards (Elmore, 1999-2000). Furthermore, as studies have demonstrated a critical link between oral language and reading (Dickinson & Tabors, 2001), speech-language pathologists in the schools are called on to support students who are facing challenges as they learn how to read (ASHA, 2001). Thus, speech-language pathologists and other reading specialists are entering classrooms and collaborating with teachers to both assess and provide intervention for children who are experiencing reading difficulties. However, specialists and teachers may use very different lenses when thinking about how best to help struggling readers.

Frequently, speech-language pathologists and reading specialists use a developmental or cognitive lens whereby they focus on the individual child's strengths and weakness compared to well-accepted developmental milestones (Hallahan, Kauffman, & Lloyd, 1999; Miller, 1981). In contrast, many teachers and educational researchers (Green & Meyer, 1991) focus on the classroom environment as a whole, on the child within the classroom environment, on individual readers in the context of multiple readers, and on the classroom as a reading community (Atwell, 1998). Explicitly or implicitly, many teachers and educational researchers use a sociocultural lens. The child is one of many, classroom dynamics are paramount, and the culture of the classroom constructs what counts as learning and what successful reading looks like (Rogers, Tyson, & Marshall, 2000).

In this chapter, we present two students. Roland, a good reader and Demario, a struggling reader. Our purpose is to provide a demonstration of classroom-based assessment that uses developmental and sociocultural lenses to advantage with each offering important but different views of children in the classroom and each providing multiple strategies to support both struggling and capable readers. Such research becomes increasingly important as school speech-language pathologists and reading specialists work with teachers to adopt a classroom-based model for assessment and intervention.

THEORETICAL FRAMEWORK

Two definitions of reading, one developmental/cognitive and the other sociocultural, afford a different view of what it means to be a reader and what constitutes the skill of reading. Depending on which definition of reading is used as a lens for looking at student readers and reading instruction, different aspects of literacy become salient. Teachers and specialists who can apply multiple definitions of reading can gain more complete understandings as to why children are struggling with reading and, in turn, better assist their students in becoming proficient readers within a reading culture.

Developmental/Cognitive Lens

Using a developmental/cognitive lens, we can describe reading as a complex cognitive activity that incorporates a set of skills that can be learned, taught, and tested (Rayner, Foorman, Perfetti, Pesetsky, & Seidenberg, 2001). Juel (1991) observes that it was not until researchers focused on the processes, traits, and skills children needed to become proficient readers rather than what teachers should or should not do in the classroom, that significant progress was made in helping children with reading difficulties. These processes and skills include attention to print, phonological and morphosyntactic awareness, understanding letter–sound relationships, word decoding, fluency, comprehension, and metacognitive strategies (Rayner et al., 2001). Comparative peer milestones, standards, and benchmarks provide the foundation for setting appropriate expectations for student achievement at particular grades. From this perspective, teachers and specialists look for their students' demonstrations of the skills they need in order to become proficient readers and then focus on instilling or improving these skills. For example, studies have found that if a child's phonological awareness is improved, then his or her ability to decode text will also improve (National Reading Panel, 2000). These studies have led to the implementation of pedagogical and curricula techniques for explicit teaching of phonological awareness and grapheme–phoneme correspondence.

Researchers investigating reading using a developmental/cognitive lens have used a wide variety of standardized tests and informal tasks. Standardized tests (e.g., Balow, Farr, & Hogan, 1992; Wiederholt & Bryant, 1992; Woodcock, 1987; Woodcock & Johnson, 1989, 1990) compare children's performance to that of a representative sample of their developmental peers. Informal tasks may be used to gain better understanding of overall reading capabilities, for example, miscue analysis (Goodman, 1972) or specific capabilities such as phonological awareness (Perfetti, Beck, Bell, & Hughes, 1987) and comprehension (e.g., (Palincsar & Brown, 1984; Pressley & Wharton-McDonald, 1997; Snow, 2001). Furthermore, research indicates that children who enter school with different language and reading abilities may need very different types of instruction (Connor, Morrison, & Katch, 2004; Connor, Morrison, & Petrella, 2004).

Sociocultural Lens

A sociocultural lens looks at reading as a situated classroom practice (Baker & Luke, 1991; Heap, 1991; Street, 1995). Using this lens reveals the importance of social and cultural features of reading within specific times and places. Reading observed as varied forms of sociocultural practices becomes what readers and teachers do together to establish what counts as reading in particular places, during certain events, and within particular relationships. Any occasion in which a piece of text is integral to the participants' interactions or their interpretative processes, as in math or science activities, is a reading occasion (Heath, 1982). Therefore learning to read or being a reader is not limited to specific moments of reading or language arts instruction.

Sociolinguists (Gumperz, 1972) and ethnomethodologists (Baker & Luke, 1991; Heap, 1991) have contributed to a social view of reading by studying it as a dialogue or interaction between the people engaged in the teaching and learning of what counts as reading during classroom activity (Bloome, 1993; Heath, 1982). As the students "read" with their teacher and classmates, they are not engaged in a generic or natural process. They are meeting the academic and social demands for participation with and about the text that are being constructed in the moment and over time in their interactions with their teacher and classmates (Green & Meyer, 1991). By understanding the sociocultural and sociolinguistic definitions of reading, specialists and teachers, working together, may take steps to shape classroom discourses to better support students' reading practices.

METHODS

Participants

Student Participant. Demario[1] and Roland were third-grade African-American boys (see Table 5.1) both of whom were in Mrs. Frank's class. Demario qualified for free and reduced lunch upon entry to school, indicating that he came from a low-income family, whereas Roland did not qualify for the free and reduced lunch program. More detailed information about the boys is provided in the results.

Teacher Participant. Mrs. Frank, who was Euro-American, had been teaching for 15 years at the time of this study and had been a Title I teacher for 4 years. She reported that, although she was discouraged, she kept teaching because, "it's the way out. It's your ticket out and these kids need a ticket out." She stated, "I wish I was affecting 80% of my class, when I'm in all probability I do believe today I'm probably only affecting 20%." When asked what she, as a third-grade teacher could do about children like Demario who have not learned to read well in first and second grade, she said, "That's a great question. I mean we [all of the teachers at the school] talk about it . . . every day. What do we do with these kids that just can't read . . . If you guys ever figure out the answer let me know." Mrs. Frank agreed to participate in the study because she wanted to learn more about how she could help Demario improve his reading

Mrs. Frank describes her approach to teaching reading as eclectic. "I do what works with these kids." However, she was trained in Project Read, which she believes is very important for working with "high-risk minority" students. She reported that she uses phonological word-attack strategies when she reviews vocabulary prior to round robin reading. She also uses "lots of literature" (e.g., *Charlotte's Web*) with the entire

---

[1]All names used are pseudonyms.

Table 5.1. Descriptive Information About Demario and Roland

	DEMARIO	ROLAND
Grade in school	Third	Third
Age at time of observation	8 years, 2 months	8 years, 1 month
Teacher report of reading ability	Struggling	Very able
Use of African-American English	Yes	Yes
Results of Metropolitan Achievement Tests–Reading (MAT) in Spring of second grade	8th percentile	97th percentile
History of special education	None	None
Percentage of appropriate related responses	100%	100%
Total number of miscues reading aloud during Reading 2	22	7

class through a whole-language approach. She describes this approach as the use of guided reading of authentic texts by applying the KWL method (What you Know; what you Want to learn; and, what you Learned) and guiding the children in using contextual clues to support their comprehension.

Mrs. Frank's classroom is located in a school in a large midwest metropolitan city in which 70% of the 506 children enrolled are African American and 34% qualify for free and reduced lunch (NCES, 1999). Her classroom and the school maintain a climate of well-controlled order. Similar to other elementary schools in the district, the school is clean, bright, and well maintained. Children are encouraged to wear uniforms and classes pass through the hallways in straight lines with arms crossed and surprisingly little chatter. State-wide standardized achievement test results have increased over the past decade; a graph comparing their school-wide performance on the tests in 1992, at the 15th percentile, with their performance in 1998, at the 54th percentile, was prominently displayed on the school office window.

Research Approach and Design

Within a developmental/cognitive lens, this study may be described as a case study. Observations in the classroom coupled with individual assessments of the two students provide an evaluation of their reading abilities as they relate to other children in the classroom, as well as to test standardization samples. In the tradition of ethnographic case studies, this study is meant as a telling case (Mitchell, 1984). "Tellings," or analytical inductions, can elaborate on understandings already in development or point to issues not yet raised. Therefore, by focusing on a particular, naturally occurring case of classroom teaching, this study is intended to "tell" us something about assessment in the classroom and classroom practices as they relate to children's reading. Combining the information gleaned using both lenses—developmental and sociocultural—provides information about the two students that would have been unavailable had one lens alone been used.

Data Collection and Analysis

Reading and oral-language assessment data for Demario and Roland were collected from school documents and from classroom observation data, which were gathered using fieldnotes, a video camera, and an audiorecording system. During classroom observations, students' written work was obtained, as were copies of the materials used (i.e., the book and the science worksheet), and Mrs. Frank and the boys were informally interviewed. Mrs. Frank was formally interviewed before and after classroom observations. Observations of the school building and classrooms within the school had been ongoing since the year prior to this study. Classroom observations, starting on the 21st day of instruction, occurred 2 or 3 days per week, leading up to the observations of the reading and science lessons on Days 24, 30, and 34. On Day 40, in a taped interview, the teacher and researcher reviewed the videotapes of the reading and science lessons. Informal and phone interviews with the teacher were conducted through the end of the school year. Demario's progress was monitored for an additional 2 years. Roland left the school district the following year.

Developmental/Cognitive Assessment. The videotapes and audiotapes were first transcribed using Child Language Data Exchange System (CHILDES), in the CHAT transcription and coding format (MacWhinney, 1994). This transcription system made possible analysis of spontaneous language samples of individual students. Approximately 15% of the transcripts were re-transcribed by a speech-language pathologist not associated with this study and reliability calculated. Comparison of the transcripts yielded 92% agreement between the two speech-language pathologists at the level of the word.

Transcripts were coded at several levels. First, using coding systems developed to quantify the features of African-American English (AAE) used by children (J. Washington, Craig, & Kushmaul, 1998), representative samples of classroom discourse were analyzed.

Additionally, these samples were coded for related verbal responses in spontaneous classroom discourse in order to rule out possible oral-language impairments. Responses to comments rather than questions may be revealing because they represent an important regulator for adults' discourse (Sacks, Schegloff, & Jefferson, 1974; Weiner & Goodenough, 1977) and for children's as well (Keenan, 1977), and reflect "formal knowledge of the structure of conversation" (Craig & Gallagher, 1986, p. 375). Furthermore, it provides an opportunity to characterize the oral-language skills children use in the classroom. This method may be particularly useful for children over 5 years of age for whom mean length of utterance (MLU) may be less informative (Miller, 1981). There is evidence that children with specific language impairment may demonstrate a greater proportion of unrelated responses that do children with typical language skills (Craig & Gallagher, 1986).

The transcripts were also used to accomplish miscue analyses of children's classroom oral readings (Goodman, 1972; Pumfrey & Fletcher, 1989; Wiederholt & Bryant, 1992). These analyses were used to assess each boy's overall reading ability as well as to investigate specific use of decoding strategies (Rayner et al., 2001).

Sociocultural Lens. On a more micro scale, using the transcripts, we observed classroom talk around texts as sequences of specific dialogue between class members. We transcribed and analyzed key sequences by applying methods that organize class members' conversation as turns of talk (e.g., Lerner, 1995). Our method of transcription made visible how speakers, through contextualization cues, respond to what their dialogue partners have said based on what they think they meant (Gumperz, 1992). Our analyses of sequences of linguistic actions and reactions during reading events made it possible to observe whether opportunities to learn about reading were or were not made available or taken up (see also (Rex, in press; Rex & McEachen, 1999)

Similar to interactional ethnographic methods (Castanheira et al., 2001) employed by Tuyay, Jennings, and Dixon (1995), we used structuration mapping. Structuration maps are any number of visual representations of the contexts constructed by participants as they interact over time (Green & Wallat, 1981). Although we made our structuration maps from videotapes, such maps can be made while observing classroom literacy events. During this study, we mapped three literacy events—Reading 1, Science, and Reading 2—to display the chronology of literate activity during the three events as phases of talk comprised of either sequences of reading activity or talk around text. Our maps represent who was talking to whom and for how long.

RESULTS

Evaluation of Children's Oral Language and Reading Abilities

Cognitive-Developmental Lens

Based on a review of his school records, Demario had no previous history of referral to special education or for speech or language therapy. During all of his interactions with the examiner, Demario was cooperative, engaging, and eager to please. Based on the analysis of transcripts, he was observed using AAE during classroom discourse and during one-on-one conversations with the first author.

According to Mrs. Frank, his teacher, Demario, was a struggling reader, especially with regard to comprehension of text. The school administered the *Metropolitan Achievement Test—Edition* (MAT: Balow et al., 1992), which is a group-administered general achievement test, to all of the first-, second-, and third-grade children in the spring of Demario's second-grade year. Demario scored at the 2nd percentile on the reading vocabulary test and at the 17th percentile on the reading comprehension test, yielding a composite score at the 8th percentile for his grade—more than a full grade level below expectations for his age and grade in school. Although caution must be used in interpreting a standardized group-administered test that is administered to African-American children (Jencks & Phillips, 1998; J. A. Washington, 1996), the results of the standardized tests appeared to confirm Mrs. Frank's assessments of Demario's reading capabilities.

According to Roland's school record, he had no history of referral to special education. He was an engaging child and was cooperative in all interactions with the investigator. He also used features of AAE during classroom discourse and during individual conversations with the examiner as evidenced in the transcripts. According to Mrs. Frank, Roland, was reading at or slightly above grade level. Results of the MAT for Roland contrasted sharply with those for Demario. Roland scored in the 97th percentile for the reading composite. The standardized test score appeared to confirm, indeed exceed, Mrs. Frank's assessment of Roland's reading abilities.

Assessment of Oral Language Skill. We completed an analysis of Demario's and Roland's related verbal responses in spontaneous classroom discourse in order to rule out possible oral-language impairments. Based on transcriptions of discourse during Reading 1 and 2, as well as Science lessons, and using the methods described previously, other-directed comments from peers, teacher, and researcher were identified. Each boy's response was then coded as no response, unrelated response, request for clarification, or related response (see Table 5.1). Nine other-directed comments were available for Demario's response. Of these, he provided a related response to all of them. For example, one was a nonverbal "thumbs-up" sign in response to the investigator's comment "I better get out of the way." Eight other-directed comments were available for Roland's response. Seven elicited related responses and one elicited a request for clarification. For example, in response to the teacher's comment, "Tripped over the trough," Roland responded, "Yeah."

Both boys were able to provide related responses. Thus, based on these analyses, in conjunction with absence of referral for special education in the school records, both Demario and Roland appeared to be capable oral communicators with no indication of specific language impairment. Although teacher report and standardized test scores indicated widely variant reading capabilities, the boys' oral-language communication skills appeared to be well within the typical range.

Assessment of Reading. Miscue analysis of oral reading was used to assess each boy's overall reading ability as well as to investigate specific use of decoding strategies. Deviations from the printed text were recorded, counted, and then categorized based on the type of decoding strategy evidenced including morphosyntactic, semantic, and phonological strategies as well as no strategy. For example, if the miscue belonged to the same syntactic class and/or shared a morpheme and did not substantially change the grammatical structure of the sentence, it was considered a morphosyntactic strategy. If the miscue did not substantially change the meaning of the text, it was considered a semantic strategy. If there existed evidence of word segmentation at the level of the phoneme, morpheme, or syllable, or if the miscue was phonologically similar to the target (at least the first three phonemes), it was considered a phonological strategy. One deviation from text might be represented by more than one strategy. Use of AAE was not (and should not be) considered a miscue (e.g., Hunt, 1974-1975). Self-corrections were also recorded (see Tables 5.2 and 5.3).

Demario had 22 miscues (see Table 5.2). For 16 of these, he waited for classmates and/or the teacher to provide the word rather than using a word-attack strategy. He made no attempt to sound out words by breaking them into their phonemic constituents and few attempts to infer them from context. Primary word-attack strategies appeared to be guessing and relying on the semantic and syntactic sense of the sentence (six of the miscues) rather than the phonological structure of the word (two of the miscues). For example, in reading the line "So far, said Zuckerman," Demario said "so then" and omitted "said Zuckerman."

Table 5.2. Demario Reading Aloud During Reading 2

	TEACHER	DEMARIO	CLASSMATES	BOOK
1	hold on a second ... Demario, you're gonna read ... go...real loud...scream			
2		When Mister &uh Zuckerman got back to the house		When Mister Zuckerman got back to the house
3		He took all his work clothes and put on his best shirt		He took off his work clothes and put on his best suit
4		Then he get into the car and		Then he got into his car and
5				
6		his car and drove to the	His car	drove to the minister's house
7	minister's			
8		minister's house ... he stayed for an hour		he stayed for an hour
9			for	and explained to the minister
10		and		
11			explained	
12		explained to to the minister that		
13			that	that a miracle had happened
14		that		on the farm
15			a miracle	

164

#				
16		a miracle had happened on the farm		
17		so then		So far
18	so far		so far	
19		xxx only four people on		said Zuckerman, only four people on earth
20	earth			
21		earth know about the this miracle … myself, you, my		know about this miracle, My self, my wife Edith
22			my	
23	hold on Demario			
24	myself		myself	
25		my wife		
26			Edith	my hired man, Lurvy
27		my		
28	hired			
29		hired man Lurvy and you		and you.
30	now only four people know about this miracle			
31	tell me who, Demario			
32	myself			
33		myself xxx		
34	read it up/ read it/ read it			
35		myself	myself	
36			my wife	

Table 5.2. Demario Reading Aloud During Reading 2 (continued)

	TEACHER	DEMARIO	CLASSMATES	BOOK
37		my wife Edith		
38			Edith	
39		my		
40	hired			
41		hired man Lurvy and you		
42	Real loud... keep going			
43		Don't tell anybody		
44			He shoulda xxx	
45		Oh yeah		
46	Don't tell anybody else			
47		Don't tell anybody else said the minister. We don't know what it means ... yet ... but ...		"Don't tell anybody else," said the minister. "We don't know what it means yet, but perhaps if I give thought to it I can explain it in my sermon next Sunday."
48	Perhaps			
49		Perhaps if I give thought to it I can explain it in my ...		
50			sermon	
51		sermon next Sunday.		

Line				
52		There can be no		There can be no doubt that you have a most unusual pig.
53		doubt that you have	doubt	
54				
55		have a	have a	
56	most unusual			
57		most unusual pig.		
58				
59		I		
60	intend		intend	
61		intend to speak about it in my sermon.	xxx	I intend to speak about it in my sermon.
62	no... sermon. And point out			and point out the fact that this community has been visited with a wondrous animal.
63		And point out this fantastic		
64	no look...point out the fact			
65		the fact that		
66	community			
67		community has been		
68			visited	
69		visted with a		
70	wondrous		wondrous	
71		wondrous animal		
72		By the way, does the pig have a name?		By the way, does the pig have a name?
73	Good Demario.... Look at the picture over there			

167

Table 5.2. Demario Reading Aloud During Reading 2 *(continued)*

	TEACHER	DEMARIO	CLASSMATES	BOOK
74		it's crowd		
75	the minister has just said, don't tell anybody ... and Zuckerman says nobody but four people... who?			
76	the minister	Mister Zuckerman	minister	
77			xxx	
78	well hold on ... the minister says who knows about it... and Zuckerman says ... me, my wife, my hired hand Lurvy, and you.			
79		me, my wife, my hired hand Lurvy, and you		
80	the minister you ... he said don't tell anybody else but look at that picture ... think anybody told?			
81		no		
82	look at the picture on eighty-three		no	
83		yes	yes	
84	looks like everybody's coming to check this out huh? Something out of the ordinary and very usual is happening here.			

Table 5.3. Roland Reading Aloud During Reading 2

	TEACHER	ROLAND	STUDENTS	BOOK
1	go Roland			
2		well I don't really know yet said Mister Zuckerman ... man		Well, I really don't know yet, said Mister Zucker (hyphen) man
3	Zuckerman... see how it went on to the next line?			
4		Mister Zuckerman		
5		but we have seen the sign ... Edith ... a mystery		But we have received a sign, Edith -- a mysterious sign
6	a mysterious sign			
7		a mysterious sign	a mysterious sign (choral response)	
8		a miracle has happened on this farm		
9		there is a large spider ... web in the doorway of the barn ... cellar right ... over the pigpen.		There is a large spider's web in the doorway of the barn cellar, right over the pigpen.
10		and when Lurvy went to feed the pig he noticed the web because ... it was foggy.		and when Lurvy went to feed the pig this morning, he noticed the web because it was foggy,
11		And you know how spider ... webs ... spider webs look very &dis ...		And you know how a spider's web looks very distinct in a fog
12	Distinct	Distinct	Distinct	
13		in a fog		

169

Table 5.3. Roland Reading Aloud During Reading 2 *(continued)*

	TEACHER	ROLAND	STUDENTS	BOOK
14		and right bang in the middle		And right spang in the middle of the web there were the, words Some Pig
15			of the web	
16		of the web there were the words some pig		
17		the words		The words were woven right into the web
18	woven			
19			woven	
20		Woven ... right into the web ... they were actually part of the web		
21		Is		I
22			&ch	
23		(Raven says next line loudly, forestalling interruption) I know because I have been down there and seen them it says some pig		I know because I have been down there.
24		just as clear as clear can be		
25		&thi there can be no mistake about it		There can be no mistake about it
26		a miracle has happened ... and a sign has appeared ... appeared		A miracle has happened and a sign has occurred here on Earth, right on our farm, and we have no ordinary pig

Line			
27	occurred	occurred	
28			
29		here on earth right on our farm and we have no ordinary pig	
30	hey Roland ... stop for a second ... we have no ordinary pig. What are they planning to do with Wilbur?		
31		kill him	
32	in fact ... the old sheep ... in that test we just took. Right? The old sheep said ... I don't like to spread bad news ... but ... they're fattening you up		
33		to kill	
34			kill
35	xxx for Christmas dinner right		
36		yeah	yeah
37	And now they're saying ... we don't have an ordinary pig here. Think they're changing their mind a little bit?		
38		yeah	yeah

Struggling readers may rely less on phonological strategies and more on semantic and syntactic cues (Stanovich, 1980; West, Stanovich, Freeman, & Cunningham, 1983) and this appeared to be the case for Demario. This analysis also revealed that Demario was relying on the teacher and his classmates to supply words rather than trying to figure them out for himself. Overall, Demario exhibited serious difficulties with reading, which required immediate intervention.

The miscue analysis of Roland's reading during Reading 2 (see Table 5.3) indicated that he had only six miscues. One was due to misreading punctuation, one differed morphologically but the base word was the same, one he started to sound out but classmates provided it for him, and in one he said, "appeared" for "occurred." Additionally, he evidenced phonological awareness in his word-attack strategies. For example, in reading the line, "There can be no mistake about it," Roland said "thi . . . there can be no mistake about it." In only two instances did he let the teacher or his classmates provide the word for him, and in one of them he sounded out the word "distinct" for himself at the same time that the teacher supplied it. In two of the miscues, there is evidence of semantic and morphosyntactic strategies, whereas in five of the miscues he demonstrated use of phonological strategies. Based on these results, Roland exhibited strong reading skills.

3-Sociocultural Lens

The teacher used a variation of round-robin reading for teaching reading. We observed closely how this method was constructed during two lessons—Reading 1 and Reading 2 events. The structuration maps for the two lessons revealed very similar structures and organization across the two events (see Fig. 5.1). Using the text *Charlotte's Web* (White, 1952), the teacher began the reading lesson by asking the entire class questions about what they had read previously in an Inquiry-Response-Evaluation (IRE) interactional sequence (Mehan, 1985). The IRE sequence—teacher asks a question; student answers; teacher evaluates student answer—is one of the most frequently observed and contested classroom instructional patterns (Cazden, 1986, 1988). Examples may be found in both Tables 5.2 and 5.3. Then the teacher called on a student to read aloud. Occasionally during the reading, the teacher interrupted to ask questions, again frequently using an IRE sequence. The child then finished reading the paragraph; the teacher asked questions, which the reading child and the other students answered, sometimes in unison; and, the next child was called on to read. If the child reading aloud paused, presumably because the next word was unknown, or if the child misread a word, other students and sometimes the teacher would immediately call out the word. The child would then repeat the word and continue reading.

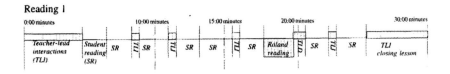

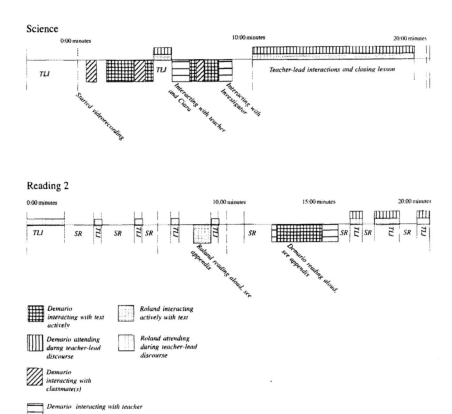

FIGURE 5.1. Structuration maps of the various discourse events, which involve the teacher, students, and investigator, occurring within the classroom during Reading 1, Science, and Reading 2. Note that shaded areas above the line represent Demario's and Roland's individual activity, whereas shaded areas below the line represent the activity of the class as a whole.

These patterns indicate that the procedural rules associated with this round-robin format were common to and consistently exercised by all members of this classroom. These patterns were evident in both Roland's and Demario's readings. This and additional evidence, some of which follows, indicate that both boys knew the social and academic rules for round-robin reading in their class. Thus, we could rule out the hypothesis that Demario did not understand what to do. When Demario failed to engage in round-robin reading it most likely did not pertain to his lack of understanding of social and academic expectations.

Analysis of the classroom observation using the structuration map for the Reading 1 lesson (Fig. 1) indicated that Demario did not actively participate in the classroom discourse. He did not interact with either teacher or classmates, did not raise his hand, or help other students with words they did not know—all common procedures in the round-robin reading. His interactions with the book may be interpreted as lacking focused engagement with text. They included flipping pages, turning the book upside down, standing the book upright on his desk, and putting his head down on his desk next to his book. Only one time during the Reading 1 observation did he track print, and video evidence indicates he was on the wrong page. The teacher did not call on him to read, nor did she interact with him during the observation time. When asked during the interview, while watching the video, about this behavior she stated, "Very common . . . very common . . . still." "Oh, I'm familiar with that . . . constant for me."

Roland's reading during the same round-robin lessons provided an important additional contribution to classroom-based assessment. For example, in this instance, Roland's reading behavior and his teacher's perception of it differed from her perception of Demario's in a number of important ways. Roland demonstrated consistent focused engagement with the text and was called on to read for a significantly longer length of time compared to other students (see structuration maps in Fig. 1); and, as miscue analysis indicated, Roland took the initiative to figure out his own meanings for the text.

This kind of observed classroom reading behavior, employing miscue analysis and structuration maps, concurs with the standardized test results and the teacher's perception of the two boys' different reading profiles. However, we have only seen Demario and Roland in a single literacy context, round-robin reading. Based on that limited view, we see Demario struggling and lacking initiative in stark contrast to Roland. Although this is useful information, it is insufficient and could lead to an incomplete intervention plan if Demario and Roland are only observed reading in a single classroom context and these are the only measures from which intervention is planned.

Multiple Views of Children's Reading

Using a sociocultural lens, we examined the discursive features of the reading activities. By situating readers within the context of a classroom culture, we investigated discourse dynamics as members of the class engaged in literacy events. From the perspective of the classroom as a discourse culture (SBDG, 1992) or speech community (Hymes, 1974), Demario's struggle with text may have built a barrier to full participation as a member of this classroom discourse community. Or, his struggle may have constructed a particular role for him within this reading culture as a deficient reader who needed particular kinds of support. In addition, his teacher may have been contributing to Demario's role as a struggling reader in the classroom through her discourse actions and the perceptions on which they were based. If these hypotheses proved to be valid, then an important aspect of intervention might include redefining the reading culture of the classroom and shaping the normative social and academic literacy practices constructed through teacher–child interactions.

These possible hypotheses led us to ask whether there were occasions during reading events in this classroom that did *not* reinforce Demario's role as a struggling reader. Given his demonstrated competence as an oral communicator, we wondered if he might be more successful within discourses that privileged oral communication as well as interaction with text, which might help him talk his text into being (Tuyay, Jennings, & Dixon, 1995). If so, the developmental perspective view of Demario's reading difficulties, established using test scores, teacher report, and miscue analysis, could be contrasted with a situated view of Demario as a reader who, within certain situations, exhibited capable reading behavior.

"Hands-on science" as practiced in Mrs. Frank's classroom offered opportunities for multiple conversations around text. For the first 9 minutes of the hands-on phase of the lesson, students were paired to promote interaction and shared observation. They worked together in pairs while the teacher and the Title I teacher wandered around the room providing feedback and encouragement. Each child was given a worksheet, a glass full of soda, some raisins, and some popcorn kernels. Students placed the raisins and popcorn kernels in the glass and then observed and reported their findings. Prior to the onset of taping, the teacher had led the children in formulating hypotheses about what would occur with the raisins and popcorn in the soda.

Our observations of literacy activities during Science showed Demario to be considerably more involved in this environment. The science structuration map (Fig. 5.1) makes visible Demario's consistent interaction with text, classmates, and his teacher throughout the 16-

minute lesson. Fully one third of Demario's time during the hands-on portion of the session was devoted to writing and reading his writing, with a fair amount of time spent erasing and rewriting. Video data indicate that he co-constructed two texts as he worked on the write-up with his student partner, Ciara, who the teacher identified as a capable student. Demario conversed with her about the worksheet text and her writing on her worksheet. For example, after observing Ciara drawing an arrow he leaned in close to the text and declared, "Got a arrow." By commenting to his partner about what she was writing on her paper, he indicated he was reading her paper, which meant he was reading the science worksheet genre and understood how to participate in the construction of such texts as well as how to comprehend the meaning of texts constructed by others. Both Ciara's and Demario's texts stated the results that Demario had raised to the teacher—"look at our raisins. . . they're melting" and both contained arrows indicating the up and down action of the popcorn seeds.

A good example of Demario's competence as a student within this discourse event is exhibited in the following example. Demario told his teacher, "The popcorn is getting heavy." His teacher responded, "That's exactly what's supposed to happen," after which many of Demario's classmates repeated, "The popcorn is getting heavier." These brief interactions between Demario and his partner and his teacher demonstrate not only his ability to engage and participate in the activity of the lesson, but also the social perception of his capabilities. By initiating the interaction with his partner, he demonstrated that he had been understanding the events of the science lesson as expected in this classroom, was cognizant of what was occurring and why, and could engage appropriately in conversation about these events.

Furthermore, when Demario pointed out the actions of the raisins in his experiment to his teacher ("Look at our raisins; look at our raisins."), he indicated that he knew the rules of this reading genre and could enter into them enthusiastically because he may have known that his report of his observation would be affirmed. Demario's understandings were corroborated when in response his teacher affirmed his observation saying, "They are still going." Demario's facility as a science reader was corroborated publicly by both the teacher and his classmates when they repeated Demario's public announcement that the popcorn is getting heavier. In this moment his teacher and classmates affirmed that he had made a useful contribution and acted as a capable member of the class. Demario's final written product was similar to his partner's and to Roland's.

Observational evidence also indicated that Roland was also affirmed as capable during hands-on science. He interacted appropriately with his student partner, initiated interactions with his teacher and was positively confirmed as a capable member of the classroom community. He completed his worksheet writing, "It went up and down" and included a picture that was similar to Demario's.

In the Science lesson, Demario may have been more successful than in Reading 1 and 2 because he had been given the opportunity to play a different role as a reader of multiple texts. He was able to talk through creating text as well as read through various texts. He was given opportunities to engage in discourses with which he was familiar and which matched the expectations for appropriate academic discourse in this kind of lesson. He was provided with learning opportunities that he took up, he initiated his own learning opportunities, and he functioned as a capable member of the classroom community. Roland was equally successful within this discourse structure suggesting that regardless of reading ability, during Science both boys were provided opportunities to learn.

The teacher's prior knowledge and interpretation of the event in question can be a critical part of classroom-based assessment. For example, Mrs. Frank was asked to what she ascribed Demario's very different levels of engagement between hands-on science and round-robin reading, as she was shown the videotape of this key reading event. Mrs. Frank's interpretation referred to Demario's temperament and not to specific reading behaviors. She believed Demario's lack of engagement during reading was because he preferred activity, "Demario loves activity. I mean that's obvious, which is why in science he was so, you know, ready to go, go, go." She went further, observing that he had difficulty focusing and staying on task, "But when it's any sort of independent sort of work . . . or work when he has to stop and think for a few minutes, he just struggles with that terribly. He struggles with that . . . very, very active . . . very difficult time staying on task or focusing on something."

In contrast to the successful opportunities to learn during hands-on science, Demario experienced notably fewer opportunities to learn during the teacher-led interactions during both Reading events and during Science. These teacher-led interactions were an important part of each lesson (See Fig. 5.1). Until Mrs. Frank called on Demario to read aloud during Reading 2, she did not call on him, even when he raised his hand, nor did she initiate an IRE sequence with him during any of the observed teacher-led interactions. In contrast, she called on Roland to read during Reading 1 and Reading 2, and engaged in extended IRE interactions during each of the videotaped observations. Thus, as we compare the two boys' experiences of the same lessons, we observe distinct differences in the opportunities to learn the teacher offered. By closely analyzing the single occasion during which the teacher did engage Demario, and his subsequent take up of reading, we may find clues as to how the specialist and teacher might proceed with focused interventions. Demario's engagement during the teacher-led interactions halfway through Reading changed from silent withdrawal to active verbal participation.[2] The structuration map for Reading 2 (Fig. 5.1) displays Demario's change in engagement. Prior to reading out loud, Demario did not join in choral responses, raise his hand, or read along in the book consistently; in fact, he kept his head on his desk. After he read aloud, he appropriately joined in choral responses, raised his hand, and looked on the correct page in the book.

While watching the videotape with Mrs. Frank, one of us (Connor) said, "Now I noticed you actually moved your chair closer to his desk when you started." Just prior to Demario's reading aloud, the videotape showed Mrs. Frank moving her chair closer to Demario and saying, "Hold on a second, Demario. You're gonna read." The teacher's response provided an important piece of information for interpreting the actions that follow. She reported, "Well, I told him he was gonna be on tape and he was gonna read, so he better pay attention." She stated further, "I gave him the eye." This was because, as she stated, "I don't know what you were looking for on tape but I wanted him . . . I don't want you to have a tape of him complete with his head down."

During the reading, Mrs. Frank asked Demario a number of questions. When she was asked during the interview and while watching the videotape, "Why did you ask him those questions right there? . . . You asked him to list who knew." She responded, "Just to see if he was even paying attention to what he was reading." By asking the teacher her reasons for responding to Demario as she did, the specialist is able to learn the teacher's assessment of the students' reading and causes of his difficulty, her approach to improving his reading, and why she uses it.

In the interview, Mrs. Frank confirmed her belief that Demario's behavior, his level of activity, and his inability to concentrate or focus were the reasons he was disengaged during the teacher-led interactions. She also observed his specific struggles with reading and particularly

---

[2]We are aware that because data collection did not begin until after Day 14, key events leading up to Demario's disengagement from the round-robin participation structure and teacher-led interaction structures are not available. Therefore, we cannot explore the interactional history preceding this episode, to determine the patterns of involvement that were constructed between the teacher and the two boys. Such a study would be valuable to provide a context for the telling events we are highlighting in this study. We can, however, investigate key events that occurred during Reading 2 to describe the observed changes in Demario's engagement in teacher-led interactions from the beginning, when he was disengaged, to the end when he was more engaged.

how they affected his ability to understand what he had read. For example, she explained, "You can tell by the way he's reading [that] he's just reading the word. And because he is struggling so much he's focusing [on] one word at a time—period. The whole sense of this paragraph or the story isn't ever flowing for him; it's just a lot of words." Nevertheless, when asked why Demario's engagement with text improved after his opportunity to read, she contributed his changed behavior to her demands that he pay attention because he was being taped.

Based on our observations, we presented an alternative to Mrs. Frank's interpretation of Demario's changed reading behavior. From a view of reading as a socially constructed and teacher-mediated activity, we posited that Demario's improved performance might have been facilitated by the teacher's particular engagement with him. First, by calling on Demario to read, and staying with him in an affirming way, she provided him with an *opportunity to learn* (Tuyay et al., 1995). She did this by identifying him as a reader and giving him a chance to demonstrate he was a competent reading member of the classroom community. Second, by talking him through the reading activity, she used Demario's competent oral-language skills to build his reading skills. Her careful and precise scaffolding of his comprehension of text while he was reading supported his reading. For example, she said to Demario, "He said, 'Don't tell anyone else.' but look at the picture. Think anybody told?" She called his attention to textual elements and strategically directed him to relate to text in explicit ways: "The minister has just said, 'Don't tell anybody.', and Zuckerman says, 'Nobody but four people.' Who?" She asked him to reread lines of text: "Read it up, read it, read it," then read it with him. This was a way of reading different from how she read with other students. One interpretation of what was occurring is that these strategies for comprehending text were implicit for other students, while for Demario they needed to be made explicit. It is important to note that in this situation, Demario was not being publicly presented as a deficit reader; rather, he was being escorted down the path of the proficient reader, and being given an opportunity to show his proficiency along the way. By taking up this opportunity, Demario experienced being a proficient reading member of his class.

However, Mrs. Frank did not scaffold word-decoding strategies with Demario, which must be considered just as important, if not more important than the comprehension strategies she did utilize. Recent research indicates that children with poor decoding, like Demario, may need as much as 20 minutes per day of explicit instruction in word decoding strategies (Connor et al., 2004a). Providing Mrs. Frank access to such strategies for Demario, as well as approaches to implement them, would be an important component of the classroom intervention.

Demario continued to fully participate in round-robin reading following his turn to read—entering in the choral responses, tracking text on the correct pages, and raising his hand to enter the reading conversations—in contrast to his behavior just prior to the event. This indicates that Demario's shift may have been a social rather than a cognitive/developmental one—especially inasmuch as the specific instruction he received was not directly supporting the skills he needed to acquire. We hypothesize that during this brief interaction, the teacher had given Demario the opportunity to join the social activity of the classroom and to experience himself as both a member and a reader. This brief analysis of the teacher's interaction with Demario illustrated for the teacher that students with reading difficulties can be also served in developing their reading skills by particular kinds of *teacher discourse moves*. It may be that changing Demario's status as a reader, and strengthening his decoding skills, will also support the development of skilled reading by increasing his motivation to read and by providing more time to practice reading within his zone of proximal development (Vygotsky, 1999).

In contrast to the scaffolding provided to Demario, Mrs. Frank provided different kinds of support to Roland as he read. For example, she connected the current text they were reading to one they had read before. This intertextual link provided another form of scaffolding and established it as an expected reading practice in this classroom. Mrs. Frank asked the children to compare what was happening in *Charlotte's Web* with a book they had read previously, *Mr. Popper's Penguins*. She framed the question carefully, "Listen up. Think for a second. How is this part of the story in *Charlotte's Web* like *Mr. Popper's Penguins*? Gotta think . . . how is what's happening right now with all these people coming around and they're not doing their work any more, how is this like *Mr. Popper's Penguins*? Although Demario did not raise his hand, Roland did and the teacher called on him. She repeated her question, "How are these two alike?" and Roland responded, "They were like the same place, and Mr. Greenbaum . . . that's how they . . . see . . . because all the people were coming there to see the penguins, and all the people are coming here to see the pig." The teacher ended the sequence with Roland by supporting and expanding his response, "So they're getting famous."

Although the interactions between the teacher and the two boys were quite different in the types of support rendered, the teacher was observed providing *opportunities to learn* that both boys took up successfully. Each boy exhibited effective round-robin reading, although our analyses make visible that their success was not a function of the round-robin format nor of the specific word-decoding strategies Mrs. Frank employed. Rather, the success was most likely related to the teacher's discursive moves within that lesson structure.

Summary of the Assessment and Recommendations

The classroom observations revealed that Demario did indeed struggle with reading, that he had not yet mastered critical decoding skills and that this interfered with his ability to comprehend the text he was reading. His reading was not fluent; in many contexts he was unengaged with text and did not actively participate in classroom discourse activities. However, he was a capable oral communicator and could use his oral-language to support his creation of text.

Classroom-based assessment revealed both strengths and weaknesses in classroom structure, procedures, and classroom discourse patterns that appeared to both support and interfere with Demario's development as a reader. In general, the round-robin format was not particularly opportune for Demario or for many other students. Specifically, the protocol did not encourage students to take initiative for figuring out words they did not know: Rather, classmates and/or the teacher provided them. Based on research about reading, encouraging strong and fluent decoding using phonological and other word-attack strategies tends to support students overall reading skills, including comprehension (Snow, Burns, & Griffin, 1998; West et al., 1983). With this in mind, the specialist and teacher can devise a plan for redesigning classroom reading events and reshaping classroom discourses during them in ways that encourage Demario and his classmates to take the initiative for figuring out words, including specific phonological and comprehension strategies.

Roland's successful reading performance during round-robin reminds us that when considering how to reshape the literacy events in the classroom to be more opportune for students like Demario, the specialist and teacher must be careful these events remain opportune for able readers like Roland. Roland's reading during the same round-robin lessons provided an important additional contribution to the classroom-based assessment. Although the specialist's primary focus should be on assisting the reading development of struggling readers, attention to only those readers may skew recommendations for classroom instruction. A teacher needs to provide reading instruction for all students—the able as well as the less able. Applying the same assessments to observe a competent reader (e.g., Roland) as those used for a less competent reader (e.g., Demario), the specialist can gain important contrastive information that will be useful to the teacher.

Demario's struggle with text may have built a barrier to his full participation as a member of this classroom discourse community. It appears that Mrs. Frank may have reinforced Demario's difficulties with reading by failing to call on him to either read or answer questions during teacher-led interactions, thereby providing fewer opportunities to learn.

This may have happened for a number of reasons and may be based on Mrs. Frank's perceptions of Demario's reading skills, including not wanting to embarrass Demario, not wanting to take time from other students, managing Demario's behavior, and tacitly but unconsciously supporting his role as a struggling reader. In this case, then, intervention might focus on redefining the reading culture of the entire classroom and the conversations between specialist and teacher might shape the social and literacy practices in the classroom so that they can become more opportune for students like Demario. For example, Demario was notably more successful during literacy events in hands-on science when he was able to talk his text into being. Focusing specifically on Demario and proceeding from an analysis of the literacy events during which Demario acted like a competent student, the specialist and teacher can begin to identify positive learning events, like the hands-on science lesson. These could be restructured to provide more focused opportunities for reading instruction, for example, focus on using phonological strategies for decoding, repeated reading to increase reading fluency, teaching reading comprehension strategies, and encouraging Demario to take more ownership of his reading (Alderman, 1999; Rayner et al., 2001; Snow, 2001).

An important part of classroom-based assessment is to illustrate where the teacher has been successful in providing opportunities to learn. During Reading 2, the teacher used skillful scaffolding to guide Demario through his reading aloud and offered him the opportunity to learn within his zone of proximal development. Thus, although she did not provide frequent opportunities to learn for Demario within the round-robin reading discourse structure, those opportunities she did provide were skillfully enacted and somewhat effective. Furthermore, by comparing her interactions with Roland, we observed that she was able to modify her discourse to provide effective opportunities to capable readers as well. Although Mrs. Frank needed to monitor which children were offered opportunities to learn and how often, as well as the content and appropriateness of her instruction (i.e., decoding for Demario; intertextual links for Roland), she did not need to change *how* she interacted with the students. Furthermore, her "round-robin" reading time might be replaced with flexible small groups (Taylor, Pearson, Clark, & Walpole, 2000) or strategies that permit more children to actively participate. One example is *Think-pair-share* (Lyman, 1992; Wolfram, Adger, & Christian, 1999). Using this strategy, Mrs. Frank could ask a question, let all of the children think about the question for 30 seconds and discuss their answers with their student partner for 1 to 2 minutes. Then Mrs. Frank could select particular students to share their answers.

Finally, Demario's clear difficulties with reading require support beyond what can be provided by any single teacher in the classroom.

Therefore, it would be appropriate to refer Demario for after-school one-on-one tutoring to remediate the specific reading-skill difficulties identified in the classroom-based assessment, including word decoding, fluency, and comprehension. After-school tutoring would be preferred because, by avoiding pull-out sessions during the day, Demario could remain a full-time member of the classroom community.

A review of Demario's school records 1 year later, when he was in fourth grade, revealed that on the state-wide reading achievement test, which was given in the winter of fourth grade Demario earned a score of 279, which placed him only 1 point below a proficient score and approaching the 25th percentile for his age. Furthermore, the school moved his designation as a "high-need" student to a "moderate-need" student. Of course, any number of factors may have contributed to this improvement, notwithstanding the classroom-based assessment and the recommendations generated. Nevertheless, this improvement is encouraging.

DISCUSSION

We have presented the literacy profiles of Roland and Demario, able and struggling readers respectively, to demonstrate the useful application of two views of reading in classroom-based assessment using both a developmental/cognitive lens and a sociocultural lens. We have done so from the point of view that speech-language pathologists' and reading specialists' will play a central role as they collaborate with classroom teachers to conduct classroom-based assessments. Examiners who can apply multiple definitions of reading across multiple contexts may be able to better assist students in becoming proficient readers. Cognitive/developmental and sociocultural assessments of children's reading performance, when taken together, can offer a wider perspective of students' reading capabilities.

Our analysis of classroom reading behavior, using a cognitive/developmental definition of reading, concurred with the standardized test results and the teacher's perception of Roland and Demario's different reading profiles. These assessments highlighted specific weaknesses in Demario's reading skills that interfered with his efforts to read capably. Specific interventions could then be focused on teaching Demario the skills he needed to become a more proficient reader. Clearly, he required more explicit instruction in decoding strategies, opportunities to gain reading fluency, as well as more constructive comprehension support (Rayner et al., 2001; Snow et al., 1998).

The sociocultural lens proceeded from a perception of Demario as a "capable" reader within certain instructional contexts (e.g., collaborative hands-on science). In the Science lesson, Demario was able to talk through creating text as well as read through various texts. He was given opportunities to engage in discourses with which he was familiar and which matched the expectations for appropriate academic discourse in this kind of lesson. Within discourses that privileged oral communication to support interactions with text, Demario was quite successful. He was both provided with and initiated his own learning opportunities. We also observed that Roland continued to be a capable student within this context. It is within these instructional contexts that students may be offered situational opportunities to learn.

A critical part of this or any successful classroom-based observation is the implicit assumption that the specialist and teacher are partners on a quest to help struggling readers become proficient readers. By using both the cognitive/developmental frame, with its focus on the individual child, and the sociocultural frame, with its focus on the classroom as a whole, we are offered insights that might not have been available using only one lens. In our study, using both lenses created a more complete, complex, and compelling assessment of Demario as a rzeader and better informed strategies to help him. It is important to note that recommendations derived from both the developmental cognitive and sociocultural definitions of reading. By having access to two theoretical lenses, languages, and repertoires of practices for reading assessment and instruction, evaluators are empowered to address elements of the complexity of the reading problem that is best served by each stance.

In conclusion, we view the implications of our study from the perspective provided by Schoenfeld (1999). He cites unifying the cognitive and the social as a central problem in educational scholarship and research that need further investigation and development. There remains a schism between "fundamentally cognitive" and "fundamentally social" studies of human thought and action (Schoenfeld, 1999, p. 5). The limitations of each lens in describing how the mind works, in context, to unravel the relationship between an individual and the environment, result in the individual having new understandings and capacities. This study demonstrates the value of exploring practical problems to produce both local and theoretically informing outcomes and attempts to reconceptualize educational research across theoretical and disciplinary boundaries, as both a pragmatic and a theory-building endeavor.

REFERENCES

Alderman, M. K. (1999). *Motivation for achievement: Possibilities for teaching and learning*. Mahwah, NJ: Erlbaum.

ASHA. (2001). *Roles and responsibilities of Speech-Language Pathologists with respect to reading and writing in children and adolescents* (Tech. Rep.). Washington, DC: American Speech Language and Hearing Association.

Atwell, N. (1998). *In the middle.* Portsmouth, NH: Boynton/Cook.

Baker, C., & Luke, A. (Eds.). (1991). *Towards a critical sociology of reading pedagogy.* Philadelphia: John Benjamins.

Balow, I. H., Farr, R. C., & Hogan, T. R. (1992). *Metropolitan Achievement Tests* (7th ed.). San Antonio, TX: Psychological Corporation.

Bloome, D. (1993). Locating the learning of reading and writing in classrooms: Beyond deficit, difference and effectiveness models. In C. Emihovvich (Ed.), *Locating learing: Ethnographic perspectives on classroom research* (pp. 87-114). Norwood, NJ: Ablex.

Castanheira, M., Crawford, T., Dixon, C., & Green, J. (2001). Interactional ethnography: An approach to studying the social construction of literate practices. *Linguistics and Education, 11*(4), 353-500.

Cazden, C. (1986). Classroom discourse. In M. E. Wittrock (Ed.), *Handbook of research on teaching* (3rd ed., pp. 432-463). New York: MacMillian.

Cazden, C. (1988). *Classroom discourse.* Portsmouth, NH: Heinemann.

Connor, C. M., Morrison, F. J., & Katch, E. L. (2004a). Beyond the reading wars: exploring the effect of child–instruction interaction on growth in early reading. *Scientific Studies of Reading, 8*(4), 305-336.

Connor, C. M., Morrison, F. J., & Petrella, J. N. (2004b). Effective reading comprehension instruction: Examining child by instruction interactions. *Journal of Educational Psychology, 96*(4), 682-698.

Craig, H. K., & Gallagher, T. M. (1986). Interactive play: The frequency of related verbal responses. *Journal of Speech and Hearing Research, 29,* 375-383.

Dickinson, D. K., & Tabors, P. O. (2001). *Beginning literacy with language.* Baltimore, MD: Paul H. Brookes.

Elmore, R. F. (1999-2000). Building a new structure for school leadership. *American Educator, 23*(4), 6-13, 42-44.

Goodman, Y. (1972). *Reading miscue inventory.* New York: Macmillan.

Green, J. L., & Meyer, L. A. (1991). The embededness of reading in classroom life: Reading as a situated process. In C. Baker & A. Luke (Eds.), *Towards a critical sociology of reading pedagogy* (pp. 141-160). Philadelphia: John Benjamins.

Green, J. L., & Wallat, C. (1981). Mapping instructional conversations—A sociolinguistic ethnography. In J. L. Green & C. Wallat (Eds.), *Ethnography and language in educational settings* (pp. 161-205). Norwood, NJ: Ablex.

Gumperz, J. (1972). Introduction. In J. Gumperz & D. Hymes (Eds.), *Directions in sociolinguistics* (pp. 1-25). New York: Holt, Rinehart & Winston.

Gumperz, J. (1992). Contextualization and understanding. In A. Duranti & C. Goodwin (Eds.), *Rethinking context* (pp. 110-120). New York: Simon & Schuster.

Hallahan, D. P., Kauffman, J. M., & Lloyd, J. W. (1999). *Introduction to learning disabilities* (2nd ed.). Boston: Allyn & Bacon.

Heap, J. L. (1991). A situated perspective on what counts as reading. In C. Baker & A. Luke (Eds.), *Towards a critical sociology of reading pedagogy* (pp. 103-140). Philadelphia: John Benjamins.

Heath, S. B. (1982). What no bedtime story means: Narrative skills at home and school. *Language in Society, 11*(1), 49-76.

Hunt, B. C. (1974-1975). Black dialect and third and fourth graders' performance on the Gray Oral Reading Test. *Reading Research Quarterly, 10*, 103-123.

Hymes, D. (1974). *Foundations in sociolinguistics: An ethnographic approach.* Philadelphia: University of Pennsylvania Press.

Jencks, C., & Phillips, M. (1998). *The Black-White test score gap.* Washington, DC: Brookings Institute.

Juel, C. (1991). Beginning reading. In R. Barr, M. Kamil, P. Mosenthal, & P. Pearson (Eds.), *Handbook of reading research* (Vol. 2, pp. 759-788). White Plains, NY: Longman.

Keenan, E. (1977). Making it last: Repetition in children's discourse. In S. Ervin-Tripp & C. Mitchell-Kernan (Eds.), *Child discourse* (pp. 163-138). New York: Academic Press.

Lerner, G. H. (1995). Turn design and the organization of participation in instructional activities. *Discourse Processes, 19*, 111-131.

Lyman, F. (1992). Think-pair-share, thinktrix, thinklinks, and weird facts: An interactive system for cooperative inking. In N. Davidson & T. Worsham (Eds.), *Enhancing thinking through cooperative learning* (pp. 169-181). New York: Teacher's College Press.

MacWhinney, B. (1994). *The CHILDES Project: Tools for analyzing talk* (2nd ed.). Pittsburgh, PA: Carnegie Mellon University.

Mehan, H. (1985). The structure of classroom discourse. In V. Dijk (Ed.), *Handbook of discourse analysis: Discourse and dialogue* (Vol. 3, pp. 120-128). San Diego: Academic Press.

Miller, J. F. (1981). *Assessing language production in children—Experimental procedures* (Vol. 1). Austin, TX: Pro-Ed.

Mitchell, J. C. (1984). Typicality and the case study. In R. F. Ellen (Ed.), *Ethnographic research: A guide to general conduct* (pp. 238-241). New York: Academic Press.

National Reading Panel. (2000). *Teaching children to read: An evidence-based assessment of the scientific research literature on reading and its implications for reading instruction* (No. NIH Pub. No. 00-4769). Washington DC: U.S. Department of Health and Human Services, Public Health Service, National Institutes of Health, National Institute of Child Health and Human Development.

NCES. (1999). URL: http://nces.ed.gov/ccdweb/school (No. School Locator): National Center for Educational Statistics.

Neuman, S. B. (2002, November). *No child left behind act.* Paper presented at the ASHA Conference, Atlanta, GA.

No Child Left Behind Act (2002). from www.whitehouse.gov

Palincsar, A. S., & Brown, A. L. (1984). Reciprocal teaching of comprehension-fostering and monitoring activities. *Cognition and Instruction, 1*, 117-175.

Perfetti, C. A., Beck, I., Bell, L. C., & Hughes, C. (1987). Phonemic knowledge and learning to read are reciprocal: A longitudinal study of first grade children. *Merril-Palmer Quarterly, 33*(3), 283-319.

Pressley, M., & Wharton-McDonald, R. (1997). Skilled comprehension and its development through instruction. *School Psychology Review, 26*(3), 448-466.

Pumfrey, P. D., & Fletcher, J. (1989). Differences in reading strategies among 7 and 8 year old children. *Journal of Research in Reading, 12*(2), 114-130.

Rayner, K., Foorman, B. R., Perfetti, C. A., Pesetsky, D., & Seidenberg, M. S. (2001). How psychological science informs the teaching of reading. *Psychological Science in the Public Interest, 2*(2), 31-74.

Rex, L. A. (1998, December). *Describing intertextuality to observe opportunities for teaching and learning language arts literacies.* Paper presented at the Annual Meeitng of the National Reading Conference, Austin, TX.

Rex, L. A., & McEachen, D. (1999). If anything is odd, inappropriate, confusing or boring, it's probably important: The emergence of inclusive academic literacy through English classroom discussion practices. *Research in the Teaching of English, 34*, 66-130.

Rogers, T., Tyson, C., & Marshall, E. (2000). Living dialogues in one neighborhood: Moving toward understanding across discourses and practices of literacy and schooling. *Journal of Literacy Research, 32*(1), 1-24.

Sacks, H., Schegloff, E., & Jeffereson, G. (1974). A simplest systematics for the organization of turn-taking for conversation. *Language, 50*, 696-735.

SBDG, Santa Barbara Discourse Group. (1992). Do you see what we see? The referential and intertextual nature of classroom life. *Journal of Classroom Interaction, 27*(1), 29-36.

Schoenfeld, A. H. (1999). Looking toward the 21st century: Challenges of educational theory and practice. *Educational Researcher, 28*(7), 4-14.

Snow, C. E. (2001). *Reading for understanding.* Santa Monica, CA: RAND Education and the Science and Technology Policy Institute.

Snow, C. E., Burns, M. S., & Griffin, P. (Eds.). (1998). *Preventing reading difficulties in young children.* Washington, DC: National Academy Press.

Stanovich, K. E. (1980). Towards an interactive-compensatory model of individual differences in the development of reading fluency. *Reading Research Quarterly, XVI*, 32-71.

Street, B. (1995). *Social literacies.* New York: Longman.

Taylor, B. M., Pearson, D. P., Clark, K., & Walpole, S. (2000). Effective schools and accomplished teachers: Lessons about primary-grade reading instruction in low-income schools. *The Elementary School Journal, 101*(2), 121-165.

Tuyay, S., Jennings, L., & Dixon, C. (1995). Classroom discourse and opportunities to learn: An ethnographic study of knowledge construction in a bilingual third-grade classroom. *Discourse Processes, 19*, 75-110.

Washington, J., Craig, H. K., & Kushmaul, A. J. (1998). Variable use of African American English across two language sampling contexts. *Journal of Speech, Language, and Hearing Research, 41*(5), 1115-1124.

Washington, J. A. (1996). Issues in assessing the language abilities of African American children. In A. G. Kamhi, K. E. Pollock & J. L. Harris (Eds.), *Communication development and disorders in African American children* (pp. 19-34). Baltimore, MD: Paul H. Brookes.

Weiner, S., & Goodenough, D. (1977). A move toward a psychology of conversation. In R. Freedle (Ed.), *Discourse relations: Comprehension and production* (pp. 213-226). Hillsdale, NJ: Erlbaum.

West, R. F., Stanovich, K. E., Freeman, D. J., & Cunningham, A. E. (1983). The effect of sentence context on word recognition in second and sixth grade children. *Reading Research Quarterly, XIX*, 6-15.

White, E. B. (1952). *Charlotte's web*. New York: HarperCollins.

Whitmire, K. (2000). Action: School services. *Language, Speech and Hearing Services in Schools, 31*, 194-199.

Wiederholt, J. L., & Bryant, B. R. (1992). *Gray Oral Reading Test* (3rd ed.). Austin, TX: Pro-Ed.

Wolfram, W., Adger, C. T., & Christian, D. (1999). *Dialects in schools and communities*. Mahwah, NJ: Erlbaum.

Woodcock, R. W. (1987). *Woodcock Reading Mastery Tests—Revised*. Circle Pines, MN: American Guidance Service.

Woodcock, R. W., & Johnson, M. B. (1989, 1990). *Woodcock-Johnson tests of achievement* (Rev. ed.). Itasca, IL: Riverside.

PART II

Applying Intertextuality to Examine an Instructional Approach

Silvia Wen-Yu Lee

Jacob Foster

When the two of us began our studies, we knew that we wanted to work in a qualitative framework. Our interests focused on teaching and learning within a small-scale setting; Wen-Yu examined a medical school dissection lab and Jake explored a teacher education study group. Given the very interactive nature of teaching and learning in these mostly unstructured activities, we thought interactional ethnography (IE) would be a good fit because it works with and values the social nature of interactions within a group.

Wen-Yu found that studying the impact of computer use on students' learning in medical school presented unexpected difficulties because her ways of collecting data were unfamiliar there. Students initially mistook Wen-Yu's video data collection as educational film-making for demonstrating the learning procedure. With that false image in mind, some students were conscious about their performance in front of the camera. The physical learning environment of the dissecting lab also imposed obstacles for IE observation. Each group of students worked around a large dissecting table and sporadically on the nearby computer. In order to have higher quality video and audiorecording, a wide-angle camera was necessary to include all the members' interactions, and a professional quality microphone was required to capture only the conversations within that group. Still, there were challenges in getting good data. Conversations from the next group sometimes overshadowed the recording of the focal group, students in the team talked over each other, and students' interactions occasionally happened outside of the camera's view. Unexpected situations such as these made the data transcribing process long and difficult.

Because Wen-Yu did not have prior experience observing an anatomy class and a dissecting laboratory, she attempted to spend as much time as possible with the students. She let the camera roll during all the dissecting sessions to capture the learning process both with and without computers. She also attended lectures and small tutoring groups with the students. All of her observations increased her understanding of what it is like to be a member of the anatomy class, and made it possible to shape research questions that took into account the culture, needs, and difficulties encountered by students in that class. Without this understanding of the medical students' learning process and the nature of medical training, she could not have meaningfully interpreted interactions in this and other studies she has since conducted in medical school settings.

Although the two of us believed from the start that the IE framework was a great fit for our work, finding, understanding, and applying the particular approach suited to our own interest and data was one of the challenges that we faced. We explored a wide variety of IE logics of inquiry in our classes with Lesley, which included many readings of IE research and discussions about methodologies with our group of graduate students. We eventually chose intertextuality as our research tool because it provided us with a framework for analysis and the terminology to describe the phenomena we observed. Jake chose intertextuality because it gave him a way to see how connections are made between theory and practice by members of a teacher education study group. For Wen-Yu, the goal of her study was to understand how and when students use computers spontaneously in relation to other resources in the dissection lab.

At first, unlike many of his classmates, Jake did not recognize intertextuality as the particular methodology that he needed because he could not understand how the concept could inform his data. However, with his classmates' urging and after much discussion, Jake came to realize that the central aspect of intertextuality was also the very basis of what he was trying to approach in his own research. Intertextuality is about drawing threads, or connections, between related texts in a social context, without assigning causality or direct influence. Jake has since completed his dissertation with intertextuality as his dominant method of analysis. His experience with intertextuality illustrates our group's learning process of making the concept "our own." Once he had committed to using it, Jake quickly realized that he could not just "plug in" his data to a method used by the researchers he had read. In beginning to apply intertextuality to his data, he came to realize that the understanding of the concept he had learned so far had both limitations and benefits. The analytical structure of intertextuality he started from was too general and vague for use in his study. This impelled Jake to learn more about the concept and how other researchers had made use of it. He was then able to modify his analytical approach so that it addressed his research interests in more detail. While tweaking the analytical framework to fit his research, Jake correspondingly tweaked his research question slightly to take advantage of the heightened value and power of the concept.

Having others to talk to and debate with as we crafted our analytical approach was significant in helping us to craft intertextuality into a useful analytic method. Our group challenged each other's ideas and helped to provide alternative interpretations of data. Our first experience of examining our own data was overwhelming. Our colleagues helped interpret interactions and focus our research questions to best fit the theories we used and themes that emerged from the data. If the conceptual and methodological argument we were developing made sense to our colleagues, we knew we were on an appropriate track. When they were confused or lost in our logic, we knew we had work to do.

6

Constructing Anatomy Literacy: Use of Computer-Based Media in a Dissecting Laboratory

Silvia Wen-Yu Lee

If there is a single area that represents the greatest change in the way physicians are preparing to enter practice in the 21st century, it is the application of computer technology to almost every aspect of their education.

—M. Brownell Anderson (2000)

Medical education is one of the areas that has been largely influenced by computer-aided instructional technologies. A great variety of computer-based and Internet-based applications have been applied for self-instruction, student assessment, problem-based learning, and distance education. In the newly published *A Snapshot of Medical Students' Education at the Beginning of the 21st Century*, it was reported that 45 out of the 130 responding medical schools require students to have their own computers upon admission to medical school (Anderson, 2000). It is not surprising that in many medical schools, course syllabi, textbooks, class notes, histology slides, patient cases, even examinations are delivered via computers. Many faculty members have developed software used in their own courses (Anderson, 2000). In particular, for facilitating anatomy instruction, numerous researchers have engaged in the development of imaging and tutoring software, online demonstration film clips (Thomson, 1998), interactive three-dimensional models (Schubert, Schiemann, Tiede, & Hohne, 1997), and virtual reality navigation through the human body (Brinkley, Bradley, Sundsten, & Rosse, 1997).

Although medical education has been largely impacted by computer- and Internet-assisted instruction, there are very few studies that have examined how computers are being used in the context of classroom discourse. In a report about literature of computer-aided instruction (CAI) in relation to medical education, the results indicate that 11% of the publications were evaluating an aspect of CAI, 13% were comparing CAI applications against other teaching media, and 60% were demonstrating applications without evaluating (Adler & Johnson, 2000). Articles about demonstration and description of computer applications have dominated the literature. Based on these observations, researchers have called for a shift in focus for how to improve the new CAI research. Two suggested research avenues are evaluations of how computers are integrated into medical curriculum and how they are incorporated into different environments (Adler & Johnson, 2000).

In anatomy education, some researchers have conducted evaluations of computer-based learning environments by measuring students' content knowledge through assessments of learning outcomes (e.g., Brinkley et al., 1997) or by scaling users' satisfaction through questionnaires (e.g., Klemm, 1998). However, few studies have addressed the associations and interactions between content provided in a particular computer application and the specific context in which anatomy is learned. Learning outcomes, in comparisons of pre- and posttests, does not depict of the actual utility of a computer application and does not characterize the learning processes of knowledge-building.

Based on the observations just stated, consequently, the research purpose of this study was twofold. First, this study was to understand and describe the situation in which students chose to use a computer in a dissecting lab. We know very little about computer utility in this kind of learning setting. In the dissecting lab studied, students worked together in groups with computer access to all of the learning materials for their class. Second, by focusing on types of emerging anatomical literacy-building opportunities, this study was also aimed at revealing how students' knowledge was built socially while using a computer. Thus, my analysis was guided by the following three questions:

1. What computer applications and anatomical content were used and how were they used by students in the dissecting lab?
2. What kind of learning opportunities emerged in socially constructed situations when students used computers in the lab?

3. How did computer use in the anatomy lab contribute to knowledge-building that leads to anatomical literacy?

By applying ethnographic and discourse-analytic methods, this study approached anatomical literacy as socially constructed phenomena. Data collection focused on students' interactions with a computer in the lab and student interviews. In the next section, I introduce the theoretical lenses that framed my perspectives of social interactions involving computer use during the dissecting lab. Through these lenses, I present three different cases of students' engagement with a computer. Each case illustrates how students expand their scope of understandings and applications of anatomical literacy through social interactions drawing on multiple computer-based media.

THEORETICAL LENSES

Literacy as a Socially Constructed Phenomena

My research was influenced by interactional ethnographic perspectives that perceive literacy as being constructed through social interactions. Literacy is a socially constructed phenomena that is situationally and dynamically defined by people in the classroom (Crawford, Castanheira, Dixson, & Green, 2001). Literacy is composed of a set of social practices that link people, media objects and strategies for meaning-making (Lemke, 1992). By working together, individuals understand, construct, and engage in literate actions contributing to both individual and group goals (Crawford et al., 2001).

Researchers in science education have suggested similar perspectives in scientific literacy. Rosebery, Warren, and Conant (1992) argued that scientific literacy is not just acquisition of facts and procedures but a socially and culturally produced way of thinking and knowing (originally cited in Roth, 1995). Collaborative use of language about scientific topics and scientific phenomena promotes scientific literacy (e.g., Lemke, 1990), and further encourages students to become attached to the discursive form of the science community (Roth & Roychoudhury, 1994).

The conceptualization of socially constructed literacy made it necessary for me to focus the study on how anatomy literacy was talked and acted into existence by students, instructors, and facilitators in the anatomy, media-rich laboratory. In this interactive and collaborative setting, I sought evidence of how people made visible to each other what counted as appropriate literate anatomy practices in the learning opportunities they took up (Crawford et al., 2001).

Intertextual Knowledge-Building and Intertextuality in Anatomy Learning

The conceptual framework of intertextual knowledge-building also was my analytical tool for observing the meaningful relationships between what group members said to each other as they socially constructed anatomy learning. Intertextuality can be generally defined as the explicit juxtaposition of texts (Fairclough, 1992). Within different scholarly works, intertextuality is viewed at various analytical levels. At a textual level, intertextuality is a characteristic existing within the text. With various degrees of explicitness, one text can be referred to by other texts (e.g., a newspaper article cites or mentions a book). At another level, intertextuality exists in a reader's mind as the reader makes connections among texts (originally cited in Bloome & Egan-Robertson, 1993). For example, students read one paragraph in one textbook and then identify the same structure on an anatomical illustration in an atlas. The meanings are made by individuals when connecting interpretations of a text or a graph to other images read, heard, or seen on other occasions (Lemke, 1992).

In addition to these two levels, intertexuality is viewed as a social phenomena and occurs when members in a learning group act and react to each other in ways that acknowledge and refer to texts to accomplish a socially agreed upon purpose (Bloome & Egan-Robertson, 1993). The socially constructed intertextual links connect between current and past texts or allows one text interpreted by means of previously composed text. Namely, the production and reception of a given text in a learning group depends on its members' knowledge of other texts (Short, 1992). In this way, social construction of intertexuality serves certain socially significant purposes for the group (Bloome & Egan-Robertson, 1993) through text-connecting practices. After group members recognize the texts being tailored, they make meaningful use of the texts in their group interactions.

Different researchers have provided their own definitions of what counts as texts within unique research settings and for specific research questions. Short (1992), in conceptualizing socially constructed intertextuality, defined texts as meaningful configurations of language intended to communicate. In this study, what counts as *text* consists of all kinds of learning materials presented by different media (i.e., images, illustrations, charts, tables, and computerized video clips and three-dimensional structures presented on the cadaver or specimen), and interpretation of anatomical concepts and structures communicated through language. A useful and crucial question for educational research is how to apply principles of intertexuality to the analysis of multimedia and hypermedia (Lemke, 1992). Hyperlinked content on a computer Web site can be inferred as intertextualized texts but only at the textual level. Jay Lemke (1992), a semiotician and scholar in science education, has suggested that the social construction of intertextuality can be a useful framework for studying technologies in society, such as interactions of teachers, peers and communities of people who are making meanings from multimedia.

Therefore, in this study, through the lens of socially constructed intertextuality, I describe students' social involvements with computer-based media toward anatomy literacy. I focused on situations that learners were engaged in text-connecting dialogue and were challenged to search for new connections collaboratively (Short, 1992). As illustrated in Fig. 6.1, I examined how literacy practices were involved and how anatomy literacy, as a result, was developed by using a computer. The process of knowledge-building by intertextuality was a channel through which both the group and individuals constructed anatomy literacy.

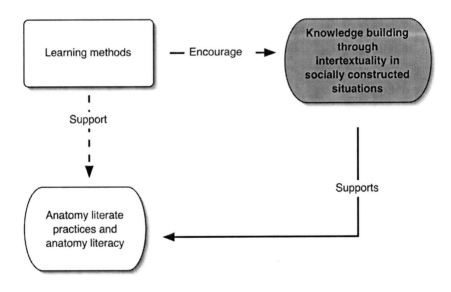

FIGURE. 6.1. The research design focused on how anatomy literate practices can be achieved through intertextuality in socially constructed situations involving computer use in the dissecting lab. Solid arrows indicate the research focus.

METHODOLOGY

Interactional Discourse Analysis

My research design was guided by an *ethnographic perspective* (Green & Bloome, 1997) to understand particular aspects of everyday-life, classroom practices in a medical school. Compared to *doing ethnography*, my approach was less comprehensive, however, more focused on discourse constructed by teachers and students within a micro-culture (i.e., the dissecting lab of the anatomy class); and my role as an observer entailed very limited direct participation. I was interested in discursive practices that provided information about what the members said and to whom, what they did with whom, under what conditions, using what resources, for what purpose, and with what social significance (Crawford et al., 2001). Discourse analysis thus is a means for me to understand the above practices and discourse through the form of speech and writing, presumes social content and cultural as well as cognitive processes (Killingsworth, 1992). Seeing through the functionalism perspective of discourse analysis, my goal was to explore what and how language communicates purposefully in particular instance and contexts, and how the phenomena found in "language in use" can be explained with reference to the communicative purposes of the interaction (Cameron, 2001).

Educational Setting

Data was collected from first-year medical students in a prematriculation gross anatomy class at a tier-one research university in the Midwest. Twenty one students enrolled in this six- week long class. This 6-week summer program was composed of 21 incoming first-year medical students. Their participation in this program was voluntary. The goal of this class was to give enrolled students a preview of the first half curriculum of the gross anatomy class and to provide retention orientation. The dissecting practices, teaching materials, and evaluation methods were identical to those used in the fall semester.

The Division of Anatomical Sciences at the university, which designs and implements the gross anatomy curriculum, has been continually seeking ways to improve anatomy instruction. One of the influential pedagogical strategies involves replacing the traditional anatomy lectures with extended hands-on experience in the dissecting lab (T. R. Gest, personal communication, June 2000). The traditional whole-class lecture and textbooks are still employed as one of the learning methods; however, they are not suggested for use as the primary resource in this class. Limited lecture time then places the responsibility on the students to prepare for dissection. Students are expected to be prepared before going to both the lecture and lab session to maximize their learning outcomes.

The two major learning resources for this class, defined by the faculty, are the online materials and the cadaver. The fact that online publication can be quickly edited and revised made it possible for designing class-specified learning materials to match the progress and special objectives of the class. Textbooks, however, which are too inflexible to be modified to match the instruction, were suggested in this class to be used in conjunction with the lab manual. Students are encouraged to read the lab manual to determine anatomical area and topics. As suggested by faculty, students should only read information that they *need* and search for information through the index in the textbook (Gest & Burkel, 2000).

Several support software applications were installed in the computers in the dissecting lab, including ATLAS*Plus* and online course materials (see Appendix B). The ATLAS*Plus* is a multimedia CD-ROM integrating text, medical illustrations and simple animations to introduce anatomical topics. The online course materials were designed and written by faculty in the Division of Anatomical Sciences to support students' learning. The materials were organized into different topics of regional anatomy corresponding to the order in which they are introduced in the class. Each different topic consists of a lab manual, review items, anatomy table of anatomical definitions, a Quicktime® dissecting movie, online multiple-choice quizzes, and clinical cases.

Students and instructors met three times a week. Each class period included a 20- to 40-minute whole-class lecture and an approximately 3-hour dissecting session. Students worked in groups of six on one cadaver in the dissecting lab. The three instructors and five facilitators walked around the room and provided assistance to all students in the lab.

Each group of students shared one dissecting table and one computer station. The computer station was set up next to the dissecting table and could be easily rolled and relocated around the table. The computer contained all the materials used for the gross anatomy class. Most of the materials were also accessible outside of the class on personal computers through Internet connections.

Literate Practices Defined by the Division of Anatomical Sciences

Anatomy, as defined by the faculty of the Division of Anatomical Sciences, is a subject that is architectural, structural, dimensional, descriptive, and also logical. The faculty suggests that the study of anatomy "should be aimed at discovering the logic and architectural necessities that eliminate the need for rote memorization" (Gest & Burkel, 2000). The institution defines that anatomy literate practices involves both *identifying* and *defining* anatomical structures (Gest & Burkel, 2000). Students are expected to understand what confirms a structure's identification by knowing its shape, color, location, and its relation to other structures. Also, students should be able to articulate the definition, the boundaries, and the characteristics of a structure in order to delineate one from the other.

To achieve anatomy literacy, the educational setting and course structure of the gross anatomy class aimed to accommodate all learning habits through a variety of instructional methods. As presented in the learning pyramid (see Fig. 6.2) this class provides students with a variety of inputs or methods to assist learning. It shows that the average retention rate increases as multiple learning methods are taken into practices. Students can achieve the above anatomy literacy through attending lecture, accomplishing suggested readings, using audiovisual materials, watching demonstrations, participating in discussion groups, practicing how to dissect, and by teaching others. These institutional definitions of anatomy literacy and learning methods framed what I counted as data and as the focus of analysis for this study of computer use and anatomy knowledge-building.

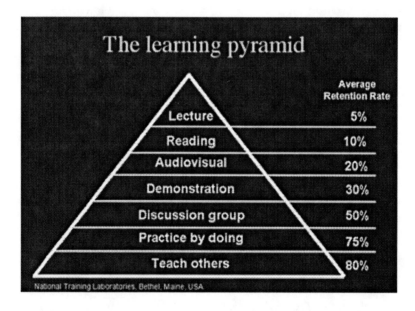

FIGURE 6.2. Teaching philosophy of the Division of Anatomical Sciences: The Learning Pyramid (originally appears in Gest & Burkel, 2000). It shows the different learning resources and learning methods that students should adapt for learning anatomy.

Data Collection

In taking an ethnographical approach, this study focused on collecting discourse data of students' interactions when using a computer in the dissecting lab. Among the interactions, I studied (a) students' interactions with computer-based media, (b) students' interactions with other members, and (c) interactions between the use of computer-based media and other practices performed by members in the dissecting lab. From the data corpus, I was most interested in illuminating anatomical literacy building during occasions of computer use.

Over the six weeks of study, 14 dissecting sessions of one selected student group were observed and videotape recorded. One video camera and one video cassette recorder (VCR) were used for data collection in the lab. The camera was set up next to the dissecting table to capture as much as possible students' conversation and interactions during dissecting (this data is referred to as *class video*). The VCR was connected to the computer to record all video output signals directly from the computer screen (this data is referred to as *process video*). Thus, by matching the class and process video data, I was able to recover the "micro"-level of computer use (knowing what was used on the computer) in the context of "macro"-level of lab discourse (knowing what happened in relation to the use of computer).

Besides collecting video data, I conducted semistructured interviews with the students and an instructor. Interview questions for the students were about general descriptions of their learning difficulties, the study they were engaged in before and after each dissecting lab, their perceptions of their learning resources and their perceptions of the use of the computer for their gross anatomy class. Questions for the instructor, however, focused on his teaching philosophy and his perception of how the computer should be used for anatomy instruction. The instructor interview provided the institutional view of what counted as anatomy literacy and literate practices for this particular class. Overall, the interview data served as an alternative resource for confirming and disconfirming evidence that can be compared to test assertions made from observational data.

Analytical Events

The data analysis process started with transcribing conversations and describing computer operations recorded in the process video. Analysis of the process video resulted in 14 different events throughout all of the research visits (see Table 6.1). An event was defined starting when one member explicitly proposed the use of computer and ending when the students engaged in an unrelated topic of activity.

Table 6.1. Events Recorded of Student Computer Use

Day	Topic	Events	Media	Participants	Theme
Day 1	Superficial Back		No computer use		
Day 2	Spine & Spinal Cord		No computer use		
Day 3	Pectoral region	1. 2:28-2:32 Cutaneous incision preparation. Ken tries to open the lab video but he is not able to do so in the first place. He opens ATLAS Plus instead, then opens the course website. Then he watches the video for the previous session.	Lab Video	students	Dissecting
		2. 2:42-2:44 Consulting lab manual for instructions. Dianne reads the lab manual. She asks Ken "We should be able to see the branches, right?"	Lab manual (online)	students	Individual
		3. 3:39-3:40 Showing the Anatomy Table to the students. Melissa discusses some anatomical structures with the students. She checks out information in the Anatomy Table and corrects something she said previously.	Anatomy Table	facilitators & students	Teaching
		4. 3:41-3:43 Searching in the Anatomy Table. Melissa reads information in the Anatomy Table again by herself.	Anatomy Table	facilitators	Individual
Day 4	Thoracic Wall	1. 2:12 Using ATLAS Plus. Ken opens the ATLAS Plus and reads some instructions to his colleagues.	ATLAS Plus	students	Dissecting
		2. 2:32 Viewing the lab video. Sandy watches the lab video but notices that the navigation bar was lost. Jen tells Sandy that she is aware of the same problem.	Lab Video	facilitators & students	Technical

Day	Topic	Activity	Lab manual (online)		
Day 5	Heart	1. 2:23pm Dianne reads the lab procedure/manual.		students	Individual
Day 6	Superior Mediastinum	1. 2:05-2:09 (3'24") Checking visual information in ATLAS Plus. Ken and Paul open the ATLAS Plus. Jen joins Ken and Paul at 2:07.	ATLAS Plus	students	Discussion
		2. 2:30-2:35 Melissa watches a lab video. Melissa discusses an anatomical structure with a student at the end of the video.	Lab Video	facilitators & students	Individual; Teaching
Day 7	Posterior Mediastinum	1. 2:35-2:37 Watching a lab video. Diane, Mary and Paul watch a lab video together. Diane walks away from the computer and starts dissecting. Mary continues watching the video and gives Dianne instructions for dissection.	Lab Video	students	Dissecting
Day 8	Abdominal Wall; Inguinal Region	1. 2:25-2:27 Watching a lab video. Dianne and Ken watch a lab video together.	Lab Video	students	Dissecting
		2. 4:30 Reading the Anatomy Table.	Anatomy Table	students	Individual
Day 9	Peritoneum		No computer use		
Day 10	Stomach & Spleen		No computer use		
Day 11	Duodenum & Liver	Facilitators download iTunes to the computer and play some music		facilitators	
Day 12	Kidney		No computer use		
Day 13	Lumbar Plexus	3:30 Reading the anatomy table. James reviews the spatial relationship of some anatomical structures with Jen and other students (from other groups). He points out information in the Anatomy Table.	Anatomy Table	facilitators & students	Teaching (Review)

In some cases, the use of computer was strongly related to preceding conversation in the group. In other cases, the searched computer content was then used in the following off-computer learning activities. Thus, in order to understand the situation that led to or resulted from the use of the computer, I transcribed class video data including what happened a few minutes before or after the computer events.

ANALYSIS

Defining Learning Events With Computer

Data interpreted from the process video including the time on-computer, content being used, participants, type of activity, and a description of each event were mapped together and listed on Table 6.1. The development of this event map serves at least three functions for my analysis: (a) to provide a time-stamped description of activities, (b) to represent the episodic nature of intertextual activities, and (c) to compare time lines of the events and phases of activity (Crawford et al., 2001). This collective information allows me to explore computer use in the lab, namely, when students used the computer, what they used and how they used it. Overall, there was a pattern that showed what the computer was used mostly in the first hour of the class. There were several occasions when the computer was used at the end of the lab sessions. But these events were only initiated or proposed by facilitators.

In looking at the data longitudinally across the whole study time, one may notice from Day 9 to Day 12 no events of computer use were observed (see data in Table 6.1). In the observed group, because certain organs inside the abdominal area were not well preserved, students could not accomplish the dissection task of the day at their own table. During those sessions, students either joined other groups or relied on other kinds of specimen. By only working together for a very short time at their own table, students did not actually engage in the learning activities as a group for those lab sessions.

Categorizing Learning Themes

The next level of analysis involves identifying patterns among events. In reviewing all the transcriptions from process video, the situation when students or facilitators used the computer were coded into five different themes namely, *individual, dissecting, discussion, teaching,* and *technical.* These codes emerged from open coding (Strauss & Corbin, 1998) of the events based on the research question of what learning opportunities emerged when students used computer.

The *individual* theme defined an event in which only one student or one facilitator looked for information on the computer. In this kind of situation where no other interactions happened, it was considered a personal individual learning opportunity. In these cases, I relied on the information on the sign-up sheet to interpret *why* the member used the computer.

Dissecting defined situations when computer use facilitated the ongoing dissecting process. According to the events observed, students either read out loud the instructional steps on the computer to inform others who were dissecting or drew the attention of the whole group to stop to watch the dissecting video. In the interview, students asserted that social meanings of doing so, in some cases, was to minimize the possible mistakes in the dissection, and in other cases to resolve problems that encountered during dissection by themselves. The ultimate goal was to help each other on move along in the dissecting process and, more importantly, to ensure that their work met the dissecting lab agenda.

The third theme was defined as *discussion*. The major difference between dissection and discussion is that for the latter, there were no indications of a relationship to the current dissecting work. The discussion in these cases centered around topics that were brought up by students. Discussion situations helped students clarify for one another some ideas that seemed confusing.

The fourth kind of situation, *teaching* was similar to discussion but involved participation of the facilitators. One characteristic of these situations is that students recognized and relied on the authority of the facilitators.

The last theme, *technical*, was conversation about technical problems regarding the computer. This situation may have been initiated by dissecting lab learning objectives but the conversation was reshaped by some technical problem with the technology.

Locating Intertextual Events for Knowledge-Building

From information revealed in the lab video, I moved to the third level of analysis to locate socially constructed intertextuality in the conversations. From the five thematic events of computer use, I selected three representative cases for illustrating how intertextuality occurred in different situations of computer use and how each of them was socially significant. I represent each case as a transcription table (see Table 6.2, case 1). Each case represents a series of turns of talk in relation to the learning methods, intertextuality, and the anatomical literate practices being socially accomplished. By presenting these three representations of computer mediation, the goal of this sort of analysis is to make visible how different media for anatomy literacy were incorporated simultaneously into the anatomy literate practices that occured in the anatomy lab. In this chapter, I purposefully put the computer at the center of the analysis due to its role as a major media for delivering and instructing the institutional view of anatomy literacy. The conversation was not only a means for students to synchronize their understandings but also a research instrument to understand the pedagogical strength of using computers in a socially constructed situation.

Table 6.2. Case 1: Constructing Literacy in the Dissecting Process (Day 7)

CONVERSATION UNIT	LEARNING METHODS	INTERTEXTUALITY	ANATOMICAL LITERATE PRACTICES
1 (P, M, and D approach the computer; M clicks the movie) (D leaves the computer) P: We should turn it up (Mary checks the volume setting) M: It's already up M: Okay, the right vagus nerve. The right vagus nerve. So Dianne, identify the right vagus nerve. D: Alright. Jen is on her way (Jen was dissecting) M: Okay.	- Using audio visuals - Practice by doing (dissecting)	Mary watches the dissecting video and provides indications to her colleagues of what what needs to be located on the cadaver. Mary, in watching Jen dissecting, confirms to Mary that they are working on it.	Identifying structures
2 M: Plexuses , pulmonary, left vagus nerve follow up the vagus nerve. Recurrent esophageal. D: Right, it goes... M: It goes under the right split D: It should be there	- Teaching each other	By hearing Mary's indications, Dianne asks how to find a specific structure. Mary provides a descriptive definition.	Describing (defining structures logically)
3 M: (M leaves the computer and gets closer to the table)	-Using audio visual	Mary checks the on-going dissecting	Identifying structures

Table 6.2. Case 1: Constructing Literacy in the Dissecting Process (Day 7)
(continued)

CONVERSATION UNIT	LEARNING METHODS	INTERTEXTUALITY	ANATOMICAL LITERATE PRACTICES
beautiful job. (5) (M: gets back to the computer) M: Is it what she just pointed out? I'm not sure what she's pointing. P: You want me check it out? M: Check it out of the mediastinum (P drags the horizontal bar on the button of the movie screen to rewind the movie. P and M watches it for 20 seconds)	-Practice by doing (dissecting)	work of her colleagues. She tries to identify the structure that Dianne pointed to her, by searching for the same structure demonstrated in the video.	
4 (M leaves the computer station and walks toward the dissecting table) (M reads the dissecting manual next to the table) M: You looked at the vagus nerve? J: Yes M: We looked at the vagus nerve a hundred times. Okay. "identify the structures of the esophagus " L: You follow the vagusXXX? D: Hey, are we going to take out this fascia? M: I don't think that matters	- Practicing by doing - Teaching each other	Mary checks the dissecting manual (paper) next to the dissecting table and discusses with her colleagues their current progress.	Knowing the procedures

Date: 07/11/01

Notation symbols: () actions; XXX inaudible words; (number) pause lasts the number of seconds; [ ] abstruse words; __ emphasis

Participants' Abbreviations: Ken - K; Paul - P; Jen - J; Mary – M; Dianne - D; Linda – L.

FINDINGS

General Observations of Using Computer-Based Media in the Dissecting Lab

In general, among all of the events of utilizing computer-based media, students tended to use computer-based media at the beginning of the lab sessions (see Table 6.1). In particular, they preferred visual presentations (i.e., the dissecting video and images in ATLAS*Plus*) and indications of the dissecting process (i.e., the dissecting video and the online lab manual). Anatomy tables (see Appendix A), on the other hand, were used at the end of the lab sessions when all the dissecting works were finished. For teaching or reviewing purposes, facilitators initiated most of the events using the anatomy table. Any event using a computer lasted two to four minutes.

Selected Cases of Intertextuality

In the three cases presented here, students used computer-based media differently. Use of the computer-based media facilitated anatomy learning in three different learning scenarios: the dissecting process, the discussion of visualization, and the mentoring of a facilitator. The three cases suggested three representative and important aspects of anatomy learning in the dissecting lab. Across the three cases, students (and facilitators in the third case) did not limit their learning by what was conveyed through a computer. They expanded their learning by posing and answering questions to each other, or by proposing other related concepts (see the conversation in dash-lines in the transcripts). The following three analyses illustrate how this process occurred differently in these three learning scenarios of intertextuality.

Case 1: Constructing Literacy in the Dissecting Process. In case 1, occurring during dissecting, interactions between Mary[1] and her colleagues involved watching in the dissecting video, conducting procedures described the lab manual, and identifying structures. They worked collaboratively to figure out the dissecting procedure and to locate the anatomical structures in different media.

The use of a computer occurred a few minutes after the lab session started. Three group members, Mary (M), Paul (P), and Dianne (D) were watching the dissecting movie together. After the movie was playing for

---

[1]All of the names shown in this chapter are pseudonyms.

one minute, Dianne left the computer, walked to the dissecting table, and joined Jen's work of dissecting.

Because of the noise in the dissecting lab, Mary and Paul could not actually hear the narrative of the movie even though they had turned the volume to its maximum. Mary interpreted the information by only watching the visual cues in the movie and identified those anatomy structures and dissecting procedures showed on the screen. She gave dissecting indications to Jen (J) and Dianne (Conversation Unit 1 in Table 6.2):

> Mary: Okay, the right vagus nerve. The right vagus nerve. So Dianne, identify the right vagus nerve.
> Dianne: Alright. Jen's on her way (Jen is dissecting)
> Mary: Okay.

Mary continued to watch the dissecting video and named more anatomical structures that needed to be located on the cadaver. Dianne asked a question of how to identify one structure (see Conversation Unit 2). Mary described to Dianne the logic of finding it.

> Mary: Plexuses, pulmonary, left vagus nerve. Follow up the vagus nerve. Recurrent esophageal...
> Dianne: Right, it goes...
> Mary: It goes under the right split
> Dianne: It should be there (Dianne looks on the cadaver)

Then Mary resumed her task by tracking the current status of the dissecting work. She checked back and forth between the dissecting table and the demonstration on computer (see Conversation Unit 3 in Table 6.2).

> Mary: (M leaves the computer and gets closer to the table) beautiful job.
> (5)
> (M gets back to the computer)
> Mary: Is it what she just pointed out? I'm not sure what she's pointing.
> Paul: You want me check it out?
> Mary: Check it out of the mediastinum (P drags the horizontal bar on the button of the movie screen to rewind the movie. P and M watches it for 20 seconds.)

Mary left the computer again and walked toward the dissecting table. She read the dissecting manual (hard copy) in order to figure out the dissecting process (see Conversation Unit 4 in Table 6.2). At the end of the conversation, Mary made a dissecting decision for the group.

Mary: You looked at the vagus nerve?
Jen: Yes
Mary: We looked at the vagus nerve a hundred times. Okay. "identify the structures of the esophagus "
Linda: You follow the vagus...?
Dianne: Hey, are we going to take out this fascia?
Mary: I don't think that matters

Described in this case is a typical collaborative situation in the dissecting lab when students chose to engage in different learning methods as individuals and carried out the dissecting task as a group. Mary's role was to convey information to support her teammates' work so that the possible errors in the procedure could be eliminated. The dissecting work performed by other members in the group, on the other hand, provided feedback for Mary (see Conversation Unit 3 and 4 in Table 6.2). This process synthesized information between some learning materials and the actual dissection on a cadaver. Literate practices were then performed collaboratively by having one student read the appropriate text description (using audiovisual aids) while others dissected (practicing by doing).

During the whole dissecting process, Dianne did not come back and watch the movie clip by herself. Dianne learned to identify a certain structure on the cadaver (see Conversation Unit 2 in Table 6.2) because Mary was able to identify the same structure on the screen and described it to her. Through posing questions and expressing ideas in language, Mary and Dianne demonstrated how knowledge-building can occur across different media.

Case 2: Developing Visualization Through Intertextuality. In the second case, throughout the whole conversation, three students concentrated on viewing anatomical images in ATLAS*Plus* and engaged in defining and identifying anatomy structures collaboratively (see Table 6.3). Intertextuality was visible when they posed questions about a medium on the computer screen and made connections to anatomical perceptions. At the end of the discussion, they conceptualized an anatomical structure that is not available on the screen by applying anatomical knowledge they had learned in the lecture.

At the beginning of this lab session, without an opportunity to dissect themselves Ken (K), Paul (P), and Jen (J) were watching other colleagues dissect. Ken suggested to Jen that they could check information on the computer. But she did not join him until a while after Paul joined.

When an anatomical image was shown on the computer screen, Ken and Paul were trying to define some of its structures. Ken suggested that the key to identifying a pulmonary vein is by how it splits. Paul was not sure about this information. He then started inquiring about the location of the veins (veins are on the back of the heart) and their relationship with the artery (one artery and four veins).

Paul: Is that a pulmonary…is that artery or vein?
Ken: Looks like it splits. So probably it's the vein.
Paul: Veins are on the back of the heart? Four of those? There is only one artery it shows?
Ken: There's only one artery, Yeah. One artery and four veins.
Paul: Is there only one? (Paul turns his head to the anatomy table and asks Jen)
Jen: Oh
Ken: Is there one pulmonary artery?
Jen: Yeah, it's coming from the right chamber
Ken: Yeah, pulmonary artery
Paul: Okay, four pulmonary veins.

A similar inquiry pattern then occurred in Conversation Unit's 4 and 5 (see Table 6.3) when they talked about the bronchi.

Jen joined Ken and Paul again and posed the question of whether the image in the ATLASPlus showed certain structures they were introduced in the lecture (Conversation Unit 6 in Table 6.3).

Jen: (voice is coming closer) Did you see all the stuff he talked about by knowing the order?
Paul: He cut it out. It's nothing in it.
Jen: no, not much
Ken: I think it is sort of cut out (Ken looks at the computer screen).
Paul: I think it is on the left side.
Ken: I think the artery is always highest. Usually. The artery looks bigger than the bronchi.
Jen: I think so
Ken: So hopefully we get to that. But artery is always higher than the veins. You think so?
Paul: Yeah
Ken: But I think he said on the anatomy table. The bronchi is lower, sort of…
Jen: In the middle
Ken: In the middle. Yeah exactly.

Table 6.3. Case 2: Developing Visualization Through Intertextuality (Day 6)

	CONVERSATION UNIT	LEARNING METHODS	INTERTEXTUALITY	ANATOMICAL LITERATE PRACTICES
1	K: (K talks to J) Should we log on to the computer? (J nods and smiles to him but still stands next to the dissecting table) (K walks to the computer and clicks on the ATLAS icon on the desktop. Then he signs up the log sheet) (20) P: What are you looking at? K: I'm going to bring up the ATLAS (opening a lesson in software) P: The Netter's? I'm ready (5)	-Using audio visual	N/A	N/A
2	P: Is that a pulmonary... is that artery or vein? K: Looks like it splits. So probably it's the vein.	-Using audio visual -Teaching each other	By viewing the pictures in the ATALSPlus, Paul and Ken starts identifying and defining the structures that they will be dissecting today.	Identifying structures
3	P: Veins are on the back of the heart? Four of those? There is only one artery it shows?			Defining structures

K: There's only one artery, Yeah. One artery and four veins.

P: is there only one? (Paul turns his head to the anatomy table and asks Jen)

J: Oh

K: Is there one pulmonary artery?

J: Yeah, it's coming from the right chamber

K: yeah, pulmonary artery

P: okay, four pulmonary veins.

4 P: take it to the next. I was too busy
(K click on the next picture)   Identifying
                                                  structures
K: Trachea
(K click on the next picture)
(3)
P: (Paul leans toward the computer screen and looks at the image)Okay...four
(3)
P: What is *that*?

K: That's the uh...I think that's the pulmonary artery.

P: That's *huge*!

K: it is huge. I guess that is huge

5 K: What is this? Is this the bronchi?   Defining
                                                        structures
P: wait, I think it is the trachea

K: I think all the veins get together,

P: Oh, that. Oh, they call it (bronchia)?

6 K: and this is the little ...ligament   Identifying
                                                        structures
P: the ligament

213

(continuity
from other
structures)

Table 6.3. Case 2: Developing Visualization Through Intertextuality (Day 6) *(continued)*

CONVERSATION UNIT	LEARNING METHODS	INTERTEXTUALITY	ANATOMICAL LITERATE PRACTICES
J: (voice is coming closer) Did you see all the stuff he talked about by knowing the order? P: He cut it out. It's nothing in it. J: no, not much K: I think it is sort of cut out. P: I think it is on the left side.		Jen asks Ken and Paul whether they have seen in ATLAS*Plus* the same structures that were taught in the lecture. Ken and Paul tries to define the locations and sizes of those structures.	Identifying structures
7 K: I think the artery is always highest. Usually. The artery looks bigger than the bronchi. XXX J: I think so K: So hopefully we get to that. But artery is always higher than the veins. You think so? P: yeah K: But I think he said on the anatomy table. The bronchi is lower, sort of... J: in the middle K: in the middle. Yeah exactly.			Defining structures (what is the shape and size of the structure; how does it relate to other structures)

Date: 07/09/01

Notation symbols: () actions; XXX inaudible words; (number) pause lasts the number of seconds; [ ] abstruse words—emphasis
Participants' abbreviations: Ken - K; Paul - P; Jen - J; S: the researcher

Paul and Ken, in responding to Jen, made a quick comparison of the content in the lecture to what was presented visually in front of them (see Appendix B). Instead of reading any text on the screen, they provided to each other their own perspectives developed in the lecture and in preparation for the lab. Although they were not able to actually see what Jen suggested on computer, Ken offered important hints for recognizing and defining the structures. The hints are "the artery looks bigger than the bronchi" and "the bronchi is lower, sort of in the middle".

An interesting pattern emerged in this conversation in that the students alternatively switched between the two important literate practices: identifying structures and defining structures. After identifying a structure on the screen, a defining process followed up. This process is particularly important for anatomical visualization. In order to recognize the same structure in different presentations (e.g., illustration, radiographic image, and the real human body), students need to know the logic of how one structure is related to others as well as how one structure is defined distinctly from one another. In this case, students co-constructed the sequence of learning and made the computer image meaningful to them in the process of knowledge-building.

Case 3: Facilitating Meaning-Making Through the use of Computer-Based Media. In the third and final case, a facilitator, Melissa, was involved in the conversation of intermedia meaning-making. Melissa recognized the confusion occurred in the conversation and highlighted certain information on a computer for them. She read and further interpreted information for the students. The group interactions allowed students to pose further questions to Melissa beyond what was shown on the computer. At the end of the conversation, the group interactions provided an opportunity for the students to correct the misconceptions that otherwise could not be easily recognized (see Table 6.4).

The students were working together at the end of the lab session to review the structure–function relationship and the innervention. Melissa was monitoring their conversation and providing information.

The students were trying to demonstrate to each other the functioning of the pect major. However, even for Melissa, they could not verbalize the definition of that muscle. The conversation became inconclusive when each of them tried to focus on different ways of defining the muscle.

> (Jen is reviewing the muscles, Dianne, Lucy (L), Melissa (Mel) and Ken are listening to Jen)
>
> Jen: So the pect major=
> Lucy: =pect major is this (Lucy lifts her arms up; Dianne & Ken are moving their arms but in different ways)

Table 6.4. Case 3: Facilitating Meaning-Making Through the Use of Computer-Based Media

CONVERSATION UNIT	LEARNING/ TEACHING METHODS	INTERTEXTUALITY	ANATOMICAL LITERATE PRACTICES
1	Mel: see what's the table about it (Melissa moves the mouse so the screen wakes up). (Mel clicks on the anatomy table) (Mel scrolls down the anatomy table) (Mel pauses at the Muscle of the Pectoral) (Mel moves the mouse along the words on the table as reading them)	-Using audio visual	(continues from previous conversation)	N/A
2	(Mel reads out loud what is on computer) Mel: okay, so the crest of the pectoralis major, "flexes and adducts the arm medially rotates the arm". So medially rotate is this(.), flexes the arm is this(.), and adducts the arm is brining it toward the center. (Mel moves her arm to demo the three movements) So it's all three, so bringing to the center (.), flexes it (.) and medially rotates (.) And then= (J and K are approaching the computer)	-Demonstration	Melissa reads and demonstrates to the students a definition in the anatomy table.	Defining structures
3	J: =what is the surface on between those, the tubercle? (J points her finger to something on the screen)= K: = lateral rotates? Mel: yes Mel: the lat? The lat also medially rotates it.	-Teaching each other	Melissa answers Jen's and Ken's questions when they approaches the computer.	Identifying structures (conversation between J & Mel) Defining structures (conversation

216

	Transcript	Codes	Notes
	(Mel demos the movement by moving her arm) J: Does it go into something, is the...? Mel: intertubercular groove? J: oh yeah. (Jen leaves the computer)		between K & Mel
4	Mel so in pect minor, "draws the scapula forward, medially, medialward and downward" (Mel reads it out loud) Mel: (scrolls down more) serratus anterior(.) K: I thought it is [leading] Mel: it is. (M scrolls down the table and reads out loud one cell on the table. M moves the mouse along the words provides some wrong on the table when reading them) "a lesion of long thoracic nerve will cause...," oh. Okay, guys, I told you this wrong. (Mel leaves the computer)	-Using audio visual -Teaching others	Defining structures Melissa reads more information from the anatomy table. Ken suggests something they discussed before. Melissa checks the information in anatomy table and realizes she conclusions.
	Mel: Guys. I told you guys wrong about one process. Here's what you want to trust. Because the serratus anterior crashes the scapula...because of the long thoracic nerve, the scapula sticks out= L: xxx (Lucy says something to Melissa) Mel: Exactly, looks like a wing. You know how you put your arms against a wall and push. Your scapula is gonna be pushed out. It gonna look like that. And there's a picture in Moore's, too. Remind me everybody if I said this wrong, C5, C6, C7... J: Yes, that's what he was saying last time. Mel: Who is that?		Based-on what Melissa found out on the computer, Melissa explains the concept to the students.

Table 6.4. Case 3: Facilitating Meaning-Making Through the Use of Computer-Based Media *(continued)*

CONVERSATION UNIT	LEARNING/ TEACHING METHODS	INTERTEXTUALITY	ANATOMICAL LITERATE PRACTICES
J: I'm in James'.			
Mel: Because the long thoracic brings C5, C6, C7 branches together to form that nerve, we cut that out, makes the scapula wing.			

Date: 06/29/01 (Day 3)
Notation Symbols: ( ) actions; XXX inaudible words; (number) pause lasts the number of seconds; [ ] abstruse words :(.) short pause
Participants' Abbreviations: Ken - K; Jen - J; Melissa - Mel (facilitator)

Mel: It's like when you go to the gym, you work on the butter-
        fly machine. You press both of them to bring your arm to
        the center. (Melissa pushing hands together to re-enact
        using the butterfly machine). And also push-up
Ken: Bring your arms to the mid-line (Melissa is nodding).
Dianne: What is the difference between minor and major?
Ken: It goes under, under, hits into the medial border scapula
Lucy: Minor is supposed to lower... the scapular, pull the scapu-
        lar
Dianne: So everything is opposite
        (Melissa walks to the computer)

Melissa took the lead of searching for related information on computer. She clicked the link to Anatomy Table and read aloud the definition of
pectoralis major on it. At the same time, she moved her left arm to
demonstrate to the students those muscle functions.

        (Melissa reads out loud the anatomy table on computer)
Mel: okay, so the crest of the pectoralis major, "flexes and adducts
        the arm and medially rotates the arm." So medially rotate is
        this, flexes the arm is this, and adducts the arm is bringing it
        toward the center. (Melissa moves her arm to demo the three
        movements) So it's all three, so bringing to the center, flexes it
        and medially rotates. And then= (J and K are approaching the
        computer)

In Conversation Unit 3, both Ken and Jean followed up with questions to further define and identify the structures. At this point, though
the conversation was inspired by information on computer, the three of
them did not directly utilize any information from computer. Instead
they built the knowledge from the conversation.

Jen: =what is the surface on between those, the tubercle? (J points
        her finger to something on the screen)=
Ken: =what the lateral rotates?
Mel: yes (Melissa answers Jen's questions))
Mel: the lat? The lat also medially rotates it. (Melissa answers
        Ken's question and demos the rotation by moving her arm)
Jen: Does it go into something, is the=?
Mel: =Intertubercular groove?
Jen: Oh yeah. (Jen leaves the computer)

In Conversation Unit 4, Melissa continued to provide information to the students by reading aloud. However, this information as recognized by Ken (Conversation Unit 4 in Table 6.4), was inconsistent with what Melissa had provided early in the group. Thus Melissa corrected the former discussion and provided students with more examples to explain the concept.

Mel: Guys. I told you guys wrong about one process. Here's what you want to trust. Because the serratus anterior crashes the scapula . . . because of the long thoracic nerve, the scapula sticks out=

Lucy: XXX (Lucy says something to Melissa)

Mel: Exactly, looks like a wing. You know how you put your arms against a wall and push. Your scapula is gonna be pushed out. It gonna look like that. And there's a picture in Moore's, too. Remind me everybody if I said this wrong, C5, C6, C7 . . .

Jen: Yes, that's what he was saying last time.

Mel: Who is that?

Jen: I'm in Jame's [discussion group].

Mel: Because the long thoracic brings C5, C6, C7 branches together to form that nerve, we cut that out, makes the scapula wing.

In this case, the intertextuality occurred *through* the facilitator. Melissa did not just locate the information on computer but also re-presented it in a way through her own understanding (see Conversation Unit 2). Her demonstration by moving her arms was a common *language* among the students that was used at the beginning of the conversation. The demonstration presented by Melissa was actually a more informative than the written text on computer-based media.

Furthermore, as a pedagogical approach, Melissa showed the students where to find the information on a computer to support their knowledge-building. She led the conversation at the end to a more comprehensive discussion of the anatomical concepts with deliberation of the short statements in the anatomy tables shown on the computer screen.

The Necessity of Collaborative Intertextuality

Anatomy knowledge and the process of learning anatomy are complex. As demonstrated, learning anatomy is not just about memorizing scientific and medical facts. Rather it involves the application of pertinent knowledge at applicable moments. Students in the dissecting group could not learn the different aspects of anatomy by using a single textbook or a single learning method. To be proficient in the anatomically related practices they performed in the class, students needed to grasp the different attributes of anatomy (architectural, structural, dimensional, descriptive, and logical) by familiarizing themselves with all the recommended learning materials and lab procedures. Some students found the construction of anatomy knowledge confusing and difficult because they had to negotiate and relate information from multiple materials. For example, in an interview, a student from the observed team defined his learning difficulty as following:

> . . . most of the people I know you'll find a good page in Netter [anatomy atlas] where it shows you what you're looking at and when you try to read, you'll read back and forth, between the two[textbook and atlas], to try to see how the relationships to the structures you're reading about. Um, but it's difficult because there's so much information out there available to us to use, so many resources, the computer, the videos and the book, the stuff we can print out of the web, you have to decide you can't learn it all, use it all because you only have a couple of days. If you present things in so many different ways, it gets confusing to make all make sense, unless you see it over and over again.

Although the relationships between information are not explicit or fully structured, intertextuality through social interaction was an approach that helped group members meaningfully relate different information. Although the computer conveyed certain intertextual relationships (at the written text level) through hyperlinks, those connections among text or media were not sufficient to teach the complexity of anatomy knowledge.

Nonetheless, this study of dissection lab interactions demonstrates that how computer use can be an effective means of knowledge construction in social situations. When students *talked about* the content on the computer they made the translation and connections between visual and verbal resources, between logic and practical information, and between definitions and identifications of the same structure. From a pedagogical standpoint, intertextuality matches and supports the level of complexity of anatomical knowledge-building. It unpacks the knowledge organization so students can experience the process of how different perceptions come to fit together. In other words, intermedia meaning-making utilizes the information seeds on the computer to extend students' perceptions in anatomy leading toward development of anatomical literate practices. In this setting, the computer was the resource for both practice-situated and practice-generated knowledge (Roth & Roychoudhury, 1994).

In looking at the result on Table 6.1, one may argue that there is a low frequency of computer use by students in the lab. In the interview, students explained that the intensive agenda for dissecting restrained their use of the computer-based media. In fact, students paid more attention to the work on the dissecting table. Also, instead of looking for information on the computer, the students, whenever possible, preferred to ask questions to the faculty. The latter was less time-consuming.

What is worth noticing here is that, as is shown in video data, the participation of faculty members in the group resulted in a different kind of interaction. Due to the fact that students viewed the faculty as the source and the authority of knowledge, most conversations became faculty-centered. The faculty members were not observed referring to or reaching out to other resources. One possible explanation is that all the content and anatomical relationships are well-organized and firmly mapped out in experts' mind. Experts' organization knowledge might differ from the evolving knowledge structure that novice (or expert–novice) students have been developing via processes for making sense from multiple learning methods (National Research Council, 2000).

The Importance of Orienting Computer Use in a Meaningful Situation

Computer design tends to require less and less technical knowledge or very little intense training. For students of this generation, computers seem to be integrated with their daily lives. However, the actions and interviews of the students in the dissection lab indicate that information shown on a computer can be ambiguous and students may have problems in recovering meanings from it. The students' problems with computer use were not "technical" issues. The actual problems were that sometimes students did not know how to use computer-based media to promote learning. In an interview, a dissection team member described his difficulty as needing someone familiar with the materials to foreground what is important for each application. He said:

> . . . by the LRC [Learning Resource Center] staff, they tried to . . . most basic levels of where things are but I don't think they have used it for the things we used for. So they don't know, they can't tell you "well, this is better than this." Or you know, I don't know the lecture slides from last year were on computer till yesterday. Like the slides they used in the anatomy lecture, the overheads are actually on the computer and I haven't known this so till yesterday. . . . It depends who gives the orientation, they can tell you how to log on, how to get to where you need to be *but they can't tell you what's there, what to do.*

... there're so much stuff on the web that need the facilitators to help us by saying "do you know about this?" "how do you use this resource on the web?" because all are these links. *But as a student you don't know which one is important. It'd help if someone else says "oh, well use the anatomy tables" because I wasn't even sure what the anatomy tables were.*

This example helps us to re-evaluate the general assumptions of students' use of a computer. In the example referred to by this student, the lecture slides were linked by one of the icons on the top of the screen. However, because the icon's importance was not *introduced* or *highlighted*, it did not attract this student's attention. In a time of information overload, when teaching students how to use computer-based media, we need to answer the questions "Why should I use a specific medium for learning?" and "When should I use it?" Also, educators should take certain things into account when integrating computers into teaching. Providing the hyperlink to some information does not necessarily imply students will be actively using it. When some people believe that computer-based media are self-explanatory, some students may not be able to find this information. Some students might be passive in exploring the different links unless they were given meaningful orientation.

DISCUSSION AND IMPLICATIONS

In this study, socially constructed intertextuality was observed in the dissecting lab as students utilized computer collaboratively for various purposes. In different situations, students co-constructed learning opportunities by integrating information they read or viewed on the computer with other learning methods. Students not only built knowledge by perceiving the learning materials on the computer, but they made that knowledge and the process of building it visible to each other. In this regard, each student with individual expertise become a significant part of the learning environment for all the others (Cazden, 2001). Both the process and result of intertextuality were significant for personal knowledge development and also for group achievement.

In the cases seen in this study, the utility of the computer was strengthened when students cross-referenced media or texts. This can be done among students or between students and their facilitators. In the first case, as students accessed learning materials to dissect, the connections between practical experience of dissecting, perceptions of anatomy, and interpretation of the media were made visible and valuable through their conversations. In Case 2, students jointly used ATLAS*Plus* to define and identify structures. Students socially constructed knowledge beyond original images provided in ATLAS*Plus*. In Case 3, Melissa apprenticed the students in using the computer-based media for learning. The information Melissa was providing to the group was not just the correct answer to their question. More important, through her action, she helped students know *where* to find the information and know the importance of utilizing this information for learning anatomy. The value of the anatomy table became valuable knowledge when it was used to eliminate confusions.

Although students may have access to all of the computer-based media individually, this study suggests it is important to provide these media in a collaborative purposeful, need-to-know environment as well. By studying individually, some new students may not be able to adapt all of the learning materials immediately particularly when complex concepts are taught and an enormous volume of information is provided to the students. Exploration strategies and navigation skills for computer-based media may be like other learning skills that have a learning curve involved (Lemke, 1998). In a collaborative environment, students and facilitators can have a chance to refer to the adequate media, which provide useful information associated with the learning practices at that moment. Students thus learn from each other and from the facilitators a way of thinking and talking about anatomy literacy.

Hypermedia and computer multimedia are capable of presenting information in various ways in alternative learning environments (e.g., the dissecting lab). Intertextuality can be implemented as a pedagogical approach. For instance, faculty or facilitators can provide situated orientation of how to use computer-based media or help conduct collaborative concept-mapping cross different media. In the future, more research in medical education should be done to examine the impact of intertextuality in complex concept development and clinical problem solving.

Finally, orientating students to be active learners in realizing the value of computer-based media has a long-term consequence for medical students. Digital information systems have become more and more integrated into medical records and decision support systems (Coiera, 1997). Medical practitioners are expected to recognize, process, and utilize information presented through different computer-based media to improve the quality of diagnosis.

APPENDIX A   SNAPSHOT OF THE GROSS ANATOMY WEB SITE AND THE ANATOMY TABLE

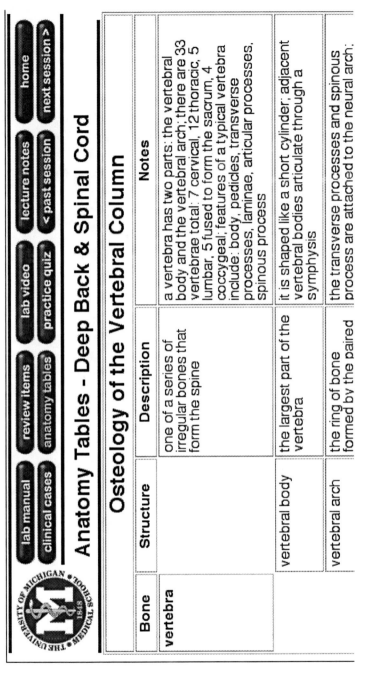

home
next session >

lecture notes
< past session

lab video
practice quiz

review items
anatomy tables

lab manual
clinical cases

Anatomy Tables - Deep Back & Spinal Cord

Osteology of the Vertebral Column

Bone	Structure	Description	Notes
vertebra		one of a series of irregular bones that form the spine	a vertebra has two parts: the vertebral body and the vertebral arch; there are 33 vertebrae total: 7 cervical, 12 thoracic, 5 lumbar, 5 fused to form the sacrum, 4 coccygeal; features of a typical vertebra include: body, pedicles, transverse processes, laminae, articular processes, spinous process
	vertebral body	the largest part of the vertebra	it is shaped like a short cylinder; adjacent vertebral bodies articulate through a symphysis
	vertebral arch	the ring of bone formed by the paired	the transverse processes and spinous process are attached to the neural arch:

(Gest and Burkel, 2000)

225

APPENDIX B SNAPSHOT OF A LESSON IN THE ATLASPLUS COMPUTER SOFTWARE

Tracheal Bifurcation

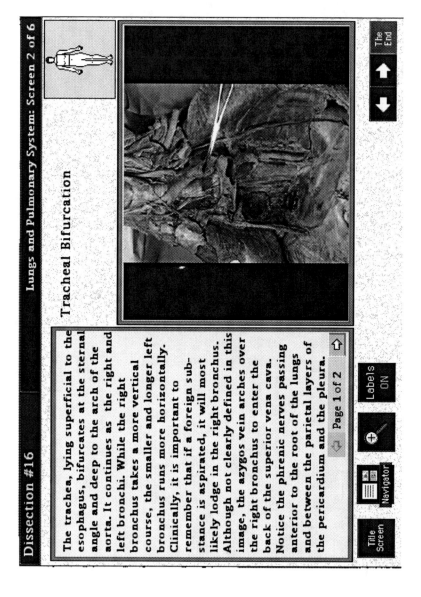

The trachea, lying superficial to the esophagus, bifurcates at the sternal angle and deep to the arch of the aorta. It continues as the right and left bronchi. While the right bronchus takes a more vertical course, the smaller and longer left bronchus runs more horizontally. Clinically, it is important to remember that if a foreign substance is aspirated, it will most likely lodge in the right bronchus. Although not clearly defined in this image, the azygos vein arches over the right bronchus to enter the back of the superior vena cava. Notice the phrenic nerves passing anterior to the root of the lungs and between the parietal layers of the pericardium and the pleura.

Page 1 of 2

Title Screen   Navigator   Labels ON

The End

226

REFERENCES

Adler, M. D., & Johnson, K. B. (2000). Quantifying the literature of computer-aided instruction in medical education. *Academic Medicine, 75*(10), 1025-1028.

Anderson, M. B. (2000). *A snapshot of medical students' education at the beginning of the 21st century: Reports from 130 schools.* Washington DC: Association of American Medical Colleges.

Bloome, D., & Egan-Robertson, A. (1993). The social construction of intertextuality in classroom reading and writing lessons. *International Reading Association, 28*(4), 305-333.

Brinkley, J. F., Bradley, S. W., Sundsten, J. W., & Rosse, C. (1997). The digital anatomist information system and its use in the generation and delivery of web-based anatomy atlases. *Computers and Biomedical Research, 30,* 472-503.

Cameron, D. (2001). *Working with spoken discourse.* Thousand Oaks, CA: Sage.

Cazden, C. B. (2001). *Classroom discourse: The language of teaching and learning.* Portsmouth, NH: Heinemann.

Coiera, E. (1997). *Guide to medical informatics, the internet and telemedicine.* New York: Oxford University Press.

Crawford, T., Castanheira, M., Dixon, C., & Green, J. (2001). What counts as literacy: An interactional ethnographic perspective. In J. Cumming & C. Wyatt-Smith (Eds.), *Literacy and the curriculum: Success in senior secondary schooling* (pp. 32-43). Melbourne, Vic.: ACER Press (The Australian Council for Education Research Ltd.).

Faircough, N. (1992). Intertextuality in critical discourse analysis. *Linguistics and Education, 4*(3-4), 269-293.

Gest, T. R., & Burkel, W. E. (2000). *Medical gross anatomy, introduction to the course.* Ann Arbor: University of Michigan. Available: http://www.med.umich.edu/lrc/coursepages/M1/anatomy/html/courseinfo/info.html [2001, 12/03].

Green, J., & Bloome, D. (1997). Ethnography & ethnographers: A situated perspective on ehtnography and ethnographers in education. In S. B. Heath (Ed.), *Handbook for research in the visual and communicative arts.* New York: Macmillan.

Killingsworth, M. J. (1992). Discourse communities—local and global. *Rhetoric Review, 11*(1), 110-122.

Klemm, W. R. (1998). New ways to teach neuroscience: Integrating two teaching styles with two instructional technologies. *Medical Teacher, 20*(4), 364-370.

Lemke, J. L. (1990). *Talking science: Language, learning and values.* Norwood, NJ: Ablex.

Lemke, J. L. (1992). Intertextuality and educational research. *Linguistics and Education, 4*(3-4), 257-267.

Lemke. J. L. (1998). Metamedia literacy: Transforming meanings and media. In D. Reinking, L. Labbo, M. McKenna, & R. Kiefer (Eds.), *Handbook of literacy and technology: Transformations in a post-typographic world* (pp. 283-301). Hillsdale, NJ: Erlbaum.

National Research Council. (2000). How experts differ from novices. In J.D. Bransford, A. L. Brown, & R.R. Cocking (Eds.), *How people learn: Brain, mind, experience and school* (pp. 31-50). Washington, DC: National Academy Press.

Rosebery, A. S., Warren, B., & Conant, F. R. (1992). Appropriating scientific discourse: Findings from language minority classrooms. *Journal of the Learning Sciences, 2*(1), 61-94.

Roth, W.-M. (1995). Affordances of computers in teacher–student interactions: The case of interactive physics. *Journal of Research in Science Teaching, 32*(4), 329-347.

Roth, W.-M., & Roychoudhury, A. (1994). Science discourse through collaborative concept mapping: New perspectives for the teacher. *International Journal of Science Education, 16*, 437-455.

Schubert, R., Schiemann, T., Tiede, U., & Hohne, K. H. (1997). Applications and perspectives in anatomical 3-dimensional modelling of the Visible Human with VOXEL-MAN. *Acta Anatomica, 160*, 123-131.

Short, K. G. (1992). Researching intertextuality within collaborative classroom learning environments. *Linguistics and Education, 4*, 313-333.

Strauss, A., & Corbin, J. (1998). *Basics of qualitative research: techniques and procedures for developing grounded theory* (2nd ed.). Thousand Oaks, CA: Sage.

Thomson, M. (1998). Multimedia anatomy and physiology lectures for nursing students. *Computers in Nursing, 16*(2), 101-108.

7

Facilitating Exploration of Theory and Practice in a Teacher Education Study Group

Jacob Foster

Learning how to teach is a process that practitioners engage in throughout their career, whether it is formalized or not. Teacher education should reflect this notion; the initial process of learning to teach is more than learning what the "methods" are, or the "most efficient" methods; more than learning particular isolated strategies and management skills; more than learning content to be taught.

> There is a strong temptation to assume that presenting subject matter in its perfected form provides a royal road to learning. What more natural than to suppose that the immature can be saved time and energy, and be protected from needless error by commencing where competent inquirers have left off? The outcome is written large in the history of education. (Dewey, 1916, p. 220)

I believe that this condition is as true for teacher education as it is for the teaching of K–12 content. Starting where more experienced "inquirers have left off" leaves little room for the personal needs, interests, and inquiries of the student teachers we are trying to engage. Teacher education programs are often structured so that student teachers experience theoretical, abstract instruction in university courses with little chance for inquiry, a sense of history, or practical connections. A number of researchers cite factors such as "traditional foundations courses that emphasize theoretical and scientific knowledge over practical, situated knowledge" (Tozer, Anderson, & Armbruster, 1990, p. 725), the timing of student teaching and university based experiences (Hollingsworth, 1989), and a mismatch in theories and strategies employed by teacher education programs (Eisenhart, Behm, & Romagnano, 1991; Lampert & Ball, 1999) as contributing to this condition. Upon completion of university courses, student teachers move into an intense, practical, contextualized experience of student teaching. In this context, there is sometimes little opportunity to explore theory and practice in direct relation to one another.

> If conceptual change is to continue we contend that the practicum experience must provide a supportive environment and multiple opportunities for preservice teachers to explore and experiment with the ideas and procedures presented in methods courses. (Mayer-Smith & Mitchell, 1997, p. 149)

One opportunity to help student teachers explore ideas and procedures from their methods course in relation to their student teaching experience is a classroom-based study group. This forum allows student teachers a chance to further consider the complex task of becoming and being a teacher while drawing connections between education theory and the practice of teaching. In the Certification and Master's of Arts in Education Program (CMAP)[1], student teachers and I organize a small study group in which we co-construct the structure, events, and flow of each session to best meet the dynamic needs and interests of the participants. This study group provides an appropriate site for me, as a teacher educator and researcher, to examine my own practice (Cochran-Smith & Lytle, 1993). In this study, I examine how theory and practice relationships are discussed in the study group forum and how I, as a facilitator, am an active influence in that exploration. The research question for this study reflects this intent: How does the facilitation of a student teacher study group encourage or discourage CMAP secondary science student teachers' consideration of the relationships between their university teacher education experiences and student teaching experiences?

The study group attempts to relate theory and practice that student teachers have previously experienced as distinct entities with little

---

[1]All program and participant names have been changed.

opportunity for juxtaposition. Through this exploration, the study group should provide an opportunity for student teachers to come to understand current science education reforms (American Association for the Advancement of Science, 1993; National Research Council [NRC], 1996); both the theoretical basis and implications for teaching. There is a wide range of aspects in current science education reforms that student teachers are asked to consider; so much so that these get compressed and shortchanged to some extent in science methods classes. The study group provides an opportunity for further, in-depth exploration of a few of the science education reform aspects that are relevant to the student teacher's needs. The focus on my facilitation in this research emphasizes an examination of my role as a science educator in how I can facilitate the exploration of a science education reform agenda. In addition, this study examines how theory can be translated into practice at the teacher education level. By drawing from current theory to inform how I approach facilitation, I can examine the benefits and challenges presented by implementing theory in the study group context.

STUDY DESIGN

Context

This study was conducted the second semester of a teacher education program at a large university. This particular program is a full-year graduate program in which all members work toward certification and a Master's of Arts in Education. During the first half of the program, student teachers focus on university coursework and spend 2 days a week observing in their classroom placements. Student teachers also take their subject methods course during this time, for which I taught the secondary science section. During the second half of the program, student teachers are in their classroom placement 5 days a week, with only a small portion of their time in university-based courses. I was the university supervisor for all four participants of this study. At the end of the science methods class, participants requested a forum for exploring issues of teaching science in more depth during their upcoming student teaching. I proposed a study group forum as a way to explore the abstract discussions and decontextualized activities of the science methods class with their contextualized student teaching experiences. Six study group sessions were held after the school day for 1 to 2 hours, at approximately 2-week intervals. Participants of the study group were not graded or assessed on their participation. Measures were taken to ensure confidentiality of the discussions as well as to separate the study group sessions from my formal supervisory observations of their student teaching.

Tenets Informing Facilitation

All participants agreed that the study group would promote exploration of student teacher interests and experiences and how they related to the science methods class. I was coordinator and general facilitator of the study group and acted in a way that was intended to allow co-construction of the agenda and discussions, while being active in facilitating links between university and student teaching experiences. As both facilitator and participant observer, I thought deeply prior to the study group sessions about how I would act to best support the student teachers and honor our design of the forum. To accomplish this, I articulated for myself how sociocultural constructivist learning theory (Cobb, 1994; O'Loughlin, 1992; Tobin & Tippins, 1993) informs my facilitation. This perspective values the prior knowledge people bring into a learning situation, suggesting that student teachers engage on the basis of experience, beliefs, and/or understandings that are relevant and authentic to them (Newman, Griffin, & Cole, 1989). The study group meets during their student teaching semester and provides a timely forum in which student teachers can explore and reflect on relevant and meaningful topics through an open, flexible agenda. Participants are welcome to bring forth ideas that are on their minds at the time; whether from an experience in their classrooms, reflection on past experiences, or connections they see to other areas of the teacher education program curriculum.

When a learner is confronted with new knowledge or a different situation, they actively work to incorporate this with their prior conceptions; people are active learners (Pintrich, Marx, & Boyle, 1993; Strike & Posner, 1992). Through social mediation provided by the study group participants and the incorporation of relevant topics and issues, each member of the study group is personally involved and actively engaged in learning. As student teachers listen, talk, and think about particular educational issues, they consider the topics of discussion in relation to their own beliefs, experiences, understandings, and future teaching plans. Science as a discipline and the process of learning are recognized as socially directed and mediated (Kuhn, 1996; O'Loughlin, 1992). Learning about a particular phenomena by an individual can never be complete; it is a process of approaching the socially accepted, distributed understanding of the phenomena (Salomon, 1993). Social mediation within the study group provides opportunities to consider multiple perspectives and alternative conceptions so all participants have a chance to build and articulate complex understandings of educational issues. Sociocultural constructivism takes into account that learning is socially embedded (Lave & Wenger, 1991; Newman et al., 1989; Vygotsky, 1978). Student teachers receive social and intellectual support in their process of learning as they share or explain their work with others in similar situations as them. A learning environment that provides this type of situation for student teachers also provides opportunities for reflection (Grimmett & Erickson, 1988) and meaning making (Singer, Marx, Krajcik, & Chambers, 2000).

As a facilitator, I draw on sociocultural constructivist learning theory to shape my role in helping student teachers explore topics in depth, in ways that apply to their work, and in an integrated manner. In discussing the role of a facilitator in social constructivist teacher education, Richardson (in press) notes that teacher educators should have the following skills and knowledge:

> Knowledge of how teacher education students learn, and how to diagnose student learning. Ability to use this knowledge quickly and flexibly during the classroom lesson. Ability and interest in determining participants' beliefs about teaching and learning and particular practices. Skill in asking sometimes difficult questions that call for deep responses for students, and the ability to do so in a non-threatening way. Knowledge of teaching practice such that current examples of practices and classroom scenes may enter the conversation. (p. 17)

Drawing on this list, learning theory, and personal experience, I articulated a suite of strategies and guiding principles for my facilitation, shown in Table 7.1.

Table 7.1. Description of Strategies and Guiding Principles Articulated for Facilitation

- Meet students where they are; draw upon their points or interests
- Be non-judgmental
- Connect student initiated topics to science methods and CMAP topics when fits with discussion
- Ground discussion in experience, student work, examples
- Emphasize depth vs. breadth
- Engage in positive reinforcement
- Identify + and -, pros and cons, approach from different perspectives
- Be honest re: agendas, rationales
- Value stories, personal experience, narratives
- Make reasoning or rationale explicit
- Let other participants respond before me
- Introduce complexities and/or background (through historical, political, logistical contexts or examples), issues and boundaries of teacher authority

Theory–Practice Relationships

Exploration of theory and practice in this study requires that I make explicit my conception of these terms. I articulated two conditions that characterize statements of *theory* by participants of the study group. First, theoretical statements are abstract understandings or positions not tied by the speaker to actual teacher practice or a particular event. Often, a speaker represents this in a way that takes the form of a philosophical or personal belief statement; of interest to me, however, is that the statement points to a larger context or generalization. I have chosen not to focus on individual participant's personal theories or beliefs, as I am concerned with the discussion and exploration of science education theory in relation to teaching of science. Second, theory in this study refers to education theory; in particular theoretical notions relevant to science education and social constructivist teaching.

I articulated *practice* as such: statements, observations, or positions made by the speaker that are based in actual teacher practice, events, or experiences. Practice is generally pragmatically oriented and dictated by context. The segment of speech presented here illustrates statements of theory and practice in a study group transcript. In this segment, Olivia (Ol) builds from practical considerations grounded in her student teaching experience to articulate a theoretical position about the organization of curriculum and its relevancy for students, a central theme in reform-based curriculum design.

> Ol: I think that the BSCS Biology, like, a molecular approach is set up completely wrong. Because, I think that kids are more interested in Ecology, and you can do some really fun activities tromping around in the woods, . . . or human impact and deforestation, . . . like look around [the district]. All the wetlands are disappearing, and . . . you talk about that, and then you go down to like homeostasis, . . . you go from Ecology to evolution and you know, so all these animals have these niches and they all fit together and then you, how do they evolve that way. And you go to evolution and then you go down from that to like, ok, these systems evolved these certain ways, so how did all these systems work? So go down to homeostasis and organs. And then you go down smaller and smaller and smaller, whereas this book starts out small, and they're studying like, acids and bases and carbohydrates and stuff and they're just like, blaaaah. You know, who cares?
>
> Ty: Right.

Ol: And I think if you keep going down, then they understand why they're, why they're studying it and why its important, and, I don't know. I think like you start with stuff that they're interested in and you go down. (Olivia & Ty, Tape 001)

In this excerpt, Olivia iterates several tenets of reform-based curriculum design theory; in particular the need for relevancy and to design curriculum from big ideas to details (NRC, 1996; Singer et al., 2000). Her talk starts in the classroom, in actual experiences and observations of her experiences in her student teaching. Her summative statement (final three lines) is theoretical in nature as they are a position statement about how curriculum should be in general, not in any one particular instance. Nowhere in this segment does Olivia use the terms *theory* or *practice*, nor does she neatly divide her comments between abstract and pragmatic statements. Instead, the practical and theoretical references are mixed throughout the transcript segment.

Intertextuality as an Orienting Perspective

As illustrated by the transcript of Olivia's talk about curriculum and student relevance, the mixing of theoretical and practical considerations requires a detailed analysis of dialogue and close study of the surrounding context. The concept of intertextuality provides a frame to examine how relations of multiple influences, perspectives, and/or events are carried out in nuanced social discourse. Intertextuality was first articulated by Julia Kristeva (1966/1986) and used extensively in literary analysis to examine how writing (and reading) is responsive to, influenced, and shaped by the social and historical context from which a text arose. While each individual constructs and articulates his or her writing or dialogue (a text) in a unique way and situated in a local discourse community, he or she is also part of larger sociohistorical conversations found in global discourse communities (Killingsworth, 1992). In this context, discourse is double-voiced and dialogic (Allen, 2000; drawn heavily from writing of Bakhtin); we talk about multiple issues or topics (such as theory and practice, curriculum and motivation) and from multiple perspectives or positions (such as student, teacher, administration) at the same time. In analyzing intertextuality, an analyst attempts to describe intertexts between local and global discourse communities, issues or topics, and perspectives or positions as they are represented in the text. Because speakers do not often attribute the influences that shape their dialogue, describing intertextuality of a text is an interpretive act (Allen, 2000; Bloome & Egan-Robertson, 1993). Employing an analytical structure that values this conception of intertextuality is described next.

METHODOLOGY

Data collection and analysis focus on interactional moves by all study group participants and particularly on how my moves as a facilitator influence exploration in discussions of theory–practice relationships.

Data Collection

My role as both facilitator and researcher requires that I be a participant observer for this study (Emerson, Fretz, & Shaw, 1995; Jorgensen, 1989). In this role, I am able to experience events then record my insights and reflections in detail after each session. For each of the six study sessions held during the semester, all but the first was videorecorded using one stationary camera to capture participant interaction and dialogue. Fieldnotes were written by me after each session (Emerson et al., 1995) and included descriptions of what happened, thoughts I had during and after a session about facilitation, member interactions, and patterns that emerged. Participant feedback on the value, structure, and function of the study group was elicited at several points during the term. I also periodically reviewed the videotapes of prior sessions to get a preliminary sense of emerging patterns or themes. Several of these themes were presented to the students during the study group reflection times embedded within the sessions. Although conducting participatory action research can be beneficial, it can also limit the analysis as I am directly involved in the context as well (Delamont, 1992; Emerson et al., 1995). I have attempted to design an analytical method that complements my research questions and provides a means of examining my participant observer status. One approach taken to illuminate my participant-observer status was to provide all participants opportunities to review and comment on my analysis and writing to confirm or challenge my work and perspective.

Data Analysis

Data analysis has been designed to reflect the organizing logic of this study, as portrayed in Fig. 7.1. Briefly, transcription and mapping of each videotape, with consideration of emergent themes recorded during this process, provide a basis for examining the topics and issues student teachers find important and relevant. Intertextuality is then employed to examine the transcripts for instances of juxtaposition of theory and practice, providing the basis to examine the role and influence of my facilitation.

Transcription of all videotapes was completed for the purpose of obtaining a record of dialogue and content. Very little symbolism was

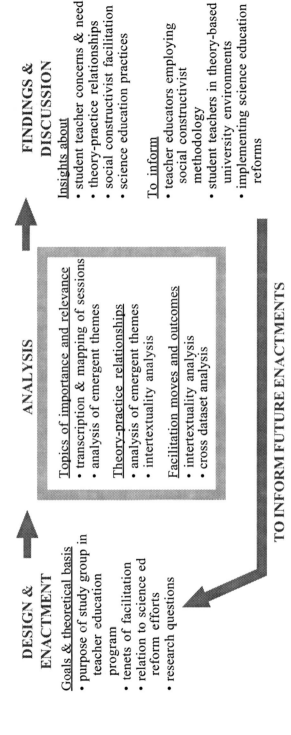

DESIGN & ENACTMENT

<u>Goals & theoretical basis</u>
• purpose of study group in teacher education program
• tenets of facilitation
• relation to science ed reform efforts
• research questions

ANALYSIS

<u>Topics of importance and relevance</u>
• transcription & mapping of sessions
• analysis of emergent themes

<u>Theory-practice relationships</u>
• analysis of emergent themes
• intertextuality analysis

<u>Facilitation moves and outcomes</u>
• intertextuality analysis
• cross dataset analysis

FINDINGS & DISCUSSION

<u>Insights about</u>
• student teacher concerns & need
• theory-practice relationships
• social constructivist facilitation
• science education practices

<u>To inform</u>
• teacher educators employing social constructivist methodology
• student teachers in theory-based university environments
• implementing science education reforms

TO INFORM FUTURE ENACTMENTS

Figure. 7.1. Organizing logic of the study.

237

used to indicate speech patterns, inflections, latching, or other characteristics. If an understanding of nuance was later needed, I returned to the original videotape. Event maps were then constructed to aid analysis; each map includes the topics discussed, time on topic, participants involved, and my moves as facilitator. Mapping sessions involved identifying events and subevents, including identification of discussion topics. For each subevent, a general summary of what happens, including facilitation moves, was written. Emergent themes were recorded as transcription and mapping took place. The remaining analysis focused on those categories relevant to current educational issues in science teaching and social constructivist learning theory. Once the transcripts and maps were complete, all statements of theory and practice made by participants were identified. These were viewed in context of the surrounding discussion and participant moves in order to identify the content and nature of the statements. In addition, for each instance I articulated how the statements were linked to the science education theory for that category. An analysis of intertextuality was then employed to examine the nature of the theory–practice relationships and the role of my facilitation within the discussion.

Intertextuality as a Framework to Examine Facilitation

Bloome and Egan-Robertson (1993) provide a structure to examine intertextuality as instantiated in socially constructed interactions for juxtapositions of both textual and nontextual references. This structure provides a frame for examining the mechanism of how intertextual juxtapositions are accomplished, and is characterized by the presence of four main components: a *proposal* that juxtaposes multiple references, *recognition* of the proposal, *acknowledgment* of the juxtaposition, the total of which leads to and includes *social significance* for the group. The conceptualization and implementation of intertextuality in this study is represented in Fig. 7.2.

A *proposal* that juxtaposes theory and practice can be introduced by any participant in the course of the conversation. Through agreement with or comments related to the proposal, other group members can recognize the proposal discourse move (*recognition*). If nobody picks up on this proposal during the subsequent conversation, the proposal is *not recognized*. Comments that indicate that other members have understood both the theoretical and practical components being juxtaposed, that the juxtaposition has meaning to them, and they are willing to take it up is considered *acknowledgment* of the proposal. When acknowledgment does not occur, exploration of the proposed juxtaposition is effectively *discouraged* as a focus of discussion. Bloome and Egan-Robertson (1993) note that

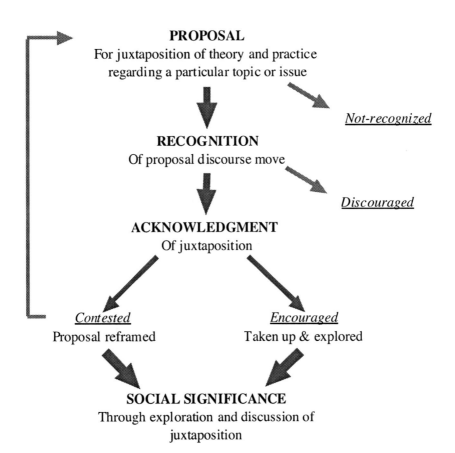

Figure 7.2. Conceptual model showing the relation of *intertextual components* with possible study group *exploration outcomes*.

both recognition and acknowledgment often occur in the same move; so often that they do not distinguish them in practice. For purposes of analysis in this study, I articulate a distinction between them. *Recognition* of a proposal indicates that others were listening to the speaker as the proposal was made, but there is not overt evidence that they understand the theory and practice issues being juxtaposed. *Acknowledgment* demonstrates *evidence* that the theory and practice components of the proposal have been understood and have meaning to others. Acknowledgment and subsequent discussion can yield two different results. The intertextual juxtaposition of theory and practice as proposed can be taken up and discussed in its original form, effectively being *encouraged* as a focus for discussion. The original proposal can also be reframed, or *contested* by any participant.

In this study, proposals for the juxtaposition of theory and practice were identified in the study group transcripts then followed through the discussion to determine the nature of the juxtaposition and the outcome of the discussion (*encouraged, contested, discouraged,* or *not recognized*). For proposals that are acknowledged or contested, an analysis of the *social significance* for the group in regards to the linking of theory and practice was undertaken. Consideration of social significance entails "identification of the social positioning and other social work done through the social construction of intertextuality as well as identifying the role the intertextuality plays in the construction of the ongoing event" (Bloome & Egan-Robertson, 1993, p. 320). In other words, this is the "social consequence" of the discussion based on the proposed juxtaposition. Analyzing social significance is an interpretive act, and as such requires careful consideration of the context and sequence of the dialogue in which the proposal is embedded, the subsequent perspectives and positions taken or considered, and connections made between topics or issues. The scope of the social significance can extend beyond the particular intertextual instance into later segments of discussion, or other sessions.

I began the analysis of social significance in this study by describing the subsequent discussion; its flow, topics and perspectives considered, and participant moves made. This was followed by an examination of how content and "others" (e.g., experienced teachers, administrators, or students) are represented through the conversation. I then articulated connections that were made between various topics or issues in the discussion. This helped me to make a tentative statement about whether there is an increased awareness or understanding of the theory–practice relationship being considered. This is a particularly interpretive step but one that I feel should be taken, as the purpose of the study group is to achieve this result. Consideration of all of these components required that I continually look for confirming and disconfirming evidence within the transcripts. The actual positions, beliefs, and understandings of the participants are only visible in as much as they are represented in their talk and actions during the discussion. Finally, to aid examination of my facilitation moves, I examined how I positioned participants, the content topics, and the theory–practice juxtapositions. This examination provides insight into how my facilitation helps or hinders student teacher's consideration of theory–practice relationships. I examined each intertextual instance on an individual basis using the approach just described, and then compared instances across the data set to describe patterns regarding the nature of the theory–practice explorations and of my facilitation moves.

FINDINGS

Intertextual Analysis

Analysis of intertextuality provides insight into the complexity of the study group dialogue. *Encouraged* intertextual instances are those discussion segments in which a juxtaposition of theory and practice become the focus of conversation. *Encouraged* instances are as short as 1 to 2 minutes, and as long as 13 or 14 minutes. Only a small proportion of *encouraged* instances of theory–practice connection making were actually initiated by me, and in one occasion I had no involvement with the theory–practice connection making in any way. Of the 12 *encouraged* instances found in the data set, 3 are based on proposals initiated by me, 2 by Olivia, 2 by Isabelle, 3 by Henry, and 2 by Ty. There is only one instance of a participant *contesting* a proposal. In total, the *encouraged* instances encompassed 32% of the study group discussion time. An additional 18 proposals are made by participants during the study group sessions but do not result in encouraged instances. These *available theory–practice* instances are those where theory and practice are either articulated but then not linked or formulated as a proposal, expressed as a proposal but *not recognized* by participants, or expressed as a proposal that was actively *discouraged*. An example of one session (Tape 201, seen in Fig. 7.3) shows *encouraged* and *available theory–practice* instances found within the session, mapped relative to the tape time, event topic, and subevent topic. Notation for each type of instance is represented as "INSTANCE" and "Available t/p," respectively, followed by the sequential number over all sessions.

TIME	EVENT TOPIC	SUBEVENT TOPIC	INTERTEXTUAL INSTANCE
0:00	Getting started		
0:36	Spring fever	everyone ready for a break	*Available t/p 3*
0:54		what doing to focus or motivate students	
1:52		attendance in class	
2:26		strategies to motivate students	
3:25	School calendar		
7:03	Spring fever (cont.)		
10:42	Lesson planning	changes in lesson planning	*Available t/p 4*
11:56	Grading	checking papers	*Available t/p 5*
14:17	Lesson planning (cont.)	effects of class attendance on planning & teaching	INSTANCE 05: value of group activities as impacted by irregular attendance
18:35	Students missing school	student motivation and attendance	INSTANCE 06: teaching to motivate students & changing low attendance
19:12		selective attendance	
21:56	Teacher performance	lack of effort or care	
23:05	Students missing school (cont.)	selective attendance (cont.)	
25:00	Teacher performance (cont.)	teacher burnout	*Available t/p 6*
27:53	Grading	importance of consistency	INSTANCE 07: assessment for fairness & feedback
29:53		student misconceptions	
31:10	Lesson planning (cont.)	relation to CT action, need for activities	*Available t/p 7*
32:29		role of CK, subject area	
34:16		strategies for engagement and management	

Time	Category	Topic	Instance
38:50	Teacher change	changing to reform based	*Available t/p 8*
41:33	Lesson planning (cont.)	need for activities (cont.)	
42:11	Curriculum issues	curriculum coverage, lack of alignment	INSTANCE 08: negative effects of repetitious curriculum (*Available t/p 9*)
44:23	Transition to first year of teaching		
49:15	Lesson planning (cont.)	need for activities, strategies for variety	*Available t/p 10*
51:28		lesson planning logistics	
57:46	Curriculum issues	time coverage	*Available t/p 11*
58:55		issues of coverage	
1:04:03		explaining CK	
1:05:52		issues of coverage (cont.)	
1:06:34		inquiry experience & teaching	
1:07:57		depth vs. breadth	INSTANCE 09: Justifying time for depth
1:09:00	Teacher change	historical context	End tape at 1:11:00

Figure 7.3. Event map of Tape 102 showing category, topic, and interactional instances.

Trends Found Across Intertextual Instances

The presence of intertextual instances show that student teachers do relate theories of science education and practices of teaching science in the study group discussions. They also demonstrate complex understandings of educational issues and can relate those to practice. The frequency of *encouraged* instances and the analysis of intertextuality show that there is success in posing and examining theory–practice relationships. In a number of instances there is evidence of an increase in participant's understanding or awareness of how practice is informed by theory (or vice versa), although this is a fairly interpretive consideration given the nature of the data. Particular intertextual instances often visit a number of topics and issues simultaneously. The topics and issues members bring to the group show a fairly high level of integration; student teachers make connections to and between general educational concepts, practices, and theories. Student teachers come to the sessions with much of this understanding, but they also note that the study group forum gives them a place to articulate their conceptions, explore connections, and gain support for their ideas and thoughts. They felt that reflection was promoted and they had a chance to process their student teaching experiences in relation to university coursework. They viewed the group as a "sounding board" to explore issues and strategies that emerge from their student teaching experiences. Although an integrated conversational pattern exists, there are, however, frequent times when the conversation moves to related connections and issues before there is a chance to explore a particular instance or issue in depth. The fairly quick transitions from one topic to the next, the higher frequency of *available theory–practice* instances, and the large amount of time not engaged with science education or social constructivist teaching topics suggest that there is room for improvement of my facilitation in future enactments of the study group.

Intertextual moves can be made by any participant; proposals are made by all members of the group and juxtapositions are *encouraged* or *discouraged* through the interactions of all participants. As the facilitator, I play an active role in the discussion, but overall *encouragement* or *discouragement* is not dependent on the moves of any one participant. In *encouraged* instances, theory is integrated with discussions of practice; theory is never discussed as a topic of its own, separate from practical application. In addition, the dialogue within *encouraged* instances generally begin and end with practical considerations; they are grounded in practice and have theoretical insertions embedded throughout. There is often a description of a classroom or teaching situation that provides the context for the articulation of a proposal. Theory is embedded in the proposal and returned to several times in the instance.

The following three examples illustrate how juxtapositions of theory–practice relations around topics of science education take shape and are discussed in the study group. In addition, they show how I am active in facilitation, both to *encourage* and *discourage* considerations of theory–practice relations. In particular, they illustrate two strategies that I have identified through the analysis: "facilitated exploration" and "embedded proposals." Considerations of patterns across my facilitation moves can be seen in the context of these three examples and are discussed afterward. Two of the examples are drawn from Tape 102 (Fig. 7.3) for consistency and to provide as deep a view of one session as possible. The structure of each example reflects the process I undertook in the analysis of intertextuality, as described earlier. To aid reading of the analysis with the transcripts (found in Tables 7.2-7.4), italicized phrases in the text are linked to corresponding phrases in the right hand column of each figure.

Facilitated Exploration

In this segment (Table 7.2), Ty introduces a *proposal* regarding ninth-grade curriculum based on his experience and observations. He juxtaposes the theoretical notion that a ninth-grade science curriculum should lay the foundation for subsequent, more advanced classes, with the practical result that students touch upon a lot of terms but achieve little depth of learning. He argues that attempts to provide a survey course with the hopes of improving subsequent performance are not successful since students do not have a chance to actually learn all the concepts for later use; a breadth-versus-depth argument (NRC, 1996). I make a comment that achieves *recognition* of the proposal, but there is not enough evidence to constitute acknowledgement. Olivia quickly points out that the situation described by Ty effectively results in a "wasted year." This statement shows that Ty's proposal is understood and has meaning for her, thereby achieving *acknowledgment*. I *agree* with their assessments and *expand its scope* by noting that the situation extends to middle school as well. Ty *agrees* with my comment by relating his own experiences in both contexts. Since curriculum over multiple years is being considered, I take the opportunity to introduce the concept of *alignment*, a notion mentioned briefly in methods class. This serves to articulate, or at least name, an aspect of the underlying theory of Ty's proposal. Olivia demonstrates that she understands alignment through her *summary* of alignment in the context of life sciences, but then notes that *in practice* the curriculum is repetitive and a little increase in detail each year just leads to a lot of wasted time. Ty then comments on how *students get bored* when they hear the same stuff over and over, to which Olivia quickly *agrees*. I take this opportunity to stress the importance of assessing student *prior knowledge* for purposes of planning to reduce overlap and not bore students by teaching material they already know. Ty notes that he *did that* recently, and Olivia reflects on the *limitations* of that strategy; students may know it but not realize it until the lesson is well underway. I provide *another possibility* based on my experience, which Olivia agrees is possible. At this point, I *summarize* the need to try to assess prior knowledge which brings this segment to a close as Ty *changes the topic* to the practical considerations of how to "do more" through implementing more activities in his teaching.

Table 7.2. Transcript of *Encouraged* Intertextual Instance 08, With Text References

INSTANCE 08, TRANSCRIPT (TAPE 102)	TEXT REFERENCES
School reform (42:11)	
Ty: = Cause we won't really get back to it. And we didn't really all that into earthquakes as much as I would have liked to, you know, but, there's not time. Its like, you just cover stuff in ninth grade. Like, =	*Proposal*
Fo: Mm-hmm.	
Ty: = you just touched on, you drop a couple words, you know, and you're gonna like, get these and more next year, or, when you take another science class.	
Fo: Yeah, that's an issue that I have with a lot of curriculum.	*Recognition*
Ty: Its like just, its such an, like, its just an intro year it seems like. Like, you're just introducing like, every tiny little thing.	
Ol: But then you have to redo all of that again. Its like a whole wasted year.	*Acknowledgment*
Fo: And in a lot of ways, you're redoing a lot of what they're doing, they've already done in scope middle school. In a lot of senses.	*Agree, expand scope*
Ol: Its wasted.	
Fo: Yeah.	
Ty: Middle school, seventh and eighth grade, seemed the same to me, they did the first, they switched books half way through or some, I don't know.	*Agree*

Fo: Yeah, different districts do it differently, but there's so much overlap, and that's what the term alignment, I don't know if you remember that term at all. Its usually in context of reform.	Introduce "alignment"
Ol: If they, even with that, they still end up having the, like, I think if =	
Fo: To redo things, right.	
Ol: = if you have like, in sixth grade they had, like, life science type stuff. ... They had like life sciences for the first half of the year, and they, all they did was study like, the self. And different organelles and stuff. Then, you don't really have to go over that again cause they covered it in so much depth that, I don't know.	Summary with example
Fo: Right. Just redoing it.	
Ol: Yeah. Then you, in, instead they =	
Ty: Well, and the problem is =	
Ol: = just like skim and then they go up again, they redo it all but they go into a little more detail, and they have so much wasted time.	But, in practice
Ty: And then kids get bored. Then they don't want to do it.	Bored students
Fo: All the more reason that you need to =	
Ol: Cause they've had it all before.	Agree
Fo: = ask them what they know already, and,	Prior knowledge
Ty: I did do that at the beginning of this one.	"Did that"
Fo: Excellent.	
Ty: I was like =	
Ol: Sometimes they think they don't know it, but then they really do.	Limitation
Fo: Sometimes they think they don't know it, sometimes they'll actually physically pretend not to know it. So,	Another possibility
Ol: So that they can have a review.	
Fo: = they get a way a, you know, from doing new stuff. So you have to know those kind of things do exist. And, you know, you can't just take things at their face value necessarily. But, it's a good start that you're doing it in some form, rather than not at all, so.	Summarize
Ty: I don't know, I would like to do more. You know?	
Fo: Yeah. I agree.	
(Ty goes on to discuss desire to incorporate more activities into his teaching.	Change topic

Ty :: Ty   Fo :: Jake (me)
Ol :: Olivia   = :: latching or overlap

Perspectives considered in this instance include a district curriculum perspective (an administrative viewpoint of sorts), in terms of the lack of alignment; and the perspective of the student, in terms of their experience in this curriculum sequence. Teachers are hardly alluded to in this segment, indicating that the curriculum positions both students and teachers as subject to an unchangeable, frustrating experience that they have little influence over. The curriculum in turn is positioned by the student teachers as "lacking" or "a waste."

Connections are made between the nature of the curriculum and the effects on students, as well as between the need for certain strategies—such as assessing prior knowledge—to avoid excess repetition. There does appear to be an understanding of the effects of such a long exposure to this sort of experience for students, who become bored and cannot (or do not) articulate what they have learned. Whether I was able to increase their awareness that they can do more as teachers in this context is not readily seen. A sense of their frustration and amazement at how things are is visible, but there is little exploration of what individual teachers might do to curb the repetition and plan for instruction based on a preliminary assessment of student understanding.

My facilitation moves within this segment consist of three components. I *agree with* Ty's assessment of the curriculum, which recognizes the proposal and gives value to the topic. I *introduce the notions of* curriculum alignment and the importance of assessing prior knowledge to aid planning. The first names and articulates the underlying theory, and the latter attempts to challenge student teacher thinking about their role by interjecting a sense of teacher control over curriculum. These points are picked up and commented on but do not change the tone or nature of the segment. At the end I *pose an alternative possibility* to Olivia's limitation from my experience, and *summarize* the need for assessing where students are. This seems to terminate the conversation as it provides an opportunity for Ty to turn to a slightly different topic.

In each of the facilitation moves throughout this instance, I am following and/or building from to something that the student teachers have introduced to the conversation. In essence, I provide the links and extensions in the conversation. Student teachers always initiate discussion with topics or issues of relevance to them that provide a basis on which proposals are made. Throughout the study group sessions there were nine instances such as this one, where a student teacher initiates the proposal and I then make interactional moves to facilitate discussion and exploration. The nine instances of this "facilitated exploration" take about 23% of the total study group discussion time and demonstrate one means of *encouraging* theory–practice relationships.

Embedded Proposals

This instance begins with 3.5 minutes of discussion initiated by the student teachers. The discussion centers on how to help students examine multiple perspectives on religion. In particular, the student teachers debate the relationship of personal views of religion (by both students and scientists) in the face of evolutionary theory. They note that students are almost exclusively focused on taking a stand based on belief and community values. As the transcript in Table 7.3 starts, I ask about the role of evidence in justifying an individual's position or belief. Ty does not seem to pick up on my intent, instead continuing the prior debate with Olivia. After a moment I rephrase my point, articulating a *proposal* that juxtaposes the practical reality that students take noncritical positions about religion and evolution with the ideal conception that a focus on evidence provides a basis to make and defend scientific choices (AAS, 1993). Ty's subsequent comment achieves *recognition* of the proposal, but it is not until a few sentences later that he makes a comment that reflects an understanding of the proposal (*acknowledgment*). In an attempt to further clarify how Ty has approached this issue with his class, I ask if he is treating the assignment as a *preliminary assessment*. Ty notes that he did *sort of* treat it as such, but he *did leave it open* for students to approach it in a variety of ways. Isabelle then suggests a *strategy for integrating the theory and practice*, outlining how a teacher can highlight evidence that supports a particular evolutionary theory and explain the rationale to students. I then make a suggestion for a *second strategy* that embeds an *assessment possibility* as well, returning to Ty's agreement that this particular assignment served multiple functions. This discussion continues on this way for another 2 minutes until a student teacher introduces a related but distinctly new issue that the group switches to.

Table 7.3. Transcript of Encouraged Intertextual Instance 02, With Text References

Intertextual instance 02, Transcript (Tape 101)	Text references
(Conversation about multiple perspectives on religion; started 28:14.)	
31:41	
Fo: So what about the role of evidence though?	
Ty: What about it? I mean, so many people still believe that God created earth in seven days, what about the evidence?	
Ol: Not that many though.	
Ty: Ok, what about evolution? I mean, there are other people that say, no that's not the way it happened. Or what about Native Americans who said that all animals existed in the sky, and then one came down and picked some mud up from the bottom of the ocean and that started the continents.	
Fo: I guess um, I guess what I'm asking in terms of what about evidence, is in terms of the student writing and defending their own theories.	*Proposal*
Ty: Mm-hmm. Oh, I did, I did say that...	*Recognition*
Fo: In terms of your	
Ty: ... I'm like, putting, just writing I believe blah blah blah blah, done, period, is not going to cut the mustard. I'm like, you gotta back it up with something. So, what I, but that was tough too cause we haven't, like I said we haven't gotten to plate tectonics, or like, fossils, or like, stuff like that so, I don't know, I have to read over them. I don't know what I got yet.	*Acknowledgment*
Fo: So this is ah, kind of preliminary before you walk into the subject, you're getting a sense of what they believe in?	*Preliminary assessment*
Ty: Yes. This was before, we just started that today, and the paper was due today.	
Fo: Ok.	
Ty: The beginning of class.	
Fo: So its kind of a pre-assessment.	
Ty: Mm-hmm. But is was like kind of creative writing too, cause it was like no one knows for sure. So if you, you know, make up your own, or if you believe in one of the things that I've presented, cause I did talk about origins of the earth before hand. Here's some scientific theories, here's some Native Americans, you know, whatever.	*Sort of, but did leave it open*

Is:	But as you learn about the different theories, you can say, ok, now that's evidence that supports this kind of theory. And if you ...	*Strategy for integrating theory and practice*
Ty:	Sure.	
Is:	... believe that, you could use that as evidence. And say that, the things that we teach in school are things that we can usually back up with evidence and that's why we're learning this, cause there's evidence. And we're not learning [made up student name?]'s theory because, your theory although good, doesn't have the evidence to back it up yet. Maybe you'll find it out or something. So, then it would tie into their papers. That sounds like what you are going to do anyway.	
Ty:	Pretty much.	
Fo:	Yeah, it'd be interesting to have them revisit the paper afterwards, you know.	*Second strategy*
Is:	Mm-hmm.	
Fo:	You know, interject those kinds of pieces to it.	
Is:	See if they've changed.	*With assessment possibility*

(Conversation continues on about role of evidence in examining theory; to 37:03.)

Fo :: Jake (me)	Ty :: Ty
Ol: : Olivia	Is :: Isabelle

Perspectives considered by the group in this instance include the point of view of the student, practicing scientists, and teachers (in this case, as mediated by the expectations of the district curriculum). The group also consider (in the last 2 minutes) the process of science (theory shaped by new evidence) and how that constitutes a perspective that can be incorporated in work with students. The student teachers seem to focus on their students as being a bit stubborn, unwilling to consider evidence in their personal stances. At the same time, Ty and Isabelle are quite explicit in providing students the space to articulate their own beliefs (perspective), and then explore strategies to help students defend those beliefs from a more scientific perspective.

Connections made among the various issues in the discussion include links between understanding students (where they are coming from re: religion and personal beliefs) with methods and approaches to promote a focus and value on evidence in defending a personal position. Connections are also made with science as a practice, both with individual scientists and their beliefs (often religious in nature) and with how the field deals with new evidence to modify theory over time. Considerations of teaching methods are made to provide student freedom in articulating their beliefs, promote a focus on evidence, and serve as a means for assessment.

Facilitation moves that I make within this instance are few but varied. When the conversation first starts, I *stay out* for a bit to see how it will develop then come in with several *clarifying questions* of Ty as he describes the assignment and student's reaction to it. As Ty and Olivia discuss how various scientists view religion, I again *stay out* until I *introduce the concept of* providing evidence (at the start of Table 7.3). Because the group does not initially pick up on this introduction, I *rephrase* my point in the context of expectations we have for students in science class (the proposal), which is where Ty began this discussion. I then ask another *clarifying question* that *links to* another teaching issue (eliciting prior knowledge via a pre-assessment). Throughout the remainder of the conversation, I both *suggest and help explore strategies* in conjunction with the student teachers.

As illustrated in this example, when I initiate proposals they are "embedded proposals," meaning that my proposals draw from points, examples, or allusions to underlying theory brought to the conversation by the student teachers. These proposals are embedded in the context created by conversation of all participants in the group. In reality, most proposals exhibit this characteristic, including student teacher proposals. Some of their proposals, however, are formulated at the start of a discussion as they introduce a new topic, situation, or request for consideration. All three occurrences of discussion in which I initiate the proposal are "embedded" in nature. The small number of discussion based on "embedded proposals" only comprise about 9% of the total study group discussion time but are seen to be successful in *encouraging* theory–practice relationships.

Potential Explorations Not Leveraged

I begin this segment (Table 7.4) with an *opening question* about how planning has developed over time. Ty relates his experience in trying to make his last teaching unit interesting and engaging but instead finding that he just had to "get through it." Ty concludes his opening comments by expressing the desire to incorporate more activities and other student-centered strategies in his planning. Ty's comments embed a *proposal* that juxtaposes the theoretical value of activities and student-centered teaching to engage and motivate students and improve learning (NRC, 1996) with his practical experience of having difficulty in finding or developing student-centered material for some topics.

Table 7.4. Transcript of Available Theory–Practice Instance 7, With Text Referenc

AVAILABLE T/P INSTANCE 7, TRANSCRIPT (TAPE 102)	TEXT REFERENCES

Exploring teaching methods (31:10)

Fo: Ahm, how about planning for the two of you? How has that gotten over time? — *Opening question*

Ty: Eh. I could use some help. Probably. I don't know. I mean, like that one chapter I asked you about, I'm like, what can I do? Your like, nothing. Everybody, I asked everybody I could possibly ask. Everyone said the same thing. Your screwed. That's a shitty chapter, get through it, you know. Ok. So I did. This chapter's a lot better. Its got a lot, I think, you know, its got cooler stuff in it. Plate tectonics, volcanoes, stuff like that, and kids are into that kind of stuff. But, I don't know. I don't know what to do, I guess. [His CT] doesn't do that, I don't think, that much, so =

Fo: Do planning that much?

Ty: No, no, no. She, I mean, she knows, she definitely plan, I think plan, well, she's been doing it for so long, she doesn't really now, you know, I don't see her do that, all that much. — *Proposal*

Fo: Mm-hmm.

Ty: = Ahm, although I know she does, I mean, we, we'll talk about it or whatever. Set up a week, but, I just would like more activities, more stuff.

Fo: So now, this is content that isn't your background necessarily, right? — *Content background*

Ty: No. Which kind of makes it harder for me to come up, I don't know. Its like, its, cause I don't know it so well, its almost easier for me to deliver it. Like that. — *Role of CK in planning*

Ol: I found that to be the opposite.

Ty: Hmm.

Ol: But I think it might be the subjects I'm teaching. — *Challenge*

Fo: How so?

Ol: Ahm, well with Physical Science it seems like there's so much you can do, when you're doing electricity and magnetism and light and reflection and stuff like that. = — *Physical science*

Ty: Yeah.

Ol: = And even now we're doing like, technology, so its like nuclear power, and computers, radio, television, stuff like that. And so, even though I'm not even going to be certified to teach some-

thing like that, at all, ahm, I've had an easier time figuring out   *Biology*
stuff to do with them than I have been with Biology, which is
my major. Cause we're in like, protein synthesis and genetics.
And with genetics there's some stuff you can do, but I feel like
there's so many really cool demos and labs and stuff that deals
with Physical Science.

Ty: That's what I'm saying.

Ol: = And that's not even something that I'm all that comfortable
with. I don't know, I think it must just, just must be the subject
area, but I don't know if its because in college all the time,   *Prior*
like all that I had in college for Biology was lecture. Or I had   *experiences*
labs that we can't do in high school. Either because of the
length of them, expense of them, =

Ty: You had an entire lab class.

Ol: Yeah. Cause I had a lab class, and so, its either like you're working
with mice, and like, you know, cutting them open, and like, having
them living still and monitoring all sort of, I mean like, just, I mean,
stuff you can't do with high school students. Like my Physiology
class. Or too much time or too expensive. You know, so, I don't
know if its just my lack of experience with that, where its so
blatantly obvious, like some real simple things to do with Physical
Science, or. I don't, I don't know. But I'm having an easier time with
the one that I don't know as much about.

(Ty expresses frustration at student behavior when doing labs or   *End*
activities. This leads to discussion of management.)   *segment*

Fo :: Jake (me)	Ty :: Ty
Ol: : Olivia	= :: latching or overlap

My immediate follow-up to Ty's proposal is a question about the relation of the subject he had been teaching to his *content background*. This elicited a response about how he believes *content knowledge plays a role* in his ability to plan for activities. Olivia *challenges* that notion by sharing her experience with physical science (not her content knowledge area) and biology (which is her area). She finds that *physical science* lends itself to activities as she has had a much easier time coming up with activities there than in *biology*. She also considers how her *own experiences* may play into this, as much of her biology preparation was lecture-based and included labs that are impractical in high schools. That *ends the segment*, as Ty shifts to a related but new topic; expressing frustration at student behavior in transitioning to nonlecture teaching.

Although the discussion following Ty's proposal is quite interesting, it is not directly related to the proposal as embedded in Ty's initial comments. Ty is looking for consideration of how to infuse all subjects with student-centered strategies and activities. We do not take this up in the conversation. We do discuss how some subjects do not lend themselves to activities, and possible reasons for that, but we do not explore possible means or value of engaging students in those topics. There is no recognition or acknowledgment of Ty's request for input or his proposal regarding the value and practice of activities. My question about content knowledge is the first move that leads away from the proposal as a focus of discussion. Perhaps I intended to explore some related point with my question, but instead directed the conversation elsewhere and it never returned to Ty. In this instance, theory and practice are juxtaposed and "available" to be taken up in the conversation, but I discourage this exploration.

These instances where theory and practice are "available" in the conversations but are not taken up can be viewed as potential explorations that are not leveraged to promote theory–practice relationship building. As illustrated in this example, *discouragement* on my part certainly does happen; on at least 18 occasions throughout the study group sessions. Several times I did not notice a proposal, was stuck on a prior topic, or shifted topics in the middle of a comment. Other ways that I hindered theory–practice exploration was by bringing in too much theory (occasionally intended as an "embedded proposal"), drawing together too many points at once, taking on a position or perspective of authority at inappropriate times, talking too much, and allowing the focus of conversation to change too soon.

Facilitation Within Intertextual Instances

My facilitation plays an active role in both *encouraging* and *discouraging* the juxtaposition of theoretical and practical considerations within the study group discussions. Two facilitation principles (Table 7.1) that I drew on regularly in *encouraged* instances were to let others talk first (Table 7.2, for example) and to draw from their points (Tables 7.2 and 7.3, for example). In the study group forum, these moves result in several characteristic strategies during *encouraged* instances, those of "facilitated exploration" and "embedded proposals." Facilitated exploration is seen in the example of *encouragement* (Table 7.2) where Ty makes the initial proposal then I make moves to broaden the scope under consideration and make explicit related theoretical and practical notions. An embedded proposal is illustrated in the example of *encouragement* (Table 7.3) where I initiate a proposal in the context of a larger discussion begun by the student teachers. Finally, Table 7.4 illustrates several examples of moves I made to discourage exploration of theory–practice relationships.

Through reflection after the sessions and analysis of successes and mishaps found in the transcripts, I have developed a revised set of facilitation principles and strategies for my future work, outlined in Table 7.5. An important learning for me in regards to facilitation is how to recognize proposals, or opportunities for proposals, as the study group conversation is going on. I have learned how to hear "in-the-moment" theory statements; the brief generalized, abstract statements that indicate a theoretical position. I continually ask myself "what is the general principle this statement represents or embodies?" I listen closely to the trends, observations, or experiences in which student teachers express amazement, frustration, or requests for input, as these often indicate underlying values and assumptions that are aligned with a particular theoretical stance. I watch for instances where I can engage in facilitated exploration and make relevant embedded proposals.

Finally, analysis of my facilitation moves highlight aspects of the content and pedagogical knowledge that I need to bring to this forum. I find that I act as a generalist of science education and social constructivist teaching to engage with and facilitate conversations initiated by the stu-

Table 7.5. Revised Guiding Principles for Facilitation, based on Lessons from Enactment, Reflection on Sessions, and Analysis of Facilitation Moves.

- Set tone and interactional style (e.g., facilitate the conversation so that it has coherence; try not to let it bounce around too much).
- Develop and maintain a safe, collegial, and confidential environment.
- Provide space for all to contribute.
- Encourage personal stories and experiences. These provide a foundation to build from.
- Encourage sharing and discussion of topics, events, situations, handouts, or student work from classrooms as examples and conversation center pieces.
- Let others respond before me. To provide others a chance to express their opinion and perspective before my "authoritative" perspective was put out.
- Incorporate participant responses or perspectives into my proposals or comments. ("Embedded proposals") As segue to this, summarize points or topics that I heard from student teachers. This often led to opportunity to link multiple topics together.
- Do not try to link too much at once, or overload with theory. How much is too much?
- Follow up on points that promote exploration of depth and theory–practice relationships. ("Facilitated exploration")
- Be part of the conversation as a participant, not out and/or above it. I am there to learn as well! An important component of 'facilitated exploration.'
- Be nonjudgmental and provide positive reinforcement.
- Identify pros and cons, approaches from different perspectives, complexities and/or background.

dent teachers. The process of learning about teaching and becoming a teacher is experienced as a holistic endeavor by the student teachers. There is not one particular aspect of teaching science that can be the exclusive focus of their teacher learning or concern. This is reflected in the degree of interrelatedness the student teachers exhibit throughout the study group sessions. Student teachers valued the open nature of the study group, as they found the forum more useful as a place to explore many facets of science education and social constructivist teaching than just on the mechanics of teaching science. As the facilitator and a co-participant, I have to be able to negotiate the many realms associated with teaching generally, and constantly remain flexible to explore a variety of issues. I find it very useful to draw upon the spectrum of my classroom experience and academic knowledge to both participate in discussions and simultaneously facilitate exploration of theory–practice relationships.

DISCUSSION AND IMPLICATIONS

This study addresses how teacher educators can work with in-the-moment student interests and experiences to facilitate discussion and thought of theory–practice relationships as they apply to classroom teaching. This study group provides an opportunity for student teachers to come to understand the theoretical basis of and implications for teaching within current science education reforms. The focus on my facilitation in this research emphasizes an examination of how science educators can facilitate the promotion and exploration of the science education reform agenda (NRC, 1996). The interactions of the study group members promote the exploration of the theoretical basis and practical implementation of current reform components. Through this exploration, student teachers explore their own practices and contribute to the thinking of others within the study group. With this said, I have found that I can also keep reform practices from being explored through facilitation moves that work against student teacher exploration. Based on their feedback comments, student teachers feel that reflection of science education reform and practice in the study group is generally promoted, and the forum provided an opportunity to consider their beliefs and personal theories in relation to their teaching practice and that of their colleagues.

Through the intertextual analysis, the study group forum is found to be successful in promoting theory–practice relationships. Although there is certainly room for improvement in the frequency of these instances, theory and practice do intertwine in the conversations. The form of the conversations and the language used is dialogic in nature (Allen, 2000) and as such require careful examination. Intertextual instances generally start and end in practice, providing student teachers a mechanism to consider different perspectives or integration of topics and issues in a slightly different way than when they started. Whether this constitutes an increase in understanding or learning is hard to say given the evidence available for this study, but consideration of the social significance in each instance provides insight to where theory–practice explorations can lead.

Interestingly, I found that the diversity of participant perspectives and experiences shared in this forum provided a more balanced discussion than was found in the methods class. In the class, discussions center around one topic and one agenda at a time. I do not have the transcripts from the methods class to compare, but this does make some sense as the methods class has a goal of helping student teachers come to understand the foundational basis of social constructivist science teaching in a forum that requires many topics to be addressed in limited time. In contrast, the open nature of the study group provides for a participant-driven exploration that necessitates consideration of the multiple perspectives they have had to wrestle with throughout their educational experience. This study indicates there is potential value of having a component of the certification program that maintains an open agenda yet promotes guided exploration or reflection. In current policy environments that are increasingly adding requirements, this may be hard to achieve. This study indicates that its presence can help achieve those policy goals and promote reform agendas.

All participants bring their own topics, questions, or concerns to the study group forum, initiate connections between topics and issues, and provide suggestions for practical teaching strategies. Participant conversation, and hence understanding of educational issues, is seen as being integrated. Through these actions, all participants appear to be involved in reflection (Grimmett & Erickson, 1988) on becoming and being a science teacher. In future studies, intertextuality (Bloome & Egan-Robertson, 1993) could be used as a means to look particularly at reflection in more depth. This may be accomplished by looking for participant proposal making, involvement in subsequent discussion of a proposal, or consideration of multiple perspectives. Intertextuality may also be employed in an examination of a particular content area or theoretical stance regarding student teacher belief and understanding.

My facilitation as the teacher educator both *encouraged* and *discouraged* participant's exploration of theory–practice relationships. By acting on my guiding principles for facilitation and adjusting as the sessions progressed, I was able to successfully *encourage* intertextual instances of theory–practice exploration. Given the limited occurrence of *encouraged* instances relative to the entire study group time, there is room for improvement. Facilitation takes practice. This study has helped me to improve in these regards and led to the articulation of a refined set of guiding principles (Table 7.5); most notably "facilitated exploration" and "embedded proposals." Use of these approaches has helped me to guide 'casual' conversations to discussions of "substance." Starting with causual conversations of grading, complaints about student lack of care, or students not following directions in lab can be led into substantive conversations about assessment, student engagement, and curriculum. Being open and flexible was important to making the experience valuable for the student teachers. I have learned how to better identify intertextual possibilities in action, and how to act on those. In examining the effect of my facilitation moves, I have become much more aware of how I can actively *encourage* or *discourage* the navigation of the two worlds of theory and practice. Through this study, teacher educators should be able to get a sense of how facilitation grounded in sociocultural constructivist learning theory (O'Loughlin, 1992) can be implemented in particular practices and some of the results that can be achieved.

Of the skills required by facilitators of constructivist forums outlined by Richardson (in press), the "ability to use this knowledge quickly and flexibly during the classroom lesson" (p. 17) is the most relevant to me at the end of this study. Working within this study group forum allows me as the teacher educator to support students in thinking about meaningful and worthwhile aspects of science teaching, but does require facilitation skills and knowledge that is more dynamic compared to what is needed in a more traditional class environment, such as the science methods class. Through this study I have become much more aware of what to look for and how to act on in-the-moment aspects of dialogue to promote theory–practice relationships. This study provides support for the value of sociocultural constructivist tenets that make exploration of theory and practice possible for student teachers.

Close examination of what student teachers bring to the study group forum provides insight into their interests and needs, both in terms of science education topics and their approach to working in a reform environment. Consideration of relevant science education topics and issues can help direct course planning and program implementation. Consideration of approaches that are promoted in this forum, such as working with each other, exploring possibilities, and articulating substantive issues, have potential long-term implications for reform. Student teachers in this study are likely to be willing to say "I don't know" or "lets try something new" to other teachers or professional developers in the future, then find the in-house support to try it out.

This study intends to inform other teacher educators who work to help students construct meaning around particular agendas in their transition from theory-based university experiences to practice-based student teaching experiences. This study hopefully provides insight into the nature of the study group forum and its applicability in other teacher education or reform programs. Engaging in this study has helped me to develop as a teacher educator and promoter of science education reforms in classroom teaching. For science educators, this study hopefully provides an illustration of practices that can be used to promote and implement reform agendas. Being explicit about my facilitation moves and the resulting conversations should provide others insight into what effect the facilitator has on a teacher's process of navigating relationships of theory and practice. With a well-grounded approach, facilitators have the ability to work within an unstructured environment in a social constructivist way to help student teachers make links between theory and practice. Through particular facilitation moves, facilitators can *encourage*, and also *discourage*, this process for student teachers. Providing this type of support to the student teachers in this study has helped them to better prepare for the demanding conditions, expectations, tasks, and environment they will experience as professional science teachers.

REFERENCES

Allen, G. (2000). *Intertextuality*. London: Routledge.

American Association for the Advancement of Science. (1993). *Benchmarks for science literacy*. New York: Oxford University Press.

Bloome, D., & Egan-Robertson, A. (1993). The social construction of intertextuality in classroom reading and writing lessons. *Reading Research Quarterly, 28*(4), 305-333.

Cobb, P. (1994). Where is the mind? Constructivist and sociocultural perspectives on mathematical development. *Educational Researcher, 23*(7), 13-20.

Cochran-Smith, M., & Lytle, S. L. (1993). *Inside/outside: Teacher research and knowledge*. New York: Teachers College Press.

Delamont, S. (1992). *Fieldwork in educational settings: Methods, pitfalls and perspectives*. Washington, DC: The Falmer Press.

Dewey, J. (1916). Science in the course of study. *Democracy and education: An introduction to the philosophy of education* (pp. 219-230). New York: The Free Press.

Eisenhart, M., Behm, L., & Romagnano, L. (1991). Learning to teach: Developing expertise or rite of passage? *Journal of Education for Teaching, 17*(1), 51-71.

Emerson, R. M., Fretz, R. I., & Shaw, L. L. (1995). *Writing ethnographic fieldnotes*. Chicago: The University of Chicago Press.

Grimmett, P. P., & Erickson, G. L. (Eds.). (1988). *Reflection in teacher education*. New York: Teachers College Press.

Hollingsworth, S. (1989). Prior beliefs and cognitive change in learning to teach. *American Educational Research Journal, 26*(2), 160-189.

Jorgensen, D. L. (1989). *Participant observation: A methodology for human studies* (Vol. 15). London: Sage.

Killingsworth, M. J. (1992). Discourse communities—local and global. *Rhetoric Review, 11*(1), 110-122.

Kristeva, J. (1986). Word, dialogue and novel. In T. Moi (Ed.), *The Kristeva reader.* New York: Columbia University Press.

Kuhn, T. S. (1996). *The structure of scientific revolutions* (Original work published 1966) (3rd ed.). Chicago: University of Chicago Press.

Lampert, M., & Ball, D. L. (1999). Aligning teacher education with contemporary K-12 reform visions. In L. Darling-Hammond & G. Sykes (Eds.), *Teaching as the learning profession: Handbook of policy and practice* (pp. 33-53). San Francisco, CA: Jossey-Bass.

Lave, J., & Wenger, E. (1991). *Situated learning: Legitimate peripheral participation.* Cambridge: Cambridge University Press.

Mayer-Smith, J. A., & Mitchell, I. J. (1997). Teaching about constructivism: Using approaches informed by constructivism. In V. Richardson (Ed.), *Constructivist teacher education: Building a world of new understandings* (pp. 129-153). Washington, DC: Falmer Press.

National Research Council. (1996). *National science education standards.* Washington, DC: National Academy Press.

Newman, D., Griffin, P., & Cole, M. (1989). *The construction zone: Working for cognitive change in school.* New York: Cambridge University Press.

O'Loughlin, M. (1992). Rethinking science education: Beyond Piagetian constructivism toward a sociocultural model of teaching and learning. *Journal of Research in Science Teaching, 29*(8), 791-820.

Pintrich, P. R., Marx, R. W., & Boyle, R. A. (1993). Beyond cold conceptual change: The role of motivational beliefs and classroom contextual factors in the process of conceptual change. *Review of Educational Research, 63*(2), 167-199.

Richardson, V. (in press). Teacher education and the construction of meaning. In G. Griffin (Ed.), *Teacher education for a new century: Emerging perspectives, promising practices, and future possibilities.* Chicago: University of Chicago Press.

Salomon, G. (Ed.). (1993). *Distributed cognitions: Psychological and educational considerations.* Cambridge: Cambridge University Press.

Singer, J., Marx, R. W., Krajcik, J., & Chambers, J. C. (2000). Constructing extended inquiry projects: Curriculum materials for science education reform. *Educational Psychologist, 35*(3), 165-178.

Strike, K. A., & Posner, G. J. (1992). A revisionist theory of conceptual change. In R. A. Duschl & R. J. Hamilton (Eds.), *Philosophy of science, cognitive psychology, and educational theory and practice* (pp. 147-176). Albany: State University of New York Press.

Tobin, K., & Tippins, D. (1993). Constructivism as a referent for teaching and learning. In K. G. Tobin (Ed.), *The practice of constructivism in science education* (pp. 1-21). Washington, DC: AAAS Press.

Tozer, S., Anderson, T. H., & Armbruster, B. B. (1990). Psychological and social foundations in teacher education: A thematic introduction. *Teachers College Record, 91*(3), 293-299.

Vygotsky, L. S. (1978). *Mind in society: The development of higher psychological processes.* Cambridge, MA: Harvard University Press.

PART III
Exploring and Building Conceptual Knowledge

Ruth Piker

Hsin-Kai Wu

The following two chapters discuss how students, through their social interactions with teachers, materials, and each other, developed their conceptual knowledge within a classroom. Hsin-Kai chose to conduct a study about conceptual knowledge because research in science education places great emphasis on students' understanding of scientific concepts. Ruth's interest in children's conceptual knowledge grew from her curiosity about how routine social practices assisted children's conceptual development and change. We found our sites of investigation to be perfect for exploring both interests. However, in applying interactional ethnographic (IE) approaches for our studies, we struggled as we shifted from one way of thinking to another.

Both of us used data that we had begun collecting prior to learning about the IE approach and prior to developing our research questions. We did not realize that we were unconsciously guided in our data collection by theoretical and methodological frameworks that were psychological and positivist, and so contrary to the frameworks informing IE. Consequently, Ruth had difficulty developing useful research questions and determining which IE approach best fit her data. At first, she tried unsuccessfully to make the data fit an approach. A more successful strategy was to evolve a research question that would be relevant to the IE approach and that could be addressed with the data she had collected. The problem that Hsin-Kai encountered was finding a theoretical or methodological connection between the IE approach and the topic in which she was interested. She did not see how an ethnographic question such as "what counts as xxxx" would be relevant to students' confusion about chemical structures. With the help of Lesley and our group members, we had to change our way of thinking about students, teachers, and classroom practices, and discover how to apply IE as a theoretical lens for interpreting what we saw happening in the classroom. Our group discussion facilitated the reframing of our research questions from previous cognitive and positivist orientations to an IE perspective that made identifying the approach easier.

During the process of applying an IE approach, the use of data was still the primary issue for us. Hsin-Kai wondered if she had collected enough data. She was not certain she could conduct an ethnographic-style study because she had not planned to pursue the members' meaning when she was collecting the data, and so had not acquired a rich corpus of relevant data to analyze. The main problem Ruth encountered was selecting the data to analyze in order to explore children's conceptual development. She had to choose between the data that would most likely produce the strongest results, which contained controversial topics, and the data that were less controversial, but contained only a handful of instances that illustrated the children's application of concepts. Additionally, Ruth felt limited by having recorded some key preschool classroom playtime events with only audio recorders and not video, which limited the type of information she had to work with. Recognizing and then taking these limitations seriously shaped the studies we eventually were able to do.

In writing up our studies, the two of us adopted similar strategies with a common purpose. First, we intentionally focused the readers' attention to a specific aspect of the study. Ruth decided to forefront children's conceptual knowledge development while down playing the curriculum and instructional practices. Similarly, while Hsin-Kai highlighted the connection between cognitive learning theories and the IE approach, she de-emphasized the differences between the two theoretical approaches. Second, we included typical examples and detailed descriptions to support our claims. The examples supporting Ruth's claims come from different times throughout the year, were gender neutral, and included rich description; whereas, Hsin-Kai provided a detailed account of her data analysis and provided segments to illustrate her findings. Finally, both of our studies provided suggestions for teaching and learning conceptual knowledge. In retrospect we realize that because we were successful in using the IE approach, our research report was guided by an implicit aim to show that IE was not only productive in terms of theory-building but also helpful for understanding classroom practices.

We think that collaborative sharing played a critical role in thinking about the approaches and their application. As we struggled to conceptually understand the IE perspective, the group and classroom discussions about the data and the approaches were invaluable. These discussions influenced the evolution of our research questions and helped us generate interpretations and finish writing our studies. We were pushed in our discussions to justify our choices of language, methods, and interpretations. In sharing the drafts of our writing among the group members, we were pushed to examine the way we had laid out the structure of our arguments and provided evidence for our claims.

8

What Does It Mean to Build Conceptual Knowledge?

Ruth Piker

Being a former early childhood preschool teacher for 6 years and an early childhood researcher provided opportunities to witness multiple pedagogies and curricula. Over the course of one academic year, I was intrigued by the way one teacher, Rachel, structured her classroom and events throughout the day, but especially by her pedagogy and interactions with the children. The classroom schedule was similar to others I had seen, including meal times, Circle Time, and Free Play inside and outside. However, each week she had different topics that she covered through multiple avenues, using props, books, field trips, posters, music, and activities. She introduced new topics and vocabulary during one daily classroom event, Circle Time, and then provided opportunities for the children to make terms their own during another, Free Play. As I shared my observations and thoughts with my colleagues, the words *conceptual knowledge* emerged from our conversations. I wondered was I observing children developing conceptual knowledge? Were the children developing their conceptual knowledge about these topics? I knew that I could only explore these questions by observing Rachel's interactions with the children over time to see the routines and ways of learning that were occurring. I hoped that a detailed examination of talk over time might reveal whether she aided the development of conceptual knowledge in the children, and if so, how.

So, what does it mean to "build conceptual knowledge"? This phrase appears in government reports focused on student learning in classroom settings (National Research Council, 1999, 2001) and position statements of professional associations (Bredekamp & Copple, 1997; Neuman, Copple, & Bredekamp, 2000) for practitioners working with young children. These reports and position statements use the terms *conceptual framework*, *concept*, and *conceptual understanding* and suggest they are a vital part of a student's development; implying concepts are an important part of student learning. These reports call on educators to build learners' conceptual knowledge; however, not one of them ever defines or illustrates what is meant by conceptual knowledge.

The research literature on conceptual knowledge refers to domain-specific knowledge, domain-general knowledge, or learning models. For example, some research literature refers to concepts as larger theoretical paradigms and set phenomena, such as biology, ontological distinction, object permanence, physics, psychology, mathematics, and literacy (Carey, 1985; Gelman & Wellman, 1991; Tyson, Venville, Harrison, & Treagust, 1997), whereas others speak of concepts as vocabulary, ideas, words and experiences (Gelman & Markman, 1986; Gentner & Namy, 1999; Murphy & Medin, 1985; Ross, Nelson, Wetstone, & Tanouye, 1986). There appears to be an assumption that everyone reading these documents shares the same interpretations and definitions of concept and conceptual knowledge. The challenge faced by educators is how to translate these statements into practices that develop children's "concepts" and "conceptual knowledge." Conceptual knowledge is the knowledge an individual possesses about a concept, whereas conceptual development and conceptual change refer to how concepts develop and mature and how they change, respectively.

Prior researchers studying conceptual development and conceptual change used experimental designs in which children follow set procedures. Only a handful of theorists have created theoretical learning models to explain and to account for the complexity of conceptual change within classroom contexts. Unfortunately, this work speaks little to educators working in preschool classrooms. This chapter is a first attempt at understanding how young children's conceptual knowledge develops and changes within a naturalistic setting of a preschool classroom. By beginning to understand how children's conceptual knowledge develops and changes within a particular context, we can start to understand how contextual factors enhance or constrain conceptual development and change.

FRAMING THE STUDY

I take a social construction perspective to studying classroom settings (Santa Barbara Classroom Discourse Group, 1992). This theoretical approach seeks to understand how routine social practices in the daily activities of the classroom contribute to gaining access to learning and to the construction of knowledge (Green & Dixon, 1994). Researchers have used the perspective of social constructivism to explain how certain aspects of classroom life are defined and constructed as social processes within the classroom (e.g., Castanheira, Crawford, Dixon, & Green, 1998; Rex, 1999; Santa Barbara Classroom Discourse Group, 1992; Tuyay, Jennings, & Dixon, 1995). They believe teaching and learning are communicative processes. Classroom members socially construct common ways of interacting, which become vehicles for defining different aspects of classroom life, for interpreting what is occurring, and for evaluating what is appropriate to know and do in the classroom (Green & Dixon, 1994; Green & Harker, 1982; Green & Meyer, 1991; Gumperz, 1982). These common understandings and ways of interacting are what students use to gain access to the knowledge and learning taking place in the classroom.

I use this theoretical lens as a way to understand how the classroom routines and ways of interacting assisted the children in socially constructing conceptual knowledge and how these common ways of interacting offered opportunities for the children to challenge and be challenged for conceptual change. The purpose of this chapter is to ask what *might* conceptual development and conceptual change look like within a preschool classroom setting. From my year-long observations and recordings of classroom practices, I raise the question: what is conceptual knowledge? Through classroom members' social interactions, I witnessed the children develop prior and new concepts, and defend and question prior conceptual understandings, which lead to conceptual change. During particular events of classroom life, the teacher and children developed common ways of interacting that enabled the children to develop their conceptual knowledge.

Rachel, the teacher in this particular classroom, used weekly thematic units as her curriculum, which provided her with a means to create daily classroom events that fostered knowledge development and change. Rachel organized classroom activities that provided the children opportunities for learning new information, using prior knowledge and developing new understandings. The two most influential events of the day were Circle Time and play time, which are described in the Findings section. During Circle Time, Rachel introduced terms and ideas relevant to the theme of the week and recalled with the children the previous days terms and activities. What the children learned each day was reinforced throughout the week during Circle Time and play time, which enabled the children to incorporate the terms and ideas introduced during Circle Time into their play. Rachel also provided at least one activity during play time that simulated a Circle Time activity. As the children incorporated these terms, ideas and activities into their play, they also had opportunities to interact and negotiate with peers, other adults, and materials.

I selected interactional sociolinguistics as a way to explore the social construction of conceptual knowledge and to describe the classroom contexts in which this knowledge construction took place. According to Gumperz (1982, 1986), the "interactional sociolinguistics approach focuses on the interplay of linguistics, contextual and social presuppositions which interact to create the conditions for classroom learning. Analysis focuses on key instructional activities that ethnographic observations have shown may be crucial to the educational process" (Gumperz, 1986, p. 65). These activities are part of everyday classroom affairs. Teachers set up learning environments, organize classroom settings, and label and define instructional tasks that students over time understand and come to expect. By establishing shared environments, teachers create the conditions that make learning possible. Through their discourse, teachers and students maintain and hold together these daily activities. The task of interactional sociolinguistics is "to chart the process by which models of educability are put into daily life practice and to uncover the implicit theory of learning that informs our choice of model" (Gumperz, 1986, p. 67).

When the teacher communicates in a consistent manner, students become familiar with the types of discourse the teacher uses in the classroom. Gumperz (1986) referred to this as schemata or an interpretive frame, which is a frame for how an activity is supposed to transpire. For example, in this classroom, Rachel set up predictable organizational structures that the children knew how to recognize, such as a frame of reference for how Circle Time was going to happen every day. If the schema was not shared, different individuals may have interpreted the same message differently. This is visible when a new student enters a classroom mid-way through the year. Although Rachel and students use words such as Circle Time and listening time, the new student will not understand these terms as well or in the same way as the students who have been in the classroom since the beginning of the school year. This student will have to create a schema for this class by negotiating with Rachel and other students about what Circle Time means.

A researcher informed by this methodology uses ethnographic methods to map the interactional patterns in the classroom over time. By understanding the consistent patterns, the researcher is able to see what learning opportunity students have access to in the classroom. Ethnography is commonly associated with describing culture (Zaharlick

& Green, 1991): "Thus, ethnographers identify and explore the cultural patterns of everyday life and the consequences for participants of being members of particular cultural groups (e.g., religious, social, ethnic, educational, and/or bluebirds reading group)" (p. 206).

Using interactional sociolinguistics, I was able to map the daily classroom activities and note how Rachel threaded terms and ideas throughout the day. Because the children were familiar with these patterns, they knew how to gain access to interactions with others. Patterns of teacher–child interactions in the classroom illustrate how conceptual knowledge was socially constructed and negotiated by students across activities and across time. Before presenting examples that illustrate conceptual development and change in one Head Start classroom, I draw on the psychology literature to define conceptual knowledge, conceptual development and conceptual change, as these are the basis for my data interpretations.

CONCEPTUAL KNOWLEDGE

From a broad perspective, a concept is a mental representation (Gelman, 1996; Murphy & Medin, 1985; Wade & Tavris, 2000). Individuals use mental representations to assist in categorizing multiple pieces of information that have common properties, such as objects, activities, abstractions, or relations (Gelman, 1996; Murphy & Medin, 1985; Wade & Tavris, 2000). Individuals utilize concepts to organize information about the world in a manageable way that allows them to make decisions quickly and efficiently, identify novel entities, solve problems, form analogies, and create figurative images (Gelman, 1996; Murphy & Medin, 1985; Wade & Tavris, 2000). Children as young as infants have structured concepts of the world, life, biology, physics, and mathematics, which are the foundation for extending old concepts and for building new ones (Carey, 1985; Gelman, 1996; Murphy & Medin, 1985). Children use their concepts to assist them in generalizing membership to other objects, activities, or experiences. The structures of these concepts—the type of information that makes them up, the links that unite this information into a membership, and the way the concept is held together—are unique to the individual.

As children gain information and knowledge about a category membership, the concept is elaborated and expanded. The child uses this membership information to generalize to other objects, abstractions, experiences, and relations to develop and expand the concept. Theorists have tried to explain how the content of concepts and their organization develop into larger systems as the child matures (Gelman, 1996); keeping in mind that young children's conceptual structures differ from those of older children and adults (Carey, 1985; Gutheil, Vera, & Keil, 1998; Tyson, et al., 1997). For example, a child's concept of special needs would differ from an adult's, which would further differ from that of a special education researcher.

CONCEPTUAL DEVELOPMENT

Research on conceptual development attends to how children develop concepts and the links that unite the information into a concept. Murphy and Medin's (1985) concept–theory approach suggests "people's theories of the world embody conceptual knowledge and that their conceptual organization is partly represented in their theories" (p. 289). This approach explains how people's theories of the world enable them to (a) create and organize conceptual knowledge and (b) hold information, objects, and facts together as concepts (see Gelman, 1996, for a review of the literature). Children use prior knowledge and experience as they create theories about the events and situations occurring around them. Concepts are coherent as long as they fit with the individual's background knowledge, regardless of whether the two objects appear similar or dissimilar (Murphy & Medin, 1985).

Researchers studying conceptual development as learning in the classroom suggest that understandings are in part knowledge-dependent. The more knowledge or information provided for the object the more developed the concept and the more likely the child is to generalize to other information. Children with more knowledge about a category were further able to generalize to new objects, especially if the objects shared the same name (Gelman & Markman, 1986; Gelman & Wellman, 1991; Gentner & Namy, 1999). For example, children who compared objects with similar novel noun labels (i.e., blicket) were able to notice more commonalities within the category membership; thus, adding more members to this category (Gentner & Namy, 1999). If the child did not have prior knowledge or information about the item, there was a 50/50 chance that the child would correctly match the objects (Gelman & Markman, 1986). In addition, how elaborate and accurate concepts are may be a function of the amount and type of knowledge the child possesses; suggesting, "that the number of different things a young child can do with an object increases the child's ability to conceptualize the object and learn the name associated with it" (Ross et al., 1986, p. 80).

The children in this classroom were given information during Circle Time about a concept; they then reinvoked this new information into their play activities, but used their theories of the world and prior conceptual understandings to make sense out of this new information. As the children socially interacted with adults, peers, or materials, they developed their conceptual knowledge of this object or relation. I offer two examples to illustrate (a) how children's concepts of special needs and being on a plane would differ from those of adults, (b) how the children use their theories of the world to make sense and organize information presented by the teacher, and (c) how the more knowledge and time spent with an object a child has assisted them in generalizing to other situations and in developing their conceptual knowledge.

Conceptual Change

Researchers studying conceptual change focus on how children's concepts change over time and the mechanism involved in this change. Carey (1985) and Tyson et al. (1997) explicitly state what they believe is required for a theory of conceptual change. A theory of conceptual change must (a) acknowledge that individuals experience big and small conceptual changes, (b) take into account the age of the individual, and (c) locate itself within a classroom setting (Carey, 1985; Gutheil et al., 1998; Tyson et al., 1997). Carey's theory of conceptual change specifically addresses the small (weak) and big (strong) changes and focuses on children between 3 and 5 years of age, but it is not located within a classroom setting. Tyson and colleagues' theory locates itself within a classroom setting and addresses the small and big changes, however the students are in high school and college classrooms.

Carey (1985) conducted a series of case studies examining how children's domain-general and domain-specific conceptual knowledge is changed or restructured in the course of acquisition. Carey refers to two types of restructuring: "weaker sense" (novice–expert shift) and "strong sense" (theory change). The weaker sense (based on the work of Chi, Glaser, & Rees, 1982, cited in Carey, 1985) is described as follows: "with expertise, new relations among concepts are represented, and new schemata come into being that allow the solution of new problems and change the solutions to old problems" (p. 5). Conceptual change in the weaker sense occurs when children gain more information about one of their concepts, and accumulation of this information might be seen as changing the conceptual structure, allowing for more advanced thinking and elaborating. Through this accumulation of new information with prior knowledge, children provided more "expertise"-type information and solutions to new and old problems. The more knowledge about a concept, the better the child is able to think in sophisticated and accessible ways (Carey, 1985; Gobbo & Chi, 1986).

Strong sense restructuring refers to fundamental changes to the individual's core concepts, also referred to as theory change. Strong restructuring is more difficult to identify, unless you systematically document the child's prior knowledge, identify and follow the learning opportunities available to the child for developing his or her conceptual under-standing, and evaluate what the child remembered and learned. This is beyond the scope of this chapter because I did not document children's prior knowledge nor did I evaluate what they learned. However, this does not imply that strong restructuring was absent.

The third requirement for a theory of conceptual change is locating itself within a classroom context. Learning theories incorporate cognitive processes, motivation, and classroom factors for explaining conceptual change. The most well-known work theorizing conceptual change as a learning model is that by Posner and his colleagues (1982, cited in Tyson et al., 1997) with high school and college-age students. Because of the sen-sitivity to age in a theory of conceptual change, Posner and his col-leagues' model of conceptual change as a learning theory would not apply to my study. Nevertheless, I identify classroom factors that might have contributed to the children's conceptual change.

I describe interactions of children alone, with other children, and with the teacher that illustrate children using knowledge they learned in another setting and applying it to new settings. It can be seen that in some situations when interacting with others, the children were observed try-ing to explain certain events using their theories of certain concepts, but then struggled to reaffirm their position or change their understandings. However, in another example, the child easily generalizes his concept of how to carry babies from one setting to another.

Children's conceptual development and change appear to be affected by the amount of knowledge and information a child possesses. In this preschool classroom, knowledge provided by Rachel becomes a crucial variable influencing the kinds of concepts a child will possess, which ulti-mately become the foundation for further knowledge acquisition. Classroom factors that appear to enhance or constrain conceptual devel-opment and change are further discussed in the Discussion section.

DESIGN

The data collected for this chapter was part of an ongoing partnership between the University and a Head Start grantee agency located in a rural county. Over the course of 3 years, the partnership developed and evolved into what was called a "community of practice" (Lubeck & Post, 2000; Post & Lubeck, 2000) involving 11 teachers. During Year 4 of the project, each teacher worked on a particular project. The director's intent was that each teacher would explore a new form of practice (e.g., teacher portfolios, child portfolios) and then share her experiences with others. I was asked to support two teachers as they developed guidelines and rec-ommendations for teacher portfolios. I worked in the classroom of both teachers over the course of one academic year (1999–2000). However for this study, I focus on one of the classrooms.

The Classroom

Teacher and Children.   Rachel, who is Euro-American, had been teaching in the Head Start program for 10 years in 1999, the year of data collection. She taught from 12:30 to 4 p.m. Monday through Thursday. The average number of children enrolled throughout the year was 16. The children came from families with low incomes. They were 3 to 5 years old and, with the exception of one African-American child, all were of Euro-American descent.

Curriculum. At the time of data collection, Rachel did not use an official curriculum, nor did she borrow kits or use pre-established units. Rather, she created her own thematic units. These themes were the major source for building children's conceptual knowledge. Each theme covered a specific topic that lasted one week (e.g., fall, Halloween, family, community helpers, weather, zoo animals, etc.). Themes for each week ranged from dinosaurs and insects to topics such as transportation, special needs, and music. Over the course of the year, Rachel used the themes to expose the children to various terms and ideas.

My use of *terms* refers to words and ideas relevant to the theme of the week. Terms were signifiers of knowledge that Rachel found important for the children to know, illustrated by their daily recall. The terms were not vocabulary words that Rachel presented and children repeated or recalled once, then ignored. Through continual presentation and reinvoking of these terms, Rachel provided opportunities for the children to take-up terms and ideas and to incorporate them into their everyday language and play. Because a concept is a mental representation of objects, activities, and relations, the children used these terms to structure their conceptual understanding of the themes. These concepts were key for negotiating and building conceptual knowledge.

Data Collection

I used three ethnographic approaches for collecting my data: participant-observations, audiotaping, and videorecording. Participant-observations enabled me to gain a broader understanding of the classroom structure and practices. I participated in conversations where the teachers and other adults discussed classroom practices, curriculum, children, and administrative issues. I joined in Circle Time, sang and played with the children, and shared meals with all members of the classroom. My participant observations occurred on 28 days for the full session each day (3.5 hours) over 8 months. In October, I worked once a week as a participant-observer in Rachel's classroom. I then observed twice a week in November and December and returned to a once-a-week schedule for the remainder of the academic year. I kept fieldnotes for each day, which consisted of documenting the events and interactions of the day, such as group activities, individual activities, child–child interactions, and adult–child interactions. My fieldnotes of observations and interactions with teachers and children provided supplemental information for all classroom recordings. Most importantly, they were crucial when recording was impossible, such as while children played outside or in a large area where recording could only record parts of conversations.

Recording devices are required for documenting teacher–child interactions showing conceptual development and conceptual change. Audio- and videotape recordings enabled me to capture teacher and child language and interaction verbatim, particularly during Circle Time and Free Play. Group activities, included circle, sharing, and Story Times, were audiotaped on 12 different days. The third method consisted of 2 hours and 50 minutes of videotaping in the classroom on five different days. I videotaped five events of the day: Gross Motor, Free Play, Circle Time, Sharing Time, and Story Time. Only parts of Gross Motor and Free Play were videotaped, whereas I generally recorded the Circle Time, Sharing Time, and Story Time events in their entirety. On one occasion, the video camera battery died and, on another, Rachel used a video for part of Circle Time. I did not video record daily for a number of reasons, including difficulty with recording equipment, being on a field trip, and having atypical days.

Data Analysis

For this chapter, I only report on data that provide evidence of conceptual development and conceptual change. During the data-collection process, I noticed the teacher's weekly thematic units followed a similar structure (see Findings section). The children became familiar with the structure that enabled them to participate in the daily classroom activities and to access the teaching and learning. These structures were critical to the development of the children's conceptual knowledge. I chose data samples from multiple time points throughout the school year to illustrate how this structure for these children facilitates conceptual development and conceptual change with different concepts and at different times. Some examples come from my fieldnotes and the remainder from the recording devices. The dialogue from the recordings included in the findings section were transcribed by dividing the speech into message units (Gumperz, 1992), in which speech is broken up with a change in intonation and use of long pauses. Notations used in the tables are explained in the keys, which are located at the bottom of each table.

FINDINGS

Rachel developed particular activities and ways of interacting with children that enabled them to socially construct conceptual knowledge with her and other children. She provided opportunities for the children to learn new information and build on prior knowledge. The children interacted with her and with other children to negotiate what they knew and what the others knew as a way to build conceptual knowledge. Rachel's established patterns of expected behavior and activities signaled to the students that it was appropriate to take information introduced during one event of the day into another event.

In this section, I describe three events of the day that I believe played an important role in assisting the children to develop and change their conceptual knowledge. I follow this with examples that may be illustrative of conceptual development and conceptual change. The children's conceptual understandings of being on a plane and categorizing special needs provide some evidence for conceptual development. Conceptual change in the weaker sense may be evident in three interactions of a papoose, time and space, and insects.

Events of the Day

Rachel established events of the day that facilitated the children's opportunities to develop and change their conceptual knowledge. Because these events were established routines with consistent daily patterns, the children were familiar with and aware of the expectations during each event. The three particular events of the day that relate to this study were Circle Time, Free Play, and Large Motor. Rachel not only introduced terms and ideas during Circle Time, but also encouraged and signaled to the children to incorporate what they learned into their Free Play and Gross Motor activities.

The main purpose of Circle Time was to introduce the theme of the week and to conduct a lesson on that theme. During the lesson time, Rachel reviewed material presented earlier in the week. Through the review, Rachel re-emphasized certain terms and ideas as important and confirmed that the children had taken up the information. After she finished the review, she began a new lesson introducing new terms and ideas related to the theme. The children may have used these terms and ideas presented during Circle Time to structure their conceptual knowledge of various topics.

Circle Time gave Rachel opportunities to introduce and reinvoke terms and concepts. The children did not sit passively listening during Circle Time. Rather, Rachel interacted with the children in ways that allowed them actively to remember terms and vocabulary, as well as actively incorporate this new information into their Free Play activities. Rachel introduced terms and repeated the terms throughout the week during Circle Time. She questioned the children to see if they recalled the terms and concepts of the previous days in a way that showed the children taking up the terms. She asked open-ended questions to elicit the students' responses to determine whether the children had understood the term, such as "what have we been talking about" or "do you remember what we did yesterday?" Rachel regularly used these types of questions (for examples, see Table 8.1). Because the children became familiar with her cues, they generally were able to reply appropriately.

Table 8.1 Transcript of Special Needs Circle Time: Special Needs[a]

START TIME: 2:11
END TIME: 2:15

LINE	SPEAKER	DIALOGUE
5	Rachel	What have we been talking about this week?
6	C	Stuff
7	C	Special stuff
8	Rachel	We call it special needs
9		It is special stuff
10		Yup, you're right
11		Um what kinds of special needs?
12	C	I know
13		Dolls
14	Rachel	Well
15	C	And crutches
16	Rachel	Crutches
17		People that need crutches
18	C	Blind
19	Rachel	What kinds of dolls did we have?
20	C	Blind

Table 8.1 Transcript of Special Needs Circle Time: Special Needs[a] *(continued)*

LINE	SPEAKER	DIALOGUE
21	C	One that can't see and ones that can see
22	Rachel	Okay
23		We have a blind doll, didn't we?
24	C	And one can't hear
25	C	One can't hear
26	Rachel	Okay, we had a doll that was (p) that couldn't hear
27	C	Yeah
28	Rachel	And
29		What did they have? ((R moves her head slightly to the left and points to her ear))
30	C	Doll that couldn't walk
31	Rachel	If you can't hear at all, how do you talk?
32	MC	With your fingers
33	Rachel	With your fingers
34		Do you remember anything we learned?
35	C	Yeah
36	C	This
37	Rachel	Do you remember what this is? ((she signs something with one hand))
38	C	Yeah
39	C	Friend
((lines have been skipped))		
63	Rachel	We have a little story we're going to listen to today about special needs
64	C	It's really hard to open ((R is trying to open a plastic container))
65	MC	((multiple children's voices and movement by R. She pulls out a white dog with a blue collar and leash))
66	Rachel	Who uses the dog to help them get around?
67		I see someone tied a leash on him
68		Who uses the dog?
69	C	Blind people
70	Rachel	Yes
71		People that can't see
72		Do you remember what else blind people use?
73	C	((unintelligible))
74	C	That ((pointing to the cane R is holding))
75	C	((unintelligible))

Table 8.1 Transcript of Special Needs Circle Time: Special Needs[a] *(continued)*

LINE	SPEAKER	DIALOGUE
76	C	That red thing ((pointing to the red portion of the cane))
((lines have been skipped))		
81	C	The red thing
82	Rachel	Yes
83		Yes
84		The cane
85		The white cane with the red tip
86		You're right
87		Very good
((lines have been skipped))		
91	Rachel	Now what do they use this for?
92	C	They tap it on the floor ((the child points to the floor))
93	MC	((a couple of kids are talking))
94	Rachel	They tap it on the floor
95	C	((unintelligible)) can't see if their stairs
96	Rachel	If there are stairs or something
97		Very good ((she nods her head))
98		Or if they have to go down a curb
99		What do we call this? ((R pulls out a miniature wheel chair))
100	MC	A wheel chair
101	Rachel	Oh boy
102		You guys are smart
103		Wow
104		You do remember this
105		Don't you?
106	C	Yeah
107	Rachel	I wish we had a real wheel chair in here
108	MC	((multiple children speak at once))
109	Rachel	Do you remember what (p) this is called (p) to help someone hear?
((she holds up a doll with a hearing aid on one ear))		
110		K (p) knows what that is
111		What is it called?
112	C	Can't hear
113		Like ((unintelligible))
114		Hearing aid
115	Rachel	A hearing aid very good

Table 8.1 Transcript of Special Needs Circle Time: Special Needs[a] *(continued)*

LINE	SPEAKER	DIALOGUE
116	C	A hearing aid
117	Rachel	K's older brother (can not hear) very well
118		So he wears hearing aids to help him hear better
119		Doesn't he K?
120	K	Yeah
121	Rachel	Does he talk with his finger too? ((K looks at her))
122		Is he learning to talk with his fingers?
123	K	((K nods))
124	Rachel	'Cause you showed me the 'K'
125		Show me the 'K' again K
126	K	((K signs the letter 'K' with his fingers))
127	Rachel	Yup there's the 'K' for K
128		K knew that ((R searches the container for something else))
129		Do you remember what we called this? ((holding a miniature walker))
130	C	How to walk
131	Rachel	Yup
132		And it's called a walker
133		You're right
134		It helps you walk and it's called a walker
135	C	Walker
136	Rachel	Where's our little guy
137		And what happened to this guy? ((R pulls out a doll with part of his leg missing))
138	MC	He broke his leg
139	Rachel	Did he break his leg?
140	MC	Yeah
141	Rachel	Uh (p) ((waits for more information from the children))
142		What happened to this guy?
143	C	His leg fell off
144	Rachel	Did it fall off?
145	C	No
146	C	I know ((the child raises her hand))
147	Rachel	What
148	C	He had an accident
149	Rachel	And what happened?
150	C	He cut his leg off

Table 8.1 Transcript of Special Needs Circle Time: Special Needs[a] *(continued)*

LINE	SPEAKER	DIALOGUE
151	Rachel	His leg probably got cut off
152		Uh huh
153		Or maybe he had a disease and they had to cut it off
154	C	Uh huh
155	Rachel	What can he do? ((the doll's arms have ski poles attached and his one foot has a ski))
156	C	Skate
157	Rachel	He can still ski can't he
158	MC	Yeah
159	Rachel	He has special things that he can ski with
160	C	Uh huh
161	Rachel	This is his ski boot
162	MC	Yeah
163	Rachel	He's not really ready to ski yet right now
164		'Cause he is just showing you
165		That he can still do things
166		Even though he doesn't have a leg
167		Sometimes people have
168		They call them fake legs ((she hunches forward))
169		They'll call them prosthesis
170		Can you say that word
171	MC	(Prosthesis)
172	Rachel	(Prosthesis)
173		It's a pretend leg that they slip on over their leg
174		And it looks like a real foot
175		And when you where pants no one can even tell that your missing a leg or a foot
176		And they can still walk on it too

[a]Transcript has been edited to include lesson related conversations

Key: R = teacher

C = a child (total of seven individual children spoke)

K = Keith is a particular child

MC = multiple children respond

(( )) = observations and/or comments

( ) = overlap in conversation

(p) = pause

The second relevant event of the day, Free Play, provided children with opportunities to illustrate what they took up during Circle Time. The children not only played with materials that were available all year in the classroom but, in addition, Rachel made available at least one other activity that related to the theme of the week. In this way, the children incorporated and illustrated their knowledge of what they remembered from Circle Time, either by interacting with an adult, with peers, or with materials. For example, during the week of zoo animals, Rachel discussed what animals were found in the zoo (e.g., giraffe and tigers), how to care for animals (e.g., bottles for babies, special foods grown in the zoo, and daily baths), what they ate (e.g., bamboo, fresh meat, and carrots), and who cared for them (e.g., zoo keeper). During Free Play, she provided various stuffed zoo animals, containers with different types of foods for the animals, and arranged blocks into several compartments. Each child received a stuffed animal that he or she fed with the food provided by Rachel. After the animals ate, a few children placed their stuffed animals in the block compartments, pretending they were cages. In ways such as these, Rachel presented terms, ideas, and materials during Circle Time, and most of the children reinvoked these within their play.

The basement of the building where the program was located was large enough for the children to ride bikes, run, and enjoy other Gross Motor activities. A climbing structure with an attached slide was located at one end of the room. On warm days, the children played outside on a tree-lined parking lot. Large motor activities, specifically while outside, allowed the children time to interact with one another, as well as to challenge and expand each other's conceptual knowledge of theme-related terms and concepts. For example, during the week on insects, Rachel told the children they could look outside for insects during Gross Motor time. As soon as the children were outside, they started looking in the grass and mulch. They huddled in groups of three and four, poking and prodding the ground. When one child found an insect, several cried out in excitement, which led the other children to huddle around them. As illustrated later, during these huddles, the children negotiated with each other what they found by discussing what they learned during Circle Time.

Conceptual Development

Being on a Plane. The following examples illustrate how children made sense of the concept of being on a plane and flying somewhere; prior to this day, none of the children had been on a plane. During transportation week, Rachel presented different forms of transportation. On one particular day, during Circle Time, Rachel discussed boats and planes. After reading a book on boats, she asked the children who drives a boat (captain), an airplane (pilot), and a bus (bus driver). She then spent a few minutes describing plane activities. She then asked the children about the people who serve the food on the plane. Rachel showed the children a stack of boarding passes to use during Free Play; she referred to them as tickets used to get on a plane. Rachel told the children she was going to set up the chairs in the housekeeping area like a plane, and they could use the "tickets" to get on the plane. She also informed the children that they could play with the cups and pitchers located in the housekeeping area. During Circle Time, Rachel provided a list of terms and descriptions that the children could draw on in their play, including boarding passes, drinks, and the main characters found on planes—pilot and flight attendants, and their responsibilities.

During the next event of the day, Free Play, Rachel set up an environment for the children to incorporate what they learned. As the children went off to play, Rachel arranged some chairs in a row to look like a plane, indicating which was the pilot's seat. Two children took turns being pilots, and three other children took turns being the flight attendants. I also participated in this play scenario. The following three scenarios occurred during the same play session. They illustrate how children used the new information presented during Circle Time and their theories of the world to develop the concept of being on a plane.

The "pilots" and "flight attendants" distributed the boarding passes to those of us sitting in the airplane seats, but then took them away almost immediately; rather than have one person collect them as we "boarded" the plane. The crew (pilots and flight attendants) tended to hold on to the boarding passes, carrying them around in their hands. It was unclear how the children decided when to distribute the "tickets" or when to gather them. They understood that they had to pass them out to "passengers" and pick them up. Have the children experienced using tickets to board a bus or train? On buses, the driver collects the money and/or gives daily bus passes. What other opportunities have they had using tickets?

During the same play session, the children pulled out the cups and pitchers. One girl asked what I wanted to drink and brought me my drink; she then asked the child sitting next to me. She would take the cup and wash it, then bring me more to drink. At one point, I tried to demonstrate how the flight attendants would go around and ask a couple people what they wanted to drink then get their drinks, using pitchers to refill the cups. However, the children appeared bored and confused so they got up and served me again instead. By my taking on the role of "server," I challenged the children's concepts of serving food on a plane. They had created their own understandings and seemed satisfied with how they interpreted how to serve drinks. However, when I tried to change the format, they stopped me. How did the children know what to do or how to serve the drinks? Had they been to a restaurant where sodas are left on tables, and then servers come and take the glass, only to return with a refilled drink? What other representations were they using to continue with their play? Unfortunately, I was not present the day Rachel discussed the events that transpire on a plane.

When it was time to fly, the pilots waited for the flight attendants to finish serving the drinks and sit down. At take off, everyone sat down on the chairs while the pilot flew and landed. Once we arrived at the destination, the flight attendants got up and started serving drinks again. One might ask why the "flight attendants" remained sitting during the "flight." Perhaps, the teacher did not explain that flight attendants serve food while the plane is in flight. In this instance, the children may be using their understanding of being in a car or on a school bus. In a car or school bus, you sit and wait until you arrive at your destination, and do not stand up or walk around.

Because the only possible exposure for the children of common happenings on a plane would be through the media, I thought it was interesting how they made sense of the concept of being on a plane and flying somewhere. During this one play episode, the children were previously given general indications and direction of plane activities. However, the children had to gather information from other sources in order to complete their plane play. They used their prior knowledge of serving food and what to do while being transported to another location. Using these other reference points, children may have been beginning to construct a concept of what happens on planes.

Special Needs. Rachel spent a week on the topic of special needs. On the two days I recorded Circle Time, she introduced eight examples of special needs (see Table 8.1). Rachel asked the children a broad question, "What kinds of special needs have we talked about that people have?" The children provided descriptions (e.g., "when you can't see"), names (e.g., blind), and objects used by individuals with special needs (e.g., crutches and wheelchairs) (see Table 8.1). Rachel taught the children the names, descriptions and objects associated with individuals identified as having a special need. Table 8.1 is a partial transcript of one Circle Time on special needs; the transcript shows a detailed description of how the terms were introduced and recalled, and how Rachel elaborated and expanded the children's prior knowledge. Rachel spent the first few minutes asking the children what they remember, elaborating prior understandings and providing new information.

Because Rachel started Circle Time asking the children about prior Circle Times and requested examples of special needs, she may have signaled to the children that the broad umbrella of special needs encompasses all the terms, ideas, and objects presented during these Circle Times. The children's conceptual knowledge of special needs not only includes terms and descriptions, but now they have a link between Keith and sign language (lines 117-128); connections between crutches (lines 11-17), walkers (lines 129-135), canes (lines 72-85), and hearing aids (lines 109-116) with individuals with special needs; and associations between accidents and missing legs—"causes of special needs" (lines 136-151). Within the children's mental representation of special needs, they included the information presented during these Circle Times.

The question is whether this is an example of the children developing conceptual knowledge or developing facts? Is it enough for the children to understand the essence of these terms (e.g., when someone can't hear, when someone can't see)? Is recalling examples of signs and objects developing conceptual understandings of special needs? During Play Time, the children had the opportunity to play and interact with the dolls and equipment. Is it enough for the children to use the walker, canes, crutches, and wheelchairs appropriately, in order to illustrate that they have a deeper understanding of the concept of special needs? How do we test whether the children have developed a conceptual understanding of special needs?

Conceptual Change

The following examples provide evidence for weaker sense restructuring. Weaker sense refers to the child adding new information to their preexisting concept and using this information for generalizing and in more abstract ways.

Papoose. This example of restructuring in the weaker sense illustrates a child incorporating information that he first learned during Circle Time three weeks prior to this interaction. During one Circle Time, Rachel shared with the children artifacts related to Native Americans; one was a female Indian doll. While pointing to parts of the doll, she asked the children to recall the names of things the female Indian doll was wearing. The children identified things like moccasins and papoose. Three weeks after this Circle Time, I sat in the housekeeping area watching the children play with the dress-up clothes. One of the boys asked me to help him put a baby doll into a baby backpack carrier. When the doll was in, he said "Papoose. This is my papoose." He appropriately carried his doll on his back for the rest of Free Play. Rachel spent a week teaching the children facts and information about Native Americans. Three weeks later, this boy was playing with dolls and perhaps did not know the name of the backpack carrier. However, he was able to recall that Native American babies were carried on their mothers' backs, and applied this concept to this new situation.

Time and Space. The following example shows how a child negotiated between her understandings of the world and information presented by the teacher. This occurred during Circle Time when Rachel discussed Native Americans. In this segment (see Table 8.2), Rachel asked the children "what kinds of meat would they [Native Americans] eat?" Different children provided a variety of accurate responses. On line 166, Rachel offers an alternative that the children had not mentioned.

Table 8.2 Transcript of Native American Circle Time: Time and Space

START TIME: 2:10:07
END TIME: 2:14:45

LINE	SPEAKER	DIALOGUE
145	Rachel	What kinds of meat would they eat
146-165		((children responded buffalo, dear, salmon, bear))
166	Rachel	They eat rabbits
167		Did you know that
168	MC	xxx
169	C	A moose
170	Rachel	A moose
171		Some people have rabbits as pets
172		And some people eat rabbits
173	C	Yew
174		I don't eat rabbits
175	C	xxx
176	Rachel	Sometimes when you go to the grocery store
177		You can buy rabbits
178		To eat
179		They
180		They didn't have chickens then
181		But they had birds that they ate
182	C	I can't see Z
183	Rachel	Pheasants

Table 8.2 Transcript of Native American Circle Time: Time and Space *(continued)*

START TIME: 2:10:07
END TIME: 2:14:45

LINE	SPEAKER	DIALOGUE
184	MC	xxx
185	Rachel	Or a different kind of bird
186	C	Like a cockatoo
187	C	Or we can buy them
188		And and
189	Rachel	Well there were no stores back then
190		A long time ago
191		There weren't
192		Stores for people to go in
193		So they had to go hunting themselves
194		To get their food

Key. (xxx) = unintelligible
C = one child
MC = multiple children – a couple or a few children
Rachel = teacher

Rachel introduced new content knowledge (eating of rabbits and birds) and the notion of time and space (past and present) (lines 166–194). She compared what was available to eat in the past with what is currently available, such as chickens (lines 171–186). One of the children responded with disgust at the thought of eating a rabbit, and stated she did not eat rabbits (lines 173–174). After the child's response to not eating rabbits, Rachael went on to clarify and justify why Native Americans ate rabbits. She compared rabbits to chickens, implying today's chickens would be a comparable substitute to the past uses of rabbits (lines 176–181). This 4-year-old child did not understand the concept of Native Americans hunting that far back in time (line 187). Rachel stated that "back then" they did not have grocery stories to buy chickens. Rachel tried to explain the past, but the children did not appear to understand what she was saying.

The children were trying to make connections between what Rachel said and their own understandings of reality. This child was grappling with her conceptual framework of rabbits as pets not as food and her conceptual understanding of where to purchase chickens instead of eating rabbits (lines 173, 174, 187). Rachel provided the children with opportunities to learn information about Native Americans, which the children then tried to forge connections with their own prior knowledge.

Insects. In a final example, insects were the theme of a week. The children challenged each other's concept of a particular insect, a beetle. During Circle Time, Rachel spoke with the children about types (e.g., ants and lady bug) and characteristics (e.g., having six legs) of insects, and showed them pictures of different insects. Rachel encouraged the children to search for insects outside in the play area and at home. The following week, half of the children continued to search through the grass and mulch outside. I noticed three children gathered around a small mulched area. They were excited and wanted to share their discovery with Rachel. However, she was on the other side of the parking lot collecting potting soil with three other children, so I walked over to see what they found. At first, they thought they found a dead insect. I asked what kind of insect they thought it was, and after a few suggestions and discussion, the children decided it was a beetle. After a few minutes, the insect started to move. They jumped back and became even more excited. A couple of other children noticed the commotion and came over to see the insect. After a couple minutes, the children dispersed and left the insect.

About 10 minutes later, however, I heard a child yell out that the insect had been found again. About five children gathered around to look at it. The children asked each other what it was. One of the original three said it was a beetle. After a few seconds of watching the insect, they all agreed. Another boy who had not seen the insect went to see it. He disagreed that it was a beetle. He reminded them that beetles are black, and this bug was not black. The other children rejected his claim and insisted it was a beetle. The children went back and forth arguing whether it was a beetle. The boy who insisted it was not a beetle became so upset because the other children would not believe him that he stepped on and killed the insect. The children called Rachel to tell her about the child stepping on the beetle. However, Rachel had called the children to line up and was occupied with cups of potting soil.

It is unclear whether the first group of children in this scenario guessed it was a beetle or used their conceptual knowledge about insects and beetles to determine that it was indeed a beetle. However, the last child disagreed and justified his answer with his knowledge about beetles being black. The children argued and tried to negotiate the true identity of the insect. The conflict between the children illustrates their struggles with verbally expressing their justifications and coming to a consensus regarding the identity of the insect. Each child was certain of his or her accuracy; however, the children were unable to scaffold the disagreement toward a resolution.

DISCUSSION

The purpose of this chapter was to examine how children develop conceptual knowledge in a Head Start preschool classroom and to learn what conceptual development and conceptual change look like in this preschool classroom. The question we must answer is: Are these events examples of conceptual development and conceptual change? According to Murphy and Medin's (1985) theory of conceptual development, individuals use their theories of the world to organize and structure their concepts. The children in this classroom playing "being on a plane" used their theories of using tickets, serving food and being transported from one location to another to complete their play. They incorporated their knowledge of other experiences into this play scenario creating new understandings and meanings of flying on a plane.

In addition, the more information a child possesses, the more able the child is in generalizing to other objects (Gelman & Markman, 1986; Gelman & Wellman, 1991; Gentner & Namy, 1999), and the more time spent with objects relevant to the concept, the more likely the child will conceptualize the object (Ross et al., 1986). Because the children in this classroom were given multiple pieces of information about a theme and given opportunities to use these terms, ideas, and objects within their play, they were able to use their theories about the world to develop and structure their concepts and to use this new concept for generalizing to other situations. The special needs example showed the children categorizing the terms, descriptions, and objects into one concept. The children generated, recalled, and generalized multiple pieces of information relevant to the special needs conversation.

The examples of conceptual change are less clear. Weak restructuring implies that children with more knowledge about something have a more structured concept and higher levels of thinking about the concept (Carey, 1985). The children applied their knowledge about objects and relations of one concept (objects used to carry babies, not eating pets, and color as predictor of group membership) to situations that either supported their understandings (e.g., papoose is a baby carrier) or challenged them (e.g., eating your pet rabbit, not having a grocery store, or color not being the sole predictor). These provide evidence showing children trying to use their prior knowledge and understandings in these situations.

In this chapter, I try to see how theories of conceptual development and conceptual change inform our understandings of preschool classroom events. The structure of the children's concepts of each of these topics is unclear. Are these really examples of conceptual development or development of facts? How do we know whether the children really developed concepts of being on a plane or of special needs? Is a child's ability to generalize prior information appropriately in a new setting illustrative of weak sense restructuring? Is a child's struggle to reaffirm and understand something evidence of restructuring? These are important questions that must be addressed before we begin to fully understand what conceptual development and conceptual change look like in a preschool classroom. Although one advantage of my study is that it occurred in a naturalistic setting, a major limitation of this study was not having a way to document the children's prior knowledge of the concept and to assess the development and change of this concept over time. Future research will need to identify and measure these at the outset.

Furthermore, educators ask how classroom contexts influence conceptual development and change. I assume conceptual development and conceptual change are socially constructed through interactions with others and materials. Children in the experiments on conceptual development and conceptual change were limited to the materials provided by the researcher. The children in this classroom had multiple opportunities for manipulating and expressing what they knew with different individuals and materials. These less controlled environments raise questions in need of further investigation. What contexts constrain development, and which provide opportunities to build conceptual knowledge? Can social interactions between child and adult constrain or enhance conceptual development and change?

In addition, I infer that the thematic units are venues for exposing children to new concepts. The children gathered information provided by Rachel during Circle Time and their experiences interacting with adults, peers and materials during Free Play enabled them to build concepts that related to that theme. Rachel also encouraged the children to take new knowledge to other areas of play and life. The ways the thematic units were incorporated throughout the day and reinforced over the week gave the children tools for interacting with others and with materials. For example, the boy was able to use the term papoose in another setting in appropriate ways.

These thematic units also constrained conceptual development and conceptual change. Although the children were not constrained to apply the information only during the week when a particular topic was being explored, they were encouraged to expand and continue to use the terms in other experiences. However, these units constrained the children's ability to carry over this information into subsequent weeks in other ways. For example, because the theme for the week was flowers and plants, the teacher did not attempt to identify or assist the children in the conflict resolution with the insect.

The thematic units limited the type of knowledge and concepts children developed. The children in each scenario were motivated to participate by responding and contributing to the interactions. Although this might be true for some children, not all children participated attentively during Circle Time nor did all the children take part in the theme-related activities. If they were not interested, they would have played elsewhere or sat quietly during Circle Time, avoiding the interactions. By avoiding these theme-related interactions, it is unclear what these children did learn or what other concepts they developed.

Rachel's interactional discourse patterns during Circle Time with the children are consistent with the initiate–response–evaluate pattern. This is one type of discourse pattern that is commonly found in elementary school classrooms. However, I do not imply that it is the correct or only discourse pattern found in early childhood classrooms. Rather this is one example of how this particular teacher developed conceptual knowledge in teacher-lead interactions. Researchers studying classroom discourse interactions found that the same activities, such as Sharing Time, differ from classroom to classroom (Cazden, 2001; Michaels, 1981). These discourse patterns are unique to each classroom, suggesting there are many other discourse patterns that might develop conceptual knowledge.

Through peer interactions, the children appeared to expand their understandings of concepts. Keith shared how he communicated with his brother who has hearing difficulties. The children negotiated with each other how to "be on a plane," allowing the play to continue. Who passed out boarding passes? Who served beverages, and when they were served? The insect example brought on conflict, permitting the children to question and challenge each other.

Regardless of the overall constraints, I believe that, in the examples I provided, the children did build some conceptual understandings of being on a plane, special needs, papoose, eating rabbits, and the characteristics of insects. The learning community of the classroom appeared to influence what the children learned, and, by extension, how they developed and changed.

CONCLUSION

I return to my original question: what does it mean to build conceptual knowledge? The National Association for the Education of Young Children's (NAEYC) guidelines for developmentally appropriate prac-

tice emphasize the importance of children developing conceptual knowledge, but overlook defining what they mean by concepts. These vague
guidelines are open to interpretation, as seen by Rachel. Rachel interpreted these expectations as building children's knowledge about animals,
community life, and general information. As evident by this study, children can develop multiple concepts in early childhood education, but do
we know exactly which concepts we want them to develop? Are these
concepts that are theme based important, necessary or relevant to young
children's development? Is this what we want young children to be learning? Some individuals may argue that a child's conceptual development
should include concepts of seriation, classification, and numeracy (e.g.,
High/Scope curriculum). However, neither version of NAEYC's guidelines for developmentally appropriate practice focuses primarily on these
concepts; rather they use the term *concept* more generally.

   Children's concepts are not easily defined. Children use their prior
knowledge and theories about the world to structure and develop their
concepts, which consist of multiple pieces of information, and use what
they know to link information into a coherent concept. Concepts consist
of more than biological, physical, and mathematical phenomena; they
also relate to life experiences and general information. One general statement by administrators and policymakers of the importance of children
developing conceptual knowledge is not enough to inform practitioners
about what children need to know. Defining and explaining concepts is
complex. Understanding how to develop and change conceptual knowledge is continuously being theorized and reevaluated. We need to first
understand what happens in the classroom and what types of knowledge
children develop in a preschool setting before we expect practitioners to
develop these skills and knowledge in young children.

REFERENCES

Bredekamp, S., & Copple, C. (1997). *Developmentally appropriate practice in early
    childhood programs* (rev ed.). Washington, DC: National Association for the
    Education of Young Children.
Carey, S. (1985). *Conceptual change in childhood.* Cambridge, MA: MIT Press.
Castanheira, M., Crawford, T., Dixon, C., & Green, J. (2000). Interactional ethnog-
    raphy: An approach to studying the social construction of literate practices.
    Linguistics and Education, 11(4), 353-400.
Cazden, C. B. (2001). *Classroom discourse: The language of teaching and learning.*
    Portsmouth, NH: Heinemann.
Gelman, S. A. (1996). Concepts and theories. In R. Gelman & T. K. F. Au (Eds.),
    Perceptual and cognitive development (pp. 117-150). New York: Academic Press.
Gelman, S. A., & Markman, E. M. (1986). Categories and induction in young chil-
    dren. *Cognition, 23*, 183-209.

Gelman, S. A., & Wellman, H. M. (1991). Insides and essences: Early understandings of the non-obvious. *Cognition, 38,* 213-244.

Gentner, D., & Namy, L. L. (1999). Comparison in the development of categories. *Cognitive Development, 14*(4), 487-513.

Gobbo, C., & Chi, M. (1986). How knowledge is structured and used by expert and novice children. *Cognitive Development, 1,* 221-237.

Green, J. L., & Dixon, C. N. (1994). Talking knowledge into being: Discursive and social practices in classrooms. *Linguistics and Education, 5*(3-4), 231-239.

Green, J. L., & Harker, J. O. (1982). Gaining access to learning: Conversational, social, and cognitive demands of group participation. In L. C. Wilkinson (Ed.), *Communicating in the classroom* (pp. 183-221). New York: Academic Press.

Green, J. L., & Meyer, L. A. (1991). The embeddedness of reading in classroom life: Reading as a situated process. In C. Baker & A. Luke (Eds.), *Towards a critical sociology of reading pedagogy* (pp. 141-160). Philadelphia, PA: John Benjamins.

Gumperz, J. J. (1982). *Discourse strategies.* New York: Cambridge University Press.

Gumperz, J. J. (1986). Interactional sociolinguistics in the study of schooling. In J. Cook-Gumperz (Ed.), *The social construction of literacy* (pp. 45-68). New York: Cambridge University Press.

Gumperz, J. J. (1992). Contextualization and understanding. In A. Duranti & C. Goodwin (Eds.), *Rethinking context: Language as an interactive phenomenon* (pp. 229-252). New York: Cambridge University Press.

Gutheil, G., Vera, A., & Keil, F. C. (1998). Do houseflies think? Patterns of induction and biological beliefs in development. *Cognition, 66*(1), 33-49.

Lubeck, S., & Post, J. (2000). Creating a Head Start community of practice. In L. Diaz Soto (Ed.), *The politics of early childhood education: Rethinking childhood* (pp. 33-57). New York: Peter Lang.

Michaels, S. (1981). Sharing time: Children's narrative styles and differential access to literacy. *Language and Sociology, 10,* 423-442.

Murphy, G. L., & Medin, D. L. (1985). The role of theories in conceptual coherence. *Psychological Review, 92*(3), 289-316.

National Research Council. (1999). *How people learn: Bridging research and practice.* Washington, DC: National Academy Press.

National Research Council. (2001). *Eager to learn: Educating our preschoolers.* Washington, DC: National Academy Press.

Neuman, S. B., Copple, C., & Bredekamp, S. (2000). *Learning to read and write: Developmentally appropriate practices for young children.* Washington, DC: National Association for the Education of Young Children.

Post, J., & Lubeck, S. (2000). Head Start–university collaborations: Widening the circle. *Childhood Education, 76*(5), 277-282.

Rex, L. A. (1999). "If anything is odd, inappropriate, confusing, or boring, it's probably important": The emergence of inclusive academic literacy through English classroom discussion practices. *Research in the Teaching of English, 34,* 66-130.

Ross, G., Nelson, K., Wetstone, H., & Tanouye, E. (1986). Acquisition and generalization of novel object concepts by young language learners. *Journal of Child Language, 13*(1), 67-83.

Santa Barbara Classroom Discourse Group. (1992). Constructing literacy in class-rooms: Literate action as social accomplishment. In H. H. Marshall (Ed.), *Redefining student learning* (pp. 143-175). Norwood, NJ: Ablex.

Tuyay, S., Jennings, L., & Dixon, C. N. (1995). Classroom discourse and opportu-nities to learn: An ethnographic study of knowledge construction in a bilin-gual third-grade classroom. *Discourse Processes, 19*(1), 75-110.

Tyson, L. M., Venville, G. J., Harrison, A. G., & Treagust, D. F. (1997). A multidi-mensional framework for interpreting conceptual change events in the class-room. *Science Education, 81*(4), 387-404.

Wade, C., & Tavris, C. (2000). *Psychology* (6th ed.). Upper Saddle River, NJ: Prentice-Hall.

Zaharlick, A., & Green, J. L. (1991). Ethnographic research. In J. Flood (Ed.), *Handbook of research on teaching the English language arts* (pp. 205-225). New York: Macmillan.

9

Connecting the Microscopic View of Chemistry to Real-Life Experiences

Hsin-Kai Wu

> Chemistry, . . . is a mix of a molecular engineering, based on extrapolations from the macroscopic to the microscopic, and a science, coming to grasp directly with the microscopic.
>
> —Hoffman and Laszlo (1991, p. 9)

Chemistry is a microscopic science. Chemical processes paradigmatically are represented by molecules and explained from a microscopic perspective. Various types of microscopic representations, such as structural formula and ball-and-stick models, are cultural tools for chemists to conduct inquiry (Nye, 1993). Instead of using different representations interchangeably, chemists schematically choose appropriate symbols and signs to generate hypothesis, present data, make predictions, and convince other scientific community members in their daily practices (Hoffman & Laszlo, 1991; Kozma, Chin, Russell, & Marx, 2000).

Given the important role of representations in chemistry, however, many studies showed that students are not able to understand microscopic representations as chemists (e.g., Ben-Zvi, Eylon, & Silberstein, 1986, 1987, 1988; Kozma & Russell, 1997; Krajcik, 1991; Nakhleh, 1992). Students' difficulties in interpreting representations (Ben-Zvi et al., 1986), providing verbal explanations for chemical processes (Kozma & Russell, 1997), and making translations between different types of representations (Keig & Rubba, 1993) indicate a lack of connections among chemical phenomena, representations, and relevant concepts (Kozma, 2000). Inspired by a social constructivist view of learning, Kozma, Chin, Russell, and Marx (2000) suggested that chemistry curricula should guide students to use multiple representations visually and verbally in conjunction with associated physical phenomena in a classroom. A learning environment needs to explicitly demonstrate the conceptual relationships among representations at the macroscopic, molecular, and symbolic levels in a problem-solving or inquiry context. Through social and discursive practices, students have opportunities to conceptually move back and forth among three levels and cognitively interact with various types of representations in a meaningful way.

However, as students' learning difficulties in understanding chemical representations have been well known and a social constructivist perspective has been proposed, some questions remain unanswered. How are microscopic representations introduced, used, and practiced in a science classroom? How are conceptual connections among life experiences, chemical representations, and conceptual entities presented and constructed by members in a science class? How does the teacher's content knowledge shape his or her ways to co-construct connections with students? To answer these questions and to capture the social and interactional nature of meaning-making process in a science class, this study analyzes classroom discourse in detail. Through a close examination of class discourse, this study investigates how class members interactionally construct meanings of chemical representations by connecting them to real-life experiences.

THEORETICAL FRAMEWORK

Researchers and educators in chemistry education have been discussing the three levels of representations in chemistry: macroscopic, microscopic, and symbolic levels (Gabel, 1998; Gabel, Samuel, & Hunn, 1987; Johnstone, 1982, 1993). At the macroscopic level, chemistry is observable as melting butter or a burning candle. To better explain these phenomena, chemists develop concepts and models of atoms and molecules. At the microscopic or molecular level, a burning candle becomes a chemical process in which carbon atoms of the wax react with oxygen molecules in the air and carbon dioxide molecules are produced. Another way to represent this process is using a chemical equation with symbols, formulas, and numbers, such as $C(s) + O_2(g) \rightarrow CO_2(g)$. As shown in this example, chemists represent sensory experiences by atoms and molecules, and translate them into symbols and formulas. Examining the evolution of the chemists' way of seeing and drawing, Hoffmann and Laszlo (1991) argued that microscopic representations currently used in chemistry have evolved from phenomenological analogies of sensory experiences at the macroscopic level. Conceptual knowledge in chemistry is embedded in representation at different levels. However, learning microscopic and symbolic representations is especially difficult for students, because these representations are invisible and abstract while students' understandings of chemistry heavily relies on sensory information (e.g., Ben-Zvi et al., 1986, 1987, 1988; Gabel et al., 1987).

Learning as Development of Individual Cognition

To ease students' difficulties, various instructional strategies, tools, and curriculum have been developed based on two research traditions. One tradition is built on theories of cognitive psychology and views learning as development of individual cognition. According to these theories, the process of understanding is restructuring the individual cognitive framework that includes a range of cognitive processing such as assimilation, accommodation, and building connections of knowledge elements (Osborne & Freyberg, 1985; White & Gunstone, 1992). It implies that one way to help students develop understanding at the microscopic and symbolic levels is to create or reconstruct their conceptual connections between existing preconceptions of observable phenomena and novel external representations (i.e., symbols and molecular models) in individual cognition. Some technological tools, such as 4M: Chem (Kozma, Russell, Jones, Marx, & Davis, 1996), were designed to facilitate the formation of conceptual connections among multiple representations in order to promote the construction of an expert-like mental model. Through cognitively interacting with microscopic and macroscopic representations simultaneously provided by tools, students relate their preconceptions to scientifically appropriate representations at the symbolic and microscopic levels and construct or restructure cognitive linkages among them.

Although conceptual connections are defined as structural linkages between knowledge elements within individual cognition (Gagne, Yekovich, & Yekovich, 1993), this model of learning has been critiqued as mentalism (Lemke, 1990) because it assumes that cognitive processes are isolated from social contexts and that all minds operate and process information in the same way. Indeed, the ways to make cognitive processes or mental representations accessible are mainly through social or discursive interactions among teachers, students, and researchers. The research methods used to investigate mental models or individual cognitive developments, such as interviews, picture drawings, thinking aloud, are already confounded with various social factors, as indicated by Kelly, Chen, and Crawford (1998).

Additionally, understanding representations is more than a construction of internal cognitive connections. The historical development of chemical representations indicates that the usage of representations are rhetorical and context-dependent (Kozma et al., 2000; Nye, 1993). Rather than using various types of representations interchangeably, chemists schematically choose appropriate symbols and signs to generate hypothesis, present data, make predictions about the chemical phenomena that are the focus of their investigation (Kozma et al., 2000). They construct various representations to convince other scientific community members (Latour, 1987; Lynch & Woolgar, 1990) and confirm their membership (Kozma et al., 2000). That is, understanding of chemical representations is observable and ties to the situated use of them across tasks and contexts. Connections are not only structurally constructed within a cognitive world, but also observable through discursive interactions among class members, textbooks, and instructional resources. Thus, although learning theories of individual cognition view understanding as connection-making or restructuring within individual cognition, studying students' conceptual understanding of representations should seriously take their contextual and discursive activities into account because both students' cognition processes and chemists' usage of representations are mediated by social practices (Kelly et al., 1998).

Learning as Sociocultural Practices Within a Community

The other research tradition, social constructivism, emphasizes that the process of knowledge construction is embedded in discursive and social interactions through which learners are encultured into scientific practices (Brown, Collins, & Duguid, 1989; Lave & Wenger, 1991; Resnick, 1987). Inspired by this theoretical tradition, Kozma et al. (2000) conducted an historical and observational study in a chemistry laboratory. Based on their findings of how chemists used representations for scientific investigation and social communication, they suggested that to develop students' understanding of chemistry, the chemistry curriculum should guide them to use multiple representations in conjunction with associated physical phenomena in the classroom. Namely, to promote students to develop conceptual understanding of chemical representations, a learning environment, including the teacher, curriculum materials, and technological tools, should explicitly demonstrate the relationships among macroscopic, microscopic, and symbolic levels in an inquiry context.

Through social and discursive practices, students conceptually move back and forth among three levels and have opportunities to cognitively interact with various types of representations in a meaningful way (Kozma, 2000).

The literature discussed here indicates that constructing conceptual connections between three levels of chemistry (i.e., macroscopic, microscopic, and symbolic) is crucial for learning chemistry and that through social and discursive practices, the cognitive process of connection-making is accessible. This study takes combining perspectives; together the cognitive psychological and social constructivist works in education provide a theoretical basis for this study. One theoretical premise of this study draws from theories of cognitive psychology that understanding chemistry involves the construction of conceptual connections among three levels of chemical representations. Yet, instead of applying quantitative methods to assess students' conceptual understanding, through a social constructivist lens, I examine how class members interactionally construct meanings of chemical representations by verbally connecting them to real situations and how the teacher's content knowledge shapes his or her ways to co-construct connections with students. In order to research these questions, I analyze qualitative data collected from a high school science class co-taught by a student teacher and an experienced teacher. Before I provide a detailed account of the data-collection process, I define what I mean by "making connections" among three levels based on related theories and empirical studies.

Connections Between the School Chemistry and Real Situations

Although making conceptual connections among three levels to help students learn chemistry is suggested by the literature, little is understood about what types of connections are constructed in the classroom, whether these connections are meaningful for students, and how teachers use connection-making as an instructional strategy. Following the implications provided by the literature, I define types of connections that could be built in the classroom.

In this study, real-life experiences refer to the ones that students have outside the school, so the first type of connection that could be made is between students' real-life experience and the macroscopic aspect of chemistry. Studies in the area of students' alternative conceptions have indicated that isolating the school science from students' real life could make students develop two unconnected knowledge systems related to science: One is used to solve science problems in schools, and the other is used for their daily lives (e.g., Osborne & Freyberg, 1985). Although

chemical processes at the macroscopic level are visible and relatively easier to be understood, in most chemistry curricula, these processes are
extracted from real situations and usually designed as laboratory activities. In these activities, students are asked to follow given procedures
instead of experiencing an iterative process of scientific inquiry. It is not
surprising that most students are not able to apply their scientific knowledge learned in schools to real situations because they do not have opportunities to do so in schools. Additionally, the same phrase may share different meanings in students' daily life and their science classroom. For
example, "organic" is commonly used to describe a type of food that is
cultivated naturally without using artificial insecticides or hormones.
However, in chemistry, "organic" refers to a type of compounds containing carbon atoms. Thus, to learn science, students must appropriate their
use of language and reconstruct meanings for terms that are commonly
used in their cultural and linguistic practices outside the school.

To fill the gap between students' daily experiences and learning
experiences in the science classroom, the first connection that could be
constructed in classroom settings is between real situations and the
chemistry content at the macroscopic level. In fact, the process of building this type of connections has been discussed as "contextualization" in
science education which means to situate the learning context in students' real-life experience (Krajcik, Czerniak, & Berger). For example,
informed by the social constructivist learning model, the project-based
science emphasizes that contextualization is a key feature of this
approach for students to make meaning of the school science (Marx,
Blumenfeld, Krajcik, & Soloway, 1997). A contextualized driving question, on which a project is centered, is anchored in an important real situation (Cognition and Technology Group at Vanderbilt, 1990). It provides
opportunities for students to see how the school science is related to their
lives and how the scientific knowledge is applied in real-life situations.

Compared with the first type of connection, the construction of connections between real situations and the chemistry content at the microscopic and symbolic levels have not received much attention outside the
area of chemistry education, although it has been documented that most
students do not understand atoms, molecules, and chemical symbols.
Therefore, this study focuses on the construction of this second type of
connections in a science classroom.

According to the history of chemistry, chemists first simplified real
situations into chemical processes and developed atomic and molecular
models to make explanations (Hoffman & Laszlo, 1991; Nye, 1993). In
general, chemical representations were developed through the sequence
of visible phenomena, chemical reactions, atomic and molecular models,
and symbols/formulas. As some researchers assume that students'

development of understanding is similar to the historical development of science (e.g., Wiser, 1995), the connections between real-life experiences (e.g., visual phenomena) and the chemistry content at the microscopic and symbolic levels (e.g., molecular models and formulas) would be difficult to build without mediators, such as simplified chemical processes or common names of chemicals. Thus, one objective of this study is to deepen the understanding of the ways in which phenomena in real-life experiences, chemical molecules/structures, and symbols are connected to each other in the classroom settings and whether some of the representations are used as mediators. By exploring the nature of this type of connection, this study could provide insight into how to help students understand chemical symbols and molecules through class interactions.

Class Discourse and Learning Community

Although most studies in the area of chemistry education adapt theoretical assumptions from cognitive psychological theories, the ethnographic aspect of this classroom-based study could contribute to understandings of the social and interactional nature of teaching and learning in chemistry. According to Lemke (1990), intertexts of oral and written texts construct ways of making social meanings. Therefore, analyzing oral and written discourse within the class learning community could be an avenue to investigate how meanings of chemical representations were socially constructed in a chemistry class. Through a close examination of classroom discourse, I identify various connections made by class members, analyze how and why they made these connections, and discuss how these connections were socially meaningful and recognized by class members.

METHODS

In order to investigate what types of connections were established in the class through social and discursive practices, and how the teachers' content knowledge shaped the connections students made, ethnographic data were collected over 7 weeks. In this section, I describe the context of this study and then provide a detailed account of data collection and analysis.

Context

This study was conducted at a small public high school in a university town in the midwest. There was a focus on the arts (drawing, painting, photography, music, and dance) at the school. The school curriculum was solid academically, although it was not high-powered and no advanced placement (AP) courses were offered. The teachers in the science program have been working with educational researchers from a local university to develop and implement a 3-year, integrated, project-based science curriculum (Marx et al., 1997) called Foundations of Science (FOS; Heubel-Drake, Finkel, Stern, & Mouradian, 1995). FOS was intended to replace separated earth science, biology, and chemistry courses at the 9th, 10th, and 11th grades. Throughout the year, students studied scientific subject matter by investigating broad questions and creating artifacts. Four essential features of FOS curriculum were project-based science; integrated curriculum; real science, local topics; and regular use of technology. Projects were designed as a driving force for the content being taught. The curriculum was "authentic" (Brown et al., 1989; Resnick, 1987) in that the teachers believed that "science is taught as it is practiced in the real world" (Heubel-Drake et al., 1995). FOS also emphasized the practical application of science in the community, so local topics and real issues were brought into the classroom to be discussed and investigated. Technology was used on a daily basis. There were Apple Powerbook 165c portable color laptop computers, and four Power Mac desktop computers in the classroom. Students had access to the Internet, the school network, and several pieces of commercial software.

Data for this study were collected from an 11th-grade science classroom of 25 students (2 Asian, 2 African, and 21 White Americans) who had previous experiences with the instructional approach in their freshman and sophomore years. The students represented a range of racial, academic, and socioeconomic characteristics that corresponded to district demographics, although the majority of students were White and middle- to upper middle-class.

The Toxin Project

This study focused on a cycle of activity—a complete set of activities, actions, or lessons around a single topic or a specific theme (Green & Meyer, 1991). The notion "cycle of activity" was used to indicate a complete series of intertextually tied activities initiated and enacted by class members (Floriani, 1993). Through these activities, class members interactionally constructed their academic and cultural knowledge with common thematic content. The cycle of activity from which data were collected was a 7-week project named "Toxin Unit." Figure 9.1 situates this cycle of activity in a larger class history.

THREE-YEAR FOUNDATIONS OF SCIENCE (FOS) CURRICULUM

FOS I	FOS II	FOS III

Foundations of Science (FOS) III

First Semester	Second Semester			
	Feb	March	April	May	June

Toxin Project

Week	Week 1	Week 2	Week 3	Week 4	Week 5	Week 6	Week 7
Day	1(M), 2(W), 3(Th)	4(M), 5(W), 6(F)	7(M), 8(W), 9(F)	10(M), 11(W)	12(M), 13(W)	14(M), 15(W), 16(F)	17(M), 18(W), 19(F)
Events	• Introduce the project • Watch water treatment video • Foul water lab • Watch movie: a civil action	• Review foul water lab • Discuss the movie and related issues • Lecture: ionic and covalent bonds • eChem I • Lecture: naming alkanes	• eChem II • Lecture: naming hydrocarbons • Manipulate physical models • eChem III • Lecture: cyclic compounds and functional groups • Watch video: Michigan at risk • Quiz	• Review quiz • Watch video: Michigan at risk • Toxin investigation • Lecture: EN, polarity, solubility • Solubility lab	• Review solubility lab • Review polarity and solubility • Toxin in my house • Lecture: TV method • Lecture: VSPER theory • Web hunt: VSPER theory	• Discuss web evaluation criteria • Watch video: Silence of spring • Demo: creating a webpage • Web page design	• Web page design • Discuss evaluation criteria of independent study • Peer critique of web pages

FIGURE 9.1. The Toxin Project situated in and across time (M: Monday; W: Wednesday; Th: Thursday; F: Friday).

During this cycle of activity, students worked with one or two other classmates and each small group conducted an investigation of a known toxin from a list provided by their teachers. Classroom activities of this cycle or unit were centered around a driving question: "Is my drinking water safe?" To answer this question, they were given lectures of relevant chemical concepts, searched information from the web, watched videos of water treatment and environmental science, did lab activities of solubility and water purification, built physical and computational models, and designed web pages for final presentations (see Fig. 9.1). Chemical concepts covered by this unit were VSEPR (Valence-Shell Electron Pair Repulsion) theory, covalent bonds, IUPAC (International Union of Pure and Applied Chemistry) nomenclature of organic compounds, molecular structures, and polarity of bonds and molecules. Throughout the project, several local topics and environmental issues were raised and discussed. For example, students watched video about the local water treatment plant and engaged in discussions about some toxic chemicals that could be found in their houses.

Teachers

Two teachers were co-teaching the class. Mark, the experienced teacher, majored in chemistry, and had 10-year teaching experience and 5-year experience with the FOS program. Maggie, the student teacher, was an undergraduate student majoring in biology and minoring in chemistry. She was assigned to teach at this school for 4 months to fulfill certification requirements. She had no instructional experience with project-based science prior to teaching this Toxin Unit. During the cycle of activity, Maggie took the main role of teaching in the class. Mark sometimes contributed his opinions about some issues or his understanding of the content to class discussions without interrupting Maggie's instruction. During the time of my class observation, Mark never showed his dissatisfaction in front of the class at what or how Maggie taught. Nor did he act in front of the students in ways that might be interpreted as undermining Maggie's authority as a teacher. The students trusted the instruction and answers that Maggie gave, and never asked for Mark's permission or acknowledgment for the activities that Maggie had them to do. They treated her as a co-teacher rather than as an inexperienced student teacher.

Data Collection

Before collecting data for the present study, I visited Mark's science class weekly and attended teachers' meetings several times. Through the 7-week data collection, I attended every class period including watching a movie outside the school on Day 3. I participated in the class as a researcher conducting this study, as a computer specialist, and as a content specialist for the Toxin Unit. I interacted with the students for their content questions and computer problems. I also attended teachers' meetings and was involved in the project planning.

I collected multiple sources of data for the study. I took fieldnotes during each of the class periods that I attended in order to capture the major events of the day and to note particular episodes related to constructing meanings for chemistry. An Hi-8 video camera recorded the classroom activity. These recordings are the primary data source for this study's transcriptions of the Toxin cycle of activity and evidence for my analytical claims.

Because FOS was an integrated and interdisciplinary science curriculum, teachers did not assign a specific textbook as the main source of information for it. Rather, they integrated the scientific information collected from multiple resources, including journal articles, the Internet, and textbooks, to write worksheets, handouts, and develop the curriculum. I collected these curriculum materials during teachers' meetings and the class periods. I used these materials to understand how teachers implemented the FOS curriculum and what they considered the content of the curriculum.

Data Transcription and Analysis

Several analytic steps were taken to understand how the teachers and students made the science content meaningful through linking it to real situations. First, the videorecordings of class activities were transcribed. During transcription, I identified chemical concepts covered during this cycle of activity, the events of each day, and the length of events. In this study, an event is defined as a bounded set of activities about a common theme on a given day. The event could contain one activity or a series of socially and academically linked activities that comprise subevents (Lin, 1993). This level of transcription provided an overview of the cycle of activity and made a range of events visible. Second, event maps of the 7-week cycle of activity were created to demonstrate that events were thematically tied to each other within the Toxin Unit (see Fig. 9.2 for event maps of Days 6, 7, and 12). Furthermore, I located and coded the subevents involving explicit links between chemistry and real situations made by class members on maps. Third, discourse segments of these subevents were transcribed and analyzed. The selections of segments were guided by the research questions. The common terms, chemical terminology, and chemical representations used by students and teachers were coded.

min	Day 6	Day 7	Day 12
5	Previewing today's activities		Previewing today's activities
10	Class discussion: reviewing ionic and covalent bonds		Class discussion: reviewing solubility lab
15			
20		Group time: Using a computer program to build virtual 3D models and practice naming rules of alkanes	Group time: manipulating 3D models to investigate polarity of molecules
25	Class discussion: homework		
30	Lecture: Defining alkanes		
35	Lecture: Nomenclature of alkanes (Segment 1: ethanol)*		
40			
45			
50	Student activity: Practicing the nomenclature of alkanes		
55		Lecture: Defining and naming alkenes and alkynes	Class discussion: polarity and solubility of toxins
60			
65		Student activity: Practice naming	
70		Student activity: Manipulating 3D physical models	Class discussion: Toxin in my house (Segment 2 & 4: Toxin in my house)*
75			
80			
85		Lecture: Introducing functional groups (Segment 3: Fish smell)*	
90			

FIGURE 9.2. Event map: events and approximate time spent on Days 6, 7, and 12. The discourse segments selected for analyses are located in the highlighted events.

The curriculum materials and fieldnotes that were collected to describe the implementation of FOS curriculum were not coded and analyzed in detail; rather, they were used to map patterns of classroom instruction and display the events of the day and particular episodes related to my research questions. The data from these two resources offered evidence for triangulating the assertions I generated from the classroom video data. I generated assertions from the transcripts of segments by searching the data corpus. Then I established an evidentiary warrant for the assertions and verified them by confirming and disconfirming evidence provided by the data corpus (Erickson, 1986).

FINDINGS

This section presents analyses of how connections between real situations and the chemistry content were co-constructed by class members through social and discursive practices. First I discuss how the intertextual links between real situations and the content at the *microscopic* level were built in the class. Then I illustrate how the student teacher and the experienced teacher used different instructional strategies to construct connections with and for students.

Connecting the Real World to the Content at the Microscopic Level

To illustrate how the connections were built in the class, I present three excerpts of class interactions on Days 6, 12, and 7. These three excerpts are selected to demonstrate patterns that emerged from the ethnographic data corpus. The first excerpt on Day 6 shows how a connection was initiated and completed by the class members. It provides a detailed account of how a connection was constructed through a student-initiated class interaction. The second excerpt (Day 12) is taken from a class discussion of homework. It reveals how teachers instigated connections selectively while interacting with students' responses. The third excerpt (Day 7) demonstrates a connection constructed solely by the teachers. It allows me to examine what content knowledge was involved in the construction of a connection.

Excerpt 1: A student-Initiated connection. This excerpt is taken from a lecture on the nomenclature of alkanes Day 6 of the Toxin Unit (see Fig. 9.2). Prior to this event, the student teacher, Maggie, reviewed bonding theory, discussed homework with the class, and introduced the definition of alkanes. During this event, Maggie showed students a chart of alkanes with chemical names and structures. This excerpt occurred right after Maggie gave a brief description of the chart. I selected this excerpt to demonstrate how a connection was initiated by a student and how the initiation was recognized by the class members.

This excerpt (Table 9.1) shows how Jack, as a student, initiated this interaction by raising a question about how ethanol was relevant to what he learned about alkanes. Ethanol was something he heard outside the class and used in real situations (lines 2, 4). Maggie signaled that this question of ethanol could be socially meaningful to all class members by saying "let's think about ethanol" (line 5). She used the pronoun "us" to redirect this Jack–teacher dialogue to a whole-class discussion. She then asked a question regarding the number of carbon atoms (5) that built on information she had given prior to Jack's question. She had said that the number of carbon atoms and the type of compounds determine a compound's name. Although she did not explicitly use the term, atom, her first question (line 5) assumed that students recognized that ethanol contains some carbon atoms. Given her introduction of the earlier information, there was a known and socially acknowledged answer for her current question (line 5). A student's incorrect response (line 6) indicated that students might not know ethanol has carbon atoms or they did not see the relationship between the prefix and the number of carbon atoms. She then explicitly linked the name "ethanol" to the prefixes shown on the chart (line 7). Evan's correct response (line 8) showed that he recognized this relationship by saying "eth for two." In response to Maggie's further question (line 9) about the meaning of the ending, "ol," more than one student showed their recognition of using a chemical name to identify structure-related information (line 10). At the time, some students had gotten the rule between the chemical name of a compound and its chemical characteristics. Maggie's conclusion (line 11) further confirmed the rule by indicating that students could have no understanding of alcohol, but they had to learn to use the prefix to identify the number of carbon atoms that could be applied for chemical names they learned from their daily lives.

In this interaction, Jack brought his understanding about an organic compound within a real-world context into the school classroom. Maggie's response signaled that what he presented was socially acceptable within the history of what counted as appropriate chemistry information in the classroom. Furthermore, she used the compound, ethanol, as an example to show students how a chemical name commonly used in their daily lives could inform them about its structure, such as the number of carbon atoms and the type of compounds. When she said "let's think about ethanol," she moved the name "ethanol" from the context of Jack's experience to the context of a science class. Her first question regarding the number of carbon atoms further connected this "ethanol"

Table 9.1. Day 6: A Student-Initiated Link

LINE	THE EXPERIENCED TEACHER	THE STUDENT TEACHER	STUDENT
1			(Jack raises his hand.)
		Jack	
2			Jack: I just come up with this idea, ethanol, that's what the wxxx perform stuff that can run cars.
3		Okay, ethanol.	
4			Jack: Is there anything to do with this sort of . . .
5		Okay, let's think about ethanol. How many carbons do you think ethanol has?	
6			Student: I have six.
7		Well, do you recognize anything in ethanol that's on this chart?	
8			Evan: Two for eth (he shows two figures).
9		It has two carbons. And do you recognize the ending O L at all?	
10			Students: alcohol
11		Alcohol. Okay, we'll get into that a little more on Monday, and how to actually name alcohols. But you know just from today, you already know that has two carbons.	

to the chemistry content at the microscopic level that ethanol was something made up of carbon atoms.

During this cycle of activities, students often volunteered their ideas about organic compounds within a real-world context. Maggie took the opportunities by using these compounds as examples to show the students how a chemical name commonly used in their daily lives informed them about its structure, such as the number of carbon atoms and the type of compounds. A common chemical name became a mediator connecting students' life experiences and the chemistry content at the microscopic level when it was meaningful in both contexts. Because a student-initiated connection revealed what students have known about the content, it provided a context for the class members to build meanings on their prior knowledge and concrete experiences. Through discursive practices, the teachers strategically linked a chemical term to the content by guiding students to rethink the conceptual relationship between the number of carbon atoms and the nomenclature of organic compounds. Even though some students may not share a common experience or may not realize what a specific term meant in chemistry, they acknowledged that the chemistry content could be connected to their daily lives.

Excerpt 1 shows how a connection was initiated by a student and established through a class discussion. However, not all students' questions initiated the construction of connections. Excerpt 2 reveals how the teacher selected students' responses as initiations and chose specific connections to make.

Excerpt 2: A Teacher Instigated Connection-Making. Excerpt 2 is taken from a class discussion on Day 12 (see Table 9.2), and the topic of this discussion was "Toxins in my house." Prior to Day 12, students had to fill out a "Home Hazardous Products Survey" as homework. This class discussion was based on the compounds that students found in their houses.

In this interaction, although the student teacher repeated the student's response "lime salt" (line 3), she did not write it on the board, nor did she ask further questions about it, as she did to Ted (line 5). Her response to ammonium chloride provided an explanation of why she ignored lime salt (lines 10, 12). Rather than putting it on the list immediately, she asked a question to the whole class as to whether ammonium chloride was organic or nonorganic (line 10). Her response (line 12) showed that to be a compound that would be put on the list or be discussed, it should be an organic toxin or at least a toxin. In this cycle of activity, all lectures were related to organic chemistry (see Fig. 9.1), so her response in this interaction re-emphasized that the chemical compounds which were socially meaningful in this interaction (and in this cycle of activity) were organic toxins. Therefore, as an inorganic nontoxin, lime salt was and should be ignored by the teacher and the class. As shown from line 9 to line 15, Jerry gave and then changed his answers three times. Receiving the teacher's signal that the organic toxin would be a legitimate answer in the class, he seemed to repair his first response and bought in organic prefixes to his second and third responses. Thus, the teacher and students interactively chose and ignored to understand specific chemical compounds and co-constructed meanings of "organic."

Table 9.2. Day 12: Links That Were Chose to Be Made

LINE	THE EXPERIENCED TEACHER	THE STUDENT TEACHER	STUDENT
1		What's something that you found in your house?	
2			Student: Lime salt.
3		Lime salt?	
4			Students: xxxx Students: Shut up. Ted: Iso-propanol.
5		Iso-propanol (she writes the name on the board). What's iso-propanol? Where did you find that, Ted?	
6			Ted: I found that on the furniture polish.
7		Okay, so Ted found iso-propanol on furniture polish. Jerry.	
8	Shh...		
9			Jerry: I found hum... ammonium chloride xxxxxxx.
10		Ammonium chloride. Is ammonium chloride toxic? Is ammonium chloride . . . that's ammonium, which is N and Hs, right? And Cl. Would that be organic? Would that be an organic toxin or non-organic toxin?	
11			Students: non-organic.
12		It would be an inorganic, because it doesn't have any carbon in it. Okay? But it is a toxin, and we put it up. What was it again?	
13			Jerry: ammonium methyl, uh . . .
14		Ohh. That was methyl ammonium.	
15			Jerry: It's dimethyl.

Table 9.2. Day 12: Links That Were Chose to Be Made *(continued)*

LINE	THE EXPERIENCED TEACHER	THE STUDENT TEACHER	STUDENT
16		So dimethyl ammonium chloride (she looks at Jerry and waits for his confirming.)	
17			Allan: what is that?
18			(Jerry turns to Allan and explains to him.)
19		A lot of people probably got some kinds of ammonium chlorite or ammonium chloride. Those are really common in things like uhh . . . toilet bowl cleaner, and lots of combination bleach cleaners. Something with ammonium chloride in it is really common.	

Additionally, in this interaction, a connection could be seen between ammonium chloride and cleaners. To help students decide whether ammonium chloride was organic or not, the student teacher told students what atoms are in it (line 10). Rather than using atoms' names (i.e., nitrogen, hydrogen, and chlorine), she described these atoms as symbols (i.e., N, H, and Cl). Thus, at the microscopic/symbolic levels, ammonium chloride was represented as a combination of atoms and symbols in this interaction. The connection between the content and real situations was completed by the student teacher's conclusion (line 19) of ammonium chloride as an ingredient of cleaners. In this interaction, ammonium chloride was used as a name across contexts, which mediated the construction of a connection by allowing the teacher to move it from the context of real situations to the context of the science class.

As shown in Excerpts 1 and 2, although connections could be initiated by students and selectively constructed through the class interactions, the content knowledge at the microscopic/symbolic levels was mainly provided or prompted by the teacher. In the first excerpt, the student teacher's questions guided students to treat "ethanol" as a compound with two carbon atoms. Her response in Excerpt 2 defined what counted as an organic compound and determined what atoms ammonium chloride consist of. By presenting a connection constructed solely by the teachers, in Excerpt 3, I analyze what content knowledge was involved in the process of making a connection.

Excerpt 3: A Connection Constructed by the Teacher. Excerpt 3 is taken from a lecture of functional groups of organic compounds on Day 7. After the student teacher introduced the functional groups of halocarbon, alcohol, ether, aldehyde, ketone, and ester, Mark, the experienced teacher gave the following talk (Table 9.3).

Table 9.3. Day 7: A Link Constructed by the Teacher: Fish Smell and Lemon

LINE	THE EXPERIENCED TEACHER	THE STUDENT TEACHER	STUDENT
1	I'm gonna show you how these [functional groups] actually work together. If you... let's say you're about to eat some fish. And fish has that funky smell that funky smell is an aldehyde. And... that funky smell you take a piece of lemon which has . . . which has citrate acid in it. It's a carboxylic acid. It's citrate acid.		
2		So this is the lemon. (She circles the general formula of carboxylic acid, and writes "citrate acid" next to it.)	
3	It's the lemon, and you pour on to the fish smell which is the aldehyde. And those things together break the aldehyde down into I think a ketone, and which doesn't smell as much. So you know, I mean you are constantly doing these types of reactions . . . umh . . . without even thinking about it. And you're changing one compound into another compound to solve the particular problem. That's just an example what's going on there.		

Instead of constructing connections through dialogic interactions with students, the teachers made connections by describing processes, showing structures, and presenting relevant information in monologic discourse. To show students "how these [compounds with functional groups] actually work together," the experienced teacher integrated chemical terminology (i.e., aldehyde, carboxylic acid, and ketone) into a daily experience. He transformed the fish smell and lemon to chemical compounds, and deodorization became a chemical process. To make all connections in this talk visible, I further transcribe this excerpt to Figure 9.3. It demonstrates how multiple representations of chemistry were juxtaposed as the experienced teacher moved back and forth between the real situation and chemistry content. This example created a context for students to rethink the functional groups they just learned and emphasized that chemistry at the three levels (i.e., the macroscopic, microscopic, and symbolic levels) was part of their daily life (line 3).

As shown in Fig. 9.3, these connections could have not been built without content-knowledge elements (i.e., aldehyde, citrate acid, and carboxylic acid). The experienced teacher must realize the chemical characteristics of these functional groups and relevant connections prior to giving the talk. Based on his understanding of students' prior knowledge and experiences, he assumed that students had experience with pouring lemon juice on a fish, because his talk would have been socially meaningless if students did not recognized either fish smell or functional groups. Thus, by creating these connections, the experienced teacher demonstrated his content knowledge of the topics and pedagogical knowledge of what students already knew and how to teach the content meaningfully. To illustrate how the teachers' content could shape the ways of making connections, I present Excerpt 4 and discuss how the student teacher and the experienced teacher constructed connections differently.

The Content Knowledge and the Ways of Making Connections

Excerpt 3 and Fig. 9.3 showed that the construction of connections involved both the teacher's content and pedagogical knowledge. To further explore this issue, I selected the fourth excerpt.

Excerpt 4: Toxin in My House. This discourse segment follows Excerpt 2 (Table 9.4); both of the segments are taken from the same event on Day 12 (see the event map in Fig. 9.2). After the student teacher concluded that ammonium chloride was a common ingredient of cleaners (see Tables 2 and 4 [line 19]), she asked Andy about the toxin he found in

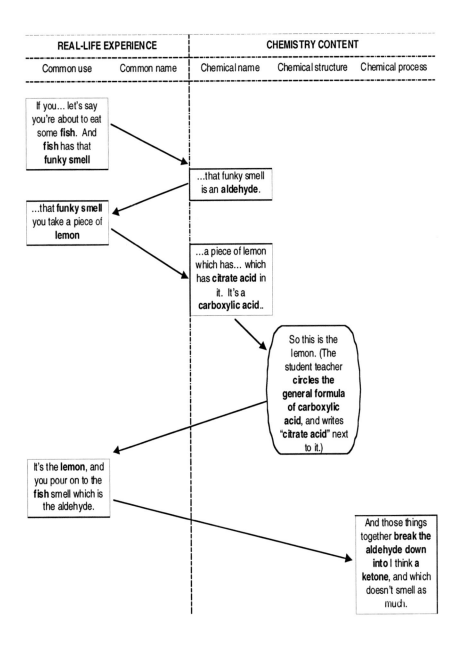

FIGURE 9.3. The connection-making process in the Fish Smell and Lemon excerpt. Boxes contain the experienced teacher's discourse. The oval contains the description provided and the action taken by the student teacher.

Table 9.4. Day 12: Toxin in My House

LINE	THE EXPERIENCED TEACHER	THE STUDENT TEACHER	STUDENT
19		A lot of people probably got some kinds of ammonium chlorite or ammonium chloride. Those are really common in things like uhh...toilet bowl cleaner, and lots of combination bleach cleaners. Something with ammonium chloride in it is really common. So Andy, what did you find in your house?	
20			Andy: Mono ethanol amine
21		Mono ethan ol amine? (She writes it on the board.)	
22			Andy: Yeah. It was in oven cleaner.
23		And what was that in?	
24			Andy: Oven cleaner.
25		Oven cleaner?	
26			Andy: right
27	Which is very interesting. It's probably the same thing, almost.		
28		Is this? (she points to dimethyl ammonium chloride)	
29	Yeah. Because dimethyl, what does dimethyl mean? It means 2 methyls, which means two carbons, right? What is ethyl?		(Some students nod.)
30			Allan: One...two carbons
31	Two carbons. Right. Amine is another way of saying ammonium, so it's another some kinds of the ammonium compound.		

his house—monoethanolamine in oven cleaner. The experienced teacher then intervened in the dialogue between the student teacher and Andy by saying that monoethylamine and dimethyl ammonium chloride were almost the same compound. He explained that both dimethyl and ethyl contained two carbon atoms, and that amine was one kind of ammonium compound.

The experienced teacher's intervention began with the comment (line 27), "which is very interesting." Rather than initiating the intervention with a complete sentence, he used "which" to slot into and continue the dialogue between the student teacher and Andy. The use of "which" made his intervention part of their dialogue rather than an interruption. As mentioned previously, during the time of class observation, he never interrupted class instruction in ways that may have undermined the student teacher's teaching authority. Continuing and becoming a part of the class discourse were strategies he frequently used.

In response to the student teacher's question (line 28), Mark, the experienced teacher, first explained the chemical meaning of dimethyl (line 29). His explanation made an intertextual link to what students had already learned about naming rules and subgroups. By including several small questions, his explanation showed his assumptions that students understood that di meant two and methyl was a subgroup with only one carbon atom. When he said "right?" he was looking for students' confirmation, which could be verbal or non-verbal expressions, such as nodding. His explanation was more like a review of what students already learned, so he expected the answers to his questions to be known by the class. Allan's response further validated the teacher's assumption that students could recognize the structural similarity between dimethyl and ethyl. In contrast with his treatment of dimethyl, his explanation of amine (line 31) did not contain any questions. He directly provided a description of how amine was related to ammonium knowing that for students ammonium was a socially recognizable compound and amine was first mentioned by a class member. Thus, in this interaction, the experienced teacher applied different instructional strategies of questioning and explaining based on his recognition of students' prior knowledge regarding naming rules and molecular structures. To introduce the compounds that were not socially recognized by the class, he used descriptions or lecturing. Furthermore, he made intertextual connections to what students had already learned by using a series of interactive questions. The student teacher applied a similar strategy in the first excerpt by prompting students to read the structure-related information from ethanol.

In this fourth interaction, the student teacher and the experienced teacher demonstrated their content knowledge through discursive practices. From chemical names of two compounds (dimethyl ammonium

chloride and monoethanolamine), the experienced teacher saw the similarity of their molecular structures. His explanations (lines 29, 31) illustrated his understanding of molecular structures, naming rules, and the
relationship between them. Yet the student teacher's response (line 28)
showed that she did not recognize the relationship when Mark first made
a comment about these two compounds (line 27). At the time, she did not
identify the similarity of structures between them as Mark did.

Figure 9.4 synthesizes the second and fourth segments and certain
elements of the connections constructed during these interactions
become visible. It can be observed that the information related to the content was mainly provided by the two teachers. In addition, the experienced teacher's explanations were all located in the chemistry domain.
As he did in Excerpt 3 (see Fig. 9.3), Mark tended to extend the chemistry
content into what students had not yet learned through describing or presenting various connections between real situations and the content at the
microscopic level. His explanations and descriptions contained many
chemical terms and required considerable content knowledge. The student teacher also provided relevant information and/or encouraged students to generate meanings related to the chemistry content. For example, Fig. 9.5 showed how the connection was constructed in the Excerpt
1. By questioning students to interpret chemical meanings from the name
"ethanol," Maggie illustrated how to read a structure from a chemical
name. However, compared with the experienced teacher, she tended to
construct intertextual connections with students by building on what students had already learned. She applied content knowledge to shape students' ways of constructing connections with the class. Her response in
Excerpt 4 could also be interpreted as a lack of content knowledge about
the relationship between ammonium and amine. Therefore, with more
understanding of the chemistry content, the experienced teacher made
connections with the class through presenting information or asking a
series of questions by oral discourse; on the other hand, the student
teacher with presumably less content and pedagogical knowledge mainly used questioning to build connections with the class.

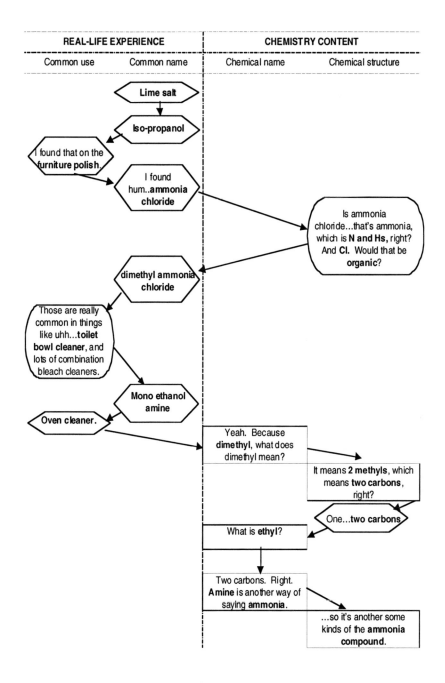

FIGURE 9.4. The connection-making process in the Toxin in My House excerpt. Boxes contain the experienced teacher's discourse. Ovals contain the student teacher's discourse. Students' responses are shown in hexagons.

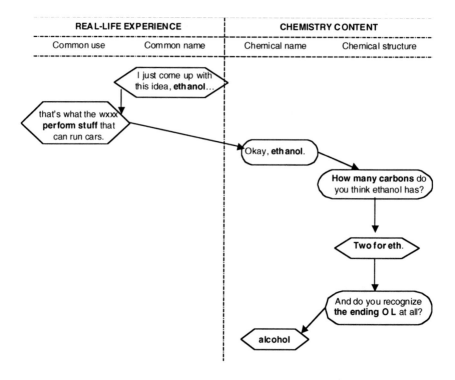

FIGURE 9.5. The connection-making process in the Ethanol excerpt. Ovals contain the student teacher's discourse. Students' questions and responses are shown in hexagons.

DISCUSSION AND CONCLUSIONS

Recent studies in science education have increasingly turned to a concern with the use of language in scientific practices (e.g., Hogan, Nastasi, & Pressley, 2000; Kelly & Chen, 1999; Kozma, 2000). Kozma indicated that the use of language in chemistry serves educational functions. Whereas the participants in Kozma (2000) studies were chemists and college students, this study illustrates how students and teachers at the high school level co-construct meanings of chemical representations through classroom discourse. Students' final artifacts demonstrate that they took up this "connection-making" as a way of presenting and learning chemistry knowledge. Figure 9.6 shows one student group's web page in which they gave an introduction to their toxin—acetone. In this page, they provided a detailed description of the chemical structure of acetone and

The **CHEMICAL PROPERTIES** of acetone are:

Solubility: It dissolves in water, and is often used as a solvent

Covalent bonding/3D Structure:

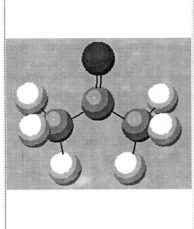

This is a ball-and-stick diagram of the molecule C_3H_6O, otherwise known as ACETONE. The grey balls represent Carbon atoms, the white balls are Hydrogen and the red ball is Oxygen. The black sticks represent bonds: single sticks represent single bonds, and double sticks represent double bonds. Therefore, there are single bonds among the Carbon and Hydrogen atoms, and among the Carbon atoms. There is one double bond in Acetone- between the Carbon and Oxygen atoms. The Carbon-Hydrogen bonds are non-polar bonds, the Carbon-Carbon bonds are neutral, and the CArbon=Oxygen bond is polar. The Carbon-Oxygen bond has stongest electronegativity value, therefore Acetone is slightly polar because the non-polar bonds among the other atoms contribute to eliminating some of the polar bond's electronegativity.

Polarity: Acetone is borderline between polar and nonpolar. In an experiment we performed, we found that non-polar substances dissolved in the acetone. In solubility, like substances dissolve like substances, and so we concluded that acetone was non-polar. However, acetone also partly dissolves in water due to it's 3-D structure as shown above, and is not strongly polar or non-polar.

Effects on the Human Body: Because Acetone can be polar and non-polar it effects many systems in the body. For example, fat is non-polar and so Acetone can attack the fat cells in your body. If you are exposed to acetone it goes into your bloodstream and is then carried to all the organs in your body. I f it is a small amount the liver breaks it down to chemicals that are not harmful and uses these chemicals to make energy for normal body functions.

FIGURE 9.6. One student dyad's web page of their toxin: Acetone.

explained how this structure causes the polarity of this compound. They then tied the information of polarity to solubility and biological effects on the human body. This page included conceptual information of the three levels of chemistry and revealed that the students' thinking of chemistry could move back and forth among phenomena (i.e., biological effects and solubility), representations (i.e., the structure and formula), and concepts (i.e., the relationship between polarity and structure). At the conceptual level, therefore, oral and written discourses could be used to make interpretations of chemical representations. Through the use of language, students in this study came to learn the conceptual knowledge embedded in symbolic and molecular representations.

Although students are capable to make connections among three levels, students' understanding are usually constrained by available resources (Kozma, 2000) and teachers' scaffolds were crucial to support students' conceptions to move beyond the perceptual experiences. The close examination of class discourse suggests that although connections could be co-constructed by the teachers and students, the chemistry terms and content at the microscopic level were mainly provided or guided by the teachers. As shown on Figs. 9.4 and 9.5, students did not actively mention any information located in the chemistry domain unless they were prompted by the teachers. Without explicit instruction, students may not be able to build connections. Therefore, due to the abstract and content-based nature of chemical representations, teachers' scaffolds are crucial to facilitate the construction of connections between chemical representations and observable phenomena.

At the social level, connection-making, a specified way of language use (Lemke, 1988), might be promoted by the design of the curriculum. Instead of learning microscopic representations through teachers' lecture or textbooks, students were encouraged to collect information from multiple sources. The learning community created a socially accepted way to bring their life experiences into the classroom context and made the content meaningful. The "authentic" feature of the curriculum may contribute to the establishment of the social norm, as the teachers emphasized the practical application and local issues of science in the community (Heubel-Drake et al., 1995).

However, although the culture of the class in this study invited students' daily experiences, teachers did not further include these related experiences into the interactional space (Heras, 1993) of class discussions. When Maggie moved a chemical name from Jack's experience into the context of the class in Excerpt 1, this process involved recontextualization. She isolated the compound "ethanol" as a chemical name from Jack's experience and recontextualized it in the context of the science class without discussing it within Jack's context or providing implications of why this compound was used as a way that Jack described. She might consider that Jack's experiences might not be socially recognized by other class members, so chose to discuss it as a chemical compound. However, if making connections and contextualization become ways of understanding science, the questions of whose context counts as "the" context of a class and how class members construct social meanings through integrating multiple contexts outside the school should not be overlooked.

Teachers' content knowledge shapes the discursive nature of scaffoldings. Carlsen (1992) indicated that insufficient content knowledge led teachers to control classroom conversion rather than encouraging an interactive dialogue between the teacher and students. The findings of this study further show that teachers' content knowledge influenced their choices of discursive strategies; however, it may not necessarily constrain the interactions between the teacher and students. In this study, although the student teacher did not have sufficient content knowledge to extend students' understanding through presenting more connections in real situations, she still promoted students to generate questions and relate the content to experiences through oral discourse.

The findings of this study provide a backdrop for further research to explore how students use connections as a way of learning, how students learn from connections that are built by different instructional strategies, and how chemistry is learned and taught in a class through the social constructivist lens.

ACKNOWLEDGMENTS

This chapter was based on work supported by the National Science Foundation (NSF) under NSF REC-9555719. Any opinions, findings, and conclusions expressed in this study are those of the author and do not necessarily reflect the views of the NSF. I thank Lesley Rex, Greg Kelly, and Joe Krajcik for their comments on an early version of the manuscript. I also thank the teachers and students who participated in this study.

REFERENCES

Ben-Zvi, R., Eylon, B., & Silberstein, J. (1986). Is an atom of copper malleable? *Journal of Chemical Education, 63,* 64-66.

Ben-Zvi, R., Eylon, B., & Silberstein, J. (1987). Students' visualization of a chemical reaction. *Education in Chemistry,* July, 117-120. (www.rsc.org/Education /Eic).

Ben-Zvi, R., Eylon, B., & Silberstein, J. (1988). Theories, principles and laws. *Education in Chemistry,* May, 89-92. (www.rsc.org/Education/Eic).

Brown, J. S., Collins, A., & Duguid, P. (1989). Situated cognition of learning. *Educational Researcher, 18,* 32-42.

Carlsen, W. S. (1992). Closing down the conversation: Discouraging student talk on unfamiliar science content. *Journal of Classroom Interaction, 27,* 15-21.

Cognition and Technology Group at Vanderbilt (1990). Anchored instruction and its relationship to situated cognition. *Educational Researcher, 19,* 2-10.

Erickson, F. (1986). Qualitative methods in research on teaching. In M. C. Wittrock (Ed.), *Handbook of research on teaching* (3rd ed., pp. 119-161). New York: Macmillan.

Floriani, A. (1993). Negotiating what counts: Roles and relationships, texts and contexts, content and meaning. *Linguistics and Education, 5*(3&4), 241-274.

Gabel, D. (1998). The complexity of chemistry and implications for teaching. In B. J. Fraser & K. G. Tobin (Eds.), *International handbook of science education* (pp. 233-248). Dordrecht, The Netherlands: Kluwer Academic Publishers.

Gabel, D. L., Samuel, K. V., & Hunn, D. (1987). Understanding the particulate nature of matter. *Journal of Chemical Education, 64,* 695-697.

Gagne, E. D., Yekovich, C. W., & Yekovich, F. R. (1993). *The cognitive psychology of school learning.* New York: HarperCollins.

Green, J. L., & Meyer, L. A. (1991). The embeddedness of reading in classroom life: Reading as a situated process. In C. Baker & A. Luke (Eds.), *Toward a critical sociology of reading pedagogy* (pp. 141-160). Philadelphia: John Benjamins.

Heras, A. I. (1993). The construction of understanding in a sixth-grade bilingual classroom. *Linguistics and Education, 5*(3&4), 275-299.

Heubel-Drake, M., Finkel, L., Stern, E., & Mouradian, M. (1995). Planning a course for success. *The Science Teacher, 62,* 18-21.

Hoffmann, R., & Laszlo, R. (1991). Representation in chemistry. *Angewandte Chemie, 30,* 1-16.

Hogan, K., Nastasi, B. K., & Pressley, M. (2000). Discourse patterns and collaborative scientific reasoning in peer and teacher-guided discussions. *Cognition and Instruction, 17*(4), 379-432.

Johnstone, A. H. (1982). Macro- and micro-chemistry. *School Science Review, 64,* 377-379.

Johnstone, A. H. (1993). The development of chemistry teaching: A changing response to changing demand. *Journal of Chemical Education, 70*(9), 701-705.

Keig, P. F., & Rubba, P. A. (1993). Translation of representations of the structure of matter and its relationship to reasoning, gender, spatial reasoning, and specific prior knowledge. *Journal of Research in Science Teaching, 30*(8), 883-903.

Kelly, G. J., & Chen, C. (1999). The sound of music: Constructing science as sociocultural practices through oral and written discourse. *Journal of Research in Science Teaching, 36*(8), 883-915.

Kelly, G. J., Chen, C., & Crawford, T. (1998). Methodological considerations for studying science-in-the-making in educational settings. *Research in Science Education, 28*(1), 23-49.

Kozma, R. B. (2000, August). *Representation and language: The case for representational competence in the chemistry curriculum.* Paper presented at the 16th biennial Conference on Chemical Education, Ann Arbor, MI.

Kozma, R. B., Chin, E., Russell, J., & Marx, N. (2000). The roles of representations and tools in the chemistry laboratory and their implications for chemistry instruction. *Journal of the Learning Sciences, 9*(2), 105-143.

Kozma, R. B., & Russell, J. (1997). Multimedia and understanding: Expert and novice responses to different representations of chemical phenomena. *Journal of Research in Science Teaching, 34,* 949-968.

Kozma, R. B., Russell, J., Jones, T., Marx, N., & Davis, J. (1996). The use of multiple, linked representations to facilitate science understanding. In R. G. S. Vosniadou, E. DeCorte, & H. Mandel (Ed.), *International perspective on the psychological foundations of technology-based learning environments* (pp. 41-60). Hillsdale, NJ: Erlbaum.

Krajcik, J. S. (1991). Developing students' understanding of chemical concepts. In R. H. Y. S. M. Glynn & B. K. Britton (Ed.), *The psychology of learning science. International perspective on the psychological foundations of technology-based learning environments* (pp. 117-145). Hillsdale, NJ: Erlbaum.

Krajcik, J. S., Czerniak, C. M., & Berger, C. (1999). *Teaching children science: A project-based approach.* New York: McGraw-Hill College.

Latour, B. (1987). *Science in action: How to follow scientists and engineers through society.* Cambridge, MA: Harvard University Press.

Lave, J., & Wenger, E. (1991). *Situated learning: Legitimate peripheral participation.* New York: Cambridge University Press.

Lemke, J. L. (1988). Genres, semantics, and classroom education. *Linguistics and Education, 1*(81-99).

Lemke, J. L. (1990). *Talking science: Language, learning and values.* Norwood, NJ: Ablex.

Lin, L. (1993). Language of and in the classroom: Constructing the patterns of social life. *Linguistics and Education, 5*(3&4), 367-410.

Lynch, M., & Woolgar, S. (Eds.). (1990). *Representation in scientific practice.* Cambridge, MA: MIT Press.

Marx, R. W., Blumenfeld, P. C., Krajcik, J. S., & Soloway, E. (1997). Enacting project-based science. *Elementary School Journal, 97*(4), 4-13, 22.

Nakhleh, M. B. (1992). Why some students don't learn chemistry. *Journal of Chemical Education, 69*(3), 191-196.

Nye, M. J. (1993). *From chemical philosophy to theoretical chemistry.* Berkeley: University of California Press.

Osborne, R., & Freyberg, P. (1985). *Learning in science: The implications of children's science.* Auckland, New Zealand: Heinemann Education.

Resnick, L. B. (1987). Learning in school and out. *Educational Researcher, 16*, 13-20.

White, R., & Gunstone, R. (1992). *Probing understanding.* London, New York: Falmer Press.

Wiser, M. (1995). Use of history of science to understand and remedy students' misconceptions about heat and temperature. In D. N. Perkins, J. L. Schwartz, M. M. West, & M. S. Wiske (Eds.), *Software goes to school: Teaching for understanding with new technologies* (pp. 23-38). New York: Oxford University Press.

PART IV

Studying the Social Positioning of Students' Roles and Identities

Sharilyn C. Steadman

Nine years of secondary teaching experience taught me that classrooms were fascinating communities built through complex moment-to-moment interactions that defined the roles that students and teachers could take up. As the bells rang each day to signal the end of one class period and the beginning of the next, a new community of students filled the classroom, and while each classroom community reflected their own negotiated patterns of social interaction and knowledge construction, they also often shared common concerns with the class before and the class after. I began to understand that an examination of the experiences of one class might inform the interactions of another. But how could I tell their stories? What language could I use? What data could I collect? Interactional ethnography (IE) offered an approach to exploring classroom life that honored the observer-participant perspective, the unique nature of each learning community, and the opportunity to compare interactions within and among classroom groups.

As a member of Lesley's introductory course in IE, I entered an English classroom seeking to collect data that would help me discover what respect *looked like* in a secondary setting. The interactions of the classroom immediately challenged my initial focus and the wisdom of entering a learning environment with *a priori* assumptions. An IE approach discourages the temptation to embrace a topic and jump to conclusions too early and instead encourages researchers to begin their investigations with a wide-angle lens that, in time and through exposure to the learning site, becomes more acute. Through this process, I came to refine my research question and identify an important aspect of my research classroom site: gendered discourse. As my study expanded to cover an entire school year, however, the large amount of data that I gathered presented my greatest dilemmas: how to decide what to foreground, what to set aside, and how to logically present my findings. I came to recognize that it was necessary to draw boundaries around certain moments in my data, privileging some events and ignoring others, but I did so reluctantly until I accepted that such decisions are necessary in this type of research

Because the first part of my study was completed for Lesley's class, I enjoyed a level of collaboration with my classmates and Lesley that contributed greatly to my study. Each time we met as a class, we attempted to articulate clearly what we were seeing in our selected investigatory sites. As we shared videotapes and transcriptions of discursive interactions, we questioned, explored, and pushed on possible interpretations, and in the process, deepened our understandings of each project and of the methods of IE.

10

Extending Opportunities, Expanding Boundaries: Addressing Gendered Discourse Through Multiple Subjectivities in a High School English Classroom

Sharilyn C. Steadman

"Awww, Ms. N., I was in the process of winning!"

Seth stood next to a group of seated male students, his voice rising above the din of the classroom. As I looked at expression of mock irritation on Seth's face and the smiles of his group members, I knew the focus of my research had suddenly shifted. In my role as a university-based researcher, I had originally intended to explore what counts as respect in Ms. Nelson's 12th grade English class; however, the events of my first day of observation in September 2000, spotlighted play as an active element of the discourse of these students. Over the course of the fall semester, I conducted an interactional ethnographic (IE) study that revealed the presence of a gendered discourse in which boys positioned themselves as "players" and girls positioned themselves as "teachers." This discourse defined the experiences of all members of the classroom community, limiting the positions that males and females could take up and shaping the teaching and learning that occurred in the class (Tuyay, Jennings, & Dixon, 1995).

The gendered discourse inhabiting this classroom presented a challenge to the teacher, a challenge she accepted; in the spring semester, Ms. Nelson launched a cycle of activity (Green & Meyer, 1991; Santa Barbara

Discourse Group, 1992; Tuyay et al., 1995; Zaharlick & Green, 1991) that
addressed the restrictions imposed by this classroom culture's historically defined gendered roles. By requiring each student to teach a poetry
term to the class, Ms. Nelson tackled the boys' limited opportunities and
reluctance to take on leadership/teacher roles while simultaneously
encouraging the entire learning community to expand its view of what
boys can and cannot do. In taking up the sanctioned role of teacher and
its accompanying academic aspects, the boys repositioned themselves
within the class. Thus, the male students' new subjectivity as teachers
and their multiple positioning as players and teachers enriched the teaching *and* learning occurring within this academic context.

NEED FOR THIS STUDY

The existence of a gender-differentiated discourse within this classroom
did not mark this community as idiosyncratic. In fact, exploration of the
gendered nature of discourse within society at large has received much
attention. Deborah Tannen's works *That's Not What I Meant: How
Conversational Style Makes or Breaks Your Relationships* (1987), *You Just
Don't Understand: Women and Men in Conversation* (1990), and *Talking
From 9 to 5* (1994b) examine the difficulties that arise when people try to
communicate across the gender line. At one time, such a topic may have
found a receptive audience only in the scholarly community; however,
public interest has placed Tannen's works on bestseller lists. Several educational researchers have also focused their efforts on this subject, studying primarily preschool and elementary classrooms for evidence of gender-differentiated language. Obviously, gendered discourse raises some
interesting topics for further study, including the origin of differences
between the ways boys and girls talk, the impact such differences may
have on the interaction between members of the community, the effect of
such differences on multiple facets of relationships. Although these and
other topics suggest significant issues regarding gendered discourse at
large, in the classroom it is teaching and learning that command fore-
most attention; therefore, when I shared the final results of the fall
semester's data collection and analysis with Ms. Nelson in January 2001,
our discussion focused on the impact of gendered discourse and gender-
affiliated roles on the teaching and learning that took place in her classroom. We discussed whether the female students, in consistently assuming the teacher role, acted as gatekeepers, thereby refusing male students
opportunities to take on leadership roles, and we explored the effect of
the boys' adherence to play discourse on the entire community. Ms.
Nelson and I both wished to continue our collaboration through the
spring semester in an attempt to expand the culturally sanctioned dis-

course of the boys and girls in her class and subsequently to influence the discursive positionings available to the members of the classroom community.

Student participation in the poetry cycle of activity designed to address the existing discursive position (boys play) provided the second semester focus of this study. As noted, such gender-specific behavior is not unique; the need to acknowledge, address, and reduce the limitations of gender-defined roles (often relating to social inequality) appears in educational and cultural studies (e.g., DeFrancisco, 1998; Eder, Evans, & Parker, 1995; O'Barr & Atkins, 1998; Weedon, 1997). Although our focus on limited teaching and learning opportunities differed from the corpus of literature, the existence of gender-differentiated positioning still generated a concern that we believed needed to be addressed. Furthermore, offering students the opportunity to assume the position of teacher within a classroom finds a foundation in established literature. In 1933, John Dewey asserted that teachers and students should frequently switch roles in order to become sufficiently sensitive to each other's contributions and, thereby, develop common understandings. Dewey (1967, cited in Fishman & McCarthy, 2000) goes on the say, however, that "the teacher is a learner, and the learner is, without knowing it, a teacher—and upon the whole, the less consciousness there is, on either side, of either giving or receiving instruction, the better" (p. 228). Although such unconscious assumption of the teaching position may be the ultimate goal for Ms. Nelson's male students, the initial step toward this goal demanded a transparent assignment that required the boys to teach, thereby positioning themselves not just as "players" within the classroom, but as instructors as well.

In exploring the students' take up of multiple subjectivities, this study initially asked: What is required for boys to position themselves as teachers in this class, a position historically assigned to girls? In focusing on the primary question, several study questions emerged:

- What particular discursive positions were available to boys previously?
- How did the boys' previous positioning give meaning to the material social relations within the class?
- Can boys assume the subjective position as teacher while simultaneously maintaining subjectivity as players?
- Will multiple subjectivity change the material reality of the class beyond the cycle of activity?

In examining these questions, I found a related body of elements allowed the boys to assume multiple subjectivities: (a) sanction by the teacher, (b) an academic aspect to the assignment, and (c) the opportunity to enact "teaching" individually. By requiring the boys to take up the teaching role, Ms. Nelson situated them to accept a new discursive position that did not threaten the historic aspect of masculinity; therefore, the boys assumed the position of teacher while retaining the position of "players," and class members accepted them as both.

To make explicit the new positioning of boys as teachers during the cycle of activity, I highlight four episodes from the fall semester's study. Comparing the male subjectivities from the fall with those assumed during the spring cycle of activity provides a rich contrast. Fall episodes include the initial event that points to boys as "players"; an interaction between a boy who joked and teased while a girl maintained a serious demeanor; a group presentation that contrasts the playful manner of the boys and the teacher-like position of the girl; and an interaction between two boys, one of whom takes up the discursive role of teacher and one who rejects this positioning.

This study enriches the conversation on gender by addressing an underresearched group: high school males. Studies of gendered discourse within school settings focus overwhelmingly on pre-school/kindergarten and elementary school children (e.g., Davies, 1989; Fichtelius, Johansson, & Nordin, 1979; Goodwin, 1998; Graddol & Swann, 1989; Maltz & Borker, 1982) or middle school students (Canaan, 1990; Eder et al., 1995), while comparatively little work addresses high school students. Current feminist, poststructural, and critical theories rely on fluid concepts of subjectivity and positioning, and, therefore, a comprehensive body of research on gender within schools cannot limit itself to the primary grades. As this ethnographically oriented study suggests, high school settings may contribute substantial data to the current understandings of gendered-discursive practices and gendered cultural norms. Similarly, researchers delving into theories of subjectivity and positioning frequently align with feminist practice and investigate women's roles and women's identities, sometimes referring to men and male positioning only in terms of their interactions with women (e.g., Coates, 1999; Weedon, 1997). Thus, little research exists on the discourse of and various discursive positions available to high school students, especially to males, within the unique context of secondary school.

THEORETICAL FRAMEWORK

Theories on IE and research on gender discourse and gendered identity inform this study. Feminist ethnographer Diane Bell endorses an ethnographic approach to studying a community's behavior: "Ethnography . . . empowers and validates everyday experiences. It brings to the threshold of consciousness the routines, rhythms and rituals of everyday life, allows us to savour the ordinary, map the mundane" (Bell, 1993, p. 298, cited in Coates, 1996, p. 15). Thus, an IE approach, foregrounding socio-cultural and sociolinguistic lenses, provides the approach used for this study. The sociocultural view asserts that communities are interactional and that interaction creates the *discourse* as the discourse simultaneously shapes the community, or as James Paul Gee (1999) states, language "always simultaneously reflects and constructs the situation or context in which it is used" (p. 82). The term discourse here refers to not only spoken language, but also to social communicative practices (Hicks, 1995; Talbot, 1998). Thus, discourse embraces both oral and written texts and "socially situated practices that are constructed in moment-to-moment interaction" (Hicks, 1995, p. 51). The sociolinguistic approach states that language is used as social action. Taking up this lens, Erving Goffman (1967) posits that discourse is an analytic resource of sociability. Consequently, the discourse of Ms. Nelson's first period class reflects and constructs the norms of the community.

A community's discourse often reflects the roles the members have accepted for their genders, thus producing a gendered discourse characterized by consistent aspects. Jennifer Coates (1995) states that "women and men talk differently" and that "male speakers are socialized into a more competitive style of discourse, while women are socialized into a more cooperative style of speech" (p. 13). Janet Holmes (1995) concurs, finding that in general men typically engage in a type of verbal sparring while women tend to engage in conversations that avoid confrontation. The foundation for this binary pair (Davies & Hunt, 2000) that suggests that male discourse is competitive/female discourse is cooperative resides in early childhood experiences. In investigating the discourse of young children, Coates draws on the ethnographically based work of Maltz and Borker (1982) who argue that same-gender play instills different conversational rules in boys and girls: Boys adopt adversarial speech patterns, and girls come to rely on collaboration and affiliation. Evidence of inequalities in classroom talk may surface when boys are far more eager to talk than girls, impatiently calling out if they are not called on quickly enough, whereas girls adhere to the "rules," raising their hands and waiting their turns to speak (Graddol & Swann, 1989). In a similar finding, a study conducted in a Swedish day school illuminated that from an early age, children learn from their social situations to act like girls or boys and what they have learned is reflected in their speech (Fichtelius, et al., 1979).

Thus, as children learn the language, they take on much more than mere words. They "learn to constitute themselves and others as unitary beings, as capable of coherent thought, as gendered, and as one who is in particular kinds of relation to others" (Davies, 1989, p.1). Examining the ways in which children interact with language, with other children, and with teachers deepens scholarly understanding of the discourse that infuses classrooms. Ethnographic studies from predominately primary classroom settings have produced evidence that the ways teachers talk to girls and boys and the ways girls and boys talk among themselves vary greatly. "Teachers routinely differentiate between girls and boys; certain forms of behavior (such as calling out) are acceptable from boys but not from girls" (Swann & Graddol, 1995, p. 135). Such data led "Katherine Clarricoates to conclude that classroom interaction is 'suffused with gender'" (Swann & Graddol, 1995, p. 135). Discourse within classrooms, therefore, is complex, multifaceted, and constantly in flux.

Poststructuralim offers a useful frame for understanding subjectivity and the power associated with various discursive positions within a society. Poststructural theory, developed from the works of Derrida, Lacan , Kristeva, Foucault, and others (Weedon, 1997), argues that individual identity is not rigid or unchanging and that it does not develop autonomously. Bronwyn Davies (1989) states that a belief in such a fixed, autonomous being obscures "our recognition of the complex and contradictory ways in which we are constantly constituting ourselves and the social world in which we live" (p. 6). Poststructuralists then posit that subjectivity—an individual's thoughts, emotions, sense of self, and relationship to the world—is constantly in process and constantly shifting, and that it is constructed in relation to and within the language of one's society and culture (Davies, 1989; McAffee, 2000; Weedon, 1997). Chris Weedon (1997) asserts that language, rather than reflecting the individual, shapes the individual and creates social reality. It is not surprising, then, that students often seek to interact in ways that allow them to maintain comfortable positions in multiple discourses (Wilson Keenan, Solsken, & Willett, 1999), thereby enriching their social realities. Thus, when students take up a new language, a new discourse, such as the discourse of teaching, they repositioned themselves within the classroom community and take on a new subjectivity.

As mentioned, language defines subjectivity, and inherent in the language is "a historically specific range of ways of giving meaning to social reality . . . [that] provides various discursive positions, including modes of femininity and masculinity" (Weedon, 1997, p. 25). These modes of femininity and masculinity, then, provided the students of Ms. Nelson's class with the basis for the positions they assumed in the fall semester, positions that suggested that boys played and girls taught. These subjectivities, however, were sometimes contradictory, presenting students with choices; one instance of contradictory subjectivities is discussed in further detail following Table 10.3. Because gender is socially produced, and thereby defined by the specific language of a community, gender must constantly be "reaffirmed and publicly displayed by repeatedly performing particular acts in accordance with the cultural norms (themselves historically and socially constructed, and consequently variable)" (Cameron, 1997, p. 49). Although an exploration of the factors involved in the development of notions of masculinity and femininity (and the power associated with those subjectivities) falls beyond the scope of this chapter, the need to constantly reaffirm such positions offers an explanation for the boys repeated joking, putting each other down, and straying from the assigned tasks. In contrast, the girls frequently returned to the role of teacher, remaining serious and staying on task.

By focusing a feminist, poststructural lens on the data collected in this study (Kamler, 1999), I am able to assert that moment-by-moment choices that students made within classroom communities—choices on whether or not to participate in the discourse, how and with whom to interact—provided opportunities for community members to constantly reposition themselves. Such repositioning reflects the participants' previous knowledge and identities and their present and future stances within the culture. By combining these theoretical approaches, I explore the participants' shift in discourse as an indicator of their willingness and ability to place themselves in new subjectivities within their community while simultaneously creating new situations with new discursive positions (Gee, 1999).

CONTEXTUAL FRAMEWORK

This study occurred at Liberty High School, a Grade 9–12 facility that serves approximately 600 students in a rural setting 8 miles from a medium-sized mid-western city. The focus community is a first-period 12th-grade English college preparation class. The teacher, Ms. Nelson, a White female in her 40s, has 20 years experience teaching high school English (17 of which have been at Liberty High School), serves as the department chair, leads in-service programs, and teaches advanced placement English and speech in addition to her college preparation classes. In addition, she advises several co-curricular clubs. Ms. Nelson enjoys a friendly relationship with her students and is well-liked and respected by them. In return, she demonstrates a genuine interest in the well-being of her students, frequently laughing and teasing students in class and in the halls between classes.

The majority of the students and the teacher in this class knew each other before the school year began, but this was Ms. Nelson's first year to teach senior college prep English. In the past, she taught sophomore and junior college prep and sophomore honors classes; therefore, she had all of her current students in class the previous year when they were juniors. In addition, several of her students were also in her sophomore classes. Asked if their familiarity with one another influenced the relationships and atmosphere of class, she said she believes that it made a definite difference in class, stating,

> I know these kids very well, and they know me very well. . . . We're very comfortable with each other. . . . It definitely helps set the tone. . . . They know me well enough now that if I tell them that there are reasons why they should be doing this, most of them take me seriously . . . and, they also know that I care about them a great deal, and they are more willing to listen. . . . They've already done all the testing and know where all the lines are.

She further explained that because she had all these students before in class, they were able to start immediately on the first day of school, since they understood the expectations for behavior and the rules of the class.

At the semester break, several students discovered the need to rearrange their schedules: four boys, one girl, and the aide transferred out and one female student transferred in. The new student had been in the school since ninth grade and was familiar with the members of the class. In the second semester then, the class shifted from predominately male (14 males, including the student aide, and 9 females) to an even mix (9 males and 9 females). Despite this shift, the gender-delineated roles established in the first semester continued into the second semester. Pseudonyms are used for all study participants.

METHODS

Study Design and Data Collection:

Ms. Nelson and I first met in person about 3 weeks after the start of the 2000–2001 school year. Until this time, we had only spoken on the phone. On my first visit, then, I entered the environment as observer, but within one class period moved to observer-participant as the students drew me into their discussions (Egan-Robertson & Willett, 1998; Emerson, Fretz, & Shaw, 1995; Green, Dixon, & Zaharlick, 2002; Green & Meyer, 1991). I collected whole-class data every Thursday for 6 consecutive weeks, from September 21 to November 2, 2000, videotaping with a digital video camera and three microphones. In addition, I conducted and audiotaped individual semistructured interviews with the teacher and six students. Fieldnotes from each session and in-person and phone conversations with the school's principal and with the teacher contributed to the corpus of information. Visiting the class on six consecutive Thursdays provided me with the opportunity to take up an essential element of an ethno-graphic-approach to data collection: comparison (Zaharlick & Green, 1991). At the end of my time with the class, I was able to compare their recent discourse to what I had witnessed weeks earlier, and to develop-ing a deeper understanding of individual actions and of the culture-defined norms.

On January 21, 2001, the teacher and I shifted our focus to designing a cycle of activity that would encourage all students to assume the teach-ing role for the second semester. Ms. Nelson suggested a starting date and an activity that focused on teaching poetry terms. The entire cycle of activity spanned twelve class days between February 12 and March 7, 2001, and I returned to the classroom on the first day of the activity cycle. Ms. Nelson introduced me to the newest member of the class and quick-ly explained to her that my presence related to my doctoral studies. My association with the class in the fall semester allowed me to re-enter the classroom environment quickly as a participant-observer with a degree of emic knowledge, bypassing the strict observer role. As the students were introduced to the new assignment and began preparing for their poetry presentations, I decided that the historical data of this class cul-ture and the opportunity for observation and interview suggested that a case study approach might work best for this portion of the study exam-ining the take up of the teacher role (Marshall & Rossman, 1999). I select-ed a pair of students as my focus: two boys who had emerged from the first study as engaging in the most obvious play acts and who had teamed up to be partners for this poetry term presentation: Seth and Josh. Seth had come to my attention in September on my first day in the class when he participated in a rock–paper–scissors game to avoid the responsibility of becoming the recorder for his small collaborative group (see Table 10.1). Josh, Seth's partner for the poetry presentation, embraced play as actively as Seth during the first semester and often ini-tiated the boys' laughter and talking. I again collected data from these class sessions using a digital video camera and two external micro-phones. In addition, I interviewed and audiotaped four students and the teacher individually and conducted follow-up interviews with Seth and Josh. Selected fieldnotes, two surveys, and a self-assessment contributed to the final corpus of information.

Table 10.1. Playing to Avoid Responsibility

LINE	SPEAKER	TALK	GESTURES
1	Ms. Nelson	Do any of you have a textbook? Your English textbook?	
2	Brian	Uh, yeah, in my locker, ummm	
3	Ms. Nelson	There's one right behind you.	
4	Mark	Should I go get mine, too, though?	
5	Ms. Nelson	No. You only need one for the group. Good try.	Pats Mark on shoulder.
6	Brian and Seth		Making hand gestures to each other
7	Ms. Nelson	You guys playing scissors, paper, rock to find out who's going to record?	
8	Seth	Yeah.	
9	Ms. Nelson	I'll make an executive decision. You are.	Points to Seth
10	Seth	Awww, Ms. N. I was in the process of winning! Aw, my God.	Stands up in mock outrage. Brian and Mark give each other a high five.
11	Ms. Nelson	Life is hard.	Laughs
12	Brian, Seth, and Mark	XXX	Laugh and smile Begin to work

NOTE. The following notations are used in Tables 10.1–10.4:
    XXX = unintelligible utterance   all capital letters = emphasized words
    each : = a 1- second pause.   ( ) = overlapping utterances

Data Analysis

Throughout this year-long study, I assumed an IE-based approach seeking to understand the beliefs, knowledge, and attitudes of this 12th-grade English class as demonstrated through their exchanges with each other and with the teacher (Zaharlick & Green, 1991). By viewing the everyday interactions of members of the learning community, I was able to analyze how class members acted as a social group to define a common culture that then dictated what they regarded as norms for actions and interactions, for making sense of "what occurs, for evaluating what is appropriate to know and do" (Green & Meyer, 1991, p. 141). Throughout the second semester's cycle of activity, I focused on identifying the students' shifts in previously constructed attitudes and beliefs about assuming a teaching role. The basis for recognizing those changing norms of actions and interactions lay in an analysis of the community members' discourse, defined as "language as action, or as interaction in specific social settings" (Talbot, 1998, p. 150), in this case, Ms. Nelson's first-period class. During the fall semester, I began my discourse analysis of the collected data by transcribing (Atkinson & Heritage, 1984; Ochs, 1979) message units (Green & Meyer, 1991). To verify my analyses, I interviewed six students and the teacher. As a result of that triangulation (Zaharlick & Green, 1991), the interpretations were confirmed and the transcription of message units became unnecessary; I moved instead to an analysis of naturally occurring discourse interactions (Schegloff & Sacks, 1973), distinguishing rhetorical pauses (Gumperz, 1977), overlapping utterances (Atkinson & Heritage, 1984), and turn-taking (Schegloff & Sacks, 1973), an analytical method I continued to use in the second semester data collection.

The actions and interactions I analyzed for the second semester's study fall into two categories: those recorded during the poetry presentations and those occurring outside the presentations. Both settings for discourse provided a conversational inference lens (Gumperz, 1977) through which to view the situated norms of the community. This cycle of activity was designed to offer all students equal opportunities to take up teaching roles, previously the domain of the female students; thus, by comparing the students' discourses before, during, and after their presentations, the degree to which each student took up the teaching role emerged. In order to triangulate this semester's findings, I compared the data collected from the different venues. I analyzed the discourse from the poetry presentations and then investigated information the students and teacher provided in interviews, on a survey, in a self-assessment, and in response to a session in which I shared the study's results with them. The triangulation of various types of data provided a "'thick description'" (Geertz, 1973, p. 5, cited in Marshall & Rossman, 1999, p.16) that yielded valuable insight into the influence of the cycle of activity on the male students' opportunities to teach.

The students' discourse during this cycle of activity reflects a change from previous discourse regarding what members may say or do, when, to whom, and with what expected outcomes (Alvermann & Commeyas, 1994; Rex, 2000). A comparison of the discourse and corresponding student positions of the fall semester to the discourse and redefined positions of the spring semester suggests a change in the community's views.

Therefore, as the students assumed a new discourse for a particular context (being a student/teacher within this classroom community), the general context (the classroom culture) itself was altered (Gee, 1999). This implies that the cycle of activity (teaching poetry terms to classmates) influenced the language the students took up, thereby providing new subjectivities in the classroom community, expanding what this social group considers appropriate for males and females to know and do.

RESULTS OF THE FIRST SEMESTER'S STUDY

During the Fall 2000 semester, the overriding discursive position available to the boys of Ms. Nelson's first-period class was as players. From September to December, all the boys except one (a quiet, introspective student) exhibited play behavior during at least a portion of each class period in which I collected data. Discussions with the teacher confirmed that this positioning was their typical subjectivity. The following four episodes highlight specific aspects of the classroom society's interactions during the fall semester. These episodes establish how students positioned themselves in this context, defining what they could and could not do, and provide a contrast to their subjectivities during the spring semester when the cycle of activity occurred.

"Rock–Paper–Scissors"

The first incident occurred during my first day in Ms. Nelson's classroom and, as noted previously, served to redirect the focus of my study from the role of respect to the role of play. Only later did I identify that play in this class was associated with the male gender. Shortly after the class had begun, Ms. Nelson asked the students to form groups of three or four to collaborate, to record their thoughts on an assigned topic, and to report back to the large group. As the students began to break into groups, three young men pushed their desks together to form a triangle, leaned forward, and began pounding their right fists into their left palms. On the count of three, they "shot," their right hands signaling a rock, paper, or scissors. They laughed, tallied the score, and hunched over their desks, ready to begin Round 2. The teacher approached.

As the all-male group featured in Table 10.1 engaged in a game of rock–paper–scissors, the members shared a goal: to avoid the role of recorder, the leadership role in this setting. Seth loudly protested his appointment by Ms. Nelson, even standing up to assert his point. The boys' desire to avoid leading the group was highlighted by their dominant discourse: play. The surrounding students did not appear to consider this behavior contrary to classroom discourse, and within that class period, additional smaller, less obvious play incidents took place; for example, three boys put on straw hats, pointed at each other, and laughed loudly. A casual conversation with a female student at the end of the period and subsequent visits to the class confirmed that male play occupied a definite role in the culture of this class. The term *play* encompasses many aspects of discourse. Although Fagot and Leinbach's (1983) definition of "play as any self-initiated active exploration of the social and physical environment by the child" (pp. 93-94) provides a framework, children of different ages and in different situations play differently. By middle childhood, gender differences in the organization of play emerge as boys' play takes on more complex facets than girls' play; boys' play interactions demonstrate greater role differentiation, interdependence between players, explicitness of goals (i.e. competitiveness), a greater number of rules, and team formation (Crawford, 1995; Etaugh, 1983). Tannen's (1994a) study of school children's conversations reveals numerous instances of boys engaging in specific acts of playful behavior and no examples of girls taking up similar behavior. These acts of teasing, mock attacks, and joking (defined as nonserious communicative behavior) serve to initiate and solidify positive relationships within male gender groups (Sherzer, 1985; Tannen, 1994). The play of the boys in this classroom echoes many of these aspects. Over the course of the first semester, I observed the male students routinely teasing each other and avoiding leadership roles, as depicted in Table 10.1, as well as downplaying errors, interrupting each other and thereby subverting the linear direction of conversation, discussing personally sensitive issues, pushing on taboo subjects, putting each other down, and engaging in self-depreciation. When their comments were taken seriously by others, the boys often dismissed their discourse with the phrase, "I was just jokin' with you."

The boys' play discourse contributed greatly to the culture in Ms. Nelson's first-period class. Male voices dominated the conversations that took place; however, it was not only frequency of turn that differentiated male and female dialogue in this classroom. The type of talk engaged in by boys was the medium of social currency by which most activity was accomplished. By disrupting the teacher-led discussions, but stopping short of angering the teacher, the boys of the class demonstrated that their play discourse possessed the power to dominate classroom teaching and learning (Canaan, 1990). When the boys were asked to position themselves as the teacher during the second semester, play again surfaced in many of their presentations. Thus, the episode described above provides evidence of the pervasive nature of play in the male discourse.

"You Broke My Pen!"

The second event from the fall semester highlights male–female interactions and provides a contrast between the subjectivity of the two students. Here the male student, Tim, assumed a joking, carefree attitude as he attempted to avoid responsibility for borrowing and then breaking Allison's pen. Aside from myself, a group of boys provided the only witnesses to the event, and they smiled as they listened to Tim's interaction with Allison (see Table 10.2).

As Tim grinned and downplayed his role in breaking Allison's pen, she steadfastly refused to enter into play discourse, holding instead to a serious tone, a tone that reflected a "teacher" voice that she and the other female students frequently assumed. Tim's refusal to accept responsibility for his actions in this context provides a vivid contrast to each boy's willingness during the second semester to accept the role of teacher, a position imbued with responsibility.

"They're Clowners"

Further evidence of this dichotomy of discourse surfaces in a five-student group (four males and one female) presentation of a proposal for a 30-second commercial. Here, rather than refusing to take responsibility

Table 10.2. The Broken Pen

LINE	SPEAKER	TALK	GESTURES
1	Allison	Tim, I gave you a pen yesterday.	
2	Tim	Yeah, I gave it back.	Smiling
3	Allison	You gave it back broken.	Serious
4	Tim	What?	Laughs
5	Allison	You broke my pen!	Angry look on face
6	Tim	I did not.	Smiles broadly
7	Allison	Yes, you did!	Voices rises in register
8	Tim	I did not, Allison. I didn't break it.	Smiles and looks away
9	Allison	Yes, you did,::and I want a new one.	Slams notebook closed

for a broken pen, the males refused to take responsibility for teaching the class about their commercial, and instead abrogated the leadership role to the lone female, Allison. Allison began the presentation and spoke for several moments until Brian interrupted her with a comment designed to provoke laughter. As Brian and Rick began to derail the presentation, Ms. Nelson reacted, saying, "I don't have a real clear picture of what you're doing here. You're gonna show Brian driving his car and he's going to deliberately hit something?" When the boys had no answer to their teacher's confusion, Allison tried to redirect the conversation back to the agreed on script by explaining that Brian would get out of the car and shake the hand of another player in the commercial. Allison maintained her serious demeanor and teacher-like approach to the situation. Her efforts were repeated later in the event when she referred to the appearance on the scene of an insurance agent. She struggled to regain control of the situation, but was obviously surprised when Brian mentioned hitting a Toyota RAV4, and she could only respond "Oh." Realizing the path Brian and Rick were taking, Allison virtually resigned her teacher role and simply listened. Her final comment reflected her reacquisition of the leader's role as she earnestly assured the class and the teacher that the group would film their idea. Brian and Rick nodded in agreement.

Allison later described her reaction to the boys' behavior with the phrase "They're clowners" and stated that the males in the class joked and played much of the time and that the females very, very rarely participated. My analysis of first-hand class interactions and of videotapes of the class meetings during the fall semester offered no instances of girls playing either with the teacher, with each other, or with the boys and thus affirmed Allison's assertion.

"I Was Just Jokin'"

Whereas the previous incident demonstrates that the community's girls, in this case represented by Allison, willingly assumed the teacher role, a male-to-male incident stands in vivid contrast to that specific discourse within this community. As the class was completing grammar worksheets in preparation for the upcoming ACT tests, Josh professed frustration with the portion of the assignment dedicated to quotation marks. Ms. Nelson laughed, possibly in an attempt to downplay Josh's lack of information and capitalize on the teaching moment. Michael, who sat two seats in front of Josh, with an empty seat between them, overheard Josh's remark and turned toward him. As Ms. Nelson seriously began to explain the uses of quotation marks, Michael interrupted. Voluntarily positioning himself as a teacher, Michael began to "teach" Josh (see Table 10.3).

Table 10.3. Who Is Allowed to Teach

LINE	SPEAKER	TALK	GESTURES
1	Josh	I hate English. I'm terrible at it. Why can't we just talk like normal people?	Smiles, leans back in chair.
2	Ms. Nelson		laughs
3	Josh	I know what they mean. What purpose does quotation marks serve?	
4	Ms. Nelson	⌈To correctly know::: ⌉	Serious.
5	Michael	⌊To show that someone ⌋	Sits two desks in front of Josh, an empty desk between them. Turns toward Josh and Ms. Nelson. Leans partway across the empty desk, toward Josh, raises left arm
6	Ms. Nelson	how to write something so people can understand it when you write it. To know how to comprehend it when you see it on paper:::which you do.	Michael continues to lean slightly across desk and look at Josh.
7	Michael	Josh, quotations show you that someone else⌈said something ⌉	Turns whole body toward Josh
8	Josh	⌊ Michael::: ⌋ listen to me.	Holds hand up, palms forward toward Michael, as if pushing away,
9	Michael	What?	Ms. Nelson turns to student behind Josh
10	Josh	I KNOW what they mean.	
11	Michael	Then why did you ask?	
12	Josh	I was just jokin'. That's all.	Smiles slightly, tightly
13	Michael	Didn't sound like that. Ms. Nelson, I have a question.	Serious

NOTE. The following notations are used in Tables 10.1–10.4:
XXX = unintelligible utterance   all capital letters = emphasized words
each : = a 1- second pause.   ( ) = overlapping utterances

Lacking Ms. Nelson's sanction to take up the role of teacher, a role assigned by this culture to the females in the class, Michael assumed a discursive position that Josh could not accept. Michael's violation of the classroom's approved discursive positioning made explicit the gendered nature of the classroom discourse. In essence, Josh's reaction put forth a clear message: You are a boy; you have not been asked to teach me; therefore, you cannot teach me. By interacting as he did with Josh, Michael also failed to acknowledge a tenet of this class's male discourse: Boys talk in a playful manner to de-emphasize the significance of a lack of knowledge. When Michael refused to engage in the culturally sanctioned manner, he positioned himself outside the male discourse and disrupted the accepted subjectivities of the community (Fagot & Leinbach, 1983). This male-to-male episode stands in direct contrast to the events that occurred in the second semester during the cycle of activity, when male students were invited by other males to teach, and highlights the importance of teacher sanction when males assume the teaching position.

The boys' positioning as players during the fall semester created material social relations for these students that insisted that boys joke. In essence, the boys' put downs, teasing, refusal to accept responsibility, and so on, became the social currency by which they interacted with each other, with the girls, and with the teacher. By placing the male students in the position where they were required to assume a sanctioned teaching role in the spring semester, Ms. Nelson and I asked them to assume multiple subjectivities: as players and as teachers. The success of their efforts speaks to the fragmented nature of the subject and the ability to assume seemingly conflicting discursive positions.

RESULTS OF THE SECOND SEMESTER'S STUDY

The students' subjective positioning during the poetry cycle of activity contrasted sharply with the positions they assumed in the early part of the school year. The take-up of the teacher-sanctioned role of instructor and the reactions of the class members to that take-up demonstrate the culture's ability to expand gendered boundaries. As Ms. Nelson's first-period class worked to socially construct the situated meaning of being a teacher, they cooperatively shifted the culture's concepts of male and female discourse. In the fall semester, the classroom community had excluded boys from the teaching role: The one time that a male student tried to teach another male student, the teacher-like actions were rejected. In allowing the boys to teach during the poetry cycle, however, the classroom community demonstrated a flexibility regarding the positioning of its members. The difference between the boys' reluctance to assume teacher/leadership roles during the first semester and their willingness to do so in the second semester may stem from the situated context. Students viewed the poetry assignment as a required event. Because the students received a grade for their efforts, males engaged in multiple subjectivity, maintaining their position as players and as teachers, and altering the material reality of the class, at least for the tenure of the activity.

Ms. Nelson introduced the poetry assignment to the class near the end of the period on February 12, 2001. As she handed out the assignment page and began to read it aloud, a mixture of males and females voiced various complaints. Ms. Nelson continued to read the assignment, ignoring the complaints and expanding on certain points. The students became quiet and listened as the teacher explained that the presentations would begin in about 1 week. As Ms. Nelson finished her explanation and moved to her desk, two girls, Allison and Sonia, immediately approached her about working together and signing up for a topic. Three male students, including Seth and Josh, talked with each other and laughed loudly. Over the next 5 school days, all the students selected topics for presentation and collaborated outside of and during class.

"You're Starting to Get the Hang of This One"

The task of assuming the unfamiliar role of teacher is complex. The male students in this class were accustomed to being receivers of knowledge (Edwards & Westgate, 1987) rather than disseminators of it. Thus, taking on the role of teacher required the male students to recognize the rhythm and discourse of student–teacher interaction (Mehan, 1985) and to envision what "being a teacher" looks like in light of contextually specific social factors. As the students presented their material, the impact that the boys' discursive position as "players" had had on determining the material reality of the class became apparent. When Grant gave the first presentation, Seth chose to participate; however, the reaction of the class reflected their assumption that Seth would contribute only humorous comments. When Seth struggled to assume a new position within the classroom community, the power of previous expectations became obvious.

Grant, a male student who engaged less often in playful behavior than many of the boys in the class, moved to the front of the room, bantering nervously with Ms. Nelson. Grant began his presentation with a definition and then asked a question about a poem he had chosen to share. Molly offered a possible interpretation of two lines of poetry. Several seconds passed and then Seth, in a serious tone of voice, suggested a different reading. Although Seth's suggestion was not humorous, the class immediately laughed, indicating that they anticipated a humorous reply. One male student said, "That was a good one, Seth." Seth smiled and then volunteered another nonhumorous interpretation. Members of the class grinned and looked at Seth, but no one laughed. Grant smiled and responded, "Seth, you're starting to get the hang of this one," and invited him to read and interpret the next line. Seth did, and Grant replied, "There you go, Seth."

The class members' responses to both Grant in the role of student/ teacher and to the other learners' actions signal the beginning of the shift in the culture notion of positioning. Early in Grant's presentation, he asked a question. Molly, the female student who transferred into the class at the semester break, quickly volunteered a response; however, she was the only student to do so. Her position as lone responder indicated her willingness to accept Grant as a teacher and may suggest a less entrenched awareness of the cultural belief that boys do not teach. In contrast, the lack of immediate response from the rest of the class may reflect a hesitation on their parts to honor Grant's take up of the teaching role. The class listened attentively as Molly offered her suggestion on the meaning of the first few lines of Grant's poem. When Seth responded, however, the students laughed even though Seth's comment was not humorous. The reaction of the class to Seth's initial participation as a serious member of the learning community signaled their anticipation of humor. When that humor failed to materialize, they could not react appropriately until Seth reasserted his discourse in the second and third responses and positioned himself as a serious participant in a classroom discussion led by a male student.

Although Josh chose not to participate in the presentation, he interacted with fellow male students immediately after Grant's presentation concluded. Rather than complete his assigned work, he teased with other boys, hiding books, tilting desks. His playful—and disruptive—behavior aligned more closely with sanctioned male discourse than Seth's and reflected a pattern the boys in the class routinely enacted.

"Man, I'd Be a Great Teacher"

The discourse Josh and Seth chose for their poetry presentations defined them as very different types of teachers. Josh's discursive position infused large amounts of play into his take up of the teacher role while Seth maintained a serious subjectivity. In addition, Josh offered playful comments and actions throughout Seth's presentation, whereas Seth's comments during Josh's presentation were instructional. The differences in their discourses, made all the more apparent by their pairing within the same presentation, served to demonstrate that subjectivity is not enacted identically by all males when taking up the teaching position, but rather is constructed by the individual's view of the available discursive position.

Several students presented their poetry terms between Grant and the team Seth and Josh formed. During a number of those presentations, Seth participated, and each succeeding time, class members demonstrated less of a tendency to laugh. Josh offered occasional comments, as well, but they were frequently "back-up" comments, reinforcing what other students had said. On the day of Seth and Josh's presentation, Josh presented his information first and adopted a blatantly playful approach to the discussion (see Table 10.4).

Following this interchange, Kathy answered again, and Ms. Nelson asked the students to think of an action. Students suggested answers, but none fit the definition of a metaphor. After some explanation by the teacher, one female student offered a metaphor, followed by two other students. Male and female voices joined in. Ms. Nelson encouraged them, and Josh wrote several responses on the overhead.

When Josh finished, Seth began his portion of the group's presentation. He asked if anyone could define a simile, and he asked the students to raise their hands when they had answers. The entire class laughed, but Seth did not. Dawn raised her hand. When Seth called on her, she gave a correct answer. The class sat quietly. Seth placed a pointer resembling a green hand on the overhead projector, and the class laughed, but Seth remained serious. At that moment, smoke began to rise from the light of the overhead projector. Josh looked at the machine and began to fan the air. Ms. Nelson came forward and cut a smoking rubber band off the mirrored section, and Seth calmly began again. He sat down on a stool and seriously read the poem on a transparency that he had placed on the overhead. As he finished, he asked where the first simile appeared. Many voices, male and female, answered. Seth underlined what they had identified. Seth asked for the next simile and called on Tom and then Allison who gave appropriate answers. When Seth asked what was being compared, Ms. Nelson clarified Seth's question by asking what part of the tree was being compared to an etching. Several students responded: branches. Seth maintained a serious demeanor throughout his presentation, asking questions, receiving answers, and leading an in-depth exploration of another poem. In their presentation's final moments, Seth read the directions for the homework assignment as Josh passed out the assignment, waving at the camera as he passed. Josh pretended that he could not get the overhead screen up, as Brian called Seth over to ask for help. Josh accompanied Seth to Brian's desk, but Brian paid little attention to him as Seth and Brian worked seriously on the assignment. The total presentation, from the moment Josh began to speak until Seth explained the homework assignment, lasted 24 minutes, longer than any other presentation.

The learning community played a vital role in this cycle of activity. Placed in a strange role, Josh and Seth, the students/teachers, had to

Table 10.4. Josh and Seth as Teachers

LINE	SPEAKER	TALK	GESTURES
1	Josh	Man I can't see. This is a metaphor. Anyone else know a metaphor?	Squints into light of overhead projector. The class offers no response
2	Josh	Come on, don't be dumb	The class laughs loudly
3	Josh	Man, I'd be a great teacher.	Smiles broadly
4	Ms. Nelson	Yeah, right.	Smirks and rolls eyes
5	Seth	If one person thinks of a metaphor, you get a mint.	
6	Josh	Yeah, you get a mint.	Turned to look toward Seth
7	Seth	Tom?	Reaches into pocket
8	Tom	XXX	
9	Josh	No, [that's wrong]	
10	Seth	[Wrong] Kathy, Kathy had a good one.	Looks at overhead
11	Josh	Okay, I'll write it up here. What did you say again?	
12	Kathy	Your eyes are stars.	
13	Josh	Okay, your eyes are stars. They actually are. Anybody got another one? That light makes you sweat. Can anybody else think of one except Kathy who gets all the answers?	
14	Class	Multiple voices and laughter	Josh writes on overhead
15	Josh	Can we all stay together as a group and focus on the poem?	
16	Seth	Can anyone else does anyone else know any kind of metaphor?	Smiling
17	Brian	H:er ey::es are st::ars	The class laughs
18	Josh	Besides her eyes are stars	Laughter

NOTE. The following notations are used in Tables 10.1–10.4:
XXX = unintelligible utterance   all capital letters = emphasized words
each : = a 1- second pause.   ( ) = overlapping utterances

negotiate terms of interaction with the class as a whole as the teaching activity unfolded. The class' acceptance was essential as "a speaker cannot maintain the positioning of a teacher without the help of (other) students" (Davies & Hunt, 2000, p. 110). Through the support of their classmates, the boys were able to position themselves as teachers without obvious frame clashes (Agar, 1994) between their discursive positions as players and as teachers. The way the boys assumed the teaching role differed. Josh's enactment of the teacher position reflected his belief in the value of play both as a subject in the male community of the class and as a subject in the student/teacher community. When Josh engaged in play before the day of his own presentation, other students frequently supported him in this role, playing along with him. Playful language such as, "Come on, don't be dumb," shaped his subjective positioning as a teacher.

Seth presented a very different enactment of teaching and met with very different results than Josh. When Brian, a classmate who often engaged in play with Josh and Seth, experienced confusion, he voiced his question to Seth, indicating his willingness to allow Seth to teach him. During the fall, a male student's attempt to teach another male was viewed as falling outside the discursive realm of male behavior. Two changes were apparent in the spring semester, however: The male student in need of help, Brian, invited the other male student, Seth, to teach him, and the event immediately followed Seth's presentation in which he had taught the entire class. Thus, by participating in a teacher-sanctioned instructional activity, Seth positioned himself to be invited to teach another male student, and by defining himself as an active participant in a boy-taught class, Brian's subjectivity became a male seeking instruction by another male. Research indicates that children "do not hesitate to let their companions know when they are crossing into the other sex's 'territory'" (Fagot & Leinbach, 1983, p. 99). The community's lack of pejorative response, therefore, reflects the degree to which the students accepted boys positioned as teachers and reflects that the material reality of the class that boys play and girls teach changed within the cycle of activity. By assuming multiple subjectivities within the class, the students relaxed the boundaries that had earlier defined their gendered discourse.

"They're Pretty Much Clowns"

One question that surfaced following the poetry cycle related to the permanence of the change in the material reality. Because subjectivity is shifting and precarious, would the members of the class still view the boys as legitimate teachers after the cycle of activity concluded? Approximately 2 months after the cycle of activity, I asked two female students to compare the girls' behavior in the class to that of the boys' during the presentations; Sonia and Allison responded with animation in overlapping talk, both agreeing that the boys were "pretty much clowns" and not as serious as the girls were about their class work.

Despite the fact that Seth did not act in a humorous manner during his portion of the presentation, the girls failed to remember Seth's delivery as being marked by serious language; instead, they focused on his membership in the male play group and compared him to Josh. They were not alone in this response. When I asked Josh if he liked working with Seth and how well Seth presented his part of the information, Josh immediately focused on humor and then moved to a more in-depth analysis: "Seth's a funny guy. . . . He did good. He's funny. That's like the whole attitude toward teaching. To get your students to like you. . . . That's really important, to get them to like you. . . . But Seth did a good job. He got his point across real good." Despite Seth's serious delivery of information, Josh also remembered Seth as employing humor. When asked to evaluate his own role within the class by comparing his earlier behavior, in which he played rock–paper–scissors to avoid being the recorder of a collaborative learning group, to his teacher-like poetry cycle demeanor, Seth saw no contradiction. He laughed and explained, "Well, I think when I have to do a job or whatever, I'm a little more mature and responsible than if we're just goofin' around to see who is gonna be recorder than when it comes to my grades." Seth's comments reflect his awareness of seemingly conflicting subjectivities: he can play in some contexts and be serious in others.

Failure by the girls and Josh to acknowledge Seth's serious discourse while enacting the teaching role highlights the differences in the way an individual may view him or herself within a situation and the way others may view that individual. Because individuals are always "under construction, always producing ourselves and each other" (McAfee, 2000, p. 129), Seth and his classmates were each involved in his subjectivity within the classroom context. In this situation, as Seth constructed a new position for himself as a teacher, the other members of the class produced his new subjectivity as well. Seth continued to view himself as a serious teacher 2 months after the cycle of activity. Seth's three classmates, however, despite their participation in his formal presentation as teacher, recalled his discourse as humor-filled. This dichotomy in views reflects that even though, "in principle, the individual is open to all forms of subjectivity, in reality individual access to subjectivity is governed by historically specific social factors and the forms of power at work in a particular society" (Weedon, 1997, p. 91). His classmates' memory of his presentation as humorous suggests that while Seth successfully assumed multiple positions (player and teacher) within the context of the poetry presentation, the existence of the social factor within this culture stating that boys play may limit male access to continuing subjectivity as a serious teacher outside the context of the cycle of activity. To examine this notion and share my study results with the students, I returned to the class several months after the poetry assignment has taken place. During our whole-class discussion, Ms. Nelson stated that the class had moved on to a unit involving a Shakespearian play and that she had noted a substantially increased inclination on the part of the boys to share information and interpretations, indicating that an increased willingness to "informally teach" the class may have accompanied the male students into the new unit. Many students nodded in agreement with Ms. Nelson's assessment. Thus, the members of this society of students may more willingly allow boys to assume the position of teachers in future situations.

DISCUSSION AND IMPLICATIONS OF BOYS ASSUMING A TEACHING ROLE

The National Council of Teachers of English standards for English Language Arts emphasize students should "participate as knowledge-able, reflective, creative, and critical members of a variety of literacy com-munities" (NCTE/IRA List of Standards for the English Language Arts, 2000). Such participation, however, is severely restricted when contextu-al social factors within a language arts classroom community limit indi-vidual access of subjectivity and thus determine that certain students can contribute only in certain ways. The social factors in Ms. Nelson first-period class, decreeing that boys played and girls taught, set up patterns of participation that directly affected opportunities for teaching and learning. A cycle of activity attempted to address the dichotomous dis-courses by positioning boys as teachers.

This study has provided a view of how boys, operating in a commu-nity that previously limited their access to the discursive role of teacher/leader, achieved teacher subjectivity during one cycle of activity. Several factors, embedded within the assignment, provide the impetus for the successful take up of the teacher role: the sanction of the take-up by the teacher, the academic aspects of the assignment, and the freedom to teach in an individually determined manner. By not merely inviting students to teach, but by requiring them to do so, Ms. Nelson formally sanctioned the take up of the instructor's role by all students. Later, as each student presented his or her poetry term, Ms. Nelson sat in a student desk and participated in the discussion, signaling her endorsement of the students' subjectivity as teachers and her willingness to be taught by them. During interviews, the boys' discourse when discussing the poetry assignment and their role in it ("taught," "teacher," "teaching") reflected their personal assumption of the position as teacher. An additional factor that encouraged the boys' involvement was the academic nature of the assignment. Comments by both Josh and Seth affirm that the academic context, with all the appurtenances of an academic task, further encouraged them to become active participants in the cycle of activity.

In contrast to the clearly defined guidelines of the assignment, the way to teach was not discussed at all. Thus, the freedom to enact teaching as they individually envisioned it offered each student wide latitude. The nine boys in this class approached the task of teaching from several different perspectives. Some of them infused their presentations with humor; others were more serious. Some interacted continually with the class members; some sought little interaction. Yet, in all cases, the community of learners accepted each male student in the teaching role. None was ignored or dismissed; none was ridiculed or mocked. The reaction of the class members seemed to suggest that these students rejected the idea that there is only one way to teach, thus signaling a willingness to allow a range of male discourses within the teaching role. Only once did Ms. Nelson comment on a student's discourse. When Josh remarked that he would "be a great teacher," as he was having difficulty beginning his presentation, Ms. Nelson smirked, rolled her eyes, and responded, "Yeah, right." She did not voice any further criticism of Josh's methods, however, and fully participated in the rest of his presentation.

In addition to the elements of the poetry assignment that encouraged boys to take up the teaching role, male students in this setting needed to feel secure that they could be a teacher in one context and still a player in another. They needed to be assured, consciously or unconsciously, that they could put aside play-infused text to assume another discourse, a serious teacher discourse, without having to put aside membership in the male camaraderie. Class data highlighting male interaction reflected no breech in the fabric of the male relationships. Indeed, from the "book hiding" incident that occurred immediately after Grant's presentation on the first day of the cycle of activity to the interactions observed after final presentation, male behavior confirms that Josh, Seth, and other boys in the class have maintained their playful manner. Furthermore, when Seth and Josh were asked to evaluate their roles within the classroom after the poetry teaching event, both asserted that they occupied the same role as they had earlier in the year; they insisted that no change had occurred, signaling their seamless repositioning within two discursive communities. Poststructural theory asserts that subjectivity is always in flux, that individuals are constantly constructing themselves and others; therefore, the existence of multiple subjectivities allowed the boys of this class to expand their discursive positions, rather than merely to substitute one subjectivity for another.

Davies (1989) support this conclusion: "The fact that a boy takes up a macho/superhero position does not mean that he is incapable of taking up other apparently contradictory positionings when this becomes appropriate" (p. 133). By looking across time and space, comparing the males' positioning in the fall semester to the cycle of activity, an intercontextual lens (Floriani, 1994) confirms that students can assume membership in multiple realms without abdicating membership in any. The ability to position oneself differently in different contexts dovetails with the concept of "endless becoming . . . [a notion that] draws upon the ethnomethodological claim that social reality is an interactional accomplishment, and that gendered social identity must be constantly upgraded and maintained in, and through, talk and interaction with other members of the culture" (Nilan, 2000, pp. 55-56). Thus, by offering students opportunities to participate in new situations requiring new discourses that offer multifaceted views of gender, teachers expand, complicate, and enrich students' roles and do not merely substitute one way of acting and interacting for another. Davies (1989) argues that children need the freedom that comes from recognizing the ways in which different discourses constitute them differently and the freedom to position themselves in multiple ways, regardless of the feminine or masculine tags these ways currently wear. Certainly, high school students as young adults need access to discourses that free them to take up a variety of roles, including that of teacher, regardless of the culturally imposed gender alignment those roles may sport.

This study has provided data that indicate that Ms. Nelson's first period male students successfully positioned themselves as teachers and students. Only by experiencing a teacher sanctioned, academically based activity were they willing to take up the teaching role; however, the ability of this classroom community to sustain its newly broadened gender roles cannot be determined with certainty. The teachers' observation that, in the weeks that followed the poetry cycle and teaching experience, the boys contributed more frequently to class discussions, in essence sharing knowledge and thereby teaching classmates, suggests the persistence of the newly defined discourse for boys in this classroom. In addition, when interviewed both Seth and Josh professed a willingness to take up the official teacher role again in the future. Although it appears that the boys and girls may have altered the discursive positions available to boys within their classroom community, expanding what this social group considers appropriate for males to know and do, a longer period of observation and data collection is required to claim with certainty the ability of the boys to position themselves repeatedly as teachers. The concept that an individual's position within a particular discourse is never final and is always open to challenge (Weedon, 1997) suggests that these students must be offered the chance to take up the teaching role on a regular basis until contextually specific social factors permit unrestricted access to this subjectivity for all students. Further study is needed to determine the benefits of positioning students as teachers on a regular basis; however, the story of Ms. Nelson's students suggests that it is not enough to offer students a chance to teach occasionally. Instead, carefully constructed experiences that respond to the socially specific factors of an individual classroom by requiring students to position themselves in new ways provides increased access to a variety of discursive subjectivities.

The goal of the poetry assignment was to offer male students the opportunity to teach, thereby expanding gender roles and enhancing opportunities for teaching and learning. At the end of the school year, teaching and leading was no longer the exclusive domain of the females of Ms. Nelson's first-period class, as males were allowed to enter that territory during the poetry teaching cycle and perhaps afterward. Such an expansion of roles relaxed the boundaries for teaching and learning: Girls were no longer required to act as gatekeepers, prohibiting males from engaging in instructional behavior, and boys no longer had to cling to play as their only "appropriate" activity in the class. Thus, this small study of gendered discourse in a high school English class affirms the possibility of shifting culturally constructed gendered roles to promote more equitable, more accessible opportunities for teaching and learning. In addition, it suggests that "[c]hildren should be free to explore the full range of positionings currently available within our narrative and interactive structure . . . and to find ways of thinking about and describing their own and other's behavior independently of what we currently think of as 'masculine' and 'feminine'" (Davies, 1989, pp. 133–134). By constructing activities that provide boys and girls with access to a variety of discursive positions, teachers enhance, complicate, and enrich students' lives. This study, then, argues for increased opportunities for students to assume multiple subjectivities that provide them with new ways to teach and learn about themselves and about others.

REFERENCES

Agar, M. (1994). *Language shock: Understanding the culture of conversation*. New York: William Morrow.

Alvermann, D. E., & Commeyras, M. (1994). Gender, text, and discussion: Expanding the possibilities. In R. Gardner & P. Alexander (Eds.), *Beliefs about text and instruction with text* (pp. 183-199). Hillsdale, NJ: Erlbaum.

Atkinson, J. M., & Heritage, J. (1984). Jefferson's transcript notation. In A. Jaworski & N. Coupland (Eds.), *The discourse reader* (pp. 158-166). London & New York: Routledge.

Cameron, D. (1997). Performing gender identity: Young men's talk and the construction of heterosexual masculinity. In S. Johnson & U. H. Meinhof (Eds.), *Language and masculinity* (pp. 47-64). Oxford: Blackwell.

Canaan, J.E. (1990). Passing notes and telling jokes: Gender strategies among American middle school teenagers. In F. Ginsburg & A. L. Tsing (Eds.), *Uncertain terms: Negotiating gender in American culture* (pp. 215-231). Boston: Beacon Press.

Coates, J. (1995). Language, gender, and career. In S. Mills (Ed.), *Language and gender: Interdisciplinary perspectives* (pp. 13-30). London: Longman.

Coates, J. (1996). *Women talk*. Oxford, England: Blackwell.

Coates, J. (1998). *Language & gender: A reader*. Oxford, England: Blackwell.

Crawford, M. (1995). *Talking difference: On gender and language*. London: Sage.

Davies, B. (1989). *Frogs, snails, and feminist tails*. Sydney: Allen & Unwyn.

Davies, B., & Hunt, R. (2000). Classroom competencies and marginal positionings. In B. Davies (Ed.), *A body of writing, 1990-1999* (pp. 107-132). Walnut Creek, CA: Alta Mira.

DeFrancisco, V. L. (1998). The sounds of silence: How men silence women in marital relations. In J. Coates (Ed.), *Language and gender: A reader* (pp. 176-184). Oxford: Blackwell.

Eder, D., Evans, C.C., & Parker, S. (1995). *School talk: Gender and adolescent culture*. New Brunswick, NJ: Rutgers University Press.

Edwards, A. D., & Westgate, D.P.G. (1987). *Investigating classroom talk*. London: Falmer Press.

Egan-Robertson, A., & Willett, J. (1998). Students as ethnographers, thinking and doing ethnography: A bibliographic essay. In A. Egan-Robertson & D. Bloome (Eds.), *Students as researchers of culture and language in their own communities* (pp. 1-32). Cresskill, NJ: Hampton Press.

Emerson, R. M., Fretz, R. I., & Shaw, L. L. (1995). *Writing ethnographic fieldnotes*. Chicago: The University of Chicago Press.

Etaugh, C. (1983). Introduction: The influences of environmental factors on sex differences in children's play. In M.B. Liss (Ed.), *Social and cognitive skills: Sex roles and children's play* (pp. 1-19). New York: Academic Press.

Fagot, B.I., & Leinbach, M.D. (1983). Play styles in early childhood: Social consequences for boys and girls. In M.B. Liss (Ed.), *Social and cognitive skills: Sex roles and children's play* (pp. 93-116). New York: Academic Press.

Fichtelius, A., Johansson, I., & Nordin, K. (1979). Three investigations of sex-associated speech variation in day school. In C. Kramarea (Ed.), *The voices and words of women and men* (pp. 219-25). Oxford, England: Pergamon Press.

Fishman, S., & McCarthy, L. (2000). Teaching for student change: A Deweyan alternative to radical pedagogy. In S. Fishman & L. McCarthy (Eds.), *Unplayed tapes: A personal history of collaborative teacher research* (pp. 223-249). Urbana, IL: National Council of Teachers of English and Teachers College Press.

Floriani, A. (1994). Negotiating what counts: Roles and relationships, texts and contexts, content and meaning. *Linguistics and Education, 5,* 241-274.

Gee, J. P. (1999). *An introduction to discourse analysis*. London: Routledge.

Goffman, E. (1967). On face-work: An analysis of ritual elements in social interaction. In A. Jaworski & N. Coupland (Eds.), *The discourse reader* (pp. 306-320). London: Routledge.

Goodwin, M. H. (1998). Cooperation and competition: Across girl's play activities. In A. D. Todd & S. Fisher (Eds.), *Gender and discourse: The power of talk* (pp. 55-94). Norwood, NJ: Ablex.

Graddol, D., & Swann, J. (1989). *Gender voices.* Oxford: Blackwell.

Green, J.L., Dixon, C., & Zaharlick, A. (2002). Ethnography as a logic of inquiry. In J. Flood, J. Jensen, D. Lapp, & J. Squire (Eds.), *Handbook of research on teaching the English language arts* (pp. 201-224). Mahwah, NJ: Erlbaum.

Green, J.L., & Meyer, L.A. (1991). The embeddedness of reading in classroom life: Reading as a situated process. In C. Baker & A. Luke (Eds.), *Toward a critical sociology of reading pedagogy* (pp. 141-160). Philadelphia: John Benjamins.

Gumperz, J. J. (1977). Sociocultural knowledge in conversational inference. In A. Jaworski & N. Coupland (Eds.), *The discourse reader* (pp. 98-106). London: Routledge.

Hicks, D. (1995). Discourse, learning, and teaching. In M. Apple (Ed.), *Review of research in education* (Vol. 21, pp. 49-95). Washington, DC: AERA.

Holmes, J. (1995). Women, men and politeness. In A. Jaworski & N. Coupland (Eds.), *The discourse reader* (pp. 336-343). London: Routledge.

Kamler, B. (1999). Beyond socialization: Critical frameworks for the study of early childhood. In B. Kamler (Ed.), *Constructing gender and difference: Critical research perspectives on early childhood* (pp. 1-11). Cresskill, NJ: Hampton Press.

Maltz, D.N., & Borker, R.A. (1982). A cultural approach to male-female miscommunication. In J. Coates (Ed.), *Language and gender: A reader* (pp. 417-434). Oxford: Blackwell.

Marshall, C., & Rossman, G. (1999). *Designing qualitative research.* Thousand Oaks, CA: Sage.

McAffee, N. (2000). *Habermas, Kristeva, and citizenship.* Ithaca, NY: Cornell University Press.

Mehan, H. (1985). The structure of classroom discourse. In T. A. Van Dijk (Ed.), *Handbook of discourse analysis 3: Discourse and dialogue* (pp. 119-131). London: Academic Press.

National Council of Teachers of English. (2000). Standards for the English Language Arts. http://www.ncte.org/standards/standdards.shtml. (11/30/00).

Nilan, P. (2000). "You're hopeless I swear to God": Shifting masculinities in classroom talk. *Gender and Education, 12*(1), 53-68.

O'Barr, W.M., & Atkins, B. K. (1998). "Women's language" or "powerless language"? In J. Coates (Ed.), *Language and gender: A reader* (pp. 377-387). Oxford: Blackwell.

Ochs, E. (1979). Transcription as theory. In A. Jaworski & N. Coupland (Eds.), *The discourse reader* (pp. 167-182). London & New York: Routledge.

Rex, L. A. (2000). Judy constructs a genuine question: A case for interactional inclusion. *Teaching and Teacher Education, 16*(2), 315-333.

Santa Barbara Discourse Group. (1992). Constructing literacy in classrooms: Literate action as social accomplishment. In H. H. Marshall (Ed.), *Redefining student learning* (pp. 119-150). Norwood, NJ: Ablex.

Schegloff, E.A., & Sacks, H. (1973). Opening up closings. In A. Jaworski & N. Coupland (Eds.), *The discourse reader* (pp. 263-274). London: Routledge.

Sherzer, J. (1985). Puns and jokes. In T. A. Van Dijk (Ed.), *Handbook of discourse analysis 3: Discourse and dialogue* (pp. 213-221). London: Academic Press.

Swann, J., & Graddol, D. (1995). Feminising classroom talk. In S. Mills (Ed.), *Language and gender* (pp. 135-148). London: Longman.

Talbot, M. M. (1998). *Language and gender: An introduction.* Cambridge, UK: Polity Press.

Tannen, D. (1987). *That's not what I meant: How conversational style makes or breaks your relationship.* New York: Ballantine Books.

Tannen, D. (1990). *You just don't understand: Women and men in conversation.* New York: Random House.

Tannen, D. (1994a). *Gender and discourse.* Oxford: Oxford University Press.

Tannen, D. (1994b). *Talking from 9 to 5.* New York: William Morrow.

Tuyay, S., Jennings, L., & Dixon, S. (1995). Classroom discourse and opportunities to learn: An ethnographic study of knowledge construction in a bilingual third grade classroom. *Discourse Processes, 19*(1), 75-110.

Weedon, C. (1997). *Feminist practice and poststructuralist theory.* Oxford: Blackwell.

Wilson Keenan, J., Solsken, J., & Willett, J. (1999). "Only boys can jump high": Reconstructing gender relations in a first/second-grade classroom. In B. Kamler (Ed.), *Constructing gender and difference: Critical research perspectives on early childhood* (pp. 33-70). Cresskill, NJ: Hampton Press.

Zaharlick, A., & Green, J. (1991). Ethnographic research. In J. Flood, J. Jensen, D. Lapp, & R. J. Squire (Eds.), *Handbook of research on teaching the English language arts* (pp. 205-225). Chanpagne-Urbana, IL: NCTE.

Author Index

A

Adger, C.T., 182, *188*
Adler, M.D., 194, *227*
Agar, M.H., 22, *29*, 59, *66*, 136, *153*, 352, *357*
Alderman, M.K., 182, *184*
Allen, G., 235, 257, *260*
Alton-Lee, A., 15, *29*
Alvermann, D.E., 341, *357*
American Association for the Advancement of Science, 231, 249, *260*
Anderson, M.B., 193, *227*
Anderson, T.H., 42, *68*, 230, *261*
Armbruster, B.B., 230, *261*
Armitage, M., 129, 138, *154*
ASHA, 155, *185*
Aspiazu, G.G., 127, 129, 130, *153*
Atkins, B.K., 333, *358*
Atkinson, J.M., 43, *66*, 341, *357*
Atwell, N., 156, *185*

B

Bailey, F., 13, *29*, 62, *66*
Baker, C.D., 5, *29*, 41, *66*, 83, *124*, 157, *185*

Bakhtin, M., 119, *124*
Ball, D.L., 230, *261*
Balow, I.H., 157, 162, *185*
Barnes, D., 119, *124*
Bauer, S.C., 127, 129, 130, *153*
Beck, I., 157, *186*
Behm, L., 230, *260*
Bell, L.C., 157, *186*
Ben-Peretz, M., 64, *66*
Ben-Zvi-R., 297-298, 299, *325*
Bergamo, H., 130, 131, 150, *153*
Berger, C., 302, *327*
Berne, J., 39, 63, *68*
Bloome, D., 10, 11, 12, 13, 25, *29*, *30*, 52(*n*4), 60, 62, *66*, *67*, 158, *185*, 196, 198, *227*, 235, 238, 239, 240, 258, *260*
Blumenfeld, P.C., 302, 304, *327*
Boostrom, R., 77, 117-118, *124*
Borker, R.A., 334, 335, *358*
Boyle, R.A., 232, *261*
Bradley, M., 130, 131, 150, *153*
Bradley, S.W., 194, *227*
Brandts, L., 2, *30*
Bredekamp. S., 268, 293, 294
Brilliant-Mills, H., 10, 13, *29*, 49, 63, *66*
Brinkley, J.F., 194, *227*

Brown, A.L., 157, *186*
Brown, J.S., 300, 304, *325*
Bryant, B.R., 157, 161, *188*
Burkel, W.E., 199, 200, 225, *227*
Burns, M.S., 129, *154*, 181, 182, *187*

C

Caldwell, J., 134, *154*
Cameron, D., 198, 227, 337, *358*
Canaan, J.E., 334, 343, *358*
Carey, S., 268, 271, 273, 290, *293*
Carlsen, W.S., 324, *325*
Castanheira, M., 4, 6, 16, *29*, 80, *124*, 130, 131, 136, 150, *153*, 161, *185*, 195, 198, 204, *227*, 269, *293*
Cazden, C., 40, 40(*n*1), 46, 47, 48, 48(t), 49, 50, 51, 56, 63, *66*, 172, *185*, 223, *227*, 292, *293*
Chambers, J.C., 233, 235, *261*
Chang-Wells, G.L., 16, *34*
Chen, C., 300, 322, *326*
Chi, M., 273, *294*
Chin, E., 297, 298, 300, *326*
Chow-Hoy, T.K., 78, *124*
Christian, D., 182, *188*
Clark, K., 182, *187*
Coates, J., 334, 335, *358*
Cobb, P., 232, *260*
Cochran-Smith, M., 230, *260*
Cognition and Technology Group, 302, *325*
Coiera, E., 224, *227*
Cole, M., 77, 125, 232, *261*
Collins, A., 300, 304, *325*
Collins, E., 8, *29*
Commeyras, M., 341, *357*
Conant, F.R., 195, *228*
Connor, C.M., 157, 179, *185*
Cook-Gumperz, J., 6, *29*
Copple, C., 268, *293*, *294*
Corbin, J., 205, *228*
Coulthard, R., 46, 64, *68*
Craig, H.K., 161, *185*, *187*
Craviotto, E., 3, *29*, *30*
Crawford, M., 343, *358*
Crawford, T., 4, 6, 16, *29*, 80, *124*, 130, 131, 136, 150, *153*, 161, *185*, 195, 198, 204, *227*, 269, *293*, 300, *326*

Cunningham, A.E., 172, 181, *187*
Czerniak, C.M., 302, *327*

D

Darling-Hammond, L., 39, *66*
Davies, B., 335, 335, 336, 352, 356, *357*, *358*
Davis, J., 299, *326*
de la Cruz, E., 2, *30*
DeFrancisco, V.L., 333, *358*
Delamont, S., 236, *260*
Dewey, J., 229, *260*
Dickinson, D.K., 155, *185*
Dixon, C.D., 2, 3, 4, 6, 8-9, 13, 15, 16, *29*, *30*, *31*, *33*, *34*, 42, 51, 65, *67*, *68*, 75, 80, 83, *124*, *125*, *126*, 130, 131, 132, 135, 136, 137, 150, *153*, *154*, 161 175, 179, *185*, *187*, 195, 198, 204, *227*, 269, *293*, 294, 295, 304, 331, 332, 338, *358*, *359*
Dugiud, P., 300, 304, *325*
Duran, R., 3, 15, *33*

E

Edelsky, C., 44, 45, *66*
Eder, D., 333, 334, *358*
Educational Researcher, vii, *viii*
Edwards, A.D., 348, *358*
Edwards, D., 8, 13, *30*
Egan Robertson, A., 12, 13, 25, *29*, 60, 62, *66*, 77, *124*, 196, *227*, 235, 238, 239, 240, 258, *260*, 338, *358*
Eisenhart, M., 230, *260*
Elmore, R.F., 155, *185*
Emerson, R.M., 236, *260*, 338, *358*
Erickson, F., 6, 11, *30*, 46, 53, 61, *66*, 78-79, *124*, 136, *153*, 209, *325*
Erickson, G.L., 233, 258, *260*
Espindola, J., 3, *29*
Etaugh, C., 343, *358*
Evans, C.C., 333, 334, *358*
Eylon, B., 297-298, 299, *325*

F

Fagot, B.I., 343, 347, 352, *358*
Fairclough, N., 196, *227*
Fallona, C., 80, 117, 120, *124*, *125*
Farr, R.C., 157, 162, *185*
Fenstermacher, G., 49, *66*, 73, 77-78, 119, *124*, *125-126*

Ferdman, R., 130, *153*
Fichtelius, A., 334, 335, *358*
Finkel, L., 304, *324*
Fishman, S., 333, *358*
Fletcher, J., 161, *186*
Floriani, A., 3, 12, 13, *30, 34,* 49, 61, 62, 66, 130, 131, 132, 150, *153,* 304, *325,* 356, *358*
Florio, S., 52-53, *66*
Foorman, B.R., 156, 157, 161, 182, 183, *187*
Fox, G.E., 127, *153*
Frank, C.R., 2, 3, 4, *30*
Franquiz, M.E., 3, 4, *30, 31, 35,* 42, *67*
Freeman, D.J., 172, 181, *187*
Freire, P., 130, *153*
Fretz, R.I., 236, *260,* 338, *358*
Freyberg, P., 299, 301, *327*

G

Gabel, D., 298, 299, *325, 326*
Gagne, E.D., 299, *326*
Gallagher, T.M., 161, *185*
Gallego, M.A., 77, *125*
Garfinkel, H., 5, 6, *30*
Gee, J.P., 41, 47, 49, 61, 62, *67,* 79, *125,* 128, 130, 131, *153,* 335, 337, 342, *358*
Gelman, S.A., 268, 271, 272, 290, *293, 294*
Gentner, D., 268, 272, 290, *294*
Gest, T.R., 199, 200, 225, *227*
Giddens, A., 17, *30*
Gobbo, C., 273, *294*
Goffman, E., 6, *30,* 42, 49, *67,* 335, *358*
Golden, J.M., 5, *31*
Goodenough, D., 161, *187*
Goodenough, W.H., 8, *30*
Goodman, Y., 157, 161, *185*
Goodwin, M.H., 334, *358*
Graddol, D., 334, 335, 336, *358, 359*
Graham, K., 5, 13, *31*
Green, J.L., 2, 3, 4-5, 6, 8-9, 10, 13, 15, 16, 17, *29, 30, 31, 32, 33, 34, 35,* 42, 51, 52, 52(*n4*), 56, 60, 62, *67, 68,* 75, 79, 80, 83, *124, 125, 126,* 130, 131, 135, 136, 137, 150, *153,* 156, 158, 161, *185,* 195, 198, 204, 227, 269, 270-271, *293, 294, 295,* 304, *326,* 331, 332, 338, 339, 340, 341, *358, 359*

Griffin, P., 129, *154,* 181, 183, *187,* 232, 261
Grimmett, P.P., 233, 258, *260*
Gumperz, J., 5, 6, 8, *29, 31, 32,* 51, *67,* 157, 161, *185,* 269, 170, 277, *294,* 341, *358*
Gunstone, R., 299, *327*
Gutheil, G., 271, 273, *294*

H

Hallahan, D.P., 156, *185*
Hansen, D.T., 73, 74, *126*
Harker, J.O., 5, 15, *31, 32,* 83, *125,* 269, *294*
Harrison, A.G., 268, 271-272, 273, 274, *295*
Heap, J.L., 5, *32,* 157, *185*
Heath, S.B., 79, *125,* 157, 158, *186*
Heras, A.I., 3, 10, 13, *29, 32,* 324, *326*
Herasimchuk, E., 5, 6, *32*
Heritage, J., 6, *32,* 43, 62, *66,* 341, *357*
Heubel-Drake, M., 304, *324, 326*
Hicks, D., 136, *153,* 335, *358*
Hobbs, J., 3, 15, *33*
Hoffman, R., 297, 299, 302, *326*
Hogan, K., 322, *326*
Hogan, T.R., 157, 162, *185*
Hohne, K.H., 194, *228*
Hollingsworth, L., 230, *260*
Holmes, J., 335, *358*
Howe, K., 14, *32*
Huerta-Macias, A., 129, 130, *154*
Hughes, C., 157, *186*
Hunn, D., 298, 299, *326*
Hunt, B.C., 163, *186*
Hunt, R., 335, 352, *358*
Hymes, D., 5, 6, 8, *32,* 51, 52, *67,* 175, *186*

J

Jackson, P.W., 40(*n2*), 42, *67*
Jefferson, G., 44, 46, *68,* 161, *187*
Jencks, C., 162, *186*
Jenkins, J.R., 129, *154*
Jennings, L.B., 3, 13, 15, *32, 34, 35,* 65, *68,* 75, 83, *126,* 130, 131, 132, *154,* 161, 175, 179, *187,* 269, *295,* 331, 332, *359*
Johansson, I., 334, 335, *358*

Johnson, K.B., 194, *227*
Johnson, M.B., 157, *188*
Johnstone, A.H., 298, *326*
Jones, T., 299, *326*
Jorgensen, D.L., 236, *260*
Juel, C., 156, *186*

K

Kamler, B., 337, *358*
Katch, E.L., 157, 179, *185*
Kauffman, J.M., 156, *185*
Keefe, D., 129, 138, *154*
Keenan, E., 161, *186*
Keig, P.F., 298, *326*
Keil, F.C., 271, 273, *294*
Kelly, G.J., 83, *125*, 300, 322, *326*
Killingsworth, M.J., 198, *227*, 235, *260*
Klemm, W.R., 194, *227*
Kovalik, S., 82, *125*
Kozma, R.B., 297, 298, 299, 300, 301, 322, *324*, *326*
Krajcik, J.S., 233, 235, *261*, 297, 302, 304, *326*, *327*
Kristeva, J., 235, *261*
Kuhn, T., 232, *260*
Kushmaul, A.J., 161, *187*
Kyratzis, A., 83, *125*

L

Laboratory of Comparative Human Cognition, 77, *125*
Lampert, M., 37(t), 43, 53, *67*, 230, *261*
Laszlo, R., 297, 299, 302, *326*
Latour, B., 300, *327*
Lave, J., 64, *67*, 232, *261*, 300, *327*
LeFevre, D., 55, *67*
Leinbach, M.D., 343, 347, 352, *358*
Lemke, J.L., 49, *67*, 195, 196, 197, 224, *227*, 299, 303, *324*, *327*
Lerner, G.H., 161, *186*
Leslie, L., 134, *154*
Lin, L., 2, 3, 9, 13, *30*, *32*, 60, *67*, 130, 131, 150, *153*, 307, *327*
Lloyd, J.W., 156, *185*
Lortie, D., 49, 64, *67*
Lubeck, S., 151, *154*, 274, *294*
Luke, A., 157, *185*
Lyman, F., 182, *186*

Lynch, M., 300, *327*
Lytle, S.L., 230, *260*

M

Macedo, D., 130, *153*
MacWhinney, B., 160, *186*
Maltz, D.N., 334, 335, *358*
Markman, E.M., 268, 272, 290, *293*
Marsh, L., 127, *154*
Marshall, C., 339, 341, *358*
Marshall, E., 156, *187*
Marx, N., 297, 298, 299, 300, *326*, *327*
Marx, R.W., 232, 233, 235, *261*, 302, 304
Mattern, C., 130, 131, 150, *153*
Mayer-Smith, J.A., 230, *261*
McAffee, N., 336, 353, *358*
McCarthy, L., 333, *358*
McEachen, D., 3, 13, 15, *33*, 161, *187*
McLaughlin, M., 39 63, *67*
Medin, D.L., 268, 271, 272, 290, *294*
Mehan, H., 47, 57(f), 64, *67*, 138, 145, *154*, 172, *186*, 348, *358*
Mejia, B., 127, 129, *154*
Mercer, N., 8, 13, *30*
Meyer, L.A., 17, *31*, 51, 52, 56, 60, *67*, 131, 137, 150, *153*, 156, 158, *185*, 269, *294*, 304, *326*, 331, 338, 341, *358*
Meyer, M., 41, *68*
Meyer, V., 129, 138, *154*
Michaels, S., 292, *294*
Miletta, A., 21, *32*
Miller, J.F., 156, 161, *186*
Mitchell, C.J., 83, *125*
Mitchell, I.J., 230, *261*
Mitchell, J.C., 21, *33*, 160, *186*
Moerman, M., 10, *33*
Moll, L.C., 130, 132, 150, *154*
Morris, K., 54, *68*
Morrison, F.J., 157, 179, *185*
Moschkovich, J., 49, *68*
Mouradian, M., 304, *326*
Mumme, J., 55(n5), *68*
Murnen, T., 3, 15, *33*
Murphy, G.L., 268, 271, 272, 290, *294*

N

Nakhleh, M.B., 297, *327*

Namy, L.L., 268, 272, 290, *294*
Nastasi, B.K., 322, *326*
National Center for Education
  Statistics, 127, *154*, 159, *186*
National Council of Teachers of
  English, 354, *358*
National Reading Panel, 157, *186*
National Research Council, vii, *viii*,
  222, *227*, 231, 235, 245, 257, *261*, 268,
  294
Nelson, K., 268, 272, 290, *294*
Nelson, M., 3, *33*
Neuman, S.B., 155, *186*, 268, *294*
Newman, D., 232, *261*
Nilan, P., 356, *358*
No Child Left Behind Act, 155, *186*
Nordin, K., 334, 335, *358*
Nuthall, G., 15, *29*
Nye, M.J., 297, 300, 302, *327*

O

O'Barr, W.M., 333, *358*
O'Loughlin, M., 232, 259, *261*
Oberman, I., 39, 63, *67*
Ochs, E., 41, 42, *68*, 341, *358*
Osborne, R., 299, 301, *327*
Osher, D., 127, 129, *154*

P

Palincsar, A.S., 157, *186*
Parker, S., 333, 334, *358*
Pattenaude, I., 3, *35*
Paxton, S., 130, 131, 150, *153*
Peacock, J.L., 77, *125*
Pearson, D.P., 182, *187*
Perfetti, C.A., 156, 157, 161, 182, 183,
  186, *187*
Pesetsky, D., 156, 157, 161, 182, 183, *187*
Petrella, J.N., 157, *185*
Petry, C.A., 129, 138, *154*
Phillips, M., 162, *186*
Pintrich, P.R., 232, *261*
Polkinghorne, D., vii, *viii*
Pool, K., 129, *154*
Posner, G.J., 232, *261*
Post, J., 274, *294*
Pressley, M., 157, *186*, 322, *326*
Psathas, G., 42, *68*
Pumfrey, P.D., 161, *186*
Putney, L., 3, 15, *33*, 83, *125*

Q

Quintero, E., 129, 130, *154*

R

Rayner, K., 156, 157, 161, 182, *187*
Rech, M., 3, *33*
Reisner, E.R., 129, 138, *154*
Resnick, L.B., 300, 304, *327*
Rex, L.A., 3, 8, 13, 15, *33*, 49, 60, *68*, 131,
  154, 161, *187*, 269, *294*, 341, *358*
Richardson, V., 77-78, 80, 117, 120, *125*,
  233, 259, *261*
Ricoeur, P., 20, *33*
Rogers, T., 156, *187*
Romagnano, L., 230, *260*
Rosebery, A.S., 195, *228*
Rosenholtz, S., 49, 64, 65, *68*
Ross, G., 268, 272, 290, *294*
Rosse, C., 194, *227*
Rossman, G., 339, 341, *358*
Roth, W.-M., 195, 221, *228*
Roychoudhury, A., 195, 221, *228*
Rubba, P.A., 298, *326*
Russell, J., 297, 298, 299, 300, *326*

S

Sacks, H., 43, 44, 46, *68*, 161, *187*, 341, *358*
Salomon, G., 232, *261*
Samuel, K.V., 298, 299, *326*
Sanger, M.G., 78, 79, *125-126*
Santa Barbara Classroom Discourse
  Group, 3, 4, 10, 13, *33*, *34*, 51, 52,
  60, *68*, 175, *187*, 269, *294*, 331-332,
  358
Saville-Troike, M., 8, *34*
Schegloff, E., 43, 44, 46, 51, *68*, 161, *187*,
  341, *358*
Schiemann, T., 194, *228*
Schiffrin, D., 41, 43-44, 52, 62, *68*
Schoenfeld, A.H., *184*, *187*
Schonmann, S., 64, *66*
Schubert, R., 194, *228*
Schultz, J., 6, 11, *30*, 47, 61, *66*
Seago, N., 55, *68*
Seidenberg, M.S., 156, 157, 161, 182,
  183, *187*
Shaw, L.L., 236, *260*, 338, *358*
Sherzer, J., 343, *359*
Short, K.G., 196, 197, *228*

Silberstein, J., 297-298, 299, *325*
Sinclair, J., 46, 64, *68*
Singer, J., 233, 235, *261*
Snow, C.E., 129, *154*, 157, 181, 182, 183, *187*
Soloway, E., 302, 304, *327*
Solsken, J., 336, *359*
Spencer, J.W., 135, *154*
Spillett, M.D., 127, 129, 130, *153*
Spindler, G.D., 14, *34*, 79, *126*
Spindler, L., 14, *34*, 79, *126*
Spradley, J.P., 17, *34*
Stanovich, K.E., 172, 181, *187*
Stern, E., 304, *326*
Strauss, A., 205, *228*
Street, B., 157, *187*
Strike, K.A., 232, *261*
Sundsten, J.W., 194, *227*
Swann, J., 334, 335, 336, *358*, *359*
Sykes, G., 39, *66*

T

Tabors, P., 155, *185*
Talbot, M.M., 335, 341, *359*
Tannen, D., 6, *34*, 50, *68*, 332, 343, *359*
Tanouye, E., 268, 272, 290, *294*
Tavris, C., 271, *295*
Taylor, B.M., 182, *187*
Taylor, C., 14, *34*
Thomson, M., 194, *228*
Tiede, U., 194, *228*
Tippins, D., 232, *261*
Titscher, S., 41, *68*
Tobin, K., 232, *261*
Tozer, S., 230, *261*
Treagust, D.F., *68*. 271-272, 273, 274, *295*
Tuyay, S., 3, 13, 14, *34*, 65, *68*, 75, 83, *126*, 130, 131, 132, *154*, 161, 175, 179, *187*, 269, *295*, 331, 332, *359*
Tyson, C., 156, *187*
Tyson, L.M., 268, 271-272, 273, 274, *295*

V

Vadasy, P.F., 129, *154*
Venville, G., 268, 271-272, 273, 274, *295*

Vera, A., 271, 273, *294*
Vetter, E., 41, *68*
Vygotsky, L.S., 232, *261*

W

Wade, C., 271, *295*
Wallat, C., 4, 5, 10, 13, *31*, 34, 51, 56, 62, *68*, 83, *125*, 161, *185*
Walpole, S., 182, *187*
Warren, B., 195, 228
Washington, J.A., 161, 162, *187*
Wasik, B.A., 129, 138, 152, *154*
Weade, R., 5, 13, *31*, *34*
Weedon, C., 333, 334, 336, 353, *359*
Weiner, S., 161, *187*
Wellman, H.M., 268, 272, 290, *294*
Wells, G., 16, *34*
Wenger, E., 64, 67, 232, *261*, 300, *327*
West, C., 42, *68*
West, R.F., 172, 181, *187*
Westgate, D.P.G., 348, *358*
Wetstone, H., 268, 272, 290, *294*
Wharton-McDonald, R., 157, *186*
White, E.B., 172, *188*
White, R., 299, *327*
Whitmire, K., 155, *188*
Wiederholt, J.L., 157, 161, *188*
Willett, J., 77, *124*, 336, 338, *358*, *359*
Wilson Keenan, J., 336, *359*
Wilson, S., 39, 63, *68*
Wiser, M., 303, *327*
Wodak, R., 41, *68*
Wolfram, W., 182, *188*
Woodcock, R.W., 157, *188*
Woolgar, S., 300, *327*

Y

Yeager, E., 3, 15, *31*, *33*, *34*, 35
Yekovich, C.W., 299, *326*
Yekovich, F.R., 299, *326*

Z

Zaharlick, A., 4, 5, 13, *30*, *35*, 52(n4), *68*, 75, *126*, 130, 131, 135, 136, 137, *153*, 270-271, *295*, 332, 338, 339, 340, 341, *358*, *359*

Subject Index

A

Academic task structures, 78, 100, 109, 119

Adjacency pair, 20, 43, 44

After school programs, 21, 22, 69, 70, 127-128, 129, 130, 132, 133, 134, 135, 144, 150, 151, 183

Anatomy education, 193, 194, 196, 199, 208, 220

Anatomy literacy, 24, 25, 194, 195, 197, 199, 200, 201, 206, 221

B

Backchanneling, 20, 44, 45

Biliteracy, 22, 127, 128, 130, 133, 135, 136, 137, 146, 148, 150

C

Call outs, 78, 119

Case study approach, 160, 339

Chemical representation, 26, 297, 298, 299, 300, 301, 302, 303, 307, 323, 324

Macroscopic, 298, 299, 300, 301, 302, 316

Microscopic, 27, 297, 298, 299, 300, 301, 302, 303, 309, 311, 312, 314, 316, 320, 323, 324

Symbolic, 297, 298, 299, 300, 301, 302, 303, 314, 316, 323

Chemistry education, 26

Circle time, 22, 127, 128, 130-131, 132, 133, 134, 135, 136, 137, 138, 141, 144, 145, 147, 148, 149, 150, 151, 152, 267, 269, 270, 272, 275, 276, 277, 278, 283, 284, 285, 286, 287, 289, 291, 292

Classroom Climate, 21, 22, 28, 74, 75, 78, 80, 117, 118, 119, 120, 121, 156, 159, 339; *see also* Classroom environment

Classroom as Culture, 13, 49, 51, 53, 54, 77, 131, 156, 182, 324, 332, 336, 339, 340, 343

Classroom

As discourse culture, 2-7, 13, 27, 63, 34, 175, 181, 292, 298, 303, 319, 324, 336, 343, 345, 347; *see also* as Discourse community

As speech community, 8, 52, 60, 64, 175

Classroom discourse, 194

Classroom management, 22, 80, 84, 117, 118, 121

Classroom-based assessment, 23, 70,
    155, 156, 159, 174, 177, 181, 182, 183
Co-constructing text, 176
Code switch, 147, 149
Cognition/learning theory, 264, 299-
    300, 301, 303
Collaboration, 15, 23, 45, 210, 220, 224,
    264
Communicative competence, 52, 59
Community circle, 75, 82, 83, 84, 96, 98,
    115-117, 118, 119
Combining perspectives, 183, 184
Community,
    Creating, 53, 128, 131, 137, 151, 335
    Discourse, 235
    Scientific, 297, 300, 303, 324
Community of learners, 39, 98, 150,
    292, 303, 324, 332, 340, 348, 349, 350,
    355
Community of practice, 64, 65, 274, 300
Community, classroom as, 8, 53, 63, 75,
    78, 105, 117, 119, 156, 177, 175, 179,
    181, 183, 329, 333, 337, 342, 347, 354,
    356
Computer based media, 24, 193, 208,
    215, 222, 223, 224
Concept, definition of, 271
Concept-theory approach, 272
Conceptual change, 26, 268, 269, 271,
    273-274, 276, 277, 286-290, 291
Conceptual development, 18, 26, 224,
    263, 264, 268, 269, 270, 272, 274, 276,
    277, 283-286, 290, 291, 293, 303
Conceptual knowledge, 25, 26, 263,
    264, 267, 268, 269, 270, 271, 272, 273,
    275, 276, 277, 278, 283, 286, 289, 290,
    291, 292, 293, 299, 323
Conceptual lens (frame), 8, 24, 69, 70,
    77, 130, 132, 155-84, 195, 264, 269,
    298, 301; see also Theoretical frame
Conceptual understanding, 18, 268,
    274, 275, 277, 286, 289, 292, 300
Confianza, 22, 130, 145, 147, 150
Connections, 298, 299, 300, 301, 302,
    303, 309, 312, 314, 316, 320, 322, 323
Consequentiality, 3, 15
Context, 6, 10, 11, 12, 13, 15, 26, 48, 50,

    52, 53, 56, 61-2, 63, 274, 300, 303
Contextualization, 6, 11, 23, 26, 302, 324
Conversation analysis, 6, 19, 20, 21, 41,
    43, 44, 46, 48, 50, 51, 52, 59, 65
Cultural knowledge, 8, 51, 135, 304
Culture as norms of practice, 8, 12, 13,
    64, 65, 91, 145, 147, 148, 334, 337,
    339, 340, 341
Critical theory, 334
Cycle of activity, 27, 56, 59, 62, 135, 204,
    304, 306, 307, 311, 312, 331, 333, 334,
    339, 341, 342, 347, 350, 352, 354, 355,
    356

D

Developmental perspective, 69, 70,
    156, 175
D/discourse, 128
Dialogue, 119, 157, 235, 319
Discourse,
    Concepts of, 335
    Gendered, 27, 28, 330, 331, 332, 334,
        335, 336, 343, 347, 349, 352, 354,
        355, 356, 357
    Microanalysis of interactions, 24,
        51, 53, 55, 77, 79, 117
    Moment to moment, 13, 335, 337
Discourse analysis, 4, 10, 17, 18, 19, 20,
    21, 22, 24, 27, 28, 39, 41, 61, 62, 65,
    75, 78, 79, 121, 135, 136, 161, 195,
    198, 298, 307, 335, 336, 341
Discourse in educational settings, 40,
    49, 50
Dissecting lab, 24, 194, 195, 198, 199,
    201, 205, 208, 210, 221, 222, 223
Domain analysis, 16, 17, 18

E

Embedded proposals, 249, 252, 254,
    255, 259
Emic, 4, 15, 75, 339; see also Insider's
    perspective
Ethnographic perspective, 3, 5, 10-11,
    13, 14, 15, 17, 21, 22, 26, 27, 53, 54,
    77, 79, 131, 135, 160, 161, 198, 201,
    264, 275, 303, 309, 334, 335, 336, 339;
    see also Ethnographic approach

Ethnography, 10, 13-14, 18, 21, 27, 52, 53, 63, 77, 78-9, 195, 201
Ethnography of communication, 5, 8, 51, 52, 335
Ethnomethodology, 5, 6, 356
Expectations, 15

F

Facilitation, 245-248, 252, 255-256, 257, 258-259
Feminist theory, 334
Frame clash, 352
Funds of knowledge, 130

G

Gatekeeping, 332, 357
Gender affiliated roles, 332, 333, 335, 338, 345, 356, 357
Boys as players, girls as teachers 28, 333, 334, 336, 338, 339, 343, 347, 348, 349, 352, 354, 355
Gendered discourse; *see also* Discourse-gendered
Gendered identity, 27, 28, 334, 356

H

Head Start, 26, 271, 274, 275, 290

I

Identity, 27
Cultural, 130
Individual, 336, 337
Situated as student, 50
Situated as reader, 131
Instructional conversations, 46-48, 49
Interaction
Student initiated, 309, 310, 312
Teacher initiated, 309, 311
Interactional ethnography, 1, 2, 4, 5-16, 18, 19, 21, 22, 23, 24, 25, 26, 27, 28, 41, 51, 56, 59, 60, 61, 62, 63, 65, 69, 70, 135, 189-191, 195, 263, 264, 265, 331, 335, 339
Interactional space, 10, 13, 15, 17
Interactional sociolinguistics, 5, 6, 8, 51, 270, 271
Intercontextuality, 3, 13, 15, 48, 62, 63, 130, 131, 132
Interpretive method, 14, 83

Intersubjectivity, 44, 45
Intertextuality, 9, 10, 11, 12, 13, 15, 16, 24, 25, 60, 61, 62, 63, 180, 190, 196, 197, 204, 205, 206, 208, 210, 220, 221, 223, 224, 235, 236, 237, 238, 239, 240, 241, 244, 245, 250, 257, 258, 259, 303, 304, 319, 320
Intervention, 20, 23, 70, 174, 175, 178, 182
IRE/F, 20, 46-47, 48, 51, 56, 138, 140, 141, 145, 172, 177, 292

J

Jeffersonian notation, 43, 44-5, 56

K

Knowledge *see also* Learning
Chemistry, 26
Co-construction, 9, 10, 12, 13, 14, 16, 21, 24, 25, 27, 263-265, 269, 271, 275, 277, 290, 299, 300, 304, 329
Content, 10, 288, 298, 309, 314, 315, 316, 320, 324
Pedagogical, 316, 320

L

Language assessment, 69, 160
AAE, 160, 162, 163
Metropolitan Achievement, 162
Miscue analysis, 161, 163, 172, 174, 175
Oral language, 161, 162-3, 175, 181
Scientific, 322
Language of the Classroom 3, 9, 10
Large motor time, 277, 278
Latching, 44, 238
Latino
Community, 22, 127, 128
Family networks, 22, 130, 132
Learning, 17, 20, 48-50, 52, 63, 65, 69, 75, 85, 90, 97, 98, 99, 119, 190, 196, 200, 204, 205, 210, 220, 224, 229, 232, 268, 299, 300, 310, 332
Literacy as socially constructed, 132, 195
Literacy as a situated practices, 130, 131, 157
Literate practices, 13, 16, 17, 18, 23, 175, 210, 221

M

Mapping
  Conversation, 10, 55, 56, 59, 60
  Event, 17, 25, 27, 55, 201, 236, 238,
    238, 271, 307, 308, 309
  Structuration, 17, 23, 24, 27, 55, 161,
    172, 173, 174, 175, 178
Meaning/understanding, 14, 20, 26,
  70, 77, 78, 83, 92, 98, 99, 109, 117, 119,
  131, 195, 215, 221, 233, 264, 298, 303,
  307, 312, 316, 322, 341
Mentoring tutors, 128, 130, 133, 135,
  136, 137, 138, 143, 144, 145, 147, 150,
  151, 152
Message units, 83, 277, 341
Multiple representations,
  In chemistry, 299, 300, 316
  For conceptual connections, 299,
    301
  Of reading, 175

O

Opportunities to (for) learn(ing), 1, 2,
  3, 8, 15, 16, 17, 18, 19, 21, 23, 26, 27,
  28, 69, 74, 75, 115, 118, 130, 131-132,
  177, 179, 180, 181, 182, 184, 194, 195,
  205, 223, 269, 270, 277, 289, 302, 333,
  357
Orienting question, 7, 8, 17
Overlapping utterances, 44, 45, 46, 341

P

Participant observation, 25, 26, 52, 78,
  134, 135, 232, 236, 275, 276, 307, 338,
  339
Participation structures, 11
Pauses, 44, 45, 46, 277, 341
Perspective; see also Conceptual lens
Play
  Discourse, 26, 331, 332, 336, 337,
    339, 342, 343, 344, 347, 348, 349,
    350, 352, 353, 355
  Free, 267, 269, 270, 276, 277, 278,
    283, 284, 286, 291
Positioning, 10, 27, 49, 50, 61, 136, 144,
  240, 248, 329, 332, 333, 334, 336, 337,
  341, 342, 343, 344, 345, 347, 348, 349,
  352, 353, 354, 355, 356, 357

Positivism, 14, 263
Postmodern, 14
Poststructuralism, 334, 336, 337, 355
Preschool, 26, 266, 267, 268, 269, 290,
  291, 293, 334
Professional development, 3, 19, 20, 21,
  39-41, 43, 48, 49, 50, 53, 54-55, 59, 62,
  63, 65, 121

Q

Questions, 48, 91, 144, 145, 149, 151,
  278, 319, 320

R

Reading
  Assessment, 155, 159, 160, 162, 163,
    178, 183
  Cognitive/developmental lens, 23,
    155, 156, 157, 159, 160, 162, 180,
    183, 184
  Comprehension, 98, 138, 140, 141,
    145, 147, 149, 151, 152, 159, 162,
    179, 181, 182, 183
  Sociocultural lens, 23, 156, 157, 158,
    160, 161, 172, 175, 183, 184
Reading practices, 22, 23, 24, 128, 129,
  131, 132, 136, 141, 144, 145, 147, 148,
  149, 150, 151, 152, 157, 158, 175, 180,
  182
Round Robin, 158, 172, 174, 177, 178,
  180, 181, 182
Recording,
  Audio, 264, 275, 276, 338, 339
  Process video, 24, 201, 204
  Video, 17, 21, 22, 24, 25, 27, 135, 160,
    161, 174, 176, 177, 178, 189, 201,
    204, 236, 238, 264, 275, 276, 307,
    309, 338, 339, 345
Rich points, 22, 136
Running record of classroom activity,
  17

S

Santa Barbara Classroom Discourse
  Group, 2-7
Science education, 195, 231, 234, 237,
  238, 244, 245, 256, 257, 259, 260, 263,
  322

Foundations of Science (FOS), 304, 305, 306, 309

Scientific literacy, 195

Showcasing students, 100, 105, 119

Social currency, 343, 347

Social construction, 4, 8, 10, 26, 69, 136, 194, 195, 196, 205, 206, 208, 223, 269, 270, 271, 277, 291, 298, 303

Social constructivism, 52, 63, 232, 234, 237, 244, 256, 257, 258, 260, 269, 300, 301, 325

Sociocultural constructivist learning theory, 25, 232, 233, 238, 259, 298, 302

Sociocultural theory, 23, 56, 69, 70, 130, 131, 157, 158, 183, 335

Sociolinguistic theory, 5, 6, 8, 28, 75, 130, 157, 158, 270, 271, 335

Speech pathology, 23, 155, 156, 160, 183

Studenting, 49

Student teacher study group, 25, 230-1, 232, 234, 241, 244, 245, 255, 257, 258, 259

Subjectivity, 332, 334, 336, 337, 342, 344, 347, 349, 352, 353, 354, 355, 357
   Contradictory, 333, 336, 353
   Multiple, 333, 347, 348, 352, 355, 357

T

Take up, 13, 21, 69, 74, 75, 83, 84, 85, 90, 97, 98, 117, 121, 128, 131, 161, 177, 179, 180, 195, 238, 240, 255, 275, 277, 278, 283, 333, 334, 336, 339, 341, 342, 343, 347, 348, 349, 354, 355, 356, 357

Teacher discourse moves, 50, 180

Teacher education, 25, 80, 229-230, 231, 232, 233, 237, 259-260

Teacher mediation, 232

Teacher talk, 50

Teacher's role,
   By students, 28, 143, 144, 147, 148, 150, 151, 152, 332, 333, 334, 336, 337, 339, 341, 343, 344-345, 347, 348, 349, 350, 352, 353, 354, 355, 356, 357

   By teachers, 46, 47, 49, 51, 63
   By tutors, 144, 145, 147, 150, 151, 152

Teaching
   Manner, 21, 70, 77, 78, 79, 80, 117, 119, 120
   Moral dimensions of, 21, 73, 74, 75, 77, 78, 80, 81, 84, 90, 91, 92, 98, 99, 109, 117, 118, 120, 121

Technical culture, 64-5

Telling case, 21, 59, 83, 160, 178

Text, 11, 16, 169, 196

Theory-practice relationship, 25, 230, 231, 234, 235, 236, 237, 238, 240, 241, 244, 245, 248, 251, 252, 255, 256, 257, 258, 259, 260

Think-pair-share, 182

Timelines, 17, 24

Transcription, 4, 16, 17, 18, 20, 23, 24, 27, 28, 41-43, 44, 45, 46, 47, 48, 53, 54, 55, 56, 70, 83, 135-136, 160, 161, 162, 190, 201, 204, 205, 208, 234, 235, 236, 237, 238, 240, 246, 249-256, 278-282, 285, 287-288, 307, 309, 316, 341
   Biases, 47
   CHILDES/CHAT, 160
   Contextualization cues, 6, 11
   Mapping, 5, 55, 56, 204, 237, 238
   Message units, 24, 341
   Political implications, 20, 42-43
   Sequences, 23, 51, 161
   Utterances, 6

Triangulation, 27, 136, 309, 341

Turn taking, 6, 20, 21, 44, 45, 46, 48, 341

Transition relevant place, 44

Turn, 44, 47, 49, 205

Tutoring programs, 21, 22, 69, 127-153

V

Visualization, 208, 215

W

Wait time, 45

Z

Zone of proximal development, 180

Printed in the United States
91177LV00004B/82-84/A

9 781572 736450